Oceania

Oceania

An Introduction to the Cultures and Identities of Pacific Islanders

Andrew Strathern

Pamela J. Stewart

Laurence M. Carucci

Lin Poyer

Richard Feinberg

Cluny Macpherson

CAROLINA ACADEMIC PRESS
Durham, North Carolina

Library of Congress Cataloging-in-Publication Data

Oceania : an introduction to the cultures and identities of Pacific Islanders / Andrew
Strathern ... [et al.].
    p. cm.
  Includes bibliographical references and index.
  ISBN: 0-89089-444-2
   1. Ethnology--Oceania. 2. Oceania--Social life and customs. 3. Oceania--Social
conditions. I. Strathern, Andrew.

  GN66 .O24 2002
305.8'00995--dc21

2001058227

Carolina Academic Press
700 Kent Street
Durham, North Carolina 27701
Phone: (919) 489-7486
Fax: (919) 493-5668
www.cap-press.com

Contents

Part II

by Richard Feinberg and Cluny Macpherson

Part III

by Laurence M. Carucci and Lin Poyer

Introduction

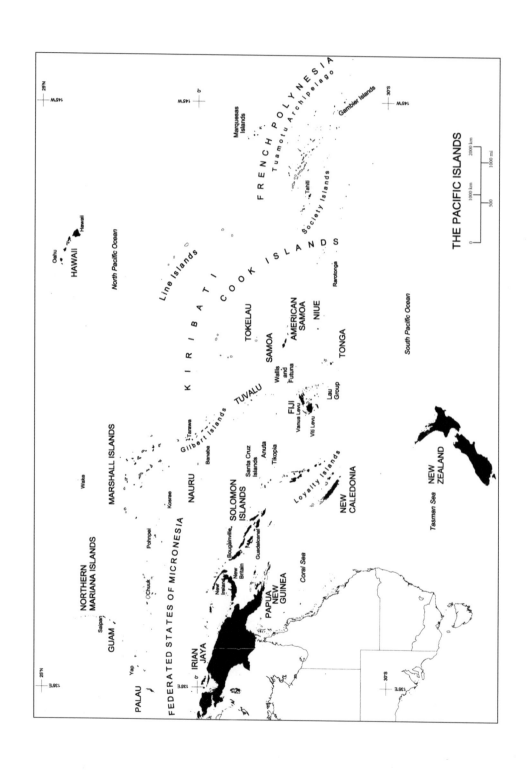

THE PACIFIC ISLANDS

Oceania: An Introduction to the Cultures and Identities of Pacific Islanders

by Pamela J. Stewart and Andrew Strathern

This book is a collaborative enterprise between six scholars who have worked in different parts of the vast island world of the Pacific with its rich diversities of cultural and historical experience. The Pacific is a major world region that stands on its own between the geopolitical worlds on its eastern and western rims, influenced by those worlds but with an identity of its own. The Pacific has been the venue of many notable anthropological studies since the earliest times of the discipline. The people of the Pacific have played important parts in world history, in their interactions with outside explorers and especially perhaps through their colonial histories and their involvement in the Pacific campaigns of World War II. Today they are people who have lived through many changes, in political, economic and religious facets of their lives, and have incorporated these changes creatively into the rhythms of their own lives. Forms of parliamentary politics, capitalist enterprise, and Christian religion have all been initially brought to these peoples as a part of the colonial impetus. In post-colonial times they continue to struggle with the historical results of that impetus and to make their own lives in its aftermath. The world of the Pacific Islanders is filled with parliaments, businesses, and churches, all of which are now parts of their own ways of life, whatever their historical genesis. Yet a concern with the ways of the ancestors, as perceived today, is often also a part of political and social innovations of the kind anthropologists call neo-traditional. We have written this book in the conviction that this Pacific world of change, adaptation, incorporation, resistance, and accommodation to the wider world around it, and now within it, is a world worth knowing, as much today as it was perceived to be by its earlier explorers, whether captains of ships or writers of books.

The aim of this book is therefore to provide an overview of ethnography, history, and contemporary changes in a broad range of societies across the Pacific region. The book is intended primarily for use in college level courses for undergraduates and can be read in conjunction with more specialized literature on specific areas. We supply references at the end of each section which instructors can use in guiding students with their readings on particular areas or issues. Overall, our shared viewpoint as co-authors is that the findings of ethnography and the anthropological analyses that have been applied to these findings are highly relevant to the understanding of contemporary processes of change, including conflict, in Pacific societies. Anthropologists have increasingly come to realize the importance of history for explaining the events and processes which they write about from their own fieldwork experiences. Adding history to the ethnographic account increases the depth of understanding which can be communicated about a given area and its problems. The overall holistic perspectives which anthropologists advocate therefore include many factors which go beyond the immediate area they write about, since the lives of peoples they study have often been greatly affected by international influences. In this book we therefore have adopted a thematic approach to achieving a synoptic view of the region as a whole, in which we see contemporary cultural and social patterns as arising out of complex sets of historical factors. Each of the three sections of the book emphasizes the cultural richness and complexity of the peoples discussed while avoiding stereotyping the peoples' lives. The overall concept of our book is to provide perspectives on Oceania as an area with great linguistic, historical, and cultural diversity. No one book could adequately survey the whole of Oceania in detail.

We also want to recognize the importance of acknowledging that Pacific Islanders have their own highly developed and extensive histories which are transmitted generation to generation. Many of these historical accounts are to be found in origin stories of the peoples. These stories contain information about the people and their placement within their landscape. For example, the Duna people of the Southern Highlands Province of Papua New Guinea call their group origin stories *malu*, which translates into "sacred knowledge, narratives of origins, genealogy." These stories establish links between spirit beings and humans and authenticate the precedence of particular groups in terms of land use and the use of the resources on that land. They convey information that establishes group identities and rights, and this knowledge is important today as it was in the past. In the 1990s *malu* knowledge was used by the Duna to present mining companies working in their area with information relevant to establishing compensation payments to the group members for environmental impacts caused by these company operations. Thus indigenous knowledge is an important factor for local people to use in their interaction with companies and "development" projects that enter into their areas (see Stewart and Strathern 2002 for further details).

Equally significant for understanding the experience of Pacific peoples are their own published accounts of their lives, which have appeared in biographical or autobiographical form. Examples of works of this kind appear in our specific bibliographies (for example Kwa'ioloa and Burt 1997; Scaglion and Norman 2000; Scaglion 2001), and a general discussion with specific examples from all over the Pacific can be found in Stewart and Strathern (eds.) 2000. As well, there is a growing tradition of collaborative writing between Pacific Island scholars and others and of independently written works by Pacific Islander historians, anthropologists, political scientists, economists, and experts in other disciplines. Some of these are brought together in B. Lal and K. Fortune's edited encyclopedia, *The Pacific Islands* (2000). While we do not discuss these works extensively, we recognize their growing importance.

In this book we present an introduction to students of anthropology and history who may be unfamiliar with the area of the Pacific and with the sophistication of the peoples living there. In the "global community" of the twenty-first century it is important for students to understand how people in Oceania are impacted by change which may arise internally or may come from outside forces; and how internal and external elements are continuously brought together in an unceasing interplay or dialectic of forces.

The book is divided into three broad sections, with specialist contributions to each of these. These sections correspond to geographical, historical, and cultural differences within the region as a whole, but we do not stress these broad divisions as such. Rather, we are interested in seeing how contemporary processes and common ethnographic themes can be seen as running like complexly interwoven threads across the region as a whole, as well as looking at the dynamic differences that exist. The regions and areas within these that anthropologists select for investigation are chosen for convenience of discussion and should not be regarded as areas with firm historical or cultural boundaries.

The term "Oceania" itself has to be understood in the light of the same considerations we have just explained. It overlaps in some ways with the term "the Pacific" as commonly used but generally does not include islands such as Taiwan or Japan, although the aboriginal inhabitants of Taiwan are Austronesian speakers with ties to the Pacific island nations. It comprises a vast range of island societies belonging to the Pacific Ocean. We include within it the Austronesian-speaking Maori populations of New Zealand but not the Aboriginal populations of Australia. We include also all of the island of New Guinea, but not the eastern Indonesian islands which actually show many correspondences to the societies of the Pacific (see for example, Strathern and Stewart 2000). We exclude Okinawa and the Ryukyu islands in the south of Japan, although these also show many parallels with Pacific island societies that we do include. From this list it can be seen that decisions to include or exclude an area within an overall region are made from particular viewpoints. We wish to stress again here that we are not concerned in this book to set up hard and fast boundaries. At the same time, we acknowledge that boundaries do exist and that the people themselves are accustomed to assessing similarities and differences between themselves and others; and we have implicitly followed this fact in our own categorizations.

The three sections of the book: the South-West Pacific, the Eastern Pacific, and the West Central Pacific, each incorporate some discussion of the following topics:

1. Basic information on the background in terms of prehistory, ecology, and linguistics, as well as a basic account of colonial and post-colonial history.
2. Basic patterns of ethnographic information, along with some detailed case studies.
3. Major patterns of change that have resulted from political and economic development.
4. The impacts of religious change, with special emphasis on Christianity and the ways that people have transformed and applied Christianity in terms of pre-existing forms of religious practices.
5. The assertions of renewed cultural and political identity that have emerged as a result of political, economic, and religious changes. This theme has become well-known in the anthropological literature under the name of "the politics of tradition" or the politics of culture and the cultural construction of traditions.

The style of presentation in the three sections is varied. This should provide the reader with different ways of looking at the topics presented. The section on the South-West Pacific is divided into short accounts of particular independent states such as Fiji, along with some more detailed case studies from each place. The island of New Guinea is treated as a whole, although it is politically divided into Papua New Guinea and Irian Jaya (West Papua). The sections on the Eastern Pacific and the West Central Pacific follow a more synoptic format, tracing major shared themes in these island societies but also paying close attention to particular studies. Instructors and students can approach all these materials either selectively or as a whole, and may choose to look further into the case studies or find similar themes on particular areas in which they are interested. Through the materials presented it will become abundantly clear that Oceania is a complex part of the world with a rich linguistic and cultural diversity. The people living throughout Oceania have been impacted historically by many forces, including the movements of peoples and environmental changes. The two main linguistic groups in the areas we discuss are called Austronesian and non-Austronesian (sometimes called

Papuan). Together these two groups include, by one reckoning, over 1,600 languages (Wurm 1975). Nowadays many young people also are familiar with English as well as their own languages. Shifting patterns of language are just one example of the historical processes of change that are continuously in action. Some aspects of societal practices change quickly while others may change little if at all over long time spans.

We can take Papua New Guinea as an example of change and diversity. It is a country with huge contrasts between its tropical coastal lands, its riverain estuaries and its montane interior. Its people are horticulturalists, fishing people, traders, hunters, business people, and politicians. Human settlement in New Guinea as a whole reaches back to 30,000 years or more before the present. The practices of Papua New Guineans have been molded by many influences including nearly one hundred years of colonial influence prior to the country becoming independent in 1975. Many factors have historically altered the lives of these people. Mining and logging companies have entered the country and established themselves. Christianity was introduced into the country and has been modified in various ways to accommodate local forms of religious beliefs and values. New diseases such as AIDS have taken a hold of the population in some areas. But in the face of all these changes and transformations the people continue to use their ingenuity and energies to craft meaningful lives, drawing on their past as an imaginative way of building their futures.

Many resources are available which provide additional information on Oceania. We provide an abbreviated list of a few of these here.

Students wishing to read further materials on the topics covered in this book may wish to look at articles published in the following journals: *Bijdragen, Journal de la Société des Océanistes, Journal of Pacific History, Journal of the Polynesian Society, Oceania, Pacific Studies, People and Culture in Oceania, The Australian Journal of Anthropology,* and *The Contemporary Pacific.*

Many other journals such as the *Journal of the Royal Anthropological Institute, American Anthropologist, American Ethnologist, Anthropos,* and *L'Homme* also publish articles on the Pacific.

A few resources that may also be helpful include:

1. Barry Craig, Bernie Kernot, and Christopher Anderson (eds.),
    1999 *Art and Performance in Oceania.* Honolulu: University of Hawai'i Press.

2. Donald Denoon (ed.) (with Stewart Firth, Jocelyn Linnekin, Malama Meleisea and Karen Nero)
    1997 *The Cambridge History of the Pacific Islanders.* Cambridge: Cambridge University Press.

3. Terence E. Hays (ed.)
    1991 *Oceania. Encyclopedia of World Cultures.* Boston: G.K. Hall.

4. Adrienne Kaeppler and Jacob Love (eds.),
    1998 *Australia and the Pacific Islands.* The Garland Encyclopedia of World Music. London and New York: Routledge.

5. Patrick Kirch
    2000 *On the Road of the Winds. An Archaeological History of the Pacific Islands before European Contact.* Berkeley: University of California Press.

6. Brij V. Lal and Kate Fortune (eds.),
    2000 *The Pacific Islands: An Encyclopedia.* Honolulu: University of Hawai'i Press.

7. Douglas L. Oliver
    1989 *Native Cultures of the Pacific Islands.* Honolulu: University of Hawai'i Press.

8. Robin Torrence and Anne Clarke (eds.)
   2000 *The Archaeology of Difference. Negotiating cross- cultural engagements in Oceania*. London and New York: Routledge.

Acknowledgments

We would like to thank Richard Feinberg, Laurence M. Carucci, Cluny Macpherson, and Lin Poyer for their collegial collaboration on this project. We have enjoyed working with them. We wish to thank Richard Feinberg for his detailed comments on both the Introduction and the South-West Pacific sections of this book. Viviana Siveroni did a splendid job on producing maps of the Pacific Islands, the South-West Pacific, and the West Central Pacific which appear in this book. We thank also the many colleagues, collaborators, and friends in the Pacific and elsewhere who have shared knowledge of their ways of life with us.

References

Kwa'ioloa, Michael and Ben Burt,
1997 *Living Tradition. A Changing Life in Solomon Islands*. Honolulu: University of Hawai'i Press.

Scaglion, Richard
2001 Juxtaposed narratives. A New Guinea Big Man encounters the colonial process. In Naomi M. McPherson ed. *In Colonial New Guinea: Anthropological Perspectives*, pp. 151–170. ASAO Monograph no. 19. Pittsburgh, PA: University of Pittsburgh Press.

Scaglion, Richard and Marie Norman
2000 Where resistance falls short: rethinking agency through biography. In Pamela J. Stewart and Andrew Strathern eds. *Identity Work*, pp. 121–138. Pittsburgh, PA: University of Pittsburgh Press.

Stewart, Pamela J. and Andrew Strathern
2000 (eds.) *Identity Work: Constructing Pacific Lives*. ASAO Monograph no. 18. Pittsburgh, PA: University of Pittsburgh Press.

2002 *Re-Making the World*. Washington, D.C.: Smithsonian Institution Press.

Strathern, Andrew and Pamela J. Stewart
2000 *The Python's Back: Pathways of Comparison between Indonesia and Melanesia*. Westport, CT: Bergin and Garvey.

Wurm, Stephen A.
1975 Papuan linguistic prehistory, and past language migrations in the New Guinea area. In *Pacific Linguistics* Series C, no. 38. Canberra: Australian National University.

Part I

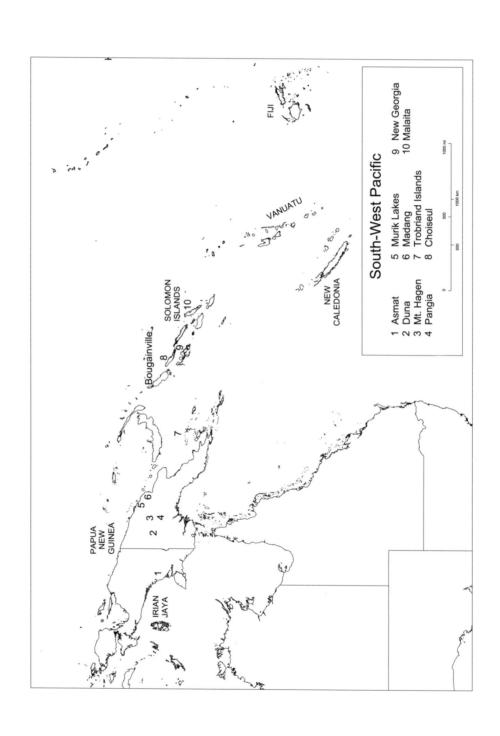

South-West Pacific

1 Asmat	5 Murik Lakes	9 New Georgia
2 Duna	6 Madang	10 Malaita
3 Mt. Hagen	7 Trobriand Islands	
4 Pangia	8 Choiseul	

The South-West Pacific

by Andrew Strathern and Pamela J. Stewart

The term South-West Pacific comprises, in our usage, the islands of New Guinea, the Solomons, Vanuatu, New Caledonia, and Fiji. We discuss each of these regions to provide an overview of the South-West Pacific, focusing on particular representative examples from these regions in our case studies.

Our area of interest in this part of the book consists of the great arc of tropical islands, beginning with the island of New Guinea that lies to the north of Australia, its western tip extending into the Indonesian archipelago. The chain of islands continues eastwards to the Solomon islands, Vanuatu (previously the New Hebrides) and New Caledonia. We include also in our purview Fiji, which lies further out in the Pacific Ocean. On ethnological grounds Fiji belongs to the Polynesian island societies as well as to our area here, which encompasses the parts of the Pacific often described as "Melanesia" by comparison with "Polynesia." In fact, although contrasts have sometimes been made between Polynesia and Melanesia, there are many continuities and similarities also, in part because of the histories of migration by people speaking versions of the languages linguists describe as Austronesian. Speakers of Austronesian languages are found in the South-West Pacific and all across the wider region of the Pacific.

The names that have been given to these islands and the designations of different areas in ethnological terms have themselves been partly a product of colonial exploration and control as well as of the classifications made by anthropologists, linguists, and others. The provenance of such names is clear when we read such terms as New Britain and New Ireland (both located in Papua New Guinea), the New Hebrides, and New Caledonia. The colonial history of these areas has also determined the development of ethnographic work. For example, Papua, the southern half of what is now the State of Papua New Guinea, was originally a British colony, and for this reason was visited by the Torres Straits scientific expedition from England in 1898 in which the ethnologist Alfred Cort Haddon played a prominent part. In some instances the metropolitan influences from a colonial or ex-colonial power remain dominant, as for example with French influence in New Caledonia, and the concern which is felt in Australia for events in Papua New Guinea, which became independent from Australia in 1975. The attention of the world is focused in a different way on the western half of New Guinea, known as Irian Jaya (or West Papua), which was until 1962 a Dutch colony. Following the Indonesian takeover there in 1962, there has been since 1964 an indigenous movement for self-determination, the Organisasi Papua Merdeka (Organization for Papuan Freedom), whose members have clashed repeatedly with the Indonesian military, especially since East Timor gained its pathway to political independence from Indonesia in 2000. Such clashes have for long given rise to arguments on human rights and political practices centering on Irian Jaya. In Fiji, arguments about political rights have in the last quarter of the twentieth century taken the form of questions of the relationship between Pacific islander Fijians and the Indian Fijian population which the British originally brought in as a labor force on sugar plantations in colonial times. New Caledonia has also been a site of arguments about self-determination and the relationship between French settlers and the indigenous peoples who were given the name of Kanaks (a Polynesian term meaning "man" or "person" that entered into the *lingua franca* of colonial New Guinea with a derogatory sense but is now adopted with pride by the indigenous New Caledonians). The Solomons, also in the year 2000, became the center of an ongoing inter-ethnic dispute between the Malaitan and Guadalcanal peoples, resulting from conflicts over political power in general and specific land rights in the vicinity of the capital city of Honiara.

These brief remarks are needed in order to indicate some of the contemporary reasons why the ethnography of the South-West Pacific is relevant to wider issues in the world today. The societies of this region, like those in many other parts of the world such as Indonesia and Africa, tend to enter into world news only when there is trouble in them. It is important, therefore, to understand both the backgrounds to these troubles and that there is much more to these societies and cultures than can be conveyed in newspaper articles. Because of the inter-connections between events and processes in all parts of the world today there is an even greater need than in earlier times for a good understanding of local cultural and social processes that are caught up in what is loosely signified by the term globalization. At the same time the people of these societies are becoming increasingly concerned to identify themselves in their own terms in this new world. Ethnography has a special part to play in both of these regards, opening the way for mutual understanding and insight to be developed. We also include here some of the findings from the Hagen, Duna, and Pangia areas of Papua New Guinea where our own ethnographic observations have been made. (See Sillitoe 1998 and 2000 for a set of overviews and case studies comparable to those we present here.)

In terms of the classic topics studied by linguists and socio-cultural anthropologists the South-West Pacific has been an area of great interest because of the diversity of its languages and of its forms of kinship and descent, as well as practices of gift exchange between persons and groups. William Foley, taking into consideration the whole sweep of areas in which non-Austronesian languages are found in the South-West Pacific, has computed that the region contains "some 1200 languages, about 20%-25% of the world's total, from a bewildering multiplicity of language families, groupings and isolates—a linguistic diversity unparalleled elsewhere on the globe" (Foley 2000: 358). About a quarter of these languages, he says, are Austronesian in type and belong to the Central-Eastern Malayo-Polynesian grouping of Austronesian languages, itself further subdivided. Most are classified as Oceanic, a sub-grouping whose speakers appear to have spread out from an ancestral area in New Britain (Foley, pp. 360–1), and may have been associated with the diffusion of the Lapita style of pottery.

Adding to this picture given by Foley, Andrew Pawley (1998) estimates a total of 900 languages for the island of New Guinea itself, of which 150 are Austronesian and are "largely restricted to the coast and offshore islands," reflecting a probable in-migration along the coastlines "less than 4000 years ago" (p. 656). He adds that "by contrast, the 750 or so non-Austronesian languages, for which "Papuan" is the traditional cover term, dominate the interior of New Guinea" (ibid.) and belong to stocks which have been present there for a much longer period of time. Following the lead of a core set of research workers at the Australian National University and elsewhere, including Professor Stephen Wurm, Don Laycock, C.L. Voorhoeve, Karl Franklin, Alan Healey, Ken McElhanon and John Z'graggen, it was proposed that a great many of these non-Austronesian languages belonged to a massive Trans New Guinea Phylum, for which forty-seven sub-groups were suggested (Pawley, p. 663). Since 1994 Andrew Pawley, Wurm's successor as Professor of Linguistics at the Research School of Pacific and Asian Studies in the Australian National University, has been re-examining the data and arguments for this phylum. He and his colleagues, particularly Malcolm Ross, have been seeking to establish the historical phonology of these languages, that is, how their various sound patterns may have changed over long periods of time, and how they may be related to a proto-form or original version from which the languages have evolved. Pawley concludes that "there is a valid genetic group which includes many of the groups of Papuan languages assigned by Wurm" (p. 683). He notes that "most of the major groups of TNG [Trans New Guinea] languages are central in the Highlands" (p. 684), and appear to have a time depth for their dispersal of at least 5000 years, which is within the period in which agriculture, probably based on taro cultivation, is known, from archaeological work at Kuk in the Western Highlands Province of Papua New Guinea, to have been practiced. Foley calls this phylum a "family", and computes that it comprises close to "300 languages, with some two million speakers, or about half the total Papuan [i.e. non-Austronesian] speaking population" (Foley 2000: 363). From this estimate, we can see both the impressive spread of historical interrelationships between these languages and also the great linguistic diversity they nevertheless represent: some 300 distinct languages, comprising a number of "sub-families" in Foley's terminology. He lists for example twelve languages in the Eastern Highlands, with a total of 200,000 speakers. How these various patterns are tied in with culture history and the movements of people over time is still not established. Foley (1998) cautions that the complexities of these historical patterns may have deeply influenced the distribution of languages today.

In terms of social organization, ideas of descent in general form an important component of how people construct their social worlds, and kin relationships are universally significant. In different regions, patrilineal, matrilineal, or cognatic principles are predominant as factors in the constitution of local groups, wider social units, and in people's overall perceptions of their social universe. Throughout the Highlands region of New Guinea patrilineal principles, reflecting ideas about male procreation and the co-operation of men in the production of social groups, are counterbalanced by an equally strong emphasis on the affective and practical significance of maternal ties. This counterbalancing in most cases results in an ideological stress on the overall agnatic character of social groups seen as political units, combined with a great deal of flexibility with regard to processes of affiliation to groups, especially with regard to the children of female agnates, who may in some instances comprise up to half of a given group's members. In other cases, such as among the Mae Enga people (Meggitt 1965), agnatic descent seems to be important both in terms of group ideology and in terms of the practical affiliations of people. Meggitt linked this situation to shortage of land among the Mae in the 1950s and 1960s, arguing that with increases in population density agnates progressively excluded others from access to group resources. Elsewhere, however, this pattern does not seem to have been necessarily followed. Many observers have pointed to an apparent disjunction between ideologies of descent and practices of affiliation. In all of these cases it turns out that there are pragmatic reasons for the situation. It is expedient for men to claim to be linked by agnatic descent, since this can be appealed to as a rhetorical norm of solidarity between them, buttressed by ideas about powers of ancestors. At the same time it is equally expedient for them to encourage non-agnatic kin to settle with them and become their clients and supporters in group affairs (A. Strathern 1972).

These group affairs most frequently involve the raising of wealth items, such as pigs and shell valuables, for use in ceremonial exchange activities that strengthen the positions of particular leaders and their groups in contests of power and status. Hence ideologies and practices in relation to descent have always to be looked at in the context of imperatives to exchange wealth between people. For the same reason, maternal ties are important, because maternal kin are important exchange partners. Women therefore also gain in importance as social agents when they are the significant links through which exchanges are made; the more so when they are important as the producers of the basic form of indigenous wealth, pigs, fed on the sweet potato which women plant and harvest.

In a few instances, notably the Huli and Duna peoples of the Southern Highlands Province in Papua New Guinea, this stress on maternal ties has developed into a full recognition of both agnatic and maternal ties in the constitution of groups, leading to an overall cognatic descent structure and an elaborate balancing of exchange obligations with both paternal and maternal kin. Within this overall structure, however, agnatic ties are recognized as primary for certain jural and ritual contexts; which is also the situation found among the Choiseulese of the Solomon Islands, as we describe in a case study below.

It is notable that some of the Austronesian speaking groups off the northern coast of the New Guinea mainland, such as in New Britain and New Ireland, and Austronesian speakers in the Massim area of South-East Papua such as the Trobriand islanders, ascribe great prominence to matrilineal descent in group constitution, particularly with regard to ritual obligations, succession to leadership, and land rights. Here also, however, we find counterbalancing tendencies. In the Trobriands for example, ties with fathers are both affectively important and significant means of obtaining resources.

As we present our different case materials, it should be borne in mind that kinship and descent, understood in indigenous terms, remain basic frameworks for understanding the world and acting in it for Pacific peoples, even if this is not foregrounded in all of our accounts. Equally, practices of the exchange of wealth, tied in with kinship, remain significant and are progressively modified as a means of coming to terms with the modern world.

Fiji

The use of singular names, such as Fiji, referring to political entities created in the wake of colonial control, tends to conceal the fact that the island polities of the region themselves consist of conglomerates of islands. Fiji, for example, consists of a large number of islands scattered over 1,290,000 square kilometers of the South Pacific ocean. Only 106 of these islands are inhabited, while another 216 potentially could be lived on but for the lack of fresh water and their extreme isolation. Most of these islands are volcanic. The two largest are Viti Levu and Vanua Levu, which together account for 87% of Fiji's land. Three quarters of the population, which is divided between Pacific islander Fijians and Indo-Fijians, live on Viti Levu. Fiji was colonized by the British in the early nineteenth century. American ships also visited for the sandalwood trade. In 1854, Cakobau, an influential Fijian chief, converted to Wesleyan (Methodist) Christianity and became king (Tui Viti) of Western Fiji with missionary support. Fiji became a British Crown Colony in 1874, and achieved independence in 1970. The British brought Indians there as indentured laborers from the late 1870s until 1916. The military coup of 1987 and the later disturbances of 2000 have brought to the fore ongoing issues of conflict between the indigenous islanders and the Indians. Some 334,000 islanders speak the Western and Eastern dialects of the Fijian language, which is classified as belonging to the Oceanic branch of the Austronesian language family. Austronesian speakers had settled there by the late second millennium b.c.e., perhaps between 1200 and 1000 b.c.e., and with them it is thought that the hand-molded, open-fired, incised and dentate-stamped pottery known by archaeologists as Lapita ware came and that this pottery also spread to Western Polynesia including Tonga (Kirch 2000: 155–158). Fiji remained in communication with societies to its west, however, and physically many of its people resemble those of "Melanesia" to the west. The principle of chiefship is highly developed in Fiji, linking it to the "Polynesian" societies lying east of it, as well as to societies with chiefly principles in the "Melanesian" islands. In the last thousand years, landscapes were highly modified through intensive taro cultivation and thousands of fortified settlements were constructed, perhaps reflecting conflict between small chiefly polities, marked apparently by the consumption of human flesh. Kirch (p. 160) suggests this practice may have been the result of "competitive involution" between local groups. Contemporary political events suggest that such competitive processes continue, perhaps expressed through factional struggles within the Great Council of Chiefs, a body originally set up by the British. Today also Lapita traditions continue in many villages where people make a variety of pots for sale to tourists. Sigatoka, an important archaeological site on the coast of Viti Levu, is also a national heritage site today, visited by tourists who pay a small entrance fee and can walk across the dunes where fragments of potsherds lie.

Case Study:

Chiefship and Political Change in Fiji

As one moves further eastwards from the island of New Guinea, through the Solomons, Vanuatu, and New Caledonia, we find an obviously increasing emphasis on chiefship as a principle of social structure, linking these areas to the Polynesian societies further to the east. This is particularly marked in Fiji, where chiefship is almost universally the dominant form of leadership, and has itself in turn greatly changed historically since it was reshaped and co-opted into the British colonial structures of power and authority.

A basic account of Fijian chiefship was given by the Fijian anthropologist Rusiate Nayacakalou and published after his death in 1975. Nayacakalou recognized the complex relationship between pressures for change and the impetus for preservation of customary forms in Fiji which forms a pan-Pacific dialectic that continues to be worked out in contexts of conflict and accommodation today. He also recognized a major factor in this impetus: economic change and the need to retain land and increase its productivity as the "only hope of competing with Indians, who dominate the national economy" (Nayacakalou 1975: 5). This statement reveals an early perception of the troubles which emerged later in Fiji in the 1980s and 1990s; of conflict that is, between the Indo-Fijians who were originally brought in by the British to work on colonial sugar plantations as indentured laborers, but subsequently settled as independent farmers and business people, and the indigenous Fijians who own the land but who are economically less prosperous than the Indo-Fijians. Nayacakalou also points to the struggle between "communalistic" ideals which underpin chiefship itself and the "individualistic" ideals of development that have been linked to "modernity". Realities, of course, are more complex, but these two notions represent ideological and discursive poles around which specific conflicts and general senses of identity tend to coalesce. Nayacakalou fully recognizes that Fijian chiefship and social organization were restructured by the colonial Native Lands Commission from the 1890s onward, after Fiji was declared a British Crown Colony in 1874. This Commission established a customary segmentary model of social structure comprising *yavusa*, founded by an immigrant "ancestor-god", divided into *matanggali*[1] founded by the ancestor's sons, and these in turn into smaller groups known as *itokatoka*. Membership of such groups became the basis of land titles established by the Commission's questionnaires administered in each village. Nayacakalou points out that the model was too simple and did not reflect village-level complexities, in which persons of different original descent co-resided and people were "taken into" groups other than those to which they were linked by patrilineal descent. *Matanggali* in this picture become local divisions of a village, not descent-based corporations. Since chiefs are recognized as authoritative leaders of their "groups", much depends therefore on what is meant by a "group" and who is in it. Further, chiefships tend to be succeeded to by primogeniture, that is, seniority of patrilineal descent, but this was not the "sole criterion for selection" (p. 33). Knowledge and ability were also important factors. Some imputation of dominance belongs to senior branches but conflicts can develop over this.

At the level of the district which includes a number of villages, there is a recognized chief called the *Tui*, followed by the name of his district or *vanua* (a term meaning in general "land" associated with a group), and he and his descendants are entitled to chiefly titles (*Ratu* for males, *Bulou* for females). This level of chief is elevated to a position of respect and surrounded by taboos which express a hierarchical relationship with followers. While the *Tui* generally succeeds to his position by seniority he may do so also by adoption and by service, or through internal conflicts and processes of selection. The

---

1. We have used /nggl/ here to represent the Fijian /q/, because this transcription indicates how the letter is pronounced.

office is political, and it is tied in with the colonially constituted Great Council of Chiefs which the British created as a part of their policy of Indirect Rule. Nayacakalou also points out (p. 50) that the Native Lands Commission could itself appoint a chief in cases of unresolved disputes. The Council of Chiefs was directly tied in with the colonial administrative hierarchy. Its function was to advise the colonial Governor on all matters involving indigenous Fijians, and its members also selected by secret ballot seven to ten officials as representatives in the colony's Legislative Council (p. 84). Deriving from this colonial structure, it is evident that the Council has a vested interest in preserving a pyramidal structure of political representation under its own control. In the name of communalism chiefs may also attempt to exploit their relationship with commoners, Nayacakalou notes, quoting the words of one prominent chief himself: "Some of us are too greedy—we just want things from our people without thinking of the return as is proper at custom" (p. 138). These observations acquire a particular poignancy in the light of subsequent conflicts.

While the details of succession to specific positions of chiefship are complex, it seems that the principle of hierarchy encapsulated in the idea of chiefship is pervasive. Christina Toren (1990) has examined this principle in a range of contexts, beginning with the spousal relationship, siblingship and matrilateral kin. She finds that while women are expected to defer to their husbands, senior women as well as men must be treated with respect and maternal kin ties are important. Equality is expressed only between persons in relationships in which joking is conventionally permitted, as for example between cross-cousins, who are also the prime marriageable category (Toren, p. 50). After a marriage between cross-cousins, the equality between them dissolves into respect. Respect is also expressed pervasively in forms of seating at church services and at formal meetings held by chiefs in connection with administrative affairs. Even when these meetings are called by elected officials, Toren shows that chiefs can dominate the proceedings through the assumption of their rights to speak at them. Chiefly status is also used to shore up elected authority (p. 166). Andrew Arno's (1993) work on talk and conflict settlement in the Lau area, begun in 1970, amply confirms this importance of talk in general, arguing that both the hierarchical context of chiefship and the egalitarian medium of joking between cross-cousins are important as channels for settling disputes.

Kinship and chiefship clearly remain important frameworks of order for Fijians. However, this does not mean that they are able to contain all possible disruptions to such order. Colonial and post-colonial politics and economics have taken their toll in this regard. The indigenous Fijians were to some extent content with their "protected" status under colonial rule, but the Indo-Fijians pushed for Independence and voting rights for themselves and Fiji became independent in 1970. When over time both the overall Indo-Fijian population and their political representatives became strong enough to stake their claims to political power, calls began for their removal. In 1987 indigenous Fijians marched to protest against Indo-Fijian membership of a coalition government, and Lt. Col. Sitiveni Rabuka led a military coup on 14 May of that year, to the surprise of the Australian and New Zealand governments. The coup overturned the Labor Party-based multiracial politics which the recent election had set up, and it was also motivated by the opposition of traditionally dominant chiefs in the Alliance Party to the rise of Dr. Timoci Bavadra, head of the coalition party, who came from Viti Levu. Rabuka led a second coup in September of 1987 and declared Fiji a republic, cutting off ties with the Commonwealth of Nations and the British crown. In 1990 the government installed by Rabuka and headed by Ratu Sir Kamisese Mara enacted a new Constitution giving the Great Council of Chiefs the power to appoint the President and twenty-four of thirty-three Senate members, and granting political and military preeminence to indigenous Fijians. This arrangement was in turn negated by the installation of a new multiracial Constitution in 1997, followed by the electoral victory of Mahendra Chaudhry, the Indo-Fijian leader of the urban-based Labor Party.

It was not long before this situation also unraveled, leading to the attempted coup by George Speight and his allies in the year 2000 and the complicated and still unresolved aftermaths of this event. Speight, a Fijian of part-Australian descent, raised the issue of Indo-Fijian domination as had Rabuka's supporters earlier, but he seems to have represented in part also the interests of some younger Fijians and of the western bloc of chiefs. He held Chaudhry and members of his government hostage in the Parliament while he negotiated for the dissolution of the new "multiracial" Constitution and Chaudhry's removal as Prime Minister, as well as the power to determine who the next President was to be. After military intervention, Speight was himself held by the authorities, but discussions on the future makeup of politics continued, with demands by the Australian and New Zealand governments that the new Constitution be fully restored. It seems evident that governments which themselves backed or acquiesced in the creation of indigenously governed nation-states elsewhere in the Pacific, such as Papua New Guinea, are faced with a difficulty in the case of Fiji, where there is major conflict between two categories of people who both have strong claims to political rights there. The conflict has no exact parallel elsewhere in the Pacific, and while its roots can clearly be traced to colonial times, it is the kind of problem that in the end can only be decided by those immediately involved, even if the forms of resolution do not agree with the views of the international community. The conflict also represents the sharpest case of the emergence of ethnic politics in the South-West Pacific to date. But this trend to the invocation of ethnicity in politics has certainly emerged in pervasive forms throughout the region, notably in the Solomon Islands (see below).

Case Study:

Medicine and Morality in Fiji

Richard Katz is an anthropologist who has studied systems of holistic medicine and healing in South Africa and Fiji. His work in Fiji was carried out in 1977–78, in the capital city of Suva and an island chain to which he gives the pseudonym of Bitu. His overall account stresses the importance of Fijian concepts such as *vu*, referring to ancestors and gods, and *mana* meaning power, including the power to heal but also the power to harm or kill if it is used disrespectfully. As in the Solomons and throughout Polynesia, these ideas have become partly blended with, partly superseded by, notions about the Christian God, owing to the long-standing presence of the Methodist and Catholic churches (Katz 1993: 24). Probably a complicated history of struggles in the past explains Katz's statement that the contemporary healers he studied had taken over this function from the ancient priestly clans because the priests had misused their *mana*. This reads like the echo of a Christian narrative of Fijian history from earlier times (p. 27).

Fijians have preserved hierarchical ideas about the correct dispositions of bodies in space in terms of higher and lower positions; and of etiquette in the mixing, serving, and consumption of kava (*yanggona*), in which respect is shown to elders and chiefs. Katz says that at ritual occasions of drinking kava the *vu* are invited to be present, and that this is why healing sessions begin with a ceremonial kava exchange (p. 54), in which the patient presents kava to the healer and asks for help. Most rural healers are older men, while in urban areas more are women and of younger age and they tend to enter into states of possession. It seems likely that the urban patterns are an innovation.

After the kava presentation the healer gives the patient a massage and mixes some herbal medicines. Healers deal with both physical ailments and conditions said to be caused by infractions against norms that have been punished by the *vu* through sending sickness. Directing *mana* so that it can heal sickness of the latter kind is called "the straight path", and is opposed to the use of power to harm others. In this regard the work of the healer becomes a microcosm of the efforts of Fijians in general to sustain their "true" ancestral custom. The domain of the healer is preserved also by the idea that sicknesses caused by the *vu* cannot be healed by western medicine. This is also a basic belief in New Guinea, and is analogous to the idea of the Duna people of the Southern Highlands Province of Papua New Guinea that witchcraft cannot be combated by Christian prayers (Stewart and Strathern 1999a). The belief in the involvement of the *vu* is maintained by a form of self-fulfilling logic. One healer whom he calls Tevita told Katz that whenever he gave a particular herbal mixture to a patient and the patient recovered he knew that the *vu* were involved (Katz, p. 128).

An interesting aspect of the healer's work is that not all of it is concerned directly with healing ailments in the human body. Tevita, for example, was consulted about problems in a fishing project, in which younger men felt that older men were jealous and might make sorcery against them. Healers are supposed to be able to combat such sorcery because it represents the evil inverse of their own *mana*, the evil they must avoid in order to continue doing good. It is apparent here that they are significant mediators in contexts of conflict over social change and economic enterprises. They are also asked to make magic to protect boats against accidents, much as Hageners of the Western Highlands in Papua New Guinea used to perform blessing ceremonies, *kela memb*, over newly purchased cars.

During Katz's fieldwork, a struggle occurred over Tevita's work. An evangelical church minister came to the village and demanded that the people give up all their indigenous medicines (*rewa*) as the instruments of Satan and come to Jesus instead (Katz, p. 239). The village was swept by a fundamentalist Christian revival (such as have occurred very widely throughout the Pacific) and the healer Tevita decided to retire. The movement's supporters held healing prayers to try to combat an epidemic of sicknesses in the village, taking the place of Tevita's work in an atmosphere of fear and crisis (Katz, p. 251). One of the leaders in these prayers was a member of the village itself, who was clearly attempting to gain prominence for himself in this way. The Christian healing groups did not abolish the belief in sorcery and people were not confident that they were able to overcome it. Katz's old mentor in Suva, Ratu Noa, commented that the church minister "was mistaken in saying that it is wrong to use Fijian traditional rituals these days" (p. 266). Ratu Noa's position was that Jesus had worked with the same *mana* that Fijian healers used, and that the Reverend's actions were not in accordance with the will of God, *Kalou*, but came from his own desire to aggrandize himself. "He is killing the very foundations of our way of life" (p. 267).

Katz's materials take us into the center of the sharp conflicts that have emerged in the past, are emerging, and will continue to emerge whenever there is a clear confrontation between evangelical Christianity and traditionalists. We will see from other case histories how such confrontations may be succeeded by phases of awkward accommodation. We also see from this Fijian case how healers are at the heart of general struggles over social change, the local working out of forces that reach out from many parts of the world and become painfully intertwined with personal interactions of individuals. The rhetoric which Tevita and Ratu Noa used to support their craft was itself very clearly shaped by these forces as well as representing a courageous attempt to answer to them and retain a sense of their own dignity and agency.

New Caledonia

New Caledonia consists of a single 400 kilometers (c. 250 miles) long island, La Grande Terre, with the Loyalty Islands chain to its east. In 1995 it had an estimated population of 185,000. French colonial possession over these territories was claimed in 1853, and the mineral-rich soils in this area gave rise from 1876 onward to a profitable nickel-mining industry. The Austronesians who entered the area around 2000 b.c.e developed over time into thirty-seven distinct language groups and built stone fortifications in dryland, karst limestone plateaus where competition for agricultural land was probably most intense (Kirch 2000: 150). On the main island taro irrigation terraces and yam mounding systems were developed. The traces of these formations possibly point to a build-up of population and emergence of chiefdoms in prehistoric times, followed by a massive demographic collapse after colonization owing to introduced diseases and the disruption of indigenous agricultural patterns brought about the colonial settlers (Kirch 2000: 155).

Captain James Cook gave the name of New Caledonia to La Grande Terre in 1774 while on his second expedition in search of Terra Australis. The terrain reminded Cook of the Highlands of Scotland, hence the name. British and American traders came searching for whales, sandalwood, and sea cucumbers (a kind of sea creature, *trepang*, boiled, dried, and used in making Chinese soup), intensifying their activities from 1840 onwards. Later in the century, the indigenous people were taken in numbers to foreign plantations as laborers, a practice known as "blackbirding". The traders' presence and behavior effected the introduction of new diseases, guns, and fierce fighting. Catholic French and Protestant English missionaries of the London Missionary Society battled one another also for control over converts to the Christian religion, giving rise to wars between rival local groups. Missionaries thought they had purchased land from the people, while the people thought they had only given the incomers permissive residence. Conflicts ensued. The French military were brought in to quell these disturbances and the emperor Napoleon III declared New Caledonia annexed to France in 1853. Convicts were shipped there from 1864 onwards, including many political radicals, and were put to work building churches and roads. Once freed they were encouraged to settle. Free settlers also came from France, and took over land for cattle farms, destroying the taro terraces. A revolt in 1878 was crushed, and the indigenous people were placed outside of French common law and forced into segregated reservations, with only 11% of the total land. Laborers were brought from Asia to work in the nickel mines which had begun in 1864. Segregation was ended only in 1946 after the Second World War, during which the US military had set up a base on La Grande Terre. Political movements for independence began in the 1950s, and their struggles grew more intense after other Pacific countries gained independence from 1970 on. In 1984 the settlers of metropolitan French origins, the Caldoches, entered into factional fighting with the indigenous Kanaks. A complicated series of political events ensued, ending in 1989 with the assassination of a noted Kanak leader Jean-Marie Tjibaou. Finally in 1998 New Caledonians agreed to a power-sharing agreement with France and to delay a further independence referendum for fifteen to twenty years. Clearly, the entrenched presence of the Caldoches is what has made a transition to independence much harder than elsewhere in the South-West Pacific. The French government has made available funding for a fine cultural center near Noumea (the capital city), named after Jean-Marie Tjibaou, as an implicit part of compensation for the turmoils of the past. The population today is only about 45% Kanaks, with 35% French or other Europeans, and smaller percentages of Asians and Polynesians from French Polynesia. One historical commentator, Robert Aldrich, noted that for the future "debates over the symbols of sovereignty (the name of the country and its flag, for example) as well as major issues such as land rights, and the division of economic and political power are likely to endure (1993: 284)."

New Caledonian indigenous cultures were founded on principles of chiefship and segmentary relations between groups, modified by interpersonal networks and the integrative functions of traditions of sacred cult pathways across the land. The Tjibaou cultural center attempts to portray some of these principles in the shape of ceremonial houses in which chiefs and elders debated issues. Anthropologists such as Jean Guiart and Alban Bensa (Guiart 1963; Bensa and Rivierre 1982) and historians such as Bronwen Douglas (1992, 1998) have done much to piece together pictures both of indigenous social organization and of colonial history and its early impacts on the peoples.

Douglas has stressed the need for a critical approach in approaching the historical ethnography of New Caledonian societies, for example in reconstructing the meanings of clashes between New Caledonian and French forces in the nineteenth century; and further in establishing the character of indigenous New Caledonian leadership (1998: 29–34) and gender relations, in which she has been concerned to recover the "traces of indigenous female agency" (1998: 114), for example women's active roles in fighting between groups (p. 115). It is likely that her own earlier generalizations regarding the mixture of elements of ascription and achievement in leadership patterns and her conclusion that "the greater the stress on kinship and descent as elements in group formation and cohesion, the more likely seniority and heredity were to be important leadership principles" will continue to stand (1998: 61, first published in 1979; see also Allen 1981).

Case Study:

New Caledonia: Chiefship and Historical Change

Alban Bensa, a French ethnologist, has written some of the major studies of chiefship in New Caledonia, following on earlier work by Maurice Leenhardt and Jean Guiart. These French traditions of scholarship clearly reflect French colonial interests in the island. Bensa's work revolves around the same kinds of interpretive issues that have occupied the attentions of scholars writing about "big-men", "chiefs", and "great-men" in New Guinea and elsewhere (Watson-Gegeo and Feinberg 1996). Bensa also takes up a theme found elsewhere in the Pacific and as far away as Eastern Indonesia: the notion that "chiefs" are pictured as prestigious immigrants with special powers taken in by the owners of the land and granted their power by these autochthonous figures, who thereby made themselves the chief's subjects (as discussed by Sahlins 1987: 73–103). Sahlins, following the work of the classical scholar Georges Dumézil on Indo-European traditions of kinship, notes that the basic idea involved here is that in societies "composed of kith and kin, of diverse lineages and clans, the ruler as above society is also considered beyond it" (1987: 78). Valerio Valeri, in his study of kingship and sacrifice in Hawai'i, notes further that the king is seen as outside society in another way, because "he is the closest instantiation of" the gods themselves and is therefore empowered to consecrate "the supreme form of sacrifice to the supreme gods" and "it is precisely this that gives him authority over men" (Valeri 1985: 142). Bensa contrasts the view of the chief as an outsider with the picture of the chief as the senior son of a male line of descent, responsible for looking after his people (Bensa 2000: 10); and further with the image of chiefs in the mid-nineteenth century as despotic fight leaders. Bensa is pointing here to the problem of historical change and the changing images of indigenous institutions created by observers. In effect all three descriptive elements pertaining to chiefship may have some validity. The idea of the chief as an immigrant stranger is preserved in origin stories; that of the chief as the senior successor in an agnatic line belongs to subsequent traditions; and the portrait of the chief as a violent leader is influenced by the heightened population movements and altered alliances occasioned by the intrusions of the French as recorded by French writers around 1850, and in particular after New Caledonia became a French colony in 1853.

One feature of chiefship, discussed by Bensa and Goromido, is quite remarkable, representing a particular application of the idea commonly found in the Pacific that "kinship" is based on commonality of substance and this is created by sharing food (often in combination with ideas about "blood" and "land"). In New Caledonia chiefs were sometimes brought in as outsiders, and in order to turn them into kin they would be offered ancient local types of yams to eat and also the sacrificed body of a man of high-ranking lineage in the local group. By consuming the flesh of this sacrifice the newcomer became one with those he served as chief. Correlatively, a chief might offer his own body as a sacrifice before his death. His liver was consumed and other parts of his body were placed on stones in a shrine dedicated to ancestors whose blessing was requested (Bensa and Goromido 1997: 98–101).

The traditions regarding one fightleader, Goodu, younger son of a chief, indicate that after pursuing vendettas against other groups he turned his aggression on his own kin, including his classificatory elder brother. The explanation given for this was that he possessed a magic stone which demanded the human flesh of victims, otherwise it would itself devour its owner. Goodu (who appears in Douglas 1992: 101 as Gondou) seems to have been a historical figure who emerged in the turbulence of early colonial times and acted in a predatory manner towards his neighbors to such a degree that some preferred to ally themselves with the French and to band together to kill him, thus inadvertently perhaps removing him as an obstacle to French control. Bensa also points out that Goodu broke the rules of the ritual consumption of human flesh which played a constitutive part in chiefship in the past, and himself indiscriminately killed and ate his own kin. As a result his mother's kin withdrew their ritual protection of him and his brothers allied themselves with the French to overthrow him.

French colonial control solidified and modified the position of the chief until the arrival of Maurice Leenhardt as a missionary there in 1902. The model of chiefship as Leenhardt saw it was in part a colonial creation—like the model of chiefship instituted by the British in Fiji —and hence Leenhardt developed his idea of the chief as a representative of his people but without power of his own (see Watson-Gegeo and Feinberg 1996: 34 on "populist" chiefs). Bensa's study neatly exemplifies the cautionary point that ethnographic descriptions belong to a particular time and place as well as to particular observers. His account of Goodu may also remind us of a debate about leadership in the Papua New Guinea Highlands shortly after the imposition of colonial rule there from the 1930s onward, as to whether some leaders might be seen as "despots" along the lines of Matoto, a Tairora "big-man" who behaved in an arrogant and ruthless fashion (Watson 1967). With hindsight, it seems possible that the accounts and traditions which developed around Matoto's name were influenced by conditions of turbulence and change associated with the colonial encroachment. Matoto was alive when the first of the Australians came to his place and was said to have threatened to shoot the intruders, but he died just prior to 1930 before Australian control was established, so we cannot argue that he was directly in conflict with the colonial presence. However, the sharp curtailment of the fighting ethos caused by the incursion of the colonial power after his death could well have generated an exaggerated legend of his prowess and outlandish deeds; and the same kind of process may have occurred with Goodu in New Caledonia. Matoto's bones were kept, and his skull was brought out by his relatives as a protective device in the 1960s when there was an eclipse of the sun (Watson 1967: 233).

Vanuatu

Vanuatu comprises 82 islands, divided into three groups. The twelve largest islands account for 93% of the land area and between them had a population of about 100,000 in 1989. The islands are composed of volcanic ash and limestone, and are still subject to earthquakes and volcanic eruptions, as well as hurricanes. The Spanish explorer Quiros named Espiritu Santo in 1606; the French explorer de Bougainville sailed between Espiritu Santo and Malekula in 1768; and Captain James Cook charted the entire group in 1774, calling it the New Hebrides because it reminded him of the misty western isles of Scotland. Garanger (1996: 8) comments that de Bougainville had called it the Great Cyclades, because it reminded him "of the luminous, gentle islands of the Aegean." Perhaps these explorers visited the area in different weather conditions. The name Vanuatu, adopted by the people after gaining their independence in 1980, means "the land that stands up," echoing the phrase in the modern Papua New Guinea *Tok Pisin* song, *Bipo Australia i lukautim yumi tasol nau yumi yet i mas sanap*, "Previously, Australia looked after us, but now we must stand up on our own."

Vanuatu's colonial history, like that of New Caledonia, has been turbulent. Sandalwood traders from 1825 to 1869 provoked violence. London Missionary Society members were killed in 1839. A Presbyterian missionary, John Paton, incited the Royal Navy to shell the island of Tanna in 1865, in response to the Tannese expelling him and his wife in 1860 following a measles epidemic (Linnekin 1997: 199). Smallpox was introduced via infected clothing from abroad. The population dropped from about 500,000 to about 40,000 in 1920; currently it is up to a total of 174,000 including foreigners. Up to the early 1900s as many as 50,000 people, males and females, were taken as indentured laborers to the sugar cane fields in Queensland, Australia (Moore 1985). French and British companies occupied indigenous land. Warships were sent to bombard coastal villages when the local people resisted this process. Joint British-French jurisdiction over the islands began in 1887. In World War II American forces established a large base on Espiritu Santo.

The British authorities succeeded in training local people (ni-Vanuatu) for government roles. In the 1970s the French tried to build a French-speaking majority, but failed. In 1971 the New Hebrides Cultural Association emerged as a resistance movement against large land purchases by an American businessman; and it soon became a nationalist political party (the Vana'aku Party), headed by an Anglican priest Walter Lini, who later became the country's first Prime Minister, against French opposition. The new government survived a rebellion on Espiritu Santo by the followers of Jimmy Stevens. British and French troops sent to Santo to disarm Stevens were replaced by a national force from Papua New Guinea under General Ted Diro, and Stevens was arrested (W. Rodman 2000). Vanuatu's subsequent political history has been marked by intense factionalism and continuing opposition between Anglophone and Francophone interests. At independence, however, unlike the situation in Papua New Guinea, all alienated land was returned to its putative indigenous holders.

Vanuatu cultures show much diversity, in line with the separation from one another of autonomous groups that is so widespread in the South-West Pacific islands. These diversities are often shown in the rich elaboration of different rituals and artistic traditions associated with them. Nevertheless, the overall themes of these rituals revolved around the importance of age-graded initiation, institutions of chiefship and competition for power, and the raising of pigs for slaughter in sacrifice and the extraction of their tusks to be used as prestigious decorations, accompanied by prestations of yams, taro, kava, and also dance forms and songs, which would require a reciprocal return. These cultural patterns clearly link Vanuatu to the Solomon Islands and New Guinea, as does its diversity of languages, with 105 separate languages, all Austronesian variants. *Bislama*, which is the national language, also closely resembles Papua New Guinea's *Tok Pisin* and Solomon Islands' *Pijin*. These are "creolised" language forms, combining a vocabulary largely based on English with grammatical patterns more typical of indigenous languages. It is remarkable that while pigs were central in the rituals in Vanuatu, the Solomons, and New Guinea, they were absent in New Caledonia until Captain Cook landed there in 1774 and was so struck by the civility of the people that he gave two dogs to one chief and two pigs to another. In other respects the prehistoric evidence for Vanuatu resembles that for New Caledonia. Pioneering fieldwork by José Garanger on the island of Efate and nearby established the first arrival of Lapita-ware people followed by locally variable "incised and applied-relief ceramics" (Kirch 2000: 135) called Mangaasi by archaeologists. The first "Lapita people" apparently came around 3,000 years ago to Erromango island. Vanuatu oral traditions have also proved a valuable source of evidence of prehistoric practices. On Retoka island there is a sacred site where according to traditions an important chief Roy Mata was interred along with the bodies of kinsfolk. Garanger excavated this site and found burials corresponding to these traditions, including a central male skeleton and pairs of male and female skeletons clutching each other. The archaeologist Matthew Spriggs notes that according to traditions the men were drugged with kava but the women were supposedly conscious at the time of burial. The bodies were ornamented with shell beads and bands and pig tusks, and the site dates to between 650 and 400 years ago, which attests to the validity of the local oral histories. The site also attests to the level of chiefly hierarchy that held sway on Retoka at the time, and possibly fits with the argument that the severe demographic collapse of island societies in the colonial period obscured strong chiefly patterns which were developed earlier (Kirch 2000: 139–140; compare the earlier discussion by Jolly 1994: 29–34).

Case Study:

Status Acquisition in Vanuatu: Art and Power

Vanuatu societies have become well-known in the ethnographic literature for their graded rituals of status acquisition. There appears to have been a complex historical circulation of cults of this type analogous to the circulation of fertility cults with their repetitions and variations of customary elements in the Western Highlands of Papua New Guinea (Strathern and Stewart 1999a). Consequently it is difficult to isolate elements from one another, although earlier anthropologists who worked in the area such as Bernard Deacon and John Layard attempted to do so, identifying separate cultural complexes which they thought had been mixed over time. Some of the elements involved were the planting of sacred shrubs and trees, the erection of carved tree-fern statues, and the construction of dolmens, stone platforms and stone circles. It is this pattern of building stone monuments that has led to the attribution of the term megalithic cultures to the Vanuatu cases (Patterson 1981: 191). In kinship terms another persistent element is the introduction of a candidate for early grades in the prestige hierarchy by maternal kin. Sacrifices of tusked boars on stone platforms and their presentation to mothers' or wives' kin were a concomitant of this practice.

Mary Patterson gives an account of three of these rituals from north Ambrym. One was *tobuan*. This consisted simply of clubbing to death boars with long circular tusks on the stone platforms and their presentation to either mother's or wife's patrilineal kin. The intending killer solicited preliminary gifts from his kin and then returned these with an increment at the time of the killing. This element of a solicitory gift followed by a greater return resembles the pattern of *moka* gifts in the Hagen area of Papua New Guinea. The kinsmen of the killer furnished the stone platform for the sacrifice and were paid for this. The killer of the boars climbed up a ladder made up by the intended recipients of the sacrifice, each rung representing a boar previously killed for the kinsfolk; and as he climbed up he announced the name of the participants who received pigs commemorated in this way. The recipients were also given a presentation of cycas palm leaves and a lily-like plant with red flowers (Patterson 1981: 195). These elements also have resonances with Hagen custom. The runged ladder resembles in its function the set of bamboo or cane sticks worn as a pendant by participants in the Hagen *moka* exchange system, in which each cross-piece indicated a set of eight or ten pearl shells given previously by the wearer to exchange partners. The leaves and the lily-like plant are reminiscent of the sacred plant objects that belong to the complex of fertility cults in the Western Highlands of Papua New Guinea. It is reasonable to suppose that they were also supposed to have life-giving powers, such as are thought in many parts of the Pacific to be bound up in the cordyline plant. The donor of the pigs at the *tobuan* could also sacrifice pigs for youths whom he wished to place in the category of his "sons", thereby binding them to him as his supporters. The *tobuan* was therefore an occasion for creating a political following: again, as "big-men" did by extended kin ties in *moka* gifts to classificatory kin in Hagen.

Patterson further notes that by means of each successive sacrifice the holder of a *tobuan* identifies himself progressively with the ancestors, ensuring for himself a place in the ancestral world. Each sacrifice in a sense marked a rebirth of the identity of the sacrificer, signaled also by the lighting of a new fire and his assumption of a new name and title. The broad equivalent of this in the *moka* is the *moka*-maker's desire to make his "name" or identity (*mbi*) widely known and therefore commemorated in the future, a form of success which is thought to depend on ancestral support as well as the individual's own determined efforts.

There is another aspect to the rite which also finds a close parallel in New Guinea custom. In north Ambrym the sacrifices had a propitiatory or apotropaic function, that is, they were made to placate spirits and avoid misfortune. They had to be continued by a man through life "in order that the spirits of his mother's kinsmen will not devour him when he dies, make him ill while he lives or even kill him" (Patterson 1981: 197). This striking point is paralleled by the common practice of making matrilateral payments in New Guinea for the same purpose of ensuring the benevolence of the mother's kin or at least averting their malevolence. Ideas of this kind tend to be enduring. Patterson notes that these practices continued in her field area during 1968–1971, the span of time of her fieldwork visits, except among those converted to the Seventh Day Adventist church. The practices had a further twist. In rituals analogous to the *tobuan* the sacrificer pointed his arrows at his mother's kin in a ritual threat to kill them, and it was explained that this was an act of transgression to express his daring in the face of his mother's agnates who were his life-givers: "the kinsmen who pass on, through their sisters and daughter, the vital blood that sustains life and who have the power to guarantee the existence of a person's spirit after death" (Patterson 1981: 217).

New rituals were continually being imported from one area to another and used as a vehicle for achieving status and prestige. In north Ambrym the *tobuan* rituals appear to have been the basic and oldest forms, closely tied in with kinship relations. The people in this area had more recently imported a system of status grades called *mage*, through which particular families were able to consolidate their high status and pass it down to their successors. The study of such importations and the prerequisites for status acquisition which went with them can provide clues to historical patterns of changes in leadership, possibly linked also to colonial influence as well as to indigenous micro-evolution. The immensely complex and aesthetically impressive Vanuatu rituals and the artistic forms that went with them were a testimony to the social drives of competition and self-aggrandizement by which they were motivated (see Bonnemaison 1996).

Bonnemaison suggests that the quest for individual prestige developed historically out of the religious sources of these rituals. This idea would be in line with Patterson's observation that in Ambrym the rituals were closely tied to kinship but also in a sense represented a transgression or transcending of the kinship order. Yet the rituals were still embedded in a fundamental ideological framework about the need for ancestral support, just as the *moka* activities were in the Hagen area. Masks were worn as the marks of the increasing status of participants. As a man rose in the graded societies he became treated as "a supernatural being, hedged about with numerous tabus and kept carefully apart from the world of the 'living'" (Bonnemaison 1996: 209). This process reveals a fundamental difference from the New Guinea Highlands processes, in which a "big-man's" prestige was tied to his own lifetime and there was no elaborate or automatic transformation of a dead "big-man" into a powerful, ranked ancestor.

Artistic productions were geared to this system of acquisition of power. Grade-takers in lower ranks had to carve tree-fern statues for their entry, and later to surround these with rows of small upright stones when they entered the intermediate grades. For the highest grades tall stones were erected. In south Malakula, high-ranking men were represented after their death in effigies, built around their modeled skulls and painted in white, blue, black, and red with marks of their rank (Bonnemaison, p. 209). Men wove special garments and constructed tapa (bark cloth) belts to mark their entry into high grades. Women decorated elaborately for many of these ritual occasions and wove important kinds of mats, some of which were used to wrap the dead while others, known on Ambae Island as *singo*, were "small, finely woven mats which are understood to be inherently powerful, capable of causing harm to those who mishandle them." They made another object from pandanus leaves which men wore folded over a belt or hanging from it to indicate a status they had achieved in the *hungwe* graded pig-killing system (Bolton 1996: 113). Women themselves wear elaborate barkcloth mats for their dances, and they are the chief contributors of decorated mats to social occasions. Bolton notes that these occasions include life-cycle rites. In Longana, she writes, "as many as 1500 mats may be exchanged at one marriage" (Bolton 1996: 114). Women have also historically invented new types of mats and passed them into networks of exchange while commemorating the names of the places where the mats were first made. It is apparent that this "mat cycle" constitutes an important sphere of social reproduction and memory-creation in relation to networks of associations between women and places that has to be seen as parallel in importance to the male drive to create personal ancestral power through the grade system. Women's artifacts were also essential to men as the artistic markers of the status they achieved while alive and as the encompassing elements which took them on their final pathway to bodily death. Maternal connections and matrilineal descent were important ongoing elements in this picture of the balanced interplay between the achievement of female and male status.

The Solomon Islands

The Solomon Islands complex abuts at its north-western end on the lower tip of Bougainville Island, which is historically a part of Papua New Guinea. The six largest islands of the Solomons chain are Choiseul, Isabel, Malaita, New Georgia, Guadalcanal, and Makira. In all there are 347 inhabited islands out of a total of 922, with a population estimated in 1995 to be 399,000. The 1999 census results indicate a current overall figure of 409,000. Archaeologically, the Solomons and Bougainville belong together. Matthew Spriggs found a ceramic sequence spanning the last 1500 years in Central Bougainville (Kirch 2000: 133). Peter Sheppard has found possible traces of Lapita occupation in the Roviana Lagoon, New Georgia (ibid.). David Roe, analyzing materials excavated in Guadalcanal, found evidence of settlement dating from about 6,400 years up to 150 years ago, demonstrating agricultural intensification, but without pottery. Burial crypts investigated by Kirch, Douglas Yen, and Paul Rosendahl on Kolombangara Island contained human skulls and shell disks of the kind anthropologists have described as being important in competitive exchange activities. Notable among these studies was Harold Scheffler's study of exchange on Choiseul Island (Scheffler 1965). The recent archaeological and ethnohistorical work of Sheppard and Shankar Aswani on Roviana promises to establish the points in time when shell valuables appeared in burial sites and the correlations with the historical intensification of chiefship patterns, also linking together the histories of coastal Austronesian with inland non-Austronesian speakers. Earlier work in social anthropological vein, such as Scheffler's, can therefore now be linked with more recent findings by prehistorians. In this regard it is also interesting to note that both Garanger and Spriggs attribute the Roy Mata burial complex in Vanuatu to an in-migration from Polynesia, in line with other back migrations from Polynesia into the Solomons in the last 1,500 years, including to Anuta (see Feinberg and Macpherson this volume), Tikopia (studied by Raymond Firth), Bellona (studied by Torben Monberg), Rennell Island (Kirch 2000: 147), and other places. The Santa Cruz islands, which lie 665 km (412 miles) to the east of Honiara, the Solomons capital, also contain both Melanesian (non-Austronesian speaking) and Polynesian peoples.

Spanish explorers came to the Solomons in the sixteenth and seventeenth centuries, as a part of the search for the treasures of El Dorado. Pedro Fernandez de Quirós called the islands the Solomons, implying they were as rich as King Solomon's fabled treasure. Malaria and conflicts with the people led to the Spanish departing. In 1767–8 Carteret and de Bougainville rediscovered Santa Cruz, Malaita, and Choiseul. In the 1830s the colonial trading phase began, sea traders purchasing shells, sea-cucumbers and sandalwood, often cheating the people and spreading disease as well as their trade goods (e.g. iron to replace stone tools). Labor recruiters between 1870 and 1910 took thousands of workers to the cane fields of Fiji and Queensland, Australia. Missionaries of the Catholic church began work on Guadalcanal and Malaita in the nineteenth century, and returning labor migrants brought back other churches. Britain declared a protectorate in the Solomons in 1893 to limit German colonial interests in Bougainville. Large coconut plantations owned by Levers and Burns Philp were established. The Japanese seized the Solomons in 1942, precipitating a fierce conflict with American military forces and the Allies, particularly in Guadalcanal. The indigenous islanders were greatly impressed by the wealth and power of the Americans and after the defeat of the Japanese they began the Ma'asina Ruru (or Masing Rule) movement for change and reassertion of indigenous custom as a means of promoting political and cultural autonomy, in reaction against the perceived indignities of British colonial rule. The term Ma'asina means a set of brothers, derived from usage among the 'Are'are people, and the aim of the movement was to unite a number of linguistic groups together in opposition to the colonial government, and to encourage the Americans, with their wealth, to return (Keesing 1992: 103). The British arrested movement leaders, and factional struggles weakened it internally also; but the authorities were constrained to set up a system of local government after 1953 starting with Malaita itself, eventually leading towards political independence for the Solomons in 1978. Since that time, there has been conflict with the Papua New Guinea state and with Australia over policies towards the separatist movement in Bougainville. The Bougainville problem has also entered into issues between Malaitans and Guadalcanal people that have resulted in interethnic conflicts around Honiara, the capital. Bartholomew Ulufa'alu, Prime Minister of the Solomons for a part of the time during these recent conflicts, was a student leader at the University of Papua New Guinea in the 1970s, and spearheaded a notable strike of students against the Papua New Guinea government at that time. Although he is himself from Malaita, he was reportedly threatened by paramilitary members of the Malaita Eagles Force during confrontations with the Guadalcanalese in the year 2000 and was constrained to resign from his post.

Timber is the Solomons' main export, and extensive logging threatens entirely to deplete the rainforests, a problem that recurrently appears in the region as a whole, including Papua New Guinea. Efforts to control logging have been made since 1993, and in 1994 the Australian government offered A$2 million in aid under the stipulation that logging leases on a proposed World Heritage site at Marovo Lagoon should be ended. However, since 1994 the government has used its own paramilitary police to protect Malaysian logging firms against local opposition, a policy instituted by the then prime Minister, Solomon Mamaloni. Solomons waters are rich in fishing grounds for tuna, and fishing is the country's second largest industry. The Japanese company Taiyo has been dominant in this enterprise, freezing most of its tuna catch for export to Japan. In 2000 the company pulled out its operations, and the government has since been left with the task of trying to reorganize the fishing business.

Case Study:

Land and Sea: Historical Changes in Marovo Lagoon, New Georgia

The Pacific in general is dominated by vast expanses of ocean, across which prehistoric navigators intrepidly made their way in order to settle in the more hospitable of its innumerable clusters of volcanic islands and atolls. Fishing has been an important part of the livelihood and culture of all the coastal groups, and rights have been maintained over areas of water just as they have over stretches of forest and gardening land.

Edvard Hviding's study of marine tenure in the Marovo Lagoon area of the Solomons illustrates this point and also many of the wider themes that inform the contemporary ethnography of the South-West Pacific. In his own words, he is concerned to show "the juxtapositions of traditionalism and modernity...and the multiple entanglements of Marovo people in ancient cultural systems, varieties of Christian religion, modern nation-state, and capitalist systems" (1996: xv). As noted earlier, Marovo has been the site of fierce conflict between customary landholders and Malaysian logging companies. The landholders see themselves as guardians of the lagoon's resources. Not surprisingly they view the loggers as exploiters, to be resisted.

Some 10,000 Marovo people belong to named kin groups, termed *butubutu*, that control stretches of land, coral reefs and sea as their estates, *puava* (Hviding 1996: 13). Membership of these groups is gained through kin ties that are bilateral, that is, ones which can be traced through either parent. These groups have proved to be strong opponents of outsiders wishing to appropriate the trees and tuna fish of their estates. Their members also control vital practical knowledge of how to find the resources of the sea and they maintain a sense of social relationship with its creatures (p. 198).

The term Marovo means "in the direction of the sunrise" (east). The Roviana Lagoon people, mentioned earlier, live on the westward side of New Georgia, and Roviana means "in the direction of the sunset." This kind of designation of people in directional terms is common also in New Guinea, where directions in the landscape are encoded in everyday speech. Kolombangara Island, also mentioned above, is a volcanic island lying on the north west tip of New Georgia. It has been the site of extensive logging recently.

The Marovo environment provides a great diversity of food resources and the people practice hunting in the forest, gathering in the lagoon and beyond, collecting shellfish, and gardening, in which they plant a variety of root crops including sweet potatoes and taro, and bananas. Forest animals hunted include feral pigs and marsupials. Puddings are made from pounded roots and *Canarium* nuts, baked in stone-lined earth ovens. This kind of "home cooking" is said by Marovo people to be an important part of their *kino*, "way of life". Although the environment is abundant, tropical storms can make canoe travel dangerous. Weather magic includes more ways of stopping rain than of making it (p. 53). As throughout the islands of the South-West Pacific, earthquakes occur, and there are active volcanoes. Island interiors consist of "extinct craters, steep summits, and pinnacles (p. 54)," but they have also been extensively inhabited in the past. Ancestral shrines are often located in the forest, and contain conch-shell trumpets, whale teeth and shell rings as well as human crania like those found in archaeological sites on Kolombangara. Their location shows a sense of spiritual linkage with the forest itself as ancestral, a sense shared by peoples in Papua New Guinea such as the Duna of the Southern Highlands Province (Stewart and Strathern 2000a).

The Marovo people are tied into a cash economy, supplying their needs for introduced goods such as soap, salt, kerosene, and matches. They manufacture small stone mortars used for pounding tubers and nuts which are in strong demand outside of Marovo. The three Christian church denominations (Seventh Day Adventist, United or Methodist, and Christian Fellowship) maintain their own separate health services, schools, sawmills, and airfields. Money is also gained by selling nassa shells (small cowries) to other islanders or sea cucumbers to outside traders, as well as by growing copra; but the most significant recent boom has been in the sale of figurative wood carvings, promoted by the Seventh Day Adventist church, mostly made by men. This case is again paralleled from New Guinea, where among the Asmat people of Irian Jaya the Catholic church encouraged a revival of carving after its earlier suppression because of its connection with head-hunting. Finally, cash remittances are also received from family members working in towns: another feature widespread in the Pacific, where people seek urban employment but wish to retain their rights and social ties to their places of origin.

In the Solomons, customary land and sea areas cannot by law be alienated from the *butubutu* groups (apart from areas already alienated under colonial control). Each village has a *bangara* or hereditary male leader, who oversees the enforcement of customary law and draws his power from his custodianship of ancestral shell valuables. New government representatives have not displaced the *bangara* from their positions, and adherence to the idea of *kastom* (custom) as a way of life remains strong. This does not mean that *kastom* is necessarily unchanging or without history. Oral histories in fact record movements and changes in the past. It does mean that the *idea* of *kastom* provides a conceptual anchor for local notions of identity, seen as rooted in the past, in a context of continual transformations in life since the nineteenth century. *Kastom* also provides the means of maintaining a sense of regulation over marine and land resources.

Kastom is used as a basis for negotiating with outside commercial interests, such as tuna fisheries; and as a framework within which tendencies to the individualization of resource ownership are internally handled. In the course of such negotiations, custom itself is reinterpreted and transformed. The greatest conflict has arisen over logging operations, earlier initiated by British and Australian companies, but since the 1990s increasingly carried out by Asian interests. Moving to the vicinity of Marovo from Kolombangara, Levers Pacific Timbers began logging there in the 1970s. In 1983 Marovo *butubutu* leaders refused to negotiate further with the Levers company, which eventually closed its operations and withdrew from the Solomons in 1986, causing a big loss in the nation's export earnings. Christian Fellowship church groups were prominent in leading resistance to the company. This church originated after World War II and "fused Methodism with strong communalism and elements of ancestor worship" (Hviding 1996: 51). It was founded by a charismatic prophet, Silas Eto, who is known as the Holy Mama ("Holy Father"), and broke with the Methodists to become a separate indigenous church in 1960 (Hviding, 122). The founder died in 1984, but was succeeded by his sons, and one of these played a leading part in organizing the opposition to Levers. Although the government had negotiated with the people on the company's behalf for logging rights, when the people saw the overall environmental damage done by the loggers they felt that this was insupportable. Further, only a few of the leaders had actually signed the logging agreement; and the people generally did not respect the company because it failed to recognize them by directly sending its personnel to come and talk with them. Although they themselves later, in 1989, invited Asian loggers into the area conflicts soon emerged again, this time about the destruction of sacred sites in the forest of the kind we have mentioned above. Hviding points out that conflicts of this sort involve the nation-state authorities in a "double bind." They must be attentive to the interests of their own local populations, but they also need revenue on a national level to promote development, which the people also demand. The authorities are unlikely to win respect either from the local people or from the multinational companies in these circumstances. Exactly the same dilemma has faced the Papua New Guinea government in relation to mining operations, as for example regarding the huge mining operation for gold and copper at Ok Tedi in the Western Province, where environmental pollution of massive proportions has finally raised a stark set of choices for the government: either lose revenue or lose the viability of the environment downstream from the mine for the foreseeable future.

Case Study:

Exchange and Social Change on Choiseul Island

Choiseul Island lies to the north of New Georgia, where Marovo lagoon people live. Its total population in the 1960s was about 5,7000 persons (Scheffler 1965: 6), with an overall population density of about 5 persons per square mile. The overall figure is not very meaningful since most of the people in the 1960s were living in villages near to the coast. (By 1999 a government census indicated a population of 20,000 for Choiseul.) Harold Scheffler worked in the Varisi-speaking area of Choiseul between 1958 and 1961. The Varisi lanuage or dialect had some 1,000 speakers of it in the 1960s and is one of six language divisions recognized on the island. The Choiseulese experienced a complex and difficult history of relations with the outside world from the 1860s onwards, with successive waves of traders for tortoise-shell and bêche-de-mer (sea cucumbers), "blackbirders" who forcibly recruited laborers and also sold guns, and from 1893 onward a colonial British government that was enmeshed in local politics by punishing raiders and killers of Europeans. The British brought down severe reprisals on the Choiseulese in an attempt to break their cycles of revenge killings. This enmeshing of the colonial power with local revenge practices is a recurrent and important feature of colonial history, and played an important part in the history of the Kwaio people of Malaita (Keesing 1992). Christian missionaries of the Anglican and Methodist denominations were prominent in bringing people together to live in enlarged coastal villages, encouraging them to trade in copra and to send their children to school. Converts and returned laborers helped to get these missionaries established, as they did elsewhere in the Pacific (Scheffler 1965: 21). Concomitantly, the colonial government gave the missionaries consistent support. Catholics and Seventh Day Adventists reached Choiseul in the 1920s. Christianity and indigenous religious ideas have to some extent been blended. God has replaced the indigenous spirits and gardeners are asked to offer first fruits to Christian preachers rather than to the local group leaders whom Scheffler calls "managers" (Scheffler 1965: 24). The indigenous gardening practices were in the past based on taro (*Colocasia*) as the main crop. Since the coming of outsiders, the sweet potato was introduced and has largely taken over from taro after the latter was affected by a severe blight.

Scheffler's account of the Varisi people is both a historical study and a reconstruction of how Choiseulese society was constituted around 1900, not long after the declaration of a British protectorate. That means his account relates largely to a period more than a century ago now. Nevertheless his study was important, in two ways. First, he gave an analysis of an unusual form of social organization, in which cognatic as well as agnatic descent was important. This might seem a very technical issue. However, it leads to comparisons with a people of the Papua New Guinea Highlands, the Duna, on whom we include a separate case study later in this text. Here, we set the scene briefly before discussing the second important aspect of this study, its elucidation of exchange practices prior to the time of full control by the colonial government and missions. In regard to this topic also it turns out that there are significant comparisons with another Highlands Papua New Guinea people, the Hageners.

Scheffler himself situates his discussion of Varisi social structure in terms of the early debates about the applicability of "African models" to the analysis of Highlands Papua New Guinea societies, with particular reference to the choices people have about where to live or which sets of people to support in their activities. Ethnographic observers found that there was considerable flexibility in the patterns of these choices in these

Highlands societies, and John Barnes suggested that this flexibility of affiliation and the fact that processes of group segmentation were not regular or chronic but "catastrophic", that is, occasioned by unpredictable conflicts, amounted to a divergence from African patterns (Barnes 1962). However, block comparisons of this sort between Africa and New Guinea are hard to make. The point here is that Scheffler found Barnes' generalizations about the Highlands of Papua New Guinea helpful in thinking about Choiseul. In Choiseul, however, flexibility was itself clearly structured. Local groups had at their cores sets of agnatic or patrilineal kin who were considered the holders of primary rights to landed estates. Among these kin one man would be recognized as the *batu*, a term which Scheffler translates as "manager", following an earlier usage by Kenelm Burridge on the Tangu people of Papua New Guinea (Burridge 1961). The *batu* was generally supposed to be the eldest son of the previous *batu*, but this position depended also on ability and could be held by another agnate. Conflicts over who should be the *batu* could arise. The group within which the *batu* held his position was called the *sinangge*, and a number of these belonged to a larger group, also called a *sinangge*, "the big *sinangge*". The *batu*'s role was significant. He was the custodian of group prosperity, especially a certain kind of shell valuable known as *kesa*. *Kesa* were circular disks made from fossilized giant clam shells (*Tridacna*), and they were needed for paying debts and rewarding allies, and for giving away in feasts known as *kelo*.

Besides the agnates and the *batu* a *sinangge* might include numbers of others, most prominently the children or descendants of natal female agnates. These might be, for example, the children of marriages known as *tamazira*, in which no brideprice was paid and the couple were then required to live at the bride's father's place in uxorilocal residence. Such marriages might in fact be arranged by a *batu* in order to claim the help of his daughters and their husbands in his activities (Scheffler 1965: 47, 196). More generally, "anyone is said to be always welcome in any...*sinangge* with which he can trace a consanguineal connection," and cognatic descendants of a group founder were all referred to as "born of women" (*popodo nggole*) whereas agnates were "born of men" (*popodo valeke*). "Born of women" members were said to be guests in the group and not as "strong" in it as the agnates. They did have rights of residence but were not expected to exercise so much influence in activities as did the leading agnates. It is this division between agnates and other cognates in the group which is comparable to the situation among the Duna (Stewart and Strathern 2002).

The second feature of Scheffler's study that is of interest here is his delineation of activities of exchange involving the *kesa* valuables. One remarkable thing about these valuables is that they were neither regularly made by the people nor were they apparently traded in by established means, as shell valuables were throughout the Papua New Guinea Highlands. The Choiseulese told Scheffler that *kesa* were "made and given to men by *bangara* Laena, a water god residing in the sea," and that "he made it specifically to be the "mark" of big-men" (1965: 200). If, then, there was a limited stock of these highly prized objects, and *batu* men largely controlled them, it is clear that *kesa* were the prerogatives of a restricted category of leaders, and could be used to control others: a situation that would fit with the myth of their origins.

Kesa were kept in sets, usually of nine cylinders, and were classified as "working" shells, used regularly in exchanges, and "large" ones kept for prestige and security and used only to fix important alliances. That is, they were not "inalienable" in the sense proposed by A. Weiner (1992) and later by M. Godelier (1997), following Weiner's influential study, but rather were used, like large, individually named pearl shells in the Highlands of Papua New Guinea, to negotiate only the most significant political connections

(Strathern and Stewart 1999b). Each cylinder was called a *mata* ("eye") and the personal histories of large *kesa* were sometimes known in detail. After the introduction of state money, equivalences were worked out between *kesa* and Australian currency.

Kesa were acquired in various ways. One was by rearing and selling pigs, which were always in demand for feasts. Such sales were supposed to be with outsiders, since within the group pigs were supposed to be given freely, although with an expectation for eventual return in kind. *Kesa* were also obtained through brideprice, and *batu* could claim the brideprices for orphans or for girls acquired as low-status adoptees. (Scheffler uses the term "slaves" for this latter category. For a study of such usages see Strathern and Stewart 2000a: 13–40.) Another major scenario was that of "helping", and here also we find a clear similarity with the Highlands of Papua New Guinea: if someone died helping another, compensaton in *kesa* could be claimed. This extended notably to help in intergroup fighting, the context which in the Mount Hagen area of Papua New Guinea triggered major payments of reparations by the initators of a fight to their military allies. As in Hagen, too, hired assassins were paid with *kesa*. The pattern of gaining a reputation as a killer on behalf of others is one that is also shared historically by the Choiseulese and the Kwaio of Malaita (Keesing 1992).

A further way of obtaining *kesa* was by visiting an exchange partner as a guest and making *nggare*. The host would steam-cook a pig, and the guest would then ask for *kesa* to go with it, which the host was obliged to supply (Scheffler 1965: 204). Later the host would become the guest and demand a return. Less coercively, young men could present gifts of baked pig and taro-pudding to their mother's brothers or father's brothers and be given *kesa* in return, so that they could enter into transactions. Such requests depended on good personal relations for their success. This notion of good relations is also carried over into the spirit realm, since spirits called *sinipa* were thought sometimes to befriend people and show them where *kesa* could be found. The human had to capture the knife the *sinipa* spirit used to cut taro and would then agree to return it "only upon promise of being shown a hoard of *kesa*" (Scheffler 1965: 205). This motif seems to recapitulate the idea of coercion. But in another scenario the *sinipa* was said to want to marry the human, who then went off to live with the spirit for some time, returning later with *kesa*. The *sinipa* were supposed to reveal *kesa* hoards that had been buried by men who then died without revealing their hiding places to their own kin. This idea of gaining wealth or good fortune as the result of a spirit marriage is widespread in Eastern Indonesia and New Guinea (Strathern and Stewart 2000a: 79–100.)

The Choiseulese at the time of Scheffler's fieldwork still valued *kesa* greatly and declared that without it people were "nobody". Managers in particular were charged with arranging *kelo* feasts at which *kesa* would be given away. Two managers of different groups might compete with each other in an escalating series of reciprocal *kelo*. Or a manager might give *kesa* as a group leader to a group whose men agreed to help them on a raid. "Allies" also helped the close kin of a person who died, by working to build a resting place for the cremated remains, consisting of slabs of stone. (Scheffler does not say so at this point, p. 209, in his text, but elsewhere in the Solomons such resting places were repositories for shell rings and for the skulls of important ancestors, as we saw for Marovo.) The close kin, known as the "bottom people" would give at least three *kesa* to the "allies". However, if they gave considerably more than this, the allies would feel they had to reciprocate or lose prestige (p. 210). They might make a small *kelo* in return; or they might give back more again than they had received, thus forcing the "bottom people" to make another return to even the transaction, perhaps slightly outdoing the allies. At any point either party could signal their willingness to quit by making only a small gift in response to the previous one received. Each sequence required a considerable amount of planning, especially in preparing large taro gardens to be harvested for the accompanying feast. Debts within the system could be inherited from father to sons, although sons might deny they knew about them or could claim they were paid. Scheffler explains in schematic detail the strategizing and manoeuvering which went on in relation to *kelo*-making in general (pp. 212–13). Making *kelo*, along with holding *kesa* shells, was seen as the hallmark of the true manager, elevating both him and his group in prestige and status. Scheffler points out that the manager's task was not just to make exchanges "but rather to initiate and manipulate those transactions which eventually resulted in exchanges of valuables" (p. 216).

It is remarkable how closely this category of *kelo* parallels the *moka* exchange system of the Mount Hagen people of Papua New Guinea, including the focus on managers or big-men, the equation of individual with group prestige, the potentially agonistic character of the exchanges, and their connection with the basic structure of "bottom" or "base" people and "allies". In Hagen this structure is expressed as the relation between the *pukl wuö*, "root man", and the *kui wuö*, "dead man", the one who died on behalf of the instigators of a particular fight. The same structure is commonly found throughout the Highlands of Papua New Guinea. The notion of escalating exchanges built around this structure is not so common, but is very characteristic of the Hagen area. We find therefore a close parallel here between the Hageners and the Choiseulese. The Mount Hagen people have become well known in the literature as the people who made *moka*. The Choiseulese could equally have become paradigmatic for agonistic exchange. Instead, however, the focus of Scheffler's meticulous ethnography was on cognatic descent, and that is how Choiseul tends to be "pigeon-holed" in anthroplogical discussions of the South-West Pacfic. Perhaps it was the lack of an ongoing *kelo* sequence during the time of Scheffler's fieldwork and the fact that much of his account is a "reconstruction" of the past that influenced this pattern. This contrasts with the Hagen situation, where *moka* was flourishing under colonial conditions and an elaborate sequence of *moka* events was observed (A. Strathern 1971). (See Strathern and Stewart 2000b, for how the *moka* system has changed and declined historically up to the end of the 1990s.)

It is interesting further to note how Scheffler, in a careful recent review of his materials on Choiseul, expresses his opinion that although agnatic and cognatic descent were both significant for the Choiseulese, the locally based *sinangge* could not be properly described as "descent groups" since filiation was a necessary but not sufficient condition for their formation (Scheffler 2001: 177; see also in this connection Feinberg 1990). He has decided to withdraw the label he gave to these groups in his earlier book (e.g. 1965: 114), although careful attention to both books shows that he makes essentially the same arguments in both regarding the actual dynamics of kinship relations and descent "constructs" or ideas about descent. Scheffler has therefore removed from the Choiseulese the analytical feature by which he had earlier made them ethnographically well known. His ethnography and his analysis of it remain, however, models of clarity and incisive discussion. Perhaps the time is right now for the Choiseulese, the Hageners, and others to be considered on a wide comparative basis as showing an emphasis on competitive or agonistic exchange, cross-cutting the supposed Austronesian and non-Austronesian division between societies in the South-West Pacific.

Case Study:

Christianity in the Solomon Islands (Kwara'ae)

The Solomon Islands, like the rest of the Pacific, has been the venue of an intensive history of missionization by Christian churches since the earliest days of colonial influence there. Ben Burt studied the Kawara'ae of Malaita, and has written specifically about this historical process for the area, which borders the area of the Kwaio worked with by R. Keesing (e.g. Keesing 1992) and David Akin (Akin 1999). Burt found that the Kwara'ae, like the Kwaio, had chosen to segregate Christians from traditionalists, unlike the pattern, found in some other places, of coexistence between these categories of people. The Kwara'ae pattern partly resulted from the fundamentalist character of the South Sea Evangelical Mission which came to the area (Burt 1994: 14). But Burt also observes that the values of their traditional religion "are actually reflected in their Christian opposition to it" (Burt, ibid.).

The Kwara'ae live in the interior of Malaita. They numbered 19,000 people at the time of study (Burt, p. 15) and are divided into clans with long genealogies of ten to twenty generations, mostly calculated in the male line. Ties with ancestors validate claims to land. Elaborate taboos protect certain relationships and values, and today's Christians represent their own traditional customs as like the Ten Commandments of the Old Testament. Burt argues that such rules also protected "the seniority and dominance of men" in the society (p. 35). Burt appears to be referring to both ritual superiority and political authority in this context. Shell money, in strings of beads, is used for bridewealth. Men who are prominent in helping and supporting others gain importance in their communities, particularly through the sponsoring of feasts. Killings had to be compensated for by shell payments, on pain of revenge in the past. Indigenous religious practices have mainly to do with maintaining good relationship with ghosts in order to avoid misfortunes and achieve success. The ghosts can ensure this if the people are "true" to them (*mamana*) and offer them sacrifices. Rules of separation hold between men and women. Both male and female ghosts are important and while male ghosts are thought of as aggressive female ones are seen as nurturant and having the power to bring calm, spoken of as "cool". Specialist priests tend the shrines set up for ancestral ghosts and oversee the preparations for festivals at which pig sacrifices are made in places where clan relics are kept. Priests can use the power of the ghosts to kill wrongdoers; the powers of sorcery are seen as used by individuals for their own ends, to cause sickness and bad luck. It appears that these fears of sorcery are still significant today, although all but a small number of Kwara'ae have converted to one or other version of the Christian religion.

Anglican Christianity was first brought back to Kwara'ae by converts who had been recruited to work on sugar plantations in Queensland, Australia, in the late nineteenth century and returned in the early 1900s. The incursion of the Christians caused a separation of traditionalists from converts, each side seeking to keep itself "pure" from the other (Burt, p. 121). This is an important historical reason for the continuing dichotomy between Christians and others, as it is also for the Kwaio. The Christians were more successful after they received government backing from the British administration, which gave protection to coastal communities of converts against the bush people. District Officer Bell, who was eventually killed by a Kwaio warrior-leader, was instrumental in extending pacification of the interior people after 1915. Retrospectively, Christians told Burt that around this time the people gave up sacrifices to the ghosts because there was too much hard work involved and the ghosts could not really help them or prevent sicknesses and the like. They cited the idea that Jesus had already been sacrificed and so there was no need for further sacrifices of pigs. Reasoning of this kind also permeates Christians' thinking in the Highlands of Papua New Guinea today (see Robbins, Stewart, and Strathern 2001; Stewart and Strathern 2000b). Between the lines here we can also read the effects of colonial control, through which the Kwara'ae were confronted with powers that did not care about their ancestors and seemed to be able to act with impunity because the Christian God was behind them. The suppression of blood feuding certainly played a part in this process (Burt, p. 133), as did epidemic diseases. Again, we can see a clear parallel with the Highlands region of Papua New Guinea, for example among the Duna in the 1950s and 1960s (Stewart and Strathern 2002). Missionaries of the South Seas Evangelical Mission (SSEM) began to provide medical services in this context and to offer a "new life", that is new protection against misfortunes as the Kwara'ae saw it. The sacrificial water from coconuts was used to "wash" people and initiate them into the new life, and this act was held to have a cooling effect like that of female ghosts in the past. Burt suggests that the prominent role of female missionaries in the SSEM may have reinforced this connection. We see, at any rate, a kind of reversal of "taboo" practices here. Christianity broke the old taboo rules incumbent on men and introduced a new set of "female" rules which also, nevertheless, drew their meanings from the indigenous religion. The SSEM propagated its teachings and new rituals by opening village "schools" to produce converts.

The Christian evangelists also began to forbid indigenous forms of feasting, presumably because of their connections with sacrifices, and to allow only festivals sponsored by the churches to take place. Local "teachers", taking over from expatriate missionaries, became a new kind of leader (again, as pastors are nowadays in Highlands Papua New Guinea and in much of Polynesia also), and were also prepared to resist the secular colonial administration, an outcome that fed into the Maasina Rule movement which emerged after the severe disruptions of World War II. Contact with American troops and their apparent generosity made the people dissatisfied with the British, and resistance to British control was spread through SSEM networks (p. 177), with new "towns" set up to organize the people for further change. At the same time the movement enjoined a return to traditional *kastom*, as the basis for social life, so that this "became a symbol of Malaitan autonomy." Maasina Rule ended with standoffs and concessions by the British after an attempt at suppression. Burt argues that the SSEM supported the Malaitans' drive for autonomy, and eventually the indigenous people gained control over their own church. Since then there has been a move (paralleled among the Kwaio) to codify traditional *kastom* in order to see "how far it was compatible with Christianity" (p. 213), and to produce clan genealogies which have now become the basis for concerted forms of political action. We see here the genesis of an "ethnic group" mentality, forged, as is often the case, in the context of state-level politics. The category of "tribal chiefs" was created by activist leaders in this context in 1975, leading up to national independence for the Solomons in 1978. Burt notes in this context that these activist leaders developed "a model of traditional political organization based on the pre-Christian ritual and political system but adapted to act as a pressure group within the developing state political system" (p. 215). Burt therefore recognizes that the idea of chiefship as such has a traditional basis among the Kwara'ae. Gegeo and Watson-Gegeo (1996) have given a detailed analysis of ideas regarding chiefship and leadership generally among the Kwara'ae, comparing these ideas to those found in Tikopia. One category they describe is *aofia*, which they say may be translated as "ruler, royalty, chief or priest" (p. 303) and compare to the Tikopian *ariki*. The term was appropriated by Anglican and Catholic translators as a title for Jesus Christ, showing the intertwining of indigenous and Christian ideas that is also commonly found in Papua New Guinea. It is interesting to note that the expanded political levels of "chiefs" here, as in Fiji, were in some regards a creation based on colonial categories of organization. The churches have acquiesced in this new order by offering blessings for chiefs at feasts held to discuss "tradition". What we are dealing with is the emergence of what some anthropologists have called "neo-traditional" frameworks of organization. Local churches of the SSEC, the South Sea Evangelical Church, are based on villages rather than clans, but villages themselves are amalgamations of clan groups whose histories have been shaped by SSEM activities and the effects of Maasina Rule. SSEC structures, as a spiritual form of organization, have slotted in as a broadly based replacement for the ghosts and their shrines. Pastors take the place of priests and hold the ritual knowledge of the Bible as priests previously held the knowledge of *kastom*. The SSEC also encourages dreams, visions, and spirit possession (Burt, p. 240) as the Pentecostal-style Assemblies of God churches do in the Papua New Guinea Highlands, sometimes stimulated by visits by international evangelists (Robbins, Stewart, and Strathern 2001). The Holy Spirit is said to inspire people for changes in the life of the spirit, and Burt argues that this makes the church indigenous in its spiritual vitality. Certain aspects of the traditional religion have therefore been incorporated into the Kwara'ae version of Christianity, in particular rules of taboos and the practice of making a spiritual relationship with Jesus, as in the traditional religion people made personal ties with ghosts through sacrifices. It is interesting to compare this process with the statement made to us by one woman belonging to the Assemblies of God church in Mount Hagen, to effect that she regarded Jesus as her "husband".

New Guinea

New Guinea is a huge tropical island that sits north of Australia, straddling an area between the Pacific region and the Indonesian archipelago. Its western half, Irian Jaya, or West Papua, formerly a Dutch colony, is a province within the Republic of Indonesia, while its eastern part, Papua New Guinea, has been an independent nation-state since 1975. Some ten thousand years ago the island was joined by the Sahul land bridge to the continent of Australia. Much more recently (1884–1906), the southern part of Papua New Guinea was a British, then (1906–1975) an Australian, colony; while the northern half was administered by Australia under mandate from the League of Nations and later the United Nations after withdrawal by the Germans in 1920 following World War I (Souter 1967: 263–7). New Guinea is thus a land that has been divided in complex ways by colonial and post-colonial history. But its great interior valleys, mountain ranges, swift rivers, and coastal swamps and plains have their own much longer history of change, including the development over many thousands of years of the lifeways of its peoples, with their multiplicities of languages, cosmologies, social forms, ingenious environmental adaptations, and struggles for prestige and power among themselves. Today these long-established indigenous complexities are overlain by and blended with a mass of changes whose reach has extended into every sphere of life. One of the characteristics of people in many parts of New Guinea is their ability to embrace novelties while still staying linked to their pasts and looking forward to the future.

Within these broad outlines the sheer variations in cultural practices that we find in different parts of New Guinea are quite remarkable. Linguists currently estimate that perhaps as many as 1,200 separate languages may be found in New Guinea and its surrounding islands of the South-West Pacific taken as a whole, about one fifth of the total number of languages in the world (Foley 2000: 358). This diversity should not be underestimated. However, areas containing distinct languages may show cultural similarities; and in some parts, notably the interior highlands, large language groups of up to 200,000 persons may be found. The smaller language groups also tend to be waning in population today as a result of out-migration, amalgamation, and the increasing use of linguae francae such as Tok Pisin ("Pidgin English") in Papua New Guinea. Population density and agricultural intensity tend to be greater in the highland valleys than elsewhere.

These highland regions in general, because of their remote and hidden locations, tended to be the last parts of New Guinea entered by explorers from the outside world. This does not mean that they were entirely cut off from the wider world inside their region. Extensive trade networks existed throughout the country through which various goods and ideas were transmitted. An important subsistence food, the sweet potato crop, reached the highlands probably between c. 1000 and 400 years ago, transforming the subsistence economy there and facilitating the growth in population density which we have just mentioned (Kirch 2000: 63–84). Earlier populations had relied on taro, bananas, sugar cane, and other cultivars, as well as on hunting and gathering. The sweet potato afforded higher yields per garden area and the possibility to plant it at higher altitudes on dry land, thus expanding settlement areas and probably stimulating patterns of migration from one center to another. It did not entirely replace other crops, but rather tended to displace them as central in sustaining life. The Mount Hagen people of the Western Highlands of Papua New Guinea proverbially say that the sweet potato is their true food and that it is like a "medicine" for them. Another bonus the sweet potato provided was that it enabled a larger population of pigs to be reared in domestic herds since it was fed to them as their main food source (Plotnicov and Scaglion 1999). This in turn increased the possibilities for large and elaborate ceremonies based on the giving of live pigs or their slaughter and distribution of their meat at festivals held for allied groups. In Irian Jaya, in the Baliem Valley, the Dani people developed elaborate wet-ditching regimens in order to sustain sweet potato production in their montane valley basins.

Although this pattern of dependence on the sweet potato, along with an emphasis on the rearing of pigs as forms of wealth, tends to be found throughout the Highlands, there are many cultural variations across this huge region. Within Papua New Guinea, anthropologists who began to work in the Highlands from the 1950s onward early on noted differences between the Eastern and Western Highlands: village-type settlements, often surrounded by stockades, in the east, and hamlets scattered within clan territories in the west; a greater intensity of warfare and initiations for young males in the east, and more stress on general fertility cults for the whole population in the west; a larger role for women in exchanges between groups in the west and a correspondingly greater importance overall of exchanges of wealth for the creation and maintenance of alliances between groups. These features seem to fit together in overall patterns of difference (see Feil 1987). Language groups are smaller in the Eastern Highlands than in the west, where the Hagen and Enga populations are both in excess of 100,000, the largest in Papua New Guinea. This is also perhaps an indication of the expansion of size in groups which have been able to utilise the sweet potato with the greatest effectiveness.

Beyond the limits of the Highlands Provinces in Papua New Guinea today lie smaller populations to the south and west. West of the Huli and Duna peoples live the Telefolmin and related peoples often described as Ok peoples. In these areas there was in the past a considerable importance of initiation practices, together with a reliance on taro rather than sweet potato as a staple crop. These Ok peoples blend across the border with peoples of the Star Mountains in Irian Jaya and westwards to the Eipo-Mek, Dani-speaking, and finally the Ekagi or Me-speaking peoples of the Wissel Lakes (formerly known in the literature as the Kapauku). The sweet potato is also important among the Dani and Ekagi.

Not only pigs are important as wealth objects throughout New Guinea. A variety of sea shells, imported into the interior of the island through intricate networks of trade routes, were also significant. The pathways of trade through which these items moved blended with or emerged into the staging of large-scale festive communal events in which complex processes of social life were negotiated and social values affirmed. Wealth items were also deeply involved in life-cycle rituals marking birth, weaning, adolescence, marriage, maturity, old age, and death. These rituals wove people and their places together in a tapestry of kinship and marriage, seen as a product of the flow of life-giving and life-enhancing substances. Wealth items themselves, such as shells and pigs, were seen as equivalents of these flows of substance through channels of kinship, hence their prominence in life-cycle exchanges. Remarkably, in many areas today, such as in Hagen, introduced money manufactured by the state has readily been substituted for shell valuables in these exchanges. This is an example of the notable facility people have for adapting to new situations and bringing old and new together in ingenious conjunctures (Strathern and Stewart 2000b). Elsewhere the old valuables are maintained and kept outside of the nexus of modern monetary exchanges. Everywhere these valuables remain in vogue as ornaments and signs of status when displayed; although many, also, find their way overseas through sales to tourists. In some places, Christian churches encourage people to wear their finery for church occasions; in others the churches discourage self-ornamentation on the grounds that it makes people too proud of their own bodies and too little concerned with their souls. There are differences between the Catholic church and the more fundamentalist Protestant churches in this respect. In Papua New Guinea the Christian churches work within a framework of government in which they have a respected place and there is no competing established religion. (There has been a Mormon church in the capital, Port Moresby, for some years; and in the year 2000 a mosque was also being built there, occasioning controversy.) In Irian Jaya the situation is different: there, the Indonesian government recognizes Islam and other religions as well as Christianity and the Christian missionizing churches depend on official tolerance for their continued presence. The Indonesian government has made its own inroads into Irian Jaya, with resettlement programs for Indonesians from elsewhere in the areas of the Dani people and others, for example; and with its ethic of secular development of various kinds.

The Highlands areas have a much shorter time span of contact with the outside world than do the coastal regions. On the other hand, they show early dates of human settlement, reaching back to 30,000 years or more before the present, comparable to those also found for the Huon peninsula on the northern coast. Moreover, archaeological work at Kuk in the Mount Hagen area has demonstrated that the cultivation of crops for subsistence there goes back at least as far as 6,000 years and possibly 9,000 years, making it one of the more ancient centers of the development of agriculture in the world (see Kirch 2000: 63–84 for a summary of archaeological work by Prof. Jack Golson and his associates in the area). The Australian explorers who entered into this region from the south and from the north in the late 1920s and early 1930s were astonished to find large, flourishing populations of people with fields of sweet potatoes, well-organized and sometimes warlike, able both to resist the incoming patrols if they wished and also to supply them with ample quantities of food when willing to do so. The newcomers were almost invariably regarded initially as spirits of the dead or outside spirits of the wild, since they were so different from other peoples of New Guinea. Their arrival caused considerable alarm; yet before long the local people were eagerly trading with them, especially when they brought the highly valued sea shells which were significant in local exchange festivals (Leahy 1991; Schieffelin and Crittenden 1990; Sinclair 1988). Encounters between the Papua New Guinea Highlanders and explorers from outside were therefore relatively benign by comparison with the early phases of contact in coastal regions which occurred from the last quarter of the nineteenth century onwards. In the southern territory of Papua the British, with Sir Hubert Murray as Governor, set up a regime designed by the outsiders to protect indigenous rights, at least to some extent. The early German administration on the northern coast was much harsher and more commercially oriented, with the expropriation of land and aggressive recruitment of workers as indentured labor on colonial plantations, together with the importation of laborers from elsewhere bringing epidemic diseases such as smallpox. The coastal areas in all parts also experienced early on the effects of Christian missionization and the introduction of new ideas and rules about work, time, the spirit world, heaven and hell, gender relations, clothing, and hygiene. In these times missionaries frequently attacked and prohibited many of the people's festivals and rituals, substituting for them Christian worship in churches. In subsequent generations, and especially after Independence in 1975 in Papua New Guinea, people have quite often taken to reviving transformed versions of their festivals and dances, sometimes with church support. Colonial history in what is now Irian Jaya (or West Papua) follows a somewhat similar pattern to that in Papua New Guinea. The Dutch first laid claims to the area in 1848 as a part of the Netherlands East Indies, but did not begin much serious "pacification" and administration until the beginning of the twentieth century. Military and civil explorations further into the interior followed. Aircraft were used to penetrate into the central highlands from the 1920s onwards, as happened also with the first patrols in Highlands Papua New Guinea, but the Baliem valley with its teeming populations of Dani speakers was not fully "opened up" until the 1950s; and in 1969, after President Sukarno of Indonesia had issued a "command to liberate" West Irian, as it was then called, from the Dutch, the United Nations supervised a form of limited representative voting, later much contested, by which the whole area became effectively a province of Indonesia instead of being allowed to become an independent state as was done in Papua New Guinea. One of the consequences of this history is that there has been less anthropological research in Irian Jaya than in Papua New Guinea subsequently, although the Baliem Valley itself and the Asmat area on the southern coast are relatively well known both through academic research and popular writings.

In the prehistoric past the whole island of New Guinea was settled by successive sets of in-migrations by peoples from South East Asia, beginning at least 40,000 years ago. These peoples populated coastal areas where they produced the large "waisted" stone blades found in the Huon peninsula, on the northern coast of Papua New Guinea. (The term "waisted" refers to the fact that these tools are narrowed in the middle, providing a grip for their users' hands.) The migrants must also have reached the interior highlands of the whole island as well as the outlying islands and eventually began the horticultural practices which archaeologists have discovered evidence for in the Mount Hagen area. In coastal parts, malaria kept population growth down. In the mountains, however, malaria was generally not present. This factor may have allowed a greater population expansion there and eventually produced a pressure to increase food supplies and to develop the cultivation of plants after the end of the Pleistocene period some 10,000 years ago. With the warmer climate of Holocene times, the movements of peoples and the growth of horticulture would have been facilitated, while rising sea levels flooded the Sahul bridge and cut off New Guinea from the Australian continent.

About 3,500 years ago it has been suggested that a new wave of peoples, referred to as the Austronesians, entered the Pacific, emanating originally perhaps from Taiwan (Pawley 1998: 656; Kirch 2000: 91). The red-slipped stamped pottery known as Lapita ware is characteristic of this period and is associated by some scholars with these Austronesian explorers and seafarers, who used and traded obsidian blades as well as shell ornaments and cooking stones from about 1500 B.C. onwards. They spread rapidly over coastal parts of New Guinea and beyond, after 1200 B.C. into the wider Pacific. The culture of New Guinea from this time developed through the intermingling and influence of the Austronesians with their much longer established non-Austronesian precursor populations (Kirch 2000).

In major parts of coastal Papua New Guinea we find strong Austronesian influence, for example in New Britain among the Tolai and in New Ireland, and in Southern Papua among the Motu and Roro and Mekeo speaking peoples and in Milne Bay Province among the Trobrianders. Given the time depth of Austronesian settlement it would be surprising if cultural uniformity held sway throughout such areas. One recurrent feature we do find (for example among the Tolai, in New Ireland, and the Trobrianders) is matrilineal descent, the tracing of group affiliation and the passing of important forms of power in the maternal line. Another is a great emphasis on death ceremonies and exchanges at death (although these are also widespread elsewhere). And a third is a recognition of hereditary chiefships, as found in the Trobriands area. The Austronesians also brought with them dogs and pigs, and pigs tend to be important, along with presentations of vegetable crops, in their exchanges (again this is not unique to them).

The Asmat of Irian Jaya belong to the general set of South Coast New Guinea cultures along with the Kiwai and others from the Papuan Gulf area of Papua New Guinea. They live scattered in a swampy plain, and in the pre-colonial past practiced warfare and head-hunting. They made funeral representations of the dead, carved in wood and painted, with the idea of capturing in these carvings the vitality of the dead, whose spirits were then thought to leave the world of the living. These carvings took the form of elaborate poles known as *bisj*. They also made elaborate shields, carved with human figures or abstract designs and these were used on head-hunting raids mounted to avenge the deaths of ancestors after whom the shields themselves were named. Shield designs were intended to terrify and confuse those attacked. Both funeral carvings and shields have more recently been made as tourist objects for sale to visitors. Indonesian control around the 1960s brought with it the destruction of many old carvings, followed by a revival of production of carvings for a museum in the area and for sale (Thomas 1995: 79–88).

In the Trobriands area of the Massim region in south-east Papua the well documented exchange of valuables in the *kula* cycle is to be found. The *kula* was first made famous by the work of Bronislaw Malinowski early in the twentieth century (Malinowski 1922). Both the institution and interest in it have endured to this day, while undergoing many transformations. Malinowski's account emphasized the competitive and aesthetic aspects of *kula*; the adventurous contexts of overseas travel in which men sailed in large canoes to other islands in order to get shell valuables (necklaces and armbands); and the way in which the system was linked to chiefship and the internal tribute of yams given to chiefs by their wives' relatives and others and stored in ceremonial yam houses. Later writers have extensively reanalyzed Malinowski's work or carried out their own. Best known perhaps among these is Annette Weiner, who established that when she worked in Kiriwina, Malinowski's earlier fieldwork location, mortuary exchanges carried out by women on behalf of their matrilineal kin had a greater importance than had appeared in Malinowski's account (Weiner 1976). Both historical change and differences of perspective help to explain this difference. Some writers, notably Mark Mosko, have reconsidered the work of both Malinowski and Weiner in the light of ideas regarding Trobriand chiefs as "fathers" of their people and of general notions of personhood (Mosko 2000).

One of the regions of Papua New Guinea that has become best known is the area of the Sepik river, made famous by the work of generations of ethnographers, collectors of artifacts, and anthropologists working on culture and society, including Margaret Mead and Gregory Bateson. The Sepik generally is associated in the popular mind with elaborately carved ritual representations of spirits; with intricate initiation practices; and with highly decorated cult-houses within which initiations were held and art objects carved. These features belong outstandingly to the middle Sepik culture areas, including the Abelam and the Iatmul. Once again it is important to stress that these features are not unique to the Sepik, nor do they exhaust all that is significant in Sepik cultures generally. However, they do form a proud part of what has overall become a cultural heritage of New Guinea as a whole. Like all other areas of the Island, the Sepik has been affected greatly by environmental changes over long runs of time, caused by the flooding of the river estuary at the end of the Pleistocene period followed by the gradual recession of the sea and the emergence of different land areas. This process perhaps encouraged an adaptiveness to change which conduced to cultural diversity, made more complex by the entry of the Austronesian language speakers and their propensity to establish wide-flung trading networks accessed by water and centered along the maritime coast (Lipset 1997: 20–21). The interior Sepik languages are non-Austronesian, including the Ndu group of languages spoken along the middle reaches of the Sepik river. This group contains seven languages, with about 100,000 speakers. Many smaller language areas are also found here, some in the process of disappearing as a result of the encroachment of Tok Pisin and English as well as out-migration, as we noted earlier.

The Highlands region in Papua New Guinea, opened up to anthropological research following World War II, has become well known for a number of themes, in particular controversies over the analysis of forms of affiliation to groups and group structure; the characteristics of leadership and the importance of ceremonial exchange; and gender relations. The various debates were integrated into a synoptic account by Feil (1987). Sillitoe (1998 and 2000) provides helpful commentaries on them also, showing how these topics are relevant also for discussions of social change. The discussion on forms of leadership and status-acquisition has in recent years tended to center on a putative contrast between "big-men" and "great-men" forms (Godelier and Strathern 1991). The category of "big-men" is one that classically portrays leaders as people who base their position on their achievements in organizing gift exchanges. The category of "great-men" is presented as composite: such leaders may be warriors, shamans or other ritual experts, noted hunters, or gardeners, sometimes with capacities seen as hereditary. By this reckoning "big-men" would be likely to be found in those societies in which the greatest value is given to ceremonial exchange; and "great-men" in those where such a stress is absent. The problem, however, is that in practice various capacities are often found together in the same leader. One early error of analysis was also to present "big-men" as secular leaders rather than as leaders in ritual or religious action. "Great-men" accordingly were seen as tending to hold their status in part because of their positions in ritual activities. Again, in practice, the power of "big-men" in exchanges is usually held to be underpinned by the favor of spirits or ancestors and this in turn leads to their importance in ritual roles (A. Strathern 1993; Strathern and Stewart 1999a, 2000d). The whole debate about "big-men" versus "great-men" was also preceded in the literature by a debate about "big-men", seen as the hallmark of "Melanesian" societies versus "chiefs", seen as the sign of "Polynesian" ones. This simple dichotomy was found to be inadequate to handle the ethnographic complexities involved. More fruitfully, we can discern an underlying interplay between ascription and achievement and between ritual and secular capacities throughout the Pacific, including in "chiefly societies". The volume edited in honor of Sir Raymond Firth by Richard Feinberg and Karen Watson-Gegeo, including the Introduction by Watson-Gegeo and Feinberg, presents a lucid and nuanced overview of many of the issues at stake in this debate (Watson-Gegeo and Feinberg 1996). We take up some of the points also in case-histories in this section.

Immense processes of change have taken in place in New Guinea from prehistoric times on, quickening in their scope and intensity with the colonial intrusions of the Germans, Dutch, British, Australians, and Indonesians, and altering further in Papua New Guinea with political independence in 1975. Papua New Guinea is set up as a Westminster-style parliamentary democracy with a formal Constitution and a civil service modeled along Australian lines. As an aspirant nation-state it has a small population of some 4 million people but with a huge diversity of cultural groups within it and very great disparities of wealth between its rural and urban areas. An immense influx of outside goods and technology has raised the demands and expectations of people to a high level, without a corresponding capacity to satisfy these wishes. The Christian churches are strongly established but also have factional relations with one another in some cases, particularly in places such as Hagen where new-style Pentecostal and charismatic movements have challenged the more long-established Catholics, Lutherans, and Anglicans. This complex blend of images from outside has sometimes been transmuted into millenarian aspirations within (Stewart and Strathern 2000b); that is, to movements which have aimed at radical reversals in the status and wealth of peoples, especially the acquisition of wealth and standing by those who feel relatively deprived of it under their present circumstances. Such movements sometimes coincide with Christian-influenced notions about the "end of the world" and the inauguration of a new epoch of time, expressed in the idea of "the millennium". Such notions came to a head in many places in the years up to 2000, seen as marking the advent of a new millennium. Subsequently, people seem to be reorganizing and continuing their lives as best they can; but millenarian ideas tend to persist also.

Deteriorating situations of civil order, with combinations of criminal violence and inter-group fighting as well as struggles over the monetary benefits from cash-cropping and mining enterprises, have posed heavy problems for ordinary citizens of the country. Allegations of corruption in politics have become commonplace. Yet, beyond all this, it is notable that to date the overall forms of introduced government have persisted, justifying in the main the transition to Independence that took place in the 1970s. With Irian Jaya (West Papua) the situation is quite different. Separatists have protested against, and have fought against, Indonesian control of their province ever since the handover by the United Nations authorities to Sukarno's government. Most recently, with the growing internal problems and conflicts within greater Indonesia and with the violent transition of East Timor to the pathway of independence, separatist proclamations have increased, only to be met by refusals on the part of the authorities and physical crackdowns on them by the Indonesian military in places such as Wamena in the Baliem valley. The situation poses a problem also for Papua New Guinea's government because of the huge areas of unpoliced borderlands between the two countries and a history of appeals for asylum by refugees and punitive incursions by Indonesian soldiers. Indonesia is unlikely to let go of Irian Jaya and to allow it to become West Papua very soon, partly because of its profitable stake in mining enterprises there, such as the huge Freeport mine in the Bird's Head area. Indonesia's new President in 2001, Megawati Sukarnoputri, has inherited this difficult problem from her predecessors.

Throughout the diverse expanse of New Guinea we tend to find a number of recurrent themes: a stress on life-cycle and political exchanges; an elaborate panoply of ritual practices connected with the overall aims of the reproduction of fertility and well-being; ingenious and successful ways of making a practical living in the environment; an interest in trading networks and external links between local groups; and a love of expressive adornment and display.

Case Study:

The Asmat of Irian Jaya: Art and Its Changing Meanings

The Asmat people, who belong to the southern coast of Irian Jaya, have become well known for their elaborate types of carvings and their former practices of revenge-taking and head-hunting. There is a museum of their carvings at Agats, within their own area. Christian missions and the Indonesian government have prohibited overt warfare and the acquisition by males of prestige through the taking of human heads. The focus of this practice lay on the augmentation of life force as well as on the appeasement of spirits of the dead who were thought to demand revenge for their own deaths. In order to sponsor a ceremonial feast for the erection of a type of ritually carved pole known as *bisj*, a warrior was supposed to qualify by personally taking six heads (Knauft 1993: 189) Reportedly, men who failed to take a head were "disparaged by women as well as men, and they could have difficulty finding a wife" (ibid.). Male leaders sometimes had more than one wife.

The Asmat area is a huge swampland, affording subsistence through the processing of sago as a staple, hunting for feral pigs, marsupials, crocodiles, rats, and birds, fishing, and the gathering of forest fruits and sago grubs (the larvae of the Capricorn beetle). In inland parts the people also clear short-term gardens for growing vegetables. The cassowary bird is important to them not only as game to be hunted but also because of its place in their mythology (see Strathern and Stewart 2000a for a comparative discussion of the symbolic meanings of the cassowary in New Guinea). Its leg bones are used to produce daggers and carving tools, as happens elsewhere in New Guinea as a whole. The crocodile, the hornbill bird, the lizard, and the turtle all have significance as spirit mediators between the living and the dead.

The Asmat are highly mobile, using rivers as waterways for their canoes. Their whole area covers an area of some 422 square kilometers, and their current total population is estimated at between 65,000 and 85,000. The coastal environment is an alluvial mud swamp, leading to the meandering reticulations of multiple rivers, which provides challenges to the endurance and ingenuity of the people. Although the forest can yield an abundance of products, the coastal area is a far cry from the rich and beneficent coastal strands that are to be found in some Pacific islands. The swamps themselves are dominated by tangles of bushes and thorns and by large trees, with heavy rainfall, and inundated by tides. Not all of the Asmat live on the coast itself: many inhabit the foothills of the Jayawijaya mountains of the interior. Because of the prevalent patterns of fighting, watchtowers were sometimes built to keep a lookout for approaching enemies. Consistent with this pattern of political fragmentation in the past, there appear to be several different language and dialect forms within the area as a whole. Political alliances have sometimes united together speakers of different languages or dialects. Disease epidemics also break up communities.

The Dutch gained sovereignty over Irian Jaya in 1793, but did not explore the region until the early 1900s. They set up a government post at Merauke, and from there they made excursions to the Asmat, establishing a post at Agats in 1938. The Indonesians took over the area in 1962.

Asmat art and ritual were deeply bound together with warfare, and many aspects of ceremonial life were forbidden by the Indonesian government. Re-appropriated as culturally valued art forms expressing local identity and also serving a tourist market, the Asmat carvings, like those of the Gogodala in the Papuan Gulf area of Papua New Guinea, later experienced a revival. This renaissance was based on a long-standing interest in the objects which had held sway in Europe from the first two decades of the 1900s, after Asmat artifacts were collected and taken there. The Indonesian authorities were concerned to build a new nation in a modernizing vein. Their officials were also afraid of the Asmat people as a result of stories of cannibalism and headhunting. The government burned down the Asmat men's houses, ritual centers in their villages, and banned dancing and drumming by Asmat people. Later, from 1968 onward, this trend was partly reversed through the United Nations Asmat Art Project and the efforts of an American Catholic bishop in Agats, Fr. Alphonse A. Sowada. Catholic missionaries of the Crosier mission from America organized from 1981 onward an annual competitive festival for Asmat villages and individual artists. Tobias Schneebaum visited Agats between 1975

and 1983, cataloguing artifacts at the Asmat Museum of Culture and Progress (Schneebaum 1990: 43).

Discussions of Asmat artifacts tend to center on the *bisj* (or *bis*) poles and on the varieties of shield designs. Both the top part of the poles and the body of shields were made
from the plank flanges of swamp mangrove trees. An expedition to obtain these flanges
was made in a ritualized manner, since the mangrove tree was treated as an enemy spirit
and was "stalked" before being cut down.

The *bisj* poles might be five to seven meters long, and were carved with a series of representations of ancestors and hornbill figures. A carved canoe at the base of the pole was
a receptacle for the life-force of victims killed in head-hunting by the pole's sponsors,
who would also be responsible for paying the carvers and for celebrating the carving by a
massive distribution of food from their sago lands, to which they gained access partly
through the practices of polygyny (Knauft 1993: 72–3). The fundamental importance of
sago and of ties gained through women in marriage is underlined by the fact that disputes over sago groves could cause the breakup of villages.

The basic idea that informed Asmat rituals may be called the cyclicity of substances
(see Stewart and Strathern 2001a on this concept). The life-force or *nammu* of the head-
hunting sponsor passed into the *bisj* pole. After the pole was carved and raised up it was
placed into the sago-bearing forest area, so that the sago palms could absorb this *nammu*.
Later, when the sago was consumed, the people would be ingesting their leader's life-force.

Head-hunting was connected with initiation ceremonies for boys. A man who took
an enemy's head would give it to an initiate, who was expected to sit in seclusion for
some time with the head, and eventually to emerge with the identity of the victim. He
even became recognized as a kinsman by the relatives of the dead victim.

The Asmat wood-carvers, called *wow-ipits*, were highly valued. In their carvings they
captured the fleeting, circulating life-force and tied it to the life-cycle of a particular
leader and his group. Since fighting was so prevalent, the carvers' skill in making shields
was also important. Artistic craftsmanship was lavished also on the carving of prows for
war canoes.

Each shield was named after a particular ancestor, whose force was thought to be
drawn into the shield itself and to help it to prevail in fighting. The shield's designs were
thought to terrify the enemy (a practice commonly seen elsewhere in New Guinea).
These designs were painted in white, red, and black. The white color comes from pearl
shells that are burned and crushed. This color is thought to give speed and protection to
canoes . The red color is made from an earth ocher which is baked to a deep red, and is
held also to make canoes move fast. Red around the eyes marks the eyes of an angry
black cockatoo and is applied with the aim of intimidating enemies. Black is made from
charcoal. When these colors are used to represent humans, white marks skin, red indicates scarifications, and black signifies hair.

Asmat shields differ in their designs according to which part of the overall area they
belong to. They show a number of commonalities. The head, or top, of the shield is
sometimes referred to as a penis, as is the fretted top part of the *bisj* poles, which is
carved from the same kind of mangrove tree flange that is taken for making shields. The
shield designs themselves represent such creatures as tree kangaroos, hornbills, fruit bats,
turtles, cassowaries, or rayfish, all of which may be thought of as strong creatures of the
wild or as embodying fertility . Shields were supposed always to be maintained upright.
Turned upside down they signified the loss of power and indicated surrender. Coastal
Asmat considered that their ancestors took the form of black cockatoos or fruit bats,
hence the representation of these on shields. The shapes of these and other creatures

such as the praying mantis become stylized designs, resembling patterns of circles and hooks. These "abstracted" patterns show most clearly in shields from the inland foothills area. The presence of circles in the "head" of a shield indicates eyes and gives the shield an overall facial expression of aggression. Other designs on shields from the different areas include whirlpools (sources of fertility), larva tracks, snakes, frog legs, river bends, fish stomachs, and water swirling down sago troughs. These kinds of designs, evoking the active creatures of the environment and showing them in close interaction with human figures, appear on the *bisj* poles, canoe prows, and incised drums, displaying a unity of aesthetic conceptions across a variety of contexts.

This unity of conceptions was originally founded on the activities of fighting and headhunting. The art forms have survived and have been transformed owing to external interest and internal pride in the carver's art. The Asmat carvers have also for long incorporated pieces of steel tools into their carving kits, replacing or supplementing the stone axe-adzes and cassowary bone gouges used previously. Prior to regular contact with the outside world, they found nails from ships' timbers washed ashore and flattened these into small chisels. Much later, following the suppression and the later revival of their art forms, Asmat carvers began modifying the old designs for sale in the tourist market, and constructing new figures, such as mother and child statues or the Indonesian national symbol, the Garuda bird, giving it a hornbill's head in accordance with the local importance of this bird. Carvers also have obtained supplies of scrap timber to work with from village sawmills set up to build mission churches and housing. They have developed a new style of openwork wood carving with these materials known as *ajour*, made from the exceptionally hard ironwood. These carvings can withstand transport to foreign places. The *bisj* poles were shortened and their protruding "phalluses" or open-work protrusions were folded upward to reduce possibilities of breakage. The carvers also make faux canoe-prows which are not designed to be attached to canoes at all, and they are commissioned to carve giant crucifixes or ornate house poles that adorn Catholic village churches, illustrating the Catholic church's policy of incorporating indigenous motifs into its own architectural forms (see Mitton 1983: 221). Headhunting has ceased, but the creativity of the *wow-ipits*, the carver, continues as does the cyclicity of life and death that the Asmat people express through their lives and their art (compare Scaglion 1999 on the Abelam).

Case Study:

Sung Ballads from the Hagen and Duna Areas of the Highlands of Papua New Guinea

In this case study we will look at an expressive art form from the Hagen and Duna areas. We have written about these genres previously (Strathern and Stewart 1997, 2000c). Long ballads that are performed by popular experts, famed for their detailed descriptive accounts, are found in only a few of the Highlands areas of New Guinea. They are also known in coastal areas such as the Trobriands (Kasaipwalova and Beier 1987; Leach 1981) and they may be or have been more common that has been recognized.

These genres bring myth, aspects of daily life, and ritual practice alive in the listener's imagination. The plots of these epic tales express the agency of the protagonists, their kin, and spirit beings, and they convey sets of moral messages and commentaries about the vicissitudes of life. They do so by highly dramatized portrayals of experience in which structures and feelings merge together to produce narrative emplotment. This form of creative expression is just one of the many ways that people in New Guinea entertained themselves and others in the past.

These ballads are relatively lengthy pieces of performance art which are highly esteemed traditionally in the cultures where they are found and are comparable in many ways with oral epic traditions found in the Greek and Balkan areas in Europe, as seen in their modes of construction and expressive presentation (Lord 1991). They are a rich source of statements on romantic and/or tragic themes that provide insightful materials on past conditions of society, changing forms of poetic composition, and diverse matters of revenge, love, hierarchy and local custom. In the Hagen area of the Western Highlands these ballads are known as *kang rom* and they are called *pikono* in the Duna area.

In the Hagen *kang rom* the stress in the stories is on overcoming distance, the desirability along with the danger of marrying at a distance, the perils of travel, the uncertain nature of relationships, and the dangers as well as pleasures of life. In the Duna *pikono* the stress instead is generally on the alliance between a young male protagonist, who is just learning about life and love, and a Female Spirit, the *Payame Ima*, who educates him in the ways of human existence and who guides him along the difficult and perilous path, filled with various adventures and exploits, toward finding a suitable wife and beginning married, adult life.

Kang rom were sung by specialists who expected payment for their efforts. Traditionally they would be chanted in a men's or women's house. Both women and men had the knowledge to produce ballads. Great care was taken in the intervals of breathing, much as an operatic aria is highly controlled to elicit heightened emotional responses in the listener.

Balladic performance was a prime form of entertainment in the past among Melpa speakers of Hagen. The stories were constructed around a limited set of plots which frequently involved a female and male and their story of courtship which had favorable or unfavorable consequences both for them and their kinsfolk. These Melpa ballads are a particular named genre that exists among the roster of sung genres, e.g., courting songs, songs for ceremonial dances, and spoken folktales. *Kang rom* are chanted in a highly characteristic, stylized, and regular manner in couplets that are shaped into sets of four lines or more which serve as a mnemonic device, enabling the singer to proceed through the lines and build on them.

The themes of these ballads are reminiscent of first origin tales (see Stewart and Strathern 2001b). But in *kang rom* the protagonists are not seen necessarily as "first people", rather they are portrayed in a sense as archetypes of human character. Individual agency and the consequences of actions are clearly portrayed in these stories—a feature shared with origin stories and courting songs.

We give an example of one *kang rom* story here, the story of Kuma Pököt and Kopon Morok.

This is a tale of the "romance of exogamy" where a young man called Pököt goes in quest of a wife and experiences trials and tribulations in his journey (Strathern and Stewart 1997).

Pököt sees a column of smoke arising in the distance just at sunset. The smoke rises and mixes with the mists of the hills. Out of curiosity Pököt wants to see what the source of the smoke is. Before leaving on his journey he bathes himself, washing away his dirt, revealing his healthy, full brown skin. He shines brightly like a star and he carefully decorates himself for the journey with a bark-belt fitted round his waist, cordyline leaves at his back, and a front-apron. As he travels toward the column of smoke he sings to himself while crossing rivers and waterways, climbing mountains and traversing barren plains. Finally he reaches a garden at the place Mukl Rupanda where he finds a grand house. Here he sees two young women. The father of the two women appears and asks Pököt what he has come for. Pököt explains that he saw the column of smoke and was curious to see who lived there. The father takes Pököt into his grand house and feeds him fresh sugar cane and prepares a fabulous earth oven feast for him. Pököt spends the night in the house and in the morning declares that he is leaving. The father offers him many fine presents (money, fine shells, and cassowaries) as departing gifts but Pököt doesn't accept them. So the father presents one of his daughters to him. Pököt prepares a great feast for his new wife and her family. He again washes himself as he had at the beginning of his journey and sets off for his home with his wife at his side. When he arrives home (his place is called Mukl Dupaim) he asks his new wife to wait in his house while he goes to tell his kinsfolk to come and greet his bride. But shortly after he leaves her alone, the suitors from her own village, who had followed closely behind during the return journey, approach her and in anger ask her why she has left to go to live elsewhere and say to her "Come on, let's go." The young bride does what she is asked to do by the suitors but before leaving she cuts off a lock of her hair, moistens it with her tears, and wraps it in a leaf, leaving it for Pököt. When Pököt returns to find his wife gone he becomes crazed and believing he has nothing to live for he hangs himself.

This particular story thus ends tragically with a death, as many of the spoken folktales also do. But some end with a young couple marrying and living together until they are old and die. In the ballads, as in life, the outcomes of "romance" are various.

Pikono is an art form that details in heroic mythical proportions practices such as *palena anda* (boys' seclusion, growth house) (for further details of Duna ritual practices see Stewart and Strathern 2002). *Pikono* are sung by men and to men who gather at nighttime in special men's houses to listen to the singing of a solitary performer which lasts well into the morning hours. The journey of the ballad takes the listener across the landscape from the edges of the familiar to the depths of the underworld (on the significance of landscape to the Duna see Stewart and Strathern 2000a). Local mountains, lakes, streams, rivers, and landmarks are named as the heroic figures move through the action of the story. A special stylized archaic form of the Duna language is used to enrich the performative aspects of presentation. This form of entertainment gives pleasure because it is contextualized inside a landscape of the day-to-day that is transformed into the landscape of the extraordinary, inhabited by powerful beings. We give here an example of how one such *pikono* begins. It was sung by an acknowledged expert performer in 1991.

"I sing of the man Yerepi Rangerakini,
As we sit here and I tell you the story.
Yerepi stayed at the place Kali,
Where the water rushes and makes a noise.
He stayed at the place Atili,
Where the water rushes and makes a noise.
At the place Mali, where the water rushes,
There he stayed, he was an orphan,
No mother, no father,
No-one to help him care for pigs or stake bananas....
So he set out from the place Apima,
Where water rang loudly, from Ateli, from Akepi,
Where water rang loudly, he went up the hill,
In the dry season, when people searched for fish
In the shallow streams, beating the water with *mbata* sticks..."

The protagonist of this story is Yerepi. Like Pököt in the Hagen ballad the narrative begins with Yerepi at home, surrounded by streams of water he had to cross when he set out on his journey. Yerepi is an orphan, with no-one to help him grow up and raise a brideprice so that he can marry. In his case, he is depicted as having chosen a pathway that led him to integrate himself in with a society of giant cannibal, the *auwape*, precursors of humans in the land. More usually heroes in these stories are helped in their quest by the *Payame Ima*, a Female Spirit who was said to look after the youths when they were secluded along with a ritual elder in the *palena anda*, the boys' growth house. She was the source of the magic of growth and physical attractiveness for these youths and therefore helped them to find wives. Heroes in the ballads are described as *pikono nane*, "balladic youths", whose journeys personify this quest for adulthood and marriage. In this regard the Hagen and Duna ballads are very similar in their basic themes.

Although ballads as such seem to be found in only a small number of the Highlands societies, the expressive imagination they reveal is found throughout the region in spoken folktales and myths. This tells us that these peoples, known in the literature more for their practices of warfare and their competitive exchanges, also possessed expressive forms of culture through which their emotions and personal sensibilities were creatively displayed (see, for example LeRoy 1985a, 1985b).

Case Study:

The Use of Natural Resources in Papua New Guinea

Extraction and processing of natural resources have for a long time been a part of the overall economy of Papua New Guinea. Along the Northern coast of the island copra, cocoa, and rubber plantations were set up. Subsequently, after World War II, coffee and later tea plantations were established in the Highlands. Shortly after Papua New Guinea gained its Independence from Australia in 1975 the Bougainville Copper Mine was set up for operation. This mining project led to local disputes. The local land holders accused the company of causing environmental pollution and of not providing sufficient shares of monetary returns from the mining operation. These events in Bougainville were followed by the armed insurrection of the Bougainville Revolutionary Army in 1988 and its demand that the island be allowed to secede from the state of Papua New Guinea. A lengthy period of police and army interventions has ensued, and the country's national parliamentarians have been embroiled in an ongoing attempt to resolve the disputes. The mine itself has long been closed. As we note later, the struggle appears to have been resolved as of August 20, 2001, with the signing of a Peace Agreement.

The huge Ok Tedi gold and copper mine opened in the Tabubil area of the West Sepik Province in Papua New Guinea in 1984. The mine brought in vast sums of money through royalties and other fees to the Papua New Guinea government and to provincial authorities, as well as to landowners. Years of controversy over the extent of the pollution from mine tailings that the company had discharged into the regional river system have led to claims for compensation by local communities living downstream from the mine whose environment has been affected by its operations.

While some mines are in the process of closure and developing exit strategies, others are preparing to open, are already opening, or their proprietary companies are exploring for potential new sites to set up operations for exploiting natural resources.

In the Southern Highlands Province oil and gas resources were discovered and began to be exploited in the 1980s. The operations were financed by the US-based oil company Chevron and by the British-based company British Petroleum. Such gas and oil ventures bring in revenue which is partially returned to the local areas in terms of services, such as hospital maintenance, schools, bridges, police barracks, jails, and airstrips. These services supplement direct government spending and in some instances exceed it. Local people come to view companies that provide these sorts of services in the way that they once viewed government. This sets up a dynamic of dependence that is difficult for the local people to break, and it also makes difficulties for the company's own operations.

In addition to services and monetary returns at both the national and local level, the mining companies make payments to compensate local people for loss of land, environmental impacts, and in some instances relocation expenses. But in many instances these payments are not seen as adequate by the local people, while at the same time the companies complain that the payments are too large. The Porgera Joint Venture gold mine in the Enga Province of Papua New Guinea was set up in 1991 and by the end of 1992 it was the third largest gold producer in the world (Banks 1996). The Porgera Joint Venture Company relocated landowning families immediately affected by its operation and paid out compensation payments to these people. In 1999 the company was preparing to expand certain aspects of its mining operation which would mean further permanent loss of land to traditional landowners and their families. More compensation payments would also need to be paid (see also Jacka 2001).

The question of adequate compensation for resource development and the ramifying effects of this on local populations is one that requires much scrutiny. Colin Filer (1996, 1997), Glenn Banks (1996) and Susan Toft (1997) have explored some of the confusing and disconcerting issues that surround the compensation system and its historical transformations.

The sorts of concerns that local people have with development in their areas are not always addressed, sometimes leaving people displaced from their former lands and confused about the true benefits of development projects that utilize natural resources.

An understanding of the complexities surrounding these kinds of issues depends on taking note of several factors The first is that the mine impacts an already existing social organization and sense of the environment among local people, and it proceeds to alter such local perceptions, gradually or catastrophically. As Filer in particular has stressed in his work, inflows of cash themselves cause alterations in local power structures and in the desires and expectations of people. This process in turn leads to heightened conflict in the local communities, which they attempt to resolve by making escalated demands on the company. If these are not met, violence is likely to ensue; and violence is also likely to occur if they are met, since there are always those who are unsatisfied with the levels of payment and are prepared to fight in order to obtain more, setting up an ineluctable sequence of spiraling conflict.

The second point is that the mine affects different people in different ways. The Porgera gold mine in the Enga province, for example, deeply and obviously affects the Porgera people themselves, but it also affects in more subtle but tangible ways those who live further away from it along the river systems into which the mine tailings go. The Duna people of the Southern Highlands Province are a case in point. Those Duna groups whose members live near to the huge Strickland River that carries mine tailings became increasingly concerned in the 1990s about the idea that these tailings were poisoning river fish, vegetation, and wild game in the adjacent bush. This concern was due in part to their cultural perception that the riverine area was part of the domain of a Female Spirit, the

Payame Ima, who was held to ensure environmental fertility, and that this spirit had left the area, or had herself died, because of the putative damage to the environment (see Strathern and Stewart 2000a for more on the *Payame Ima* and Stewart and Strathern 2002 for more on the environmental issues). Mining operations thus impact not only ecosystems but cultural systems of thought and ritual action bound up with these systems.

Third, mining operations involve interests at many different scales or levels, from the global down to the local. Arguments over these interests may arise between local people and, for example, national governmental agencies; between national and provincial authorities at odds over the division of royalties; and between local communities whose members disagree about their relative rights to receive compensation payments based on their ancestral claims to certain environmental areas. International non-governmental organizations, such as Greenpeace, sometimes interpose themselves in these conflicts, turning locally based issues into global ones or pointing to the global causes of local problems.

Most of these considerations apply to major logging and fishing operations as well as to mineral extraction enterprises. In the long run, the problems that areas experience are not only ones connected with the distribution of profits and immediate payments, but also have to do with the long-term sustainability of the environment itself. Logging and fishing companies in particular have tended to deplete resources without adequately renewing them. Our case history on Marovo Lagoon in the Solomon Islands has shown how local resistance to such projects can build up because of indigenous ideas regarding the proper "stewardship" of the land and sea and perceptions of potential wholesale destruction. (See the studies in Howitt, Connell and Hirsch eds. 1996, including the chapter by Hviding and Baines on Marovo Lagoon.)

Case Study:

Agriculture and Change in the New Guinea Highlands

Everywhere in the South-West Pacific the growing and management of food plants and trees for regular human consumption is of considerable significance for the people's way of life. In many places this is combined with activities of fishing, gathering wild plants and fruits, or hunting for game; and in some areas of rain-forest at lower altitudes these activities have assumed primary importance, accompanied by less elaborate gardens and a wider range of physical movement in search of game. In the Highlands areas relatively heavy population densities and the adoption prior to colonial times of the sweet potato as a staple crop have meant that gardening has become more intensified and in the areas most densely occupied hunting has become less frequent although myths and folktales speak eloquently to its importance in the past. Hunting and the collection of forest fruits and plants such as ferns retain a place in people's imaginations, and images of the forest enter into their spells and in their ideas about fertility spirits whose beneficence is seen as being vital for gardens themselves. Forest and garden are seen as in a symbiotic relationship, pictured in the idea of a magically fruitful garden cut with spirit help in a secret part of the forest itself, as we see in some myths from the Duna area (Stewart and Strathern 2002).

It should be emphasized that within the overall region of the Highlands and its adjacent areas such as the Strickland-Bosavi and Ok-Sibil areas as well as the Paniai Lakes further west in Irian Jaya, there is a tremendous range of diversities in gardening systems, which can be imaged not only in terms of a quantitatively based notion of least intensive to most intensive forms of land use, but also in the specific collections of food plants that are grown and in the methods of tillage and fencing. William Clarke has given an evocative account of Maring gardens, showing their complexity and something of the people's feelings about them (Clarke 1971), combining this with an assessment of the ecological context as seen by a human geographer. Edward Schieffelin has explained how the Kaluli people of the Strickland-Bosavi area fell trees in the forest and leave them in place while planting crops in between them. The trees form a barrier against soil erosion (Schieffelin 1975). Axel Steensberg has given a detailed account of ground clearing, fencing, and indigenous tools used in gardening in the Hagen and Duna areas (Steensberg 1980). George Morren has made a detailed account of both gardening and hunting among a "people on the move", the Miyanmin of the Ok area in Sandaun Province, Papua New Guinea, extending the theoretical discussion of both hunting and gardening as modes of ecological adaptation. One of his pictures also illustrates excellently the image of the "magical garden" in the forest to which we have alluded above (Morren 1986: 104).

Morren raises in his book the question of the relationship between pigs and people which is central to discussions of the development of agricultural intensification. The Miyanmin hunt wild pigs as well as keeping small domestic herds of them. As gardening has intensified in areas of heavy population density, so the size of domestic pig herds has increased while wild pigs are no longer available to be hunted. In the Aluni Valley among the Duna people, however, wild pigs are concentrated in large grassland areas close to the Strickland River where no gardening is possible, and people travel in hunting parties from their hillside settlements to burn the grasses in dry season times and shoot these pigs. At home, they keep substantial herds of domestic pigs year-round. They thus participate in both hunting and horticulture geared to pig-rearing. Domestic and wild pigs both require that strong fences be made around gardens, necessitating an expenditure of labor on this task. Peter Dwyer (1990) has organized an account of ceremonial activities among the Etoro (or Etolo) people of Strickland-Bosavi around a statement made to him that the pigs had entered a garden and eaten its produce, necessitating their killing in a ceremonial feast. In fact, the people had deliberately let the pigs into their gardens in order to fatten them up! A similar pattern showed itself in one part of the Highlands, Pangia, in the Southern Highlands Province, during 1967, when people declared that they had to kill their pigs because there were no gardens bearing sweet potatoes from which they could be fed. In fact, they had used up their garden supplies to fatten the pigs, but were also currently faced with a shortfall in the crop. The study by Roy Rappaport (1968) of pig killing festivals among the Maring remains perhaps the most detailed study of the relationship between festivals and environmental carrying capacity, although Rappaport found that the Tsembaga people, whom he studied, held their pig-killings, accompanied by elaborate politically oriented rituals, well in advance of any environmental degradation.

Pigs are central, then, to both subsistence and to politics in the Highlands, and this has probably been true for a long time. Much attention has been concentrated on the areas in the Highlands with the highest population densities and the greatest concentration of pigs per capita (see, for a good survey, P. Brown 1978). Daryl Feil, building on earlier work, has developed a whole scheme of thinking about the evolution of political organization in the Highlands based on the idea of intensification and the importance of pigs in ceremonial payments between groups (Feil 1987). In part, he has drawn on work by J.B. Watson (e.g. 1977) who drew attention to the role of pig-rearing in escalating competition for land among groups. Watson at first thought that the whole process of competition might be recent, based simply on the arrival of the sweet potato in the last three to four hundred years, but this supposition was eliminated by the work of Jack Golson and his numerous collaborators at the Kuk site in the Wahgi Valley of the Western Highlands Province.

Golson's work, conducted from the 1970s through to the present, showed early on that in the swampy area of Kuk there had been considerable gardening activity at least as far as 6,000 years BP, and possibly as far back as 9,000 years ago. Current work is testing the earliest dates, but in any case the evidence shows extensive labor inputs in the form of drainage trenches used for swamp control for several thousand years, an impressive finding which has placed the site at the forefront of archaeological interest on an international scale (Golson 1982; see also Strathern and Stewart 1998a).

The work at Kuk has contributed to the terms of an interesting question regarding the crops that may have been used before the coming of the sweet potato as well as to the issue of when the sweet potato itself reached the Highlands, since some interpretations of the evidence suggest that the date may have been earlier than c. 400 BP by several hundreds of years. The most plausible suggestion for a pre-Ipomoean staple is *Colocasia* taro, along with sugar cane, bananas, and a variety of indigenous vegetable greens and shoots. Elsewhere in the Pacific, where the sweet potato is not dominant, taro holds pride of place as an ancient and esteemed crop and its cultivation is often accompanied by magic and ritual. The same is true for yams (*Dioscorea* spp.). It is interesting to note that in the Hagen area, where Kuk is located in the territory of the Kawelka people, bananas and sugar cane are traditionally the foods a man should offer to a guest; whereas women tend to be in charge of taro, yams, vegetable greens, and sweet potatoes. This suggests an early division of labor with regard to crops in which the sweet potato has been added to an existing female domain. Folktales also record this pattern. One other crop, the *Pueraria lobata*, a root crop with a tuber that grows slowly but reaches a considerable size, has been suggested (by Watson 1965) as a pre-Ipomoean staple. This hypothesis appears to have been dropped from subsequent consideration, with the ascendancy of the idea that taro was likely to be dominant in wetland gardening. The question of how ancient gardening in general is in other parts of the Highlands, for example in swampy conditions comparable to Kuk such as at Lake Kopiago in the Duna area of Papua New Guinea or the Baliem Valley among the Dani people, is not settled.

Golson's work drew attention not only to swamp management by drains but to tillage methods generally. Brookfield and Hart (1971) have provided a comprehensive survey of data on this and other aspects of gardening in their comparison of forty-four places (1971: 94–124). They rank these places from low intensity to highly intensive systems of agriculture, rating many parts of the Highlands, such as Chimbu, Enga, and Dani, as high. They also use a comprehensive list of cultivation methods (p. 101), with 14 components or variables, ranging from the use of fire and ash, through tillage and use of compost, to the control of fallow cover, including the planting of fallow trees such as *Casuarina oligodon*. They further distinguish three basic techniques of ground preparation: "complete tillage, gridiron ditching, and mounding" (p. 112). With complete tillage, the soil is turned with digging sticks and arranged in beds with groove drains or small mounds. This is the pattern seen in the Eastern Highlands of Papua New Guinea, as shown by illustrations in Sorenson (1976: 44). In Pangia and in the Duna area fields are often seen in which some drains have been cut and the ground briefly tilled, then sweet potatoes and other crops interspersed with them have been planted continuously (Sillitoe, Stewart, and Strathern 2002). As the garden ages, it is re-tilled more completely and mounding is begun, in which large areas of soil are drawn together and sometimes compost is laid in the center of the mound. This constitutes the mounding method in Brookfield and Hart's scheme, which is used extensively in the Southern Highlands and in Enga province. It is classically associated with high altitude conditions (see Waddell 1972 for a detailed study in the Raiapu Enga area), but is found in a range of locations and altitudes. The third method, gridiron ditching, is employed predominantly in the Wahgi Valley and across to the Chimbu area. It is associated with efficient water drainage and the creation of top-soil for the beds by the earth removed from the trenches. It began, perhaps, with gardening in or near to the Wahgi Valley swamps themselves.

Both gridiron ditching and mounding are nowadays used especially for growing the sweet potato, but perhaps may also have been used for other purposes. Taro gardens tend to be made differently, with sufficient drains to remove water but plenty of water catchment also; so possibly gridiron and mounding patterns are relatively new adaptations. Along with this pattern goes an overall tendency for gardens to be divided into near-monocrop sweet potato areas and mixed gardens in which a variety of vegetables including *Colocasia* are grown. Michael Bourke and David Lea, writing on the Enga area, distinguished between mixed staple gardens, mixed supplementary gardens, and taro gardens (Bourke and Lea 1982: 80–82). These categories reflect a probable evolution of gardening types in the region as a whole. Mixed staples are a probably original type of garden found in non-intensive conditions. The mixed supplementary gardens, we suggest, have developed in high intensity areas as an analog or replacement of the mixed staple type. The sweet potato and taro monocrop gardens represent relatively new and relatively old forms of intensive gardening. The study of garden types today can therefore offer us clues to the past.

Such a study is also relevant to the present and the future. Since the 1950s cash crops geared to marketing have been introduced throughout the Highlands. In addition large amounts of land have been alienated and developed for coffee and tea plantations or for cattle ranches. These large-scale areas at first were managed by mostly Australian expatriates. More recently they have been taken over by indigenously owned land groups and government authorities with a complex mixture of results. The new economy, however, is by no means restricted to these plantations and their demands for capital, labor, processing plants and fleets of vehicles. Rather the economy has spread into every settlement which has access to vehicles through extensive smallholder plantings. Coffee has become an integral part of the way of life of Highlanders and the money from it has been used variously to feed into local exchanges, to pay compensation for killings, to build new-style houses, and to be spent on vehicles and alcohol consumption.

Coffee growing does not come without costs to the ecology and social life of these areas. Through it people become accustomed to being dependent on the cash economy generally. Village communities are disrupted by drunken behavior at the time of the coffee season. Thefts of coffee berries lead to disputes. Most significantly in the longer term, as more land is turned over to a semi-permanent tree crop, there is less space for the growing of mixed crops with their varieties of nutritious vegetables and there is also less flexibility in the reallocation of land, which leads to land shortages and disputes and a greater dependence on store-bought foods. These are results which are beginning now to show their effects. In an interesting, if ironic, conjuncture of events, the site of J. Golson's fundamental work on the prehistory of Highlands agriculture at Kuk has become the focus of a complicated legal, social, cultural, and political situation as the Kawelka people have reclaimed, for the expansion of their coffee plantings, the same land, used previously for a now-abandoned government research station, on which Golson's archaeological investigations were carried out. This has led to discussions on possible trade-offs between the demand for land on which to grow coffee and the national and provincial-level interest in the area for national cultural heritage purposes (Strathern and Stewart 1998b).

In the early years of the introduction of coffee, Ben Finney carried out a study of emergent entrepreneurs growing coffee in the Goroka area of the Eastern Highlands of Papua New Guinea (Finney 1973). Finney was optimistic at the time for the future of the area. He saw the "big-men" who enthusiastically involved themselves in the money economy as the harbingers of a new order and as also marking the "pre-adaptation" of the Highlands to change through their existing emphasis on competitive achievement. Finney's work belongs to a wider debate on forms of personhood in New Guinea, in which some scholars stress the individual and some the relational or collective aspects of people's senses of themselves (Stewart and Strathern 2000c). In fact, both aspects need to be stressed in order to understand the complexities of change. Finney's entrepreneurs ran into difficulties later when their group members found themselves at a disadvantage by comparison, and when inter-group fighting broke out over a range of problems generated through social change.

Case Study:

Warfare, Exchange, and Gender Relations in New Guinea

These are complex topics which have taken up much anthropological interest, particularly with reference to societies in the Highlands. It is not possible, or even desirable, to attempt to generalize across the great ranges of diversity that we find. Instead, we will point to some themes and questions that run across and between cases. Before doing so, however, we should first point out how warfare, exchange, and gender relations are in general interconnected. Warfare, or at least intergroup fighting of various kinds, has often been regarded as universal in these societies, and there is little doubt that this is in general the case. Warfare, of course, is itself a general term, and fighting can vary in its purposes and duration. Throughout the Highlands, warfare was linked to exchange. Many exchanges between groups grew out of sequences of fighting. An increasing emphasis on exchanges leads to the phasing down of hostile encounters, but disputes over exchanges can themselves lead to further fighting. In any case, warfare and exchange of wealth are co-implicated. Gender relations in turn tend to be strongly influenced by fighting and inter-group alliances and hostilities. Where hostile groups nevertheless intermarry there is obviously greater tension between spouses owing to their potentially opposing loyalties. If marriages form a part of friendly ongoing exchanges this situation is clearly mitigated. Violence against spouses is sometimes attributed as a pattern to societies in which male warriorhood is valued and marriages occur between enemy groups. Polygyny, associated with competitive leadership by "big-men", also influences gender relations. In societies where matrilineal descent is important, such as in New Ireland, New Britain, and the Massim area of Milne Bay Province (notably the Trobriands), high value is usually attributed to women's social reproductive powers. But a similarly high value is found, as is gradually being recognized, in societies with an emphasis on group membership being obtained through the father, and this is in line with the universal recognition of the importance of maternal ties in these same societies; and, equally, with the significant presence of ideas and rituals directed towards female spirits (see Strathern and Stewart 2000a). The issue of gender relations is therefore particularly complicated. As well, rapid changes in many spheres of life are continually altering the patterns that are found. In the Sepik area, where male initiations were practiced in the past, the maternal kin of the initiates usually played an important role in caring for the boys, thus acting in a nurturant capacity. David Lipset has argued for the Murik Lakes area in the Sepik region that a "maternal schema" based on the idea of the "uterine body" underlies much of Murik culture and must be considered in counterpoint to patterns of male aggressiveness and prominence in ceremonial affairs (Lipset 1997).

Three questions that have caused debate are as follows. One is the question of whether warfare has been equally important throughout New Guinea. The second is the debate on leadership and the distinction between so-called big-man, great-man, and chiefly systems. The third is the question of equality or inequality in gender relations. To the first question a relatively straightforward answer can be given. Warfare or fighting was of quite variable significance to social reproduction; but in most of the societies where obligatory male initiation was stressed, there was a dual concern with effectiveness in fighting and maturation in terms of sexual development and marriage. Sometimes, as was explicitly the case for the Asmat of Irian Jaya, this linkage was emphasized by the rule that the initiation of a boy into manhood required the taking of an enemy's head, whose strength was then supposed to pass into the boy (Schneebaum 1990; Knauft 1993). Among the Fore people of the Eastern Highlands of Papua New Guinea a boy was not supposed to marry until he had killed someone in fighting (Berndt 1962). Such stipulations are common enough in societies in which warriorhood was central. It is notable that they do not appear to have existed in the Western Highlands of Papua New Guinea, even though bravery in fighting was an admired and applauded characteristic there. The greater emphasis in the Western Highlands on exchange and marital alliance explains this difference, although the difference is one of degree or emphasis only.

A different connection between warfare and exchange has been suggested by Paul Sillitoe, basing his work on his long-term and in-depth study of the Wola people of the Southern Highlands Province of Papua New Guinea. (Sillitoe 1978). Sillitoe suggested that "big-men", whose influence ostensibly depended on their prowess in exchanges, also stimulated conflicts and fights between groups, in order to increase their own influence and standing, including by the practice of raising compensation payments for deaths but also as a means of eliminating rivals from elsewhere. This holds for other areas, such as Hagen, where "big-men" were often accused of procuring the death of important enemies by sorcery, and on their own death suspicions of sorcery having been made against them were characteristically raised with assertions that someone had "taken the cordyline" for them, i.e. had passed on a secret message about their death and its cause. O'Hanlon (1989) notes the significance for the Komblo people of the Wahgi Valley of the fear of betrayal to the enemy by one's own group-mates, which he describes as *kum*, a term identical to that used in Hagen for witchcraft but with the added meaning of betrayal. And in Hagen, whenever dancing of a particular kind (*mölya*) took place at the time of a festival it was thought that this could coincide with the news of the death of an enemy. The enemy's kin would hear the singing and surmise accordingly. It is notable that *mölya* dancing was also an occasion on which young people could seek out and interact with potential marriage partners, reflecting a kind of zero-sum approach to reproduction. The group celebrated the enemy's loss by an expression of its own feelings of strength and exuberance. Taking this discussion in a rather different way, Pierre Lemonnier (1990) has pointed out how in a number of societies it is leaders who mediate disputes by prominently arranging payments of valuables. He sees such leaders as intermediate, or historically transitional, between the category developed as an analytical term by Maurice Godelier and called "great-men" and the competitive, self-aggrandizing portrait of the Western Highlands "big-man". Lemonnier has produced a very useful survey on the Highlands in this vein. Here two further points should be added. First, the "great-man" category is diffuse, covering capacities from ritual to productive agricultural work to shamanistic powers, making it hard to know how to include or exclude cases in regard to it. It works best as a term for the range of leaders found among the Baruya Anga people with whom Godelier worked (see Godelier 1982). Second, as we have already noted above, the leaders called "big-men" *also* often had important capacities in regard to ritual and warfare (see A. Strathern 1993; Strathern and Stewart 2000b). Thus, these two categories partially merge into one. "Big-men" did not base their position solely on prowess in exchange seen separately from their wider place in the order of things (see Strathern and Stewart 1999a and Strathern and Stewart 2000d, for descriptions of how leaders were involved in promoting important ritual activities of their communities).

In indigenous usage, the Tok Pisin term *bikman* is widely used to designate any type of leader or important person, crossing over the putative difference between "big-man" and "great-man" made by the anthropologists. Vernacular languages usually contain a wealth of expressions regarding leadership, which cannot be easily summarized under a single label such as "great-man". They also often identify categories of female prominence and leadership in ritual or politics. All of these considerations should be borne in mind in evaluating the "big-man" versus "great-man" debate. Analytically, however, there is some merit in recognizing that in some societies leadership has tended historically to be based on prowess in exchange activities (the "big-man" type), while in others spheres of leadership are differentiated or fragmented into different kinds of capacities (the "great-man" type). In certain cases there may also have been an evolution from "great-man" to "big-man" configurations, as suggested by Feil (1987). Our overall point is that in all places, including those with chiefship systems, leadership is a complex matter, involving several components or dimensions of both ideology and practice.

Since the time of Independence in Papua New Guinea in 1975, fighting between groups in the Highlands has returned and increased considerably. The large-scale complexes of exchange alliance that had been built up prior to colonial contact in the 1930s and effloresced markedly in the years following "pacification", crumbled in the face of a variety of forces: new politics, lack of interest by younger people, influence of the churches, and an increase in struggles over land occasioned by dissatisfaction with a colonial freeze on alterations in land ownership (Meggitt 1977). On the other hand, killings continued to occur and to implicate widely flung groups as the result of travel by vehicles and car accidents. Great problems of compensation have therefore emerged, and in Hagen these exercise the skills and efforts of a new generation of leaders, often ones who are also Councillors or Representatives in Parliament. Payments of many thousands of kina (the Papua New Guinea currency note) have become an important component of these compensation payments, and the money is largely raised from coffee sales. The whole complex thus hinges on agricultural production, this time in the cash sector, just as the production of pigs depends on the sweet potato. Ramifying issues to do with compensation also implicate modern politics in a wide sense, and in general the growing scale of social relations and their implication with agricultural and industrial development has led to a huge range of contemporary problems (see Scaglion 1981, Strathern and Stewart 2000b; 2000e). These problems have recently gained the attention of political scientists, who have followed in the footsteps of anthropologists by studying elections in Papua New Guinea and the associated patterns of violence which often accompany election campaigns (Dinnen 2001). In Hagen modified versions of exchange practices are being woven into election campaigns themselves. Votes themselves are regarded as a commodity to be "bought". But the idioms in which this modern idea is expressing itself is that of soliciting a *moka* gift. Money is given in order to obtain a return in votes, and this in turn is woven into further exchanges of wealth.

The underlying importance of production in the high-intensity agricultural areas of the Highlands is generally correlated with a gendered division of labor in which the labor of women and their particular significance in pig-rearing is widely acknowledged. Women do a great deal, although not all, of the work on pigs, especially in harvesting the sweet potatoes which the pigs eat. Highlanders universally recognize this contribution, and in Hagen it was explicitly signaled by the lavish and expensive decorations women, as well as men, wore in the past for ceremonial occasions. In the Anga-speaking areas, on the eastern fringes of the Highlands proper, according to Maurice Godelier's writings, this pattern of value accorded to complementary labor and its concomitants, is not found. Godelier (1982, 1986) writes that men dominate social life in its entirety and women are excluded from ownership of axes and other tools as well as from participation in "male cults" of initiation. He presents a relatively relentless picture of male domination, down to the details of the distribution of meat from pigs, in which women receive the intestines and tongue, regarded he says as offal, while men eat the liver, "the seat of the animal's strength" (Godelier 1986: 16). This vision of Baruya gender relations seems to overlook various aspects of the people's lives and their own relationships. In fact, many details that Godelier himself includes in his ethnographic accounts and which represent what the Baruya people actually say counteract and balance this impression. It turns out, for example, that a husband has to supply his wife with tools for her work and would not dare to ask for a tool back. Women have rights to say to whom pork should be given, and husbands tend to respect this for fear of provoking a violent argument. Women also expect their husbands to share with them money they earn from cash employment. Husbands and wives together decide to whom they should allocate garden strips for sharing and women possess and control magic for pig breeding, sweet potato and taro growing, and childbirth (Godelier 1986: 16–17). Thus, one might just as easily say the Baruya women control certain domains or aspects of social life that allow the reproduction of the society. This does not fit with a model of absolute male domination.

We also learn that when girls are initiated in Baruya society senior women teach them sexual proprieties, for example to accept their husband's wish to have sexual relations and not to "cry out, or you will be heard and from shame he will hang itself"; also not to laugh if his front genital covering is not on straight, because he would be ashamed (p. 43). These last two points show a reliance on senses of shame rather than on force. They appeal to the woman's own cultural and personal sensibility and feelings for the husband rather than the threat that he may kill her, a threat which actually is cited but only in the extreme case of inappropriate behavior, adultery (ibid.). Assessing all these varied matters and coming to a simple decision regarding hierarchy or domination might seem to be complex (see Knauft 1993 for an exploration of this issue for South Coast New Guinea cultures).

Godelier's arguments depend on an overall proposition of hierarchy as it is presented by analysis from his research, conducted mostly with Baruya men. Unfortunately, this analysis does not take into consideration materials that the anthropologist also collected but did not use in his theoretical interpretations. The same is perhaps true to some extent for the tiny group of Etoro in the Strickland-Bosavi area, given prominence in the literature by the detailed studies of Raymond Kelly. Kelly (1993) also discusses questions of assessing equality and inequality in "simple societies" in a broad theoretical way, concluding for the Etoro and other cases that "the cosmologically derived system of moral evaluation is central" (1993: 512). He argues that among the Etoro "male products possess superior prestige value" and that "certain male products likewise possess spiritual consumption values that female products lack" (p. 512). The hierarchy that is created in this way is essentially an ideological artifact and he calls it in the title of this book "the fabrication of a hierarchy of virtue." Godelier does the same for the Baruya. If this is so, mythology must be an important diagnostic source for determining what the hierarchy is supposed to be. Interestingly, at one point in Kelly's text he notes that men and women interpret differently a myth that deals with reproduction and gender differences (pp. 188–194). Nevertheless Kelly argues that "both men and women live in a conceptual world shaped by a male-centered cosmology" (p. 191); even while he recognizes that women privately criticize this cosmology and have their own views about it (p. 192). Thus, we can see from these two examples that it is important to listen to both men and women when attempting to construct a model of what a "society" is like and what roles both men and women play in that social order.

For other areas in the great and populous band of societies in the Central Highlands on whose peripheries relatively small population groups such as the Baruya (c. 2000 speakers of this dialect of Anga in 1979) and the Etoro (750 speakers in 1981) (Godelier 1986: 1; Kelly 1993: 30) live, the certainties of a proposition of male dominance would not hold. Although men claim pre-eminence in the activities of ceremonial exchange and politics in these societies their myths and rituals reveal a considerable importance attributed to female spirits and the powers of fertility and prosperity which they can confer on men and women alike. Women's place in these societies as pig-rearers, gardeners, and political links has brought them a balanced and complementary role which is recognized in the intricate "fabrications" of myth and ritual as well as in daily practices. Paul Sillitoe, while to some extent arguing for the pre-eminence of men in exchange and in dance decorations among the Wola, has also argued in theoretical vein that the Highlands societies are essentially set up in ways that pre-empt the permanent installation of social inequalities, including in gender relations; hence his observation "divide and no-one rules" with regard to the gendered division of labor (Sillitoe 1985). Of course, such an argument does not maintain that true equality existed, only that no long-term relations of inequality were established.

The background to arguments of this kind is found in discussions surrounding the applicability of marxist theories of exploitation to gender relations in New Guinea and elsewhere. Maurice Godelier's early work was done in the traditions of marxist analysis, with its critique of the supposedly "egalitarian" relations of "tribal societies". Paul Sillitoe's argument was explicitly constructed in opposition to this view. Moving outside of New Guinea to Vanuatu, we find that Margaret Jolly has also addressed these issues for South Pentecost. Jolly argues that there may be a hierarchy of values, just as we saw in the work of Godelier and Kelly (and also is found in Modjeska 1995). She suggests that women's work is not erased but it is encompassed, that is, "rendered inferior to the superior value of male work" (Jolly 1994: 85). In other words she appeals to the values granted to work, as the source of inequality and thus also of hegemony in the way Kelly argues for in the Etoro case. But again, the entire social picture needs to be examined, including ritual and religious spheres, in order to try to determine the placement and "worth" of women and men in their societies.

Such arguments about hierarchy may in the last analysis be hard to evaluate because they depend on the idea that there is, in effect, an overall ideology encapsulated in practices that Pierre Bourdieu (1977) has called "habitus", a largely unconscious orientation to the world. Perceptions and evaluations of such a habitus depend to a large extent on the anthropologist and by picking out different features of social life it is possible to come up with divergent overall pictures. Similar issues have emerged even in the analysis of societies with matrilineal descent such as the Trobriands of Milne Bay, on which Annette Weiner established the significant roles and statues of women in modification of the picture given by Bronislaw Malinowski, summarizing her argument in the striking title of her book "Women of Value, Men of Renown" (1976). Perhaps it is better to consider a nuanced set of approaches to different domains of social life when considering the "worth" of individuals in any culture. Similar debates occur in relation to life in "western" societies, such as America for example, and the concerns and issues in these societies have to some extent been carried over by anthropologists to the societies of New Guinea. This process is inevitable, but it is also one that can lead to analytical pitfalls and problems. Anthropologists have to try to understand societies "in their own terms"; but they are bound to see these societies also in terms of the categories and concerns of the societies to which they themselves belong. They need to seek a balance between these different viewpoints.

Similar problems arise in the assessment of types of leadership or prominence in a society. We have mentioned the question of "big-men" versus "great-men", a typology which also has the built-in assumption that women hold no significant leadership positions. These two categories, big-men and great-men, merge with each other in certain respects, although the emergence of prominence through exchange as against warfare or other criteria undoubtedly has had a historical significance in the Highlands of both Papua New Guinea and Irian Jaya. Both of these terms, big-men and great-men, are analytical labels for important leadership categories. Many different terms are used by people in their own indigenous languages to refer to actual leaders and these terms do not easily translate simply into either of these two categories. The terms used by the people themselves to describe their leaders may be the best guide to the complexities involved; while at the same time the use of analytical terms also has its place in anthropological discussions of data. As we have seen earlier, warfare and exchange go together as well as, in some respects, being opposed to each other. And principles of succession to leadership positions, which we tend to associate with chiefship, can be subtly intertwined in either of the categories, "big-man" or "great-man". For example, among the Duna, lines of agnatic successors to leading status within local groups were the most likely to produce both ritual experts and men prominent in exchange known as *kango*; so that a *kango* might be both a "big-man", a "great-man" and in some respects a "chief". The term "chief" is best reserved for societies such as that of the Mekeo or the Trobrianders, among whom chiefship was of encompassing or overall significance (see Scaglion 1996). Yet, even in these societies, elements of competition and indeterminacy of succession show that to become a recognized chief a leader might have to demonstrate "big-man" style capacities. The status gained by senior women through the parts they play in rituals of initiation of younger females and feasting in general also needs to be taken into account. (See, on these topics, Lutkehaus and Roscoe 1995).

Case Study:

Ancestors and Christianity in Mount Hagen, Papua New Guinea

Lutheran and Catholic missionaries came to Mount Hagen in the Western Highlands Province of Papua New Guinea in the 1930s and have remained as a major presence ever since. They came shortly after the initial government patrols following the intrusion of the first Australian explorers there. And they have themselves been responsible for significant ethnographic studies in the area (Vicedom and Tischner 1943–8, Strauss and Tischner 1962).

In the indigenous Mount Hagen religion the ghosts of the dead (*kor kui*) were highly significant as the background forces influencing health and prosperity, as they were among the Kwara'ae in the Solomons. When people fell sick, ritual experts practiced divination with a special kind of arrow (*el mong*) in order to find out which ghost was responsible for the sickness to make an appropriate sacrifice to appease it. The ghosts were thought to be hungry for pork, as people are, and to send sickness as a way of obtaining sacrifices; but they did not do so randomly. In some cases, as spells spoken by experts indicate, it was thought that they withdrew their protection from people who had done wrong, allowing wild spirits of the bush to enter and make them sick. Sometimes the only wrong a person had done was simply to fail to sacrifice pigs and show a proper respect for the ghosts. Anger or frustration (*popokl*) could also lead to sickness, which could not be cured unless the sick persons revealed (*nimba mot ndurum*) their anger and the reason for it (see Strathern and Stewart 1999c and 2000b for further on these points). It was said that in this case ghosts made the person sick out of pity (*kaemb*, literally "liver") in order to draw the attention of kinsfolk to their complaint. Sacrifice was needed in this scenario also. Analogously, confession of wrong-doing was needed in order to avoid sickness and death, especially if persons had sworn an oath on the sacred divination substance (*mi*) of the group declaring their innocence (Strathern and Stewart 2001). The *mi* would find them out and punish them with sickness and death unless they confessed and made atonement. The support of the ghosts was also needed in the past to avoid being killed in battle. When motor vehicles were introduced into Hagen in colonial times after the 1960s and people began to use money from coffee income to purchase them, they often performed a blessing ceremony (*kela memb enditing*) over a new car so as to avoid being killed in traffic accidents. The collectivity of ghosts, seen as ancestors, was thought to work in conjunction with the influence of major spirits such as the Female Spirit (*Amb Kor*), to whom periodic cult sacrifices had to be made in order to ensure the continuity of fertility (Stewart and Strathern 1999b). These spirits, too, could cause sickness if they were not treated with proper respect.

It is apparent from this brief sketch that spirits were considered to be omnipresent and important in all branches of life; that the ghosts of dead kin in particular were guardians of morality; that rituals towards spirits were geared to the experiences of sickness and misfortune; and that attitudes to them were a compound of fear, respect, and trust, as might be expected of dead parental figures. When the first Christian missionaries came they expounded their view that the Christian God was in charge of all of the things that had been attributed to the spirits and that basically the spirits of the dead were bad (*kor kit*) and worship of them should be discontinued in favor of rituals to God, in order to ensure entry after death into Heaven. God as the guardian of morality had a natural place in the scheme of things for the Hageners, either as a superordinate force imposed on the ghosts or as a total replacement for them. By labeling spirits of the dead as bad, however, missionaries in a sense perpetuated belief in their existence, as happened also in the Solomons. Hageners complied with missionary requests on the surface by abolishing the special houses in which they had kept the skulls and other bones of significant dead (*kor manga, peng manga*). In a deeper sense, whenever a pig is killed, it is still regarded as a sacrifice. Christian prayers are regularly substituted for prayers to the ghosts on these occasions, as also has happened in Polynesian cases.

From the 1950s onwards further churches entered the mission field, including Seventh Day Adventists and the Pentecostal-Style Assemblies of God. These began to compete for people's allegiance and to dispute the authority and validity of the Lutheran and Catholic versions of the Christian message which were in themselves a source of internal disagreement already in communities. Seventh Day Adventists have had a relatively minor impact. They forbid the consumption of pork, which militates against the basic value of the pig and of sacrifice in the Hagen world view. They have been successful with families whose members actually wished to opt out of the demanding routines of exchange and sacrifice that underpin indigenous social life. The Pentecostal-style churches have, by contrast, had a huge impact, appealing to a younger and more urbanized generation of people with their vigorous and emotive styles of prayer, singing, and guitar-playing, their revival meetings, and their ideas of possession by the Holy Spirit, of prophecy, and of speaking in tongues. The Assemblies of God organization also encourages the local independence of its churches, which suits with the local social structure. This church can further be seen as an "adjustive" movement, encouraging people to move away from "the old times" and embrace a new world (Stewart and Strathern 2001c).

All this raises the question of the relationship to morality and the ghosts of the dead. For Assemblies of God worshipers great stress is placed on Jesus as a personal savior and guide to behavior. Morality is seen as in a sense inspirational, inspired by personal faith, devotion, and love—notions that of course inform "mainstream" Christianity also but are foregrounded in Pentecostal-type congregations. The old morality of the ghosts, centered on punishment of wrong-doing by sickness, fits well with the Old Testament background to Christianity as a whole but has less of a place in the Pentecostal scheme of things. This point is in line with another transformation which has occurred; whereas in the old system anger was regarded as in a sense justifiable because it led to the righting of wrongs or at least their revelation, in the Pentecostal scheme anger is itself seen as a sin and as such a cause of sickness. Its revelation thus becomes the confession of sin. Such a formulation again leaves no legitimate room for action by the ghosts, although in a formulation given to us by one woman the ghosts were said to go to God and ask for permission to send sickness to living kin with whom they were annoyed, so that they were incorporated into a hierarchical pantheon in this novel way (Stewart and Strathern 1998).

For a decade up until the year 2000 the Assemblies of God churches found a more effective and dramatic way of enforcing morality. The threat of the possibility of world's end was used to make people repent of their wrongdoings and confess them and thus enter into the "new life" of the church so as to have the chance of going to Heaven. During this millenarian phase of activity, dreams and prophecies which blended together old and new images including the visitations of angels, the Devil, and dead kin, flooded into people's discussions of religion (Stewart and Strathern 1999c). Old themes jostled with new ones relating to fasting, visions, and dedication to church rituals. The religious landscape was greatly transformed by these events, shifting people further away from the old religion in some senses and back to it in others. A "new world" way of thinking grew up out of the "world's end" scenario of the 1990s, and in the years following 2000 this remains to be worked out, in contexts of considerable difficulty for Mount Hagen and the country as a whole, with significant economic and political problems. Ideas about ghosts and morality are likely to remain as a dormant, but occasionally tapped into, resource of explanations regarding misfortune as people try to find their way in post-millennium times.

Case Study:

"Cargo Cults" and Millenarian Movements as Objects of Study

The phenomenon of cargo cults is an "old favorite" in the anthropology of the South-West Pacific. The term refers to a variety of rituals and movements that have occurred historically in colonial and postcolonial times, notably in New Guinea, focused variously on obtaining by magical or ritual means the wealth items brought into the area by Europeans. "Cargo" is a general Tok Pisin term for such objects of wealth, which might vary from boxes of tinned meat and other foods to large supplies of money itself, depending on the historical stages of contact and the desires of the people. Political and moral concerns were invariably deeply woven into these desires. The movements can be seen as protests against the inequalities imposed by colonial rule; as new political organizations developed to resist colonial power; as searches for moral redemption through the establishment of equality between outsiders and indigenous people; and as a means of rectifying injustice seen as brought about by the trickery of the colonial intruders, sometimes linked with the idea that an indigenous ancestor had gone away to the lands of the "white people" and had intended to send back cargo to his kinsfolk, but the colonial powers had blocked this and taken the wealth for themselves. Ideas of this kind have offered ample scope for the commentaries and analyses by anthropologists concerned with the ethical and political dimensions of colonialism. Other anthropologists have been led to point out that the category of "cargo cult" was in some instances foisted on the people by a colonial administration that was nervous about people's aspirations and resentments and used the label of the "cult" to delegitimize the people's movements of resistance to colonial rule and their attempts to help themselves. A strong statement of this perspective is to be found in Martha Kaplan's book on Fijian political history (Kaplan 1995). Kaplan argues that cults exist "not necessarily as Pacific or nonwestern phenomena but instead as a category in western culture and colonial practice... Cults and movements were "things" to colonial officers and have come down to us as such in their records and in administrative practice" (p. xiv). Monty Lindstrom has traced the history of anthropological ideas about cargo cults in Melanesia in order to deconstruct these into their "component elements and generic stipulations" (1993: 11) and he argues that "within anthropology, of course, from the 1950s to the 1980s, cargo cult became the orthodox term for Melanesian social movements" (p. 38). He refers also to the term's "gauche ancestry" and models of its stressing the desire for goods, the imminent expected arrival of spirits, and the like as "cargo cult at its crudest" (p. 39). He also cites the earlier argument by Nancy McDowell (1988: 21) that "cargo cults do not exist, or at least their symptoms vanish when we start to doubt that we can arbitrarily extract a few features from context and label them as an institution." While Lindstrom and others call into question the motivations of those who have used the term, relating them to colonialism, McDowell was pointing out one of the difficulties of making cross-culturally valid definitions in general. Her point was perhaps that the element of "cargo" had been picked out in social movements, whereas these movements in fact contained many other aspects. Martha Kaplan argues the same point, writing that the movement she studied in Fiji "was never primarily about goods," but rather was "focused on issues of leadership, authority and autonomy" (1995: xiv).

These strictures are important. On the other hand, many significant studies have been made that indicate a "search for wealth" as basic to certain movements. Wealth, however, in the South-West Pacific, is frequently seen by people as a means of attaining a sense of self-worth or equality with others. This is hardly surprising, since exactly the same can be said of some patterns of attitudes in western, class-based societies. But in the present context we must recognize that wealth also has magico-religious significance. Wealth is seen by many peoples as a sign of cosmic well-being, of proper relationships with the spirit world, and therefore the lack of it is seen as the reverse, a sign of the cosmos and spirit-world being out of balance, requiring ritual and sacrifice to set it to rights. This is the basis for all indigenous fertility practices which we also label, in an innocuous descriptive sense as "cults", without implying that they are "strange" or politically subversive. Again, we need to remove this basic idea from any sense of "the exotic" by reminding ourselves that in the Christian religion also prayers are traditionally made for the well-being of the land and its crops and thanksgiving services are held for harvest-time. Such notions are found in the hymn that begins "We plough the fields and scatter/ the good seed on the land/ but it is fed and watered/ by God's almighty hand." For the South-West Pacific and especially New Guinea anthropologists have ceaselessly emphasized the symbiosis of persons and things, the spiritual significance of material wealth, and the characteristics of wealth objects as living parts of social relations and ideas of the person: all notions that in fact go back to the early work of Marcel Mauss on the gift (Mauss 1954). In the light of this, it would be surprising if movements for social change did *not* focus, at least in part, on the acquisition of wealth. That this focus is inextricably bound up with historical relations between outsiders and Pacific Islanders, in the context of colonial history, is brought out well, for example, in the work by Andrew Lattas in his work among the Kaliai of East New Britain in Papua New Guinea between 1985 and 1986 (Lattas 1998). Lattas's detailed study also recognizes the stimulus, argued long ago by Margaret Mead, of the events of World War II and in particular the experience of seeing the huge amounts of technical gear, firepower, and foodstuffs brought in by American troops in the Pacific campaigns to stem the Japanese invasions. Similar points have been made by Keesing (1992) on Maasina Rule in Malaita. The main points to make here are (1) that the desire for such goods is always seen as integral with a desire to achieve moral and political parity; and (2) that the leaders of movements always try to set up elaborate forms of social organization in order to meet their ends and these forms are seen by the people as a type of "work": work that can lead to their political reassertion and their achievement of prosperity in the widest sense.

It is also extremely important to apply Nancy McDowell's caveat in a historical way. The element of "cargo" and its significance varies considerably according to the contact history and the stage reached in it by the people. In Mount Hagen, for example, a movement known by the people as "wind work" (*köpkö kongon*) and described as "the red box

money cult" flourished between about 1968 and 1971 (Strathern 1979–80 ; Strathern
and Stewart 2000d:10–15). This movement actually was centered on a ritual for the acquisition of large quantities of money, to be brought by spirits of the dead (who were
said to prefer now to be known as "wind people") and placed into the kinds of red
wooden boxes in which plantation laborers used to bring back their wages and goods
from the coast when they returned home. Boxes filled with stones and metal were expected to be transformed into containers of money through the rituals performed. The
cult ended when the money did not materialize. By contrast, in some other areas, ideas
and movements have a much longer history, transforming themselves over time and developing complex organizational forms and aims. These tend to be areas with a long history of early colonial contact and mission influence and persistent problems of economic development. In these areas, movements that held within them magico-religious
elements also have tended to have inbuilt ambitious projects of self-help and economic
effort, a fact which is remembered by the descendants of their adherents today, who accordingly stress themes in these movements that resonate with, and have helped to
shape, the views of contemporary anthropological observers. It is also helpful when anthropologists work in areas with a span of recorded history, especially if their own fieldwork has been conducted at different times, which can assist in understanding better the
contexts into which movements for change have been set. Panoff (1997), in discussing a
movement between 1966 and 1981 among the Maenge of New Britain, makes this point.
This was the Pomio Kivung movement, which became connected with the name of Ko-
riam Urekit, a Member of the national House of Assembly for the area, and has been
studied in detail by Harvey Whitehouse (1995). Panoff stresses that over time the magical and religious aspects of people's ideas were replaced with forms of organization for
economic development. This same quasi-evolutionary historical viewpoint is shared by
various writers. Others again take the view that movements which were actually directed
towards "rational" ways of achieving change were dubbed as "irrational" by colonialist
observers. A middle of the road position, by contrast, is that we need to recognize the intertwining of magico-religious ideas with secular ones in the organization of many drives for change. Turning our attention back again to western societies, we find that this
feature is also found. Many trends in western societies show elements of "cargo thinking": for example, the adoption of diets and lifestyles that are expected magically to preserve the youth and health of those who follow them; sure-fire get rich quick schemes
based on playing the stock market; and endless self-help courses aimed at increasing
one's social effectiveness or success in the world. All of these syndromes of activity combine certain desires and ritualistic ways of attaining them along with much practical organization and effort, and could therefore be called "cargo cults" in some sense. From
this we might well conclude that such cults exist everywhere rather than nowhere.

A classic early study by Peter Lawrence of cargo beliefs and movements on the Rai
coast of the Madang area in Papua New Guinea, anticipated by many years the later
trend in anthropology to a historical viewpoint (Lawrence 1964). Beginning with an account of the indigenous cosmic order (another approach which has proved to be of enduring value, see for example Stewart and Strathern 2001a), Lawrence traces a history of
five different stages of activity, three from 1871–1933, the fourth from 1933–1945, and
the fifth from 1948–50, all interspersed with discussions of colonial society and the effects of administration activity. Lawrence also makes it clear how the indigenous appropriation of Christian teachings was an important component throughout these periods
of time (e.g. p. 85). He quotes Tok Pisin versions of such teachings which he says were interpreted in cargoistic terms, such as "*Long Heven i nogat trobel, i nogat pen. Em i fulap*

long ol gutpela samting...Em i ples bilong peim ol gutpela man." Lawrence translates this as "Heaven is a place without trouble or pain. It is filled with every good thing...It is a place where good men are rewarded" (loc. cit.). Here we must comment that it is the rich potential for ambiguity in Christian ideology itself, as much as anything else, that lends itself to varying historical interpretations; and the connection between Christianity and millennarian aspirations has also been shown much more recently in the years leading up to 2000, as we have noted earlier (Robbins, Stewart, and Strathern 2001).

Lawrence's account of the fifth phase of cargo activity from 1945 onward centers on the leader Yali, whose father had been a master of "traditional sacred knowledge" (Lawrence 1964: 117), among the Ngaing people. Yali became an indigenous official of *tultul* of Sor village and he accompanied Australian Patrol officers on their rounds. Later he joined the police force and was in the coastal city of Lae at the time the war began in Europe in 1939. While with the police he heard much talk of resentment against the Australians and of various cargo movements in the region (p. 122). Yali was involved in war duties, was promoted to Sergeant, and was sent to Queensland in Australia for jungle training. He saw the Australian cities of Brisbane and Cairns, visited factories, and noted the emphasis on suburban order (p. 123). Later, he was sent back to New Guinea, and made a notable escape from Hollandia (Jayapura) back to Aitape, gaining the reputation of a war hero. He appears to have been encouraged through all this time by promises made to New Guinea recruits that the Australians would help them to gain better material things after the war (p. 129). He had also been shown exhibits of New Guinea material culture at the Queensland Museum, and had heard a fellow New Guinean ask why the missionaries had told them to give these things up while other Australians had collected them and put them in a house in their own country. This kind of incident may later have fed into the rumor made about Yali that while he was in Australia he had seen the cargo deity, variously known as God, God-Kilibob, or Jesus-Manup (p. 136). Yali became the accepted leader in this area of a renewed version of cargo thinking. Lawrence is at pains to point out that Yali himself did not necessarily share all the ideas and beliefs that came to center on him. He is reported by Lawrence, however, to think that the Administration would honor the promises to help his people which he had heard during the war effort. His failure to secure this end on a visit to Port Moresby in 1947 turned him against the government. He also turned against the missionaries when he heard that some Australians believed in evolution rather than in divine creation and that the missionaries had hidden this secret from New Guineans (p. 176). He decided to reorganize paganism, as a means of gaining the help of indigenous spirits to obtain good crops, game, and pigs.

Yali at this time came partly under the influence of Gurek, trained as a Catholic catechist. Gurek claimed to have had visions of spirit soldiers (*lain masalai soldia* in Tok Pisin) drilling in the bush and preparing to bring rifles and other Western goods to the people. The people, he said, could not see these soldiers because they had anger in their hearts and were always quarreling. They must live in peace, follow him, and they would find the "road to the cargo". This road was therefore pictured as lying through the agency of indigenous deities of the area. Yali adopted Gurek's position, partly out of revenge for what he saw as the trickery of the Australian administration. A feature of the new rituals mimicked the practice of Europeans of decorating tables with flowers, which Yali had seen in Brisbane, combined with food offerings to deities. Yali set up a new political organization which covered the whole southern Madang and Bogia region, with himself at its apex (a form of structure surely derived from colonial models), and the new cargo rituals spread widely throughout this region. Yali himself patrolled in it, counseling the people on how to carry out these rituals and avoid the displeasure of the administration in doing so. During this period, the people turned away from Christianity. However, after the prophet Gurek left the Rai Coast, people began to be disillusioned by the lack of results of the pagan rituals. The Lutheran Mission built a dossier against Yali, alleging corruption and misbehavior. Charges were eventually brought against Yali (not including any charge of promoting cargo cult) and he was jailed, after which he lost political influence.

Lawrence recognizes that the impressive political organization Yali developed was a mark of the widening political aspirations of people disappointed with both government and missions and could therefore be construed as a rudimentary form of revolutionary nationalism (p. 222). This kind of analysis was advanced earlier by Peter Worsley, with examples from many different parts of New Guinea and the Solomons (Worsley 1957). That the movements often contained elements of political rebellion and resistance is clear. Perhaps, however, they are to be seen in local and regional, rather than nationalist terms, since the concept of Papua New Guinea as a nation was hardly present in the 1940s and 1950s. We can see them as precursors of nationalism in the sense of being forms of opposition to colonial rule, but here too their emphasis was on "broken promises" rather than on the premises of government itself. At any rate, Lawrence's blow by blow account comes over convincingly as a historical narrative at the biographical level. Many years later the extended effects of that biographical history still continue. Elfriede Hermann and Wolfgang Kempf, who have worked more recently in the Madang area, have found that ideas about Yali are still very important among the descendants of those who were called the "flower girls" in his rituals. Hermann points out that an indigenous discourse of kastom, opposed to the colonial discourse of "cargo cult", has emerged as a means of combating the stigma of the term "cargo cult" itself (Hermann 1997: 88). A part of this stigma arose from Yali's conflicts with the Lutheran mission as we have mentioned above. After Yali's trial and fall, perhaps, people experienced shame. They have subsequently attempted to rehabilitate the indigenous rituals which formed a part of what Yali sponsored as examples of kastom and not kago kalt (cargo cult). The people of Yasaburing, Yali's home village, nowadays distance themselves from the flower rituals and say that these were not a part of kastom (i.e. not "authentic"). Women who took some part in these rituals explain that they did so only because by kastom women were needed to help with male rituals, and they did so in order simply to show they were willing to assist.

Hermann's account does not attempt to refute Lawrence's history of Yali's activities. It does show that as time moves on people develop new forms of discourse, just as anthropologists also do (see Jaarsma 1997). Perhaps it may be worthwhile to note here that the Institute of Papua New Guinea Studies published in 1986, with financial assistance from the Lutheran Church, a translation into Tok Pisin by Bill Tomasetti of the whole of Lawrence's book with the title Rot Bilong Kago. It would be interesting to know what the reception of this translation was and what its long-term effects may have been in the Madang region. This was an early attempt at the kind of "repatriation" of materials that has since become a topic for discussion.

The debates among anthropologists about the label "cargo cult" and the problems of understanding and analysis continue. The "stigma" which Hermann refers to has led some anthropologists to distance themselves from the use of the term. Others, as we have done here, point out the relevance of the idea for western societies as well as for New Guinea. The underlying questions which Yali asked, about how wealth comes into being and how it can be obtained, can be answered in various ways. We need to recognize that those answers always tend to be constructed within particular forms of discourse. Telling Yali that the Australians were more wealthy than New Guineans because of their historical access to technology in general, because New Guineans were weakened by colonial epidemics, or because Westerners found ways to make guns and use them, would hardly have been likely to satisfy his or his people's deeper epistemological and historical concerns, which had to do with issues of equality and issues concerning the powers that shape the cosmos as a whole; points that Peter Lawrence made clear in his ethnography.

The deeper message to be found in the study of historical movements for change in the South-West Pacific is not simply that "cargo cults" are a fiction of the colonial period or a figment of westerners' imaginations, but that movements of this kind which combine religious, political, and economic aims and ideas are a recurrent part of history and experience everywhere.

Case Study:

Myth and Change (Duna, Papua New Guinea)

At times of historical change new myths or narratives tend to emerge as ways in which people try to adjust to and gain some control over events in their lives. Such myths are reformulations of the past which also are ways of trying to formulate the future. They appeal to people through their striking images and their reduction of complex issues into a narrative form. This has been true of most of the movements described variously as cargo cults or millenarian movements that have been so prevalent in the disturbed histories of the South-West Pacific since colonial times (see the preceding case study). In their earlier, pre-colonial forms also we may suppose that myths were important for Pacific people in giving them a sense of identity and of authenticity and self-awareness in their landscape, since myths often combined an account of first origins with a narrative of migration and settlement.

One of the areas in Papua New Guinea where we work in addition to the Hagen and Pangia regions is the Duna area (Stewart and Strathern 2000a, 2002). For these Duna people of the Aluni Valley near to the Strickland River in the Lake Kopiago area of the Southern Highlands Province such origin myths are important for each separate large, named group or category whose members trace their origins to a specific locality and set of empowering events that occurred there. This is the same basic pattern as holds widely true in the Highlands, including Mount Hagen. The Duna call these origin stories their *malu*. Agnatic descendants of the putative original progenitors of a group are the custodians of these *malu*. Only a few leading men would both know of and have the right to recite such a *malu*, as might arise in the case of disputes over land rights. *Malu* fall into two parts. The first part tends to deal with supernatural origins involving spirits (*tama*) who are seen as the original group founders. The second part is a recitation of successive father to son links from the ancestor to the speaker of the narrative, through some seven to ten generations or so. The genealogy authenticates the speaker's claim to tell the story and links him and his agnatic line, with its cluster of related cognatic kin, to the magical powers evinced by the originary beings. Other people may in practice know parts of this recitation or versions of it, but only the acknowledged agnatic descendants (*anoagaro*) have a proprietary right to it.

Associated with the *malu* complex is the idea that each group has its traditional territory (*rindi*) to which it is linked by its *malu* and within which certain important non-ancestral spirits, as well as ancestral spirits themselves, have their domains of power. The ancestor spirits were thought in the past to manifest themselves by emerging out of the ground in the shape of round, black, heavy volcanic stones sometimes said to be their petrified hearts and called *auwi*. Shrines for sacrifice to these dotted the landscape. Since the adoption of Christianity in the 1960s these shrines have all but disappeared, though their locations are still known (Stewart and Strathern 1999c). Three categories of major non-human spirits were thought to exist permanently in bush areas outside of the settlements. These were the *Tsiri*, a male spirit of riverbanks and watercourses who was thought to have given cowrie shell valuables to humans in exchange for the sacrifice of an ancestor's sister; the *Tindi Auwene*, a powerful male spirit of the territory itself, thought to live in the high forest; and the *Payame Ima*, a powerful female spirit with ubiquitous associations, primarily the high forest also but including pools in various locations (*ipa ane*) and the great Strickland River itself (Strathern and Stewart 2000a). While notions about ancestors and *auwi* stones have receded from people's consciousness and those regarding the *Tsiri* are also muted today, the two categories of *Tindi Auwene* and *Payame Ima* have not only remained vivid in people's minds but most recently have become entwined with modern processes of development that have impacted the Duna environment.

For several decades the Aluni Valley Duna have been accustomed to prospectors for mineral resources entering their area in search of gold, copper, and more recently oil. They have also been aware of the growth of huge mining complexes in language areas adjacent to their own: the Ok Tedi copper and gold mine to the west and the Porgera gold mine in Enga Province. Numbers of Aluni Valley men have worked at or visited Ok Tedi, and Valley leaders have been involved in negotiations over compensation for environmental use and disturbance with the Porgera Joint Venture Company because of the discharge of mine tailings into a river system leading to the Strickland River. Mining and its effects have been a major part of the Valley people's historical experience with the outside world, and they have joined in the formation of the Strickland-Kulini Landowners' Association in attempts to represent their interests politically. Issues over the Strickland River running red with cyanide and putatively causing sickness and death in vegetation, fish, and game living along its banks, focused the people's concerns on the negative aspects of mining development which the Porgera Joint Venture mining company has sought to counter by offering health and community services to the people and paying statutory amounts of compensation for their use of the Strickland's water to dispose of tailings.

At the same time the people keenly want mining developments to occur in their own area so as to gain some of the wealth they have seen generated immediately around the Ok Tedi and Porgera mine sites. They were therefore happy when a company arrived to drill for oil in 1999 near to the Strickland River itself and beside a recently constructed airstrip of the Evangelical Church of Papua New Guinea at a place called Egali which we went to visit in order to interview the people about their feelings regarding the company. The company drilled for oil to a considerable depth and then met rock which their drilling bits could not penetrate, despite their conviction that oil was probably present at a greater depth based on geological indications.

The Aluni people developed a new "myth" or narrative out of these historical events. The myth took the *Tindi Auwene* and *Payame Ima* as prime actors in a drama of change. The story was said to have been invented by a leading figure in one of the groups whose *malu* is linked to the area where the drilling took place and which therefore stands to gain from royalties if oil is found. The story details how a boy of this group fell down a slope and was taken underground by two young women (instantiations of the *Payame Ima*) who took him to a place where everything, including the houses and streets, was made of money and a huge man (the *Tindi Auwene*) lay in trouble with a drilling bit pointed at his heart. He told the boy to take a pipe and strike the bit aside, which he did, thus saving the *Tindi Auwene*'s life. He was rewarded with gifts and escorted safely back up to the outside world. The *Tindi Auwene* had holes in other parts of his body that represented mine sites elsewhere in Papua New Guinea, but the present site threatened him more because it was poised above his heart.

The story reveals a complex and ambivalent set of ideas about mining. It tells us that mining can destroy the land(in the person of the *Tindi Auwene*), but that local agency may prevent this. It stakes a claim to royalties and the great wealth that comes from mining, shown by the town made of money, here seen as also belonging to the *Tindi Auwene* and the *Payame Ima*. It symbolizes resistance and acceptance at the same time. It reflects both national and local consciousness. In short, it powerfully encapsulates historical events in a cosmic drama, a new myth for a new time. We may expect that comparable myths, in this sense, are being and will be generated by local people in New Guinea and elsewhere as a means of asserting themselves and making sense of the world in the face of perplexing challenges and opportunities resulting from globalizing processes.

Case Study:

Medicine and Change in the Highlands of Papua New Guinea

Sickness and its treatments figured prominently in the indigenous religious practices in New Guinea, since adverse happenings to the body were often attributed to the agency of spirits, if not to the effects of witchcraft and sorcery (Strathern and Stewart 1999c). The indigenous medical systems were largely of the kind medical anthropologists have called personalistic, meaning that sickness is seen as the result of intentional agencies, spirits or humans. Sickness was equally closely connected to politics and morality, since attacks by hostile agents were interpreted as political or as motivated by a wish to punish or take revenge on the sick person. Magical spells and ritual actions including the sacrifice of pigs were therefore directed to altering the relationship with spirits and to restore it to a state of amity and support.

A personalistic system of this kind differs sharply from the tenets of western biomedicine which was introduced into the Highlands from the 1930s onward, with increasing impetus just before and after Independence came to Papua New Guinea in 1975. Yet the Highlanders as a whole took to the introduced medicine with alacrity when they saw that it was effective against conditions that bothered them, for example yaws, wounds and bites, fevers and stomach upsets. Like people in many places, Highlanders are quite pragmatic in these regards. They accepted and sought after medicine just as they accepted the steel tools which the newcomers brought with them as trading goods and which had obvious advantages by comparison with their own steel and wooden tools.

It might appear, therefore, that western medicine would rapidly replace all kinds of indigenous practices and patterns of thought in this sphere. This has not happened. As in other domains of activity, for example politics and economics, the Highlanders' concern with deeper explanations and patterns of cause and effect, tied in with their own socio-cosmic view of the world, have precluded any such simple result. This is because biomedicine offers no moral reasons for sickness (other than those connected with social hygiene), and these reasons continue to be sought by Highlanders in the religious sphere. In some cases God is simply cited as the cause and ritual actions are prescribed to restore the relationship with him. In other instances the ghosts of the dead or spirits of the environment are still involved, explicitly or implicitly, and sacrifices are made to appease them. Meetings of kin are held to determine what wrongdoing a person's sickness may portend. This does not mean that biomedical options are not taken. People try their best to gain access to these options, but they may be discouraged by the need to walk long distances, or the cost of a visit to town, or the overcrowding and fears of contamination in hospital themselves, or the prices of medicines bought from pharmacies. Still, they will try to make use of both biomedical solutions and Christian prayers or sacrifices to ghosts; or they will seek diagnoses of sorcery. Such a situation is called one of *medical pluralism*, the conscious use by people of more than one way of trying to overcome sickness. Pluralistic approaches of this kind are sometimes said to reflect situations of class-based inequality of access to biomedicine. As we have seen, this is partially true; but we have also seen that biomedicine does not meet at all some of the perceived needs involved in sickness from the people's own viewpoint. In certain cases, such as the concern over sickness and death caused by witches among the Duna people, neither biomedicine nor Christian prayers are thought to be effective, and there have been moves to return to indigenous methods of divination for witchcraft or to develop hybrid forms of ritual expertise that encompass both indigenous and introduced Christian ideas.

To date these forms of adaptation have taken place outside of the cognizance of biomedical doctors for the most part, and although there have been attempts and programs to study indigenous medicinal plants, there has been little attempt to integrate biomedical with indigenous cultural ways of dealing with sickness in all its aspects. Christian prayers and rituals have therefore been drafted in to meet this need; leaving, however, certain gaps, for example with regard to sacrifices of pigs or the payment of compensation for wrongdoing; or the ridding of harmful substances from the body which was dealt with by indigenous rituals such as those in Mount Hagen which involved the extraction of "bad blood" from a body by applying pieces of sugar cane skin to the skin and sucking at it. The results of this pluralistic situation are therefore an uneasy compromise and coexistence of different practices, loosely integrated through being focused on the sick body. The people energetically seek improved biomedical care, especially in the rural aid posts remote from towns such as are found among the Aluni Valley Duna people. They are also puzzled by the gaps we have noted: how to handle witchcraft, for example. In addition they have realized that their own government is not able to deliver medical health services to them and so they have sought these instead from companies such as the Porgera Joint Venture mining company, which was installing a new health center at Aluni in the year 1999, thus creating a pluralistic set of supply sources for medicines along with a pluralistic set of ideas regarding the causes of sickness. From the point of view of the Duna, and New Guineans in general, what is important is to find medicine that they think works for them, physically and socially. In this regard effective health care delivery is still only a contingent potentiality for the rural populations away from urban centers. (For further studies see Frankel and Lewis 1989.)

An Overview of Political Problems: The Legacies of Colonial and Post-Colonial Practices in the South-West Pacific

In 1970 Ratu Sir Kamisese Mara brought Independence to Fiji and remained its Prime Minister for most of the time until 1987, the year of the first coup there. Vanuatu won its Independence after a nationalist struggle, led by the Vanua'aku Party under Father Walter Lini of Pentecost Island in 1980. The Solomons progressed more peacefully to Independence in July of 1978, following a pathway of change set earlier by Papua New Guinea in 1975 under the leadership of Michael Somare, often known subsequently as "the Chief". The British in fact brought independence to the Solomons before many Solomon Islanders felt they were ready for it, and the subsequent problems their country has experienced have tended to confirm their earlier misgivings. The same is true for the older generation of leaders in the Highlands of Papua New Guinea. New Caledonia awaits full Independence and the resolution of the problems of its settlers, the Caldoches, vis à vis the indigenous Kanak people. All of these countries have experienced at least some turbulence leading up to and subsequently to the achievement of their Independence. The problems involved are classic for small countries with only peripheral trading and production status in the world economy, a legacy of internal divisions, and difficulties in achieving stable parliamentary governments that adequately represent their people's needs. In spite of this there is an impressive emphasis on democratic forms of political activity, in the broad sense, that persists throughout most of the region and which we can recognize as itself a positive legacy of the forms of political organization that held, at local levels, in the past.

In this final section we will review some of these problems, looking in particular at (1) ethnic and quasi- or emergent ethnic divisions; (2) related issues of "law and order"; and (3) further related issues of political party formation and maintenance. Needless to say, overall economic security is often at the heart of dissent and sometimes open violence in political affairs. To overcome these problems governments have often appealed to the idea of common culture as a source of pride and unity, as explained by many of the contributors to Foster (1995). Local movements of cultural revival also seek to foster respect for themselves and to forge senses of identity either in opposition to or in conjunction with the creation of an overall nation-state identity. Cultural issues have become a part of politics and have fed into arguments over ethnic identities. In Papua New Guinea, at any rate, and perhaps elsewhere, unresolved issues of the relationship with the ex-colonial power, Australia, and its citizens who work within the country for the indigenous government or for commercial companies must be seen as a part of the problems of class and ethnicity also.

In Fiji the main and obvious problem inherited from colonial times is obviously the relationship between indigenous Fijians and Indo-Fijians, as the events of 1987 and 2000 amply demonstrate. The ethnic and cultural contrasts here are clear, as are the economic issues. Mahendra Chaudhry's ascent to the Prime Ministership resulted, however, from his general support in the urban sector of the economy as well as the ethnic vote for him from Indo-Fijians. The issue which immediately precipitated the attempted coup against him was the question of possibly increasing the rents paid by Indo-Fijian sugar cane farmers to indigenous Fijian landowners, a move he may have sought to block, seeing it as an attempt to drive Indo-Fijians off the land. The underlying economic struggles are evident here as the basis for "ethnic" attitudes. They will not be made to go away simply by constitutional changes, although an agreed constitutional footing for Fiji is obviously needed, not only in international terms, but also as a foundation for peaceful interactions generally there.

In the Solomons it appears that the background to the turbulence of 1998 onward may be traced to the colonial history of Malaita. As a result of the Maasina Rule movement, Malaita was the first place to be granted its own local government council as a concession by the British colonial government in 1953; and this would appear to be the foundation for Malaitan separatist feelings that emerged clearly later. The proximate causes for conflict lay in Malaitan settlement in Guadalcanal around the capital city of Honiara and the tensions this resulted in with the Guadalcanal people, which polarized in the emergence of the Malaita Eagles Force and the Isatabu Freedom Movement as rival militias prepared to use force to achieve their aims.

Keesing (1992: 174–182) gives some clues to the background of Malaitan-Guadalcanal relations from the perspective of the pagan Kwaio with whom he worked up until 1991 and some of whom were low-paid laborers as migrants in Honiara. These migrants tended to form gangs engaged in theft and backed up by their reputation as warriors and the idea that they had "magic" as the support of their ancestors. Such actions would also obviously breed resentment. Keesing continues: "Strong resentment and hostility have been building up for years among the people of the Guadalcanal coastal zone who are faced with increasing numbers of Malaita squatters, Malaita dominance of Honiara and its Town Council, and the depredations and violence of the Malaita riff-raff, especially the Kwaio" (p. 178). This resentment was fueled further by vengeance killings wreaked on Guadalcanal villagers by Kwaio who saw themselves as obliged by ancestral custom to act in this way. Keesing also comments here that the Kwaio claim to autonomy "provides a context in which clandestine murder and blood vengeance can be construed as assertions of freedom" (p. 179). Guadalcanal villagers petitioned the Prime Minister to evict the Malaitans from Honiara. The formation of militias from communities of educated but unemployed youths, the kidnapping of the Solomons Prime Minister, and the Malaitan demands for autonomy as an aftermath of their being forcefully driven out by the Isatabu Freedom Movement, all seem relatively easy to understand given this historical context. In addition, the Malaitans are a populous group, with some 122,000 people, and they have been drawn to the capital Honiara through land shortages in their own area and the attraction of jobs and education in the city. Their cultural pride and assertiveness has sometimes led them to dominate others, leading to conflicts in this instance with the Guadalcanal people.

Papua New Guinea has had its own separatist problems for many years, chiefly from the threatened secession by the Bougainville Revolutionary Army (BRA) from 1988 onward. The main issues here were profits and environmental pollution from the Bougainville Copper Mine, now long closed by the actions of the BRA. Ethnicity came into the political arena in the form of assertions of difference between the dark-skinned Bougainvilleans and their lighter-skinned compatriots, especially those from the Highlands Provinces. Once again, we may note here how economic conditions influenced politics, and how claims of ethnic difference crystallized only through political conflict, although they were also based on certain perceived physical and cultural characteristics.

In the Bougainville case, there was a demand for autonomy long before the emergence of the BRA, brought on by the advent of independence itself and the creation of a centralized indigenous state government in 1975. Bougainville politicians sought a separate status for their island, and the provincial government system was set up in order to accommodate some of their concerns at the time, leading to a two-tiered system of government for the whole country, not just the North Solomons Province within it. The Provinces were based on the old colonial Districts. The Bougainville mine generated much needed income for a newly independent government; but its long-term political costs were also great. Secessionist sentiments had already existed in the colonial era and they were formed again in the 1980s among the Nasioi people, on whose land the mine was built and who suffered from its environmental effects (Denoon 1997: 384), leading to the BRA rebellion. After many previous attempts to reach an agreement, a comprehensive settlement was signed on August 30 2001, including "an agreement covering autonomy arrangements, a referendum on independence within ten to fifteen years following the installation of an autonomous Bougainville government and phased implementation of a weapons disposal plan" (Papua New Guinea *Post-Courier*, August 30th, 2001). The PNG Minister for Bougainville Affairs, Moi Avei, was praised for his efforts in this process. On the day of the signing itself, festive dancing groups performed in the capital city of Arawa, including a youth wearing an *Upe* hat as a mark of his status as an initiand. Young men traditionally wear this hat and let their hair grow into it, removing it at their final initiation into manhood. The hat is featured on the province's flag. The occasion was attended by the Prime Minister of Papua New Guinea, Sir Mekere Morauta, and by the Bougainville Governor, John Momis, a veteran politician. Appealing to forms of symbolism with Biblical resonances, Momis spoke of the Peace Agreement as "a new covenant washed in the blood of so many of our people of both sides of the conflict." Joseph Kabui, another long-term leader in Bougainville, spoke of the future in religious terms also as a time when "in the place of guns and soldiers will come a civil society governed by the laws of man under the watchful eyes of Almighty God." The governments of Australia, New Zealand, Vanuatu, Fiji, and the Solomon Islands were all praised by these leaders also for their roles in helping to shape the peace deal (all quotes are from the Papua New Guinea *Post-Courier*, August 31st 2001)

All political conflicts of this kind impinge on the wider economy of the countries involved and therefore lead to further problems. Questions of law and order are rapidly implicated. Large-scale development projects such as mines bring in revenue to government, but they also breed resistance, escalating demands for compensation, internal political conflict, and factional struggles between politicians themselves over their benefits. This point applies to the Ok Tedi and Porgera mines and to the oil and gas operations by Chevron in the Southern Highlands Province. A cycle of unintended consequences tends to set in, and proves hard to break. And mining operations do over time tend to produce environmental damage as has now been recognized to have occurred on a massive scale downstream from Ok Tedi.

With the fierce competition for resources and access to money, the political process in all these countries, notably Papua New Guinea, becomes highly valued by local populations and intense competitions for office, funded by operations of vote buying and outbreaks of violence in association with elections, are a further inevitable consequence. The formation of stable political parties based on clear ideologies has been inhibited by these processes of faction fighting, and successive votes of no-confidence in governments weaken the continuity of governments in the eyes of the people. Successive Prime Ministers have tried hard to combat all these problems as well as retaining the support of international lending agencies, but their positions are constantly made vulnerable by party defections, individual demands, and the threats of no-confidence votes. Parliamentary politics tend to be at least as volatile as those at village level, and for analogous reasons. On the other hand, cross-cutting ties and switches of allegiance do form a brake on accumulations of power by any one set of people over time.

Despite all of these severe difficulties, the South-West Pacific nations have tended to survive. As small-scale countries blessed with rich resources and warm tropical climates they all have the potential to meet their aims over time, to give a good standard of living to their citizens, and to provide attractive places for people to visit from elsewhere.

Two parts of this region still lie under foreign political control: New Caledonia and Irian Jaya (West Papua). The future for both places is unclear. There are orderly moves toward final independence for New Caledonia which may prove successful if the settler problem can be resolved. In Irian Jaya, the West Papua Freedom Movement has for long campaigned politically and fought militarily against Indonesian control, perhaps encouraged by the final emergence of a battered East Timor as an independent country. Dissidents are still regularly rounded up and jailed or shot and activist international organizations continue to protest against these processes. The fate of Irian Jaya is bound up with the overall fate of Indonesia as a single Republic, a topic that falls outside of our purview here but is of obvious importance for the whole South-East Asian region and for Australia and the Pacific in general. The Indonesian government offered special autonomy status to the province, granting it 70% of the royalties from mining and allowing it to be renamed Papua in legislation due to take effect on December 22, 2001. Pro-Independence campaigners, however, declared they would reject this arrangement.

1. Mount Hagen, Papua New Guinea. Male mourners at a funeral for the death of a prominent man in the 1970s charge onto a ceremonial ground where the body is displayed on a platform, waving bundles of arrows and sticks. Their bodies are plastered with white and yellow clay signifying their grief. Such patterns of mourning are also political statements of support for the bereaved group in case they seek revenge on those who may be determined to have caused the death by sorcery. This kind of display at funerals was revived in the 1970s after an earlier ban by Christian missions, and still forms a part of political statements at funerals today. (Photo: Stewart/Strathern Archive)

2. A female mourner on the same occasion as in photo 1. Behind her women's netbags are suspended from a tree. The women cluster together and sing mourning songs separately from the men; but the overall work of grieving is collaborative and communal. The mourner here has covered her body with introduced tradestore cloth which was already popular by the 1960s, and subsequently became the universal mode of daily dress. (Photo: Stewart/Strathern Archive)

3. A male dancer at a *moka* occasion in Mount Hagen, Papua New Guinea, 1960s. His array of bird plumes includes eagle and yellow bird of paradise feathers. A baler shell sits above his forehead and a large conus shell is suspended from his pierced nasal septum. Long crest feathers of the King of Saxony bird project from either side of his nose. At his chest he wears a set of tally sticks indicating pearl shells he has given away to exchange partners in the *moka*. Decorations of this kind are worn only for cultural shows nowadays. (Photo: Stewart/Strathern Archive)

4. A newly constructed ceremonial tub or *pokla mbo* at a ceremonial ground recently cleared in Mount Hagen in the 1970s. The tub is made from sharpened stakes and tree bark. Magic stones to increase fertility and prosperity may be buried in its soil. The cordyline plant growing in it is a mark of the group's vitality and longevity. The ceremonial ground here belonged to Ndamba of the Kawelka Kundmbo clan, who was prominent in the *moka* in the 1960s and 1970s. With the decline of *moka* in the 1990s no such new tubs are being constructed, and the construction of "men's houses" at ceremonial grounds is tied in with parliamentary election campaigns. (Photo: Stewart/Strathern Archive)

5. Mount Hagen, 1970s. Lengths of sugar cane and bananas are laid out for a distribution during a funeral sequence. The provision of these special foods, grown by men, is a mark of hospitality on ceremonial occasions. Today, guests may be fed with tradestore rice and tinned meat if these traditional foods are not available. (Photo: Stewart/Strathern Archive)

6. Pangia, Papua New Guinea, 1960s. A newly married bride carries a set of fine pearl shells in her netbag as a part of the bridewealth paid for her. The rear of her body is draped in brightly colored trade-cloth. Bridewealth remains important in most parts of the Highlands, but money has replaced shells since the 1960s and the monetary component has become inflated. Some of the Christian churches have tried to curb the size of bridewealth payments made. (Photo: Stewart/Strathern Archive)

7. Duna area, Papua New Guinea, 1990s. In a shady clearing beside the fieldworkers' [Stewart and Strathern] residence an older man, Tukaria, who is the local Baptist pastor, kneads the valued sauce from the fruit pandanus onto banana leaves. A younger man does the same. Small-scale regular consumption of garden foods helps to hold the members of a settlement together. These Duna people have far less access to urban goods than do the Hageners today, but they have a greater abundance of forest plants. (Photo: Stewart/Strathern Archive)

8. A home-made shotgun in a forest enclosure among the Duna people in 1998 signifies the return of these people to a situation in which they feel the need to protect themselves in possible intergroup fighting. Guns of this kind have been made widely throughout the Highlands region since the 1980s. Ostensibly the guns are also used for shooting forest game. An axe and bushknife used for gardening lie at the gun's butt and its barrel rests on a netbag. In the foreground is a small camera case belonging to the fieldworkers [Stewart and Strathern]. (Photo: Stewart/ Strathern Archive)

9. Porgera, Enga Province, Papua New Guinea, 1999. A view from inside the compound of the huge goldmine, looking to a road and tin-roofed stores just beyond it, where local people buy goods. The fence separates the two interdependent worlds of the mine and the local people on whose land the mine is situated. Large-scale developments of this kind exist in several locations in Papua New Guinea and in Irian Jaya (West Papua/Papua), bringing in royalty revenues and compensation payouts but also turbulent social problems and violence. (Photo: Stewart/Strathern Archive)

References

Akin, David
1999   Cash and shell money in Kwaio, Solomon Islands. In D. Akin and J. Robbins eds. *Money and Modernity*, pp. 103–130. ASAO Monograph no. 17. Pittsburgh: University of Pittsburgh Press.

Aldrich, Robert
1993   *France and the South Pacific Since 1940.* Honolulu: University of Hawai'i Press.

Allen Michael ed.
1981   *Vanuatu. Politics, Economics and Ritual in Island Melanesia.* London and New York: Academic Press.

Arno, Andrew
1993   *The World of Talk on a Fijian Island. An Ethnography of Law and Communicative Causation.* Norwood, NJ: Ablex Publishing Corporation.

Banks, Glenn
1996   Compensation for mining: benefit or time-bomb? The Porgera gold mine. In R. Howitt et al. eds. *Resources, Nations and Indigenous Peoples*, pp 223–235. Melbourne: Oxford University Press.

Barnes, John A.
1962   African models in the New Guinea Highlands. *Man* (o.s.) 62: 5–9.

Bensa, Alban and Jean-Claude Rivierre
1982   *Les Chemins d'Alliance.* Paris: SELAF.

Bensa, Alban and Antoine Goromido
1997   The Political order and corporal coercion in Kanak societies of the past (New Caledonia). *Oceania* 68: 84–106.

Bensa, Alban
2000   Le chef kanak. Les modèles et l'histoire. In A. Bensa and I. Leblic eds. *En Pays Kanak*, pp. 9–48. Paris: Éditions de la Maison des Sciences de l'Homme.

Berndt, Ronald M.
1962   *Excess and Restraint.* Chicago: University of Chicago Press.

Bolton, Lissant
1996   Tahigogana's sisters: women, mats and landscape on Ambae. In J. Bonnemaison et al. eds. *Arts of Vanuatu*, pp. 112–119. Bathurst, Australia: Crawford House Publishing.

Bonnemaison, Joël
1994   *The Tree and the Canoe. History and Ethnography of Tanna*, translated and adapted by José Pénot-Demetry. Center for Pacific Islands Studies. Honolulu: University of Hawai'i Press.

1996   Graded societies and societies based on titles: forms and rites of traditional political power in Vanuatu. In J. Bonnemaison et al. eds. *Arts of Vanuatu*, pp. 200–203. Bathurst, Australia: Crawford House Publishing.

Bourdieu, Pierre
1977   *An Outline of a Theory of Practice*, trans. Richard Nice. Cambridge: Cambridge University Press.

Bourke, Michael and David Lea
1982   Horticultural systems. In B. Carrad, D. Lea and K.K. Talyaga eds. *Enga: Foundations for Development*, pp. 39–77. Armidale: University of New England, Department of Geography.

Brookfield, Harold C. and D. Hart
1971   *Melanesia: a Geographical Interpretation of an Island World*. London: Methuen.

Brown, Paula
1978   *Highland Peoples of New Guinea*. Cambridge: Cambridge University Press.

Burridge, Kenelm O.
1961   *Mambu: A Melanesian Millennium*. London: Methuen and Co.

Burt, Ben
1994   *Tradition and Christianity. The Colonial Transformation of a Solomon Island Society*. Amsterdam: Harwood Academic Publishers.

Clarke, William C.
1971   *Place and People. An Ecology of a New Guinean Community*. Berkeley: University of California Press.

Denoon, Donald
1997   Redefining mineral resources. In D. Denoon et al. (eds.) *The Cambridge History of the Pacific Islanders*, pp. 383–9. Cambridge: Cambridge University Press.

Denoon, Donald with Stewart Firth, Jocelyn Linnekin, Malama Meleisea and Karen Nero (eds.)
1997   *The Cambridge History of the Pacific Islanders*. Cambridge: Cambridge University Press.

Dinnen, Sinclair
2001   *Law and Order in a Weak State. Crime and Politics in Papua New Guinea*. Honolulu: University of Hawai'i Press.

Douglas, Bronwen
1992   Doing ethnographic history: the case of fighting in New Caledonia. In J. Carrier ed. *History and Tradition in Melanesian Anthropology*, pp. 86–115. Berkeley: University of California Press.

1998   *Across the Great Divide. Journeys in History and Anthropology*. Amsterdam: Harwood Academic Publishers.

Dwyer, Peter
1990   *The Pigs that Ate the Garden. A Human Ecology from Papua New Guinea*. Ann Arbor: University of Michigan Press.

Feil, Daryl
1987   *The Evolution of Papua New Guinea Highlands Societies*. Cambridge: Cambridge University Press.

Feinberg, Richard
1990   New Guinea models on a Polynesian outlier. *Ethnology* 29(1): 83–96.

Feinberg, Richard and Karen Ann Watson-Gegeo (eds.)
1996   *Leadership and Change in the Western Pacific. Essays Presented to Sir Raymond Firth on the Occasion of his Ninetieth Birthday*. London: The Athlone Press.

Filer, Colin
1996   The social context of renewable resource depletion in Papua New Guinea. In
        R. Howitt, J. Connell, and P. Hirsch eds. *Resources, Nations, and Indigenous
        Peoples*, pp. 289–299. Melbourne: Oxford University Press.

1997   Compensation, rent, and power in Papua New Guinea. In S. Toft ed. *Compensation for Resource Development in Papua New Guinea*, pp. 156–190. Port
        Moresby: National Research Institute.

Finney, Ben R.
1973   *Big Men and Business. Entrepreneurship and Economic Growth in the New
        Guinea Highlands.* Canberra: Australian National University Press.

Foley, William A.
1998   Toward understanding Papuan Languages. In J. Miedema, C. Odé, and R.
        Dam (eds.) *Perspectives on the Bird's Head of Irian Jaya, Indonesia*, pp.
        503–518. Amsterdam: Rodopi.

2000   The languages of New Guinea. *Annual Review of Anthropology* 29: 357–404.

Foster, Robert ed.
1995   *Nation Making. Emergent Identities in Postcolonial Melanesia.* Ann Arbor:
        University of Michigan Press.

Frankel, Stephen and Gilbert Lewis eds.
1989   *A Continuing Trial of Treatment. Medical Pluralism in Papua New Guinea.*
        Dordrecht: Kluwer Academic Publishers.

Garanger, José.
1996   In Jöel Bonnemaison, Christian Kaufmann, Kirk Huffman and Darrell Tryon
        eds. *Arts of Vanuatu*, pp. 8–11. Bathurst, Australia: Crawford House Publishing.

Gegeo, David W. and Karen Ann Watson-Gegeo
1996   Priest and prince: integrating *kastom*, Christianity and modernization in
        Kwara'ae leadership. In R. Feinberg and K. Watson-Gegeo (eds.) *Leadership
        and Change in the Western Pacific*, pp. 298–342. London: The Athlone Press.

Godelier, Maurice
1982   Social hierarchies among the Baruya of New Guinea. In A. Strathern ed. *Inequality in New Guinea Highlands Societies*, pp. 3–34. Cambridge: Cambridge
        University Press.

1986   *The Making of Great Men. Male Domination and Power among the New
        Guinea Baruya.* Cambridge: Cambridge University Press.

1997   *L'Énigme du Don.* Paris: Fayard.

Godelier, Maurice and M. Strathern (eds.)
1991   *Big Men and Great Men: Personifications of Power in Melanesia.* Cambridge:
        Cambridge University Press.

Golson, Jack
1982   The ipomoean revolution revisited: society and the sweet potato in the upper
        Wahgi Valley. In A. Strathern ed. *Inequality in New Guinea Highlands Societies*, pp. 109–136. Cambridge: Cambridge University Press.

Guiart, Jean
1963   *Structure de la Chefferie en Mélanésie du Sud.* Paris: Institut d'Ethnologie.

Hermann, Elfriede
1997   Kastom versus cargo cult. Emotional discourse on the Yali movement in Madang Province, Papua New Guinea. In T. Otto and A. Borsboom (eds.) *Cultural Dynamics of Religious Change in Oceania*, pp. 87–102. Leiden: The KITLV Press.

Howitt, R., J. Connell and P. Hirsch eds.
1996   *Resources, Nations, and Indigenous Peoples.* Melbourne: Oxford University Press.

Hviding, Edvard.
1996   *Guardians of Marovo Lagoon. Practice, Place, and Politics in Maritime Melanesia.* Center for Pacific Islands Studies. Hololulu: University of Hawai'i Press.

Jaarsma, Sjoerd R.
1997   Ethnographic perceptions of cargo: fragments of an intermittent discourse. In T. Otto and A. Borsboom (eds.) *Cultural Dynamics of Religious Change in Oceania*, pp. 67–86. Leiden: The KITLV Press.

Jacka, Jerry
2001   Coca-Cola and *kolo*: land, ancestors and development. *Anthropology Today* 17(4): 3–8.

Jolly, Margaret
1994   *Women of the Place. Kastom, Colonialism and Gender in Vanuatu.* Amsterdam: Harwood Academic Publishers.

Kaplan, Martha
1995   *Neither Cargo Nor Cult. Ritual Politics and the Colonial Imagination in Fiji.* Durham, N.C.: Duke University Press.

Kasaipwalova, John and Ulli Beier
1978   *Yaulabuta. An Historical Poem from the Trobriand Islands.* Port Moresby: Institute of Papua New Guinea Studies.

Katz, Richard
1993   *The Straight Path. A Story of Healing and Transformation in Fiji.* New York: Addison-Wesley Publishing Company.

Keesing, Roger M.
1992   *Custom and Confrontation. The Kwaio Struggle for Cultural Autonomy.* Chicago: University of Chicago Press.

Kelly, Raymond
1993   *Constructing Inequality. The Fabrication of a Hierarchy of Virtue among the Etoro.* Ann Arbor: University of Michigan Press.

Kirch, Patrick
2000   *On the Road of the Winds. An Archaeological History of the Pacific Islands before European Contact.* Berkeley: University of California Press.

Knauft, Bruce M.
1993   *South Coast New Guinea Cultures.* Cambridge: Cambridge University Press.

Kwa'ioloa, Michael, and Ben Burt
1997   *Living Tradition. A Changing Life in Solomon Islands.* Honolulu: University of Hawai'i Press.

Lattas, Andrew
1998   *Cultures of Secrecy. Reinventing Race in Bush Kaliai Cargo Cults.* Madison: The University of Wisconsin Press.

Lawrence, Peter
1964   *Road Belong Cargo. A Study of the Cargo Movement in the Southern Madang District, New Guinea.* Manchester: Manchester University Press.

Leach, Jerry
1981   A Kula folktale from Kiriwina. *Bikmaus* 2(1): 50–92.

Leahy, Michael J.
1991   *Explorations into Highland New Guinea 1930–1935*, ed. by Douglas E. Jones, foreword by Jane C. Goodale. Tuscaloosa and London: The University of Alabama Press.

Lemonnier, Pierre
1990   *Guerres et Festins. Paix, Échanges et Compétition dans les Highlands de Nouvelle-Guinée.* Paris: Éditions de la Maison des Sciences de l'Homme.

LeRoy, John
1985a   *Kewa Tales,* translated by John LeRoy. Vancouver: University of British Columbia Press.

1985b.   *Fabricated World: An Interpretation of Kewa Tales.* Vancouver: University of British Columbia Press.

Lindstrom, Lamont
1993   *Cargo Cult. Strange Stories of Desire from Melanesia and Beyond.* Honolulu: University of Hawai'i Press.

Linnekin, Jocelyn
1997   New political orders. In Donald Denoon et al. (eds.) *The Cambridge History of the Pacific Islanders,* pp. 185–217. Cambridge: Cambridge University Press.

Lipset, David
1997   *Mangrove Man: Dialogics of Culture in the Sepik Estuary.* Cambridge: Cambridge University Press.

Lord, Albert B.
1991   *Epic Singers and Oral Tradition.* Ithaca: Cornell University Press.

Lorens, Pita
1986   *Rot Bilong Kago,* tanimtok Bil Tomaseti. Port Moresby: Institute of Papua New Guinea Studies.

Lutkehaus, Nancy and Paul B. Roscoe eds.
1995   *Gender Rituals.* London and New York: Routledge.

Malinowski, Bronislaw
1922   *Argonauts of the Western Pacific.* London: Routledge and Kegan Paul.

Mauss, Marcel
1954   *The Gift,* trans. Ian Cunnison. London: Cohen and West.

McDowell, Nancy
1988   A note on cargo cults and cultural constructions of change. *Pacific Studies* 11: 121–134.

Meggitt, Mervyn J.

1965   *The Lineage System of the Mae Enga of New Guinea*. Edinburgh: Oliver and Boyd.

1977   *Blood is their Argument*. Palo Alto: Mayfield Publishing Company.

Mitton, Robert

1983   *The Lost World of Irian Jaya*. Melbourne: Oxford University Press.

Modjeska, Nicholas

1995   Rethinking women's exploitation: the Duna case and the material basis of Big Man systems. In A. Biersack ed. *Papuan Borderlands*, pp. 265–286. Ann Arbor: University of Michigan Press.

Moore, Clive

1985   *Kanaka. A History of Melanesian Mackay*. Port Moresby: Institute of Papua New Guinea Studies.

Morren, George E.B., Jr.

1986   *The Miyanmin. Human Ecology of a Papua New Guinea Society*. Ann Arbor, MI: UMI Research Press.

Mosko, Mark

2000   Inalienable ethnography: keeping-while-giving and the Trobriand case. *Journal of the Royal Anthropological Institute* 6(3): 377–96.

Nayacakalou, Rusiate

1975   *Leadership in Fiji*. Melbourne: Oxford University Press.

O'Hanlon, Michael

1989   *Reading the Skin. Adornment, Display, and Society among the Wahgi*. London: British Museum Publications.

Panoff, Michel

1997   A cargo cult among the Maenge. In T. Otto and A. Borsboom (eds.) *Cultural Dynamics of Religious Change in Oceania*, pp. 59–66. Leiden: The KITLV Press.

Patterson, Mary

1981   Slings and arrows: rituals of status acquisition in North Ambrym. In M. Allen ed. *Politics, Economics and Ritual in Island Melanesia*, pp. 189–236. London and New York: Academic Press.

Pawley, Andrew

1998   The Trans-New Guinea Phylum hypothesis: a reassessment. In J. Miedema, C. Odé and R. Dam (eds.) *Perspectives on the Bird's Head of Irian Jaya, Indonesia*, pp. 655–690. Amsterdam: Rodopi.

Plotnicov, Leonard and Richard Scaglion (eds.)

1999   *Consequences of Cultivar Diffusion*. Pittsburgh: Ethnology Monographs, no. 17.

Rappaport, Roy A.

1968   *Pigs for the Ancestors. Ritual in the Ecology of a New Guinea People*. New Haven: Yale University Press.

Robbins, Joel, Stewart, Pamela J. and Andrew Strathern, guest eds.

2001   Charismatic and Pentecostal Christianity in Oceania. Spec. Issue, *Journal of Ritual Studies*, 15(2).

Rodman, William
2000   Outlaw memories: biography and the construction of meaning in postcolonial Vanuatu. In P. J. Stewart and A. Strathern eds. *Identity Work: Constructing Pacific Lives*, pp. 139–156. ASAO Monograph no. 18. Pittsburgh: University of Pittsburgh Press.

Sahlins, Marshall
1987   *Islands of History* (paperback edition). Chicago: University of Chicago Press.

Scaglion, Richard
1996   Chiefly models in Papua New Guinea. *The Contemporary Pacific* 8: 1–31.

1999   Yam cycles and timeless time in Melanesia. *Ethnology* 38: 211–225.

Scaglion, Richard ed.
1981   *Homicide Compensation in Papua New Guinea: Problems and Prospects.* Port Moresby: Law Reform Commission, Monograph 1.

Scheffler, Harold W.
1965   *Choiseul Island Social Structure.* Berkeley: University of California Press.

2001   *Filiation and Affiliation.* Boulder, CO: Westview Press.

Schieffelin, Edward L.
1975   Felling the trees on top of the crop. *Oceania* 46: 25–39.

Schieffelin, Edward L. and R. Crittenden
1990   *Like People You See in a Dream. First Contact in Six Papuan Societies.* Stanford: Stanford University Press.

Schneebaum, Tobias
1990   *Embodied Spirits. Ritual Carvings of the Asmat.* Salem, Mass.: Peabody Museum of Salem.

Sillitoe, Paul
1978   Big-men and war in New Guinea. *Man* (n.s.) 13: 252–71.

1985   Divide and no-one rules: the implications of sexual divisions of labour in the New Guinea Highlands. *Man* (n.s.) 20: 494–522.

1998   *An Introduction to the Anthropology of Melanesia: Culture and Tradition.* Cambridge: Cambridge University Press.

2000   *Social Change in Melanesia. Development and History.* Cambridge: Cambridge University Press.

Sillitoe, Paul, Pamela J. Stewart and Andrew Strathern
2002   *Horticulture in Papua New Guinea: Case Studies from the Southern and Western Highlands.* Pittsburgh: Ethnology Monographs, no. 18.

Sinclair, James
1988   *Last Frontiers. The Explorations of Ivan Champion of Papua.* Queensland: Pacific Press.

Sorenson, E. Richard
1976   *The Edge of the Forest. Land, Childhood, and Change in a New Guinea Protoagricultural Society.* Washington, D.C.: Smithsonian Institution Press.

Souter, Gavin
1967   *New Guinea: The Last Unknown.* New York: Taplinger Publishing Co., Inc.

Steensberg, Axel
1980   *New Guinea Gardens. A Study of Husbandry with Parallels in Prehistoric Eu-
            rope.* London and New York: Academic Press.

Stewart, Pamela J. and Andrew Strathern
1998   Life at the end: voices and visions from Mount Hagen, Papua New Guinea.
            Zeitschrift für Missionswissenschaft und Religionswissenschaft 82 (4):
            227–244.

1999a   "Feasting on my enemy." Images of violence and change in the New Guinea
            Highlands. *Ethnohistory* 46(4): 645–669.

1999b   Female spirit cults as a window on gender relations in the Highlands of
            Papua New Guinea. *Journal of the Royal Anthropological Institute* 5(3):
            345–360.

1999c   Time at the end: the Highlands of Papua New Guinea. In C. Kocher
            Schmid ed. *Expecting the Day of Wrath: Versions of the Millennium in
            Papua New Guinea*, pp. 131–144. Port Moresby: National Research Insti-
            tute.

2000a   Naming places: Duna evocations of landscape in Papua New Guinea. *People
            and Culture in Oceania* 16: 87–107.

2000b   (eds.) Millennial Countdown in New Guinea. Special Issue, *Ethnohistory*
            47(1).

2000c   Introduction: Narratives Speak. In P.J. Stewart and A. Strathern, eds. *Identity
            Work: Constructing Pacific Lives*, pp. 1–26. ASAO Monograph no. 18. Pitts-
            burgh: University of Pittsburgh Press.

2001a   *Humors and Substances: Ideas of the Body in New Guinea.* Westport, Conn.:
            Bergin and Garvey.

2001b   Origins versus creative powers: the interplay of movement and fixity. In A.
            Rumsey and J. Weiner eds. *Emplaced Myth: Space, Narrative and Knowledge
            in Aboriginal Australia and Papua New Guinea Societies*, pp. 79–98. Hon-
            olulu: University of Hawai'i Press.

2001c   The great exchange: moka with God. Special Issue, Charismatic and Pente-
            costal Christianity in Oceania, ed. J. Robbins, P.J. Stewart and A. Strathern.
            Journal of Ritual Studies 15(2): 91–104.

2002   *Re-Making the World: Myth, Mining, and Ritual Change among the Duna of
            Papua New Guinea.* Washington, D.C.: Smithsonian Institution Press.

Strathern, Andrew
1971   *The Rope of Moka. Big -Men and Ceremonial Exchange in Mount Hagen, New
            Guinea.* Cambridge: Cambridge University Press.

1972   *One Father, One Blood. Descent and Group Structure among the Melpa People.*
            Canberra: Australian National University Press.

1979–80   The red box money cult in Mount Hagen 1968–71, parts 1 and 2. *Oceania* 50:
            88–102, and 161–175.

1993   Big-man, great man, leader: the link of ritual power. *Journal de la Société des
            Océanistes* (2): 145–158.

Strathern, Andrew and Pamela J. Stewart

1997 Ballads as popular performance art in Papua New Guinea. *JCU Centre for Pacific Studies Discussion Papers Series*, no. 2. Queensland: James Cook University.

1998a (eds.) *Kuk Heritage: Issues and Debates in Papua New Guinea*. Pittsburgh: Department of Anthropology, University of Pittsburgh.

1998b Money, politics and persons in Papua New Guinea. *Social Analysis* 42(2): 132–149.

1999a *The Spirit is Coming! A Photographic-Textual Documentation of the Female Spirit Cult Performance in Mount Hagen*. Ritual Studies Monograph no. 1. Pittsburgh: Department of Anthropology, University of Pittsburgh.

1999b Objects, relationships, and meanings: historical switches in currencies in Mount Hagen, Papua New Guinea. In D. Akin and J. Robbins eds. *Money and Modernity: State and Local Currencies in Melanesia*, pp. 164–191. ASAO Monograph no. 17. Pittsburgh: University of Pittsburgh Press.

1999c *Curing and Healing. Medical Anthropology in Global Perspective*. Durham, NC: Carolina Academic Press.

2000a *The Python's Back: Pathways of Comparison between Indonesia and Melanesia*. Westport, Conn.: Bergin and Garvey.

2000b *Arrow Talk. Transaction, Transition and Contradiction in New Guinea Highlands History*. Kent, OH: The Kent State University Press.

2000c Melpa ballads as popular performance art. In D. Niles and D. Crowdy eds. *Ivilikou* pp. 76–84. Papua New Guinea Music Conference and Festival. Boroko: Institute of Papua New Guinea Studies.

2000d *Stories, Strength, and Self-Narration: Western Highlands, Papua New Guinea*. Adelaide, Australia: Crawford House Publishing.

2000e Accident, agency, and liability in New Guinea Highlands compensation practices. *Bijdragen* 156(2): 275–295.

2001 Rappaport's Maring: the challenge of ethnography. In E. Messner and M. Lambek eds. *Ecology and the Sacred*, pp. 277–290. Ann Arbor: University of Michigan Press.

Strauss, Hermann and Herbert Tischner

1962 *Die Mi-Kultur der Hagenberg Stämme*. Hamburg: Cram, de Gruyter and Co.

Thomas, Nicholas

1995 *Oceanic Art*. London: Thames and Hudson.

Toft, Susan ed.

1997 *Compensation for Resource Development in Papua New Guinea*. Port Moresby: National Research Institute.

Toren, Christina

1990 *Making Sense of Hierarchy. Cognition as Social Process in Fiji*. London: The Athlone Press.

Valeri, Valerio

1985 *Kingship and Sacrifice. Ritual and Society in Ancient Hawai'i*. Chicago: University of Chicago Press.

Vicedom, Georg F. and Herbert Tischner
1943–8   (3 vols.) *Die Mbowamb*. Hamburg: Friederichsen, de Gruyter & Co.

Waddell, Eric
1972   *The Mound Builders. Agricultural Practices, Environment and Society in the Central Highlands of New Guinea*. Seattle: University of Washington Press.

Watson, James B.
1965   From hunting to horticulture in the New Guinea Highlands. *Ethnology* 4: 295–309.

1967   Tairora. The politics of despotism in a small society. In Ronald M. Berndt and Peter Lawrence eds. *Politics in New Guinea*, pp. 224–275. Nedlands: University of Western Australia Press.

1977   Pigs, fodder, and the Jones effect in post-Ipomoean New Guinea. *Ethnology* 16: 57–70.

Watson-Gegeo, Karen Ann and Richard Feinberg
1996   Introduction: Leadership and Change in the Western Pacific. In R. Feinberg and K. Watson-Gegeo (eds.) *Leadership and Change in the Western Pacific*, pp. 1–55. London: The Athlone Press.

Watson-Gegeo, Karen Ann and David W. Gegeo
1990   Shaping the mind and straightening out conflicts: the discourse of Kwara'ae family counseling. In K. Watson-Gegeo and G. White (eds.) *Disentangling: Conflict Discourse in Pacific Socieities*, pp. 161–213. Stanford: Stanford University Press.

Weiner, Annette
1976   *Women of Value, Men of Renown*. Austin, TX: University of Texas Press.

1992   *Inalienable Possessions. The Paradox of Keeping-While-Giving*.Berkeley: University of California Press.

Whitehouse, Harvey
1995   *Inside the Cult. Religious Innovation and Transmission in Papua New Guiena*. Oxford: The Clarendon Press.

Worsley, Peter
1957   *The Trumpet Shall Sound. A Study of 'Cargo Cults' in Melanesia*. London: Macgibbon and Kee.

Wurm, Stephen ed.
1975   Papuan Languages. *Pacific Linguistics* C38: 1–1084.

Part II

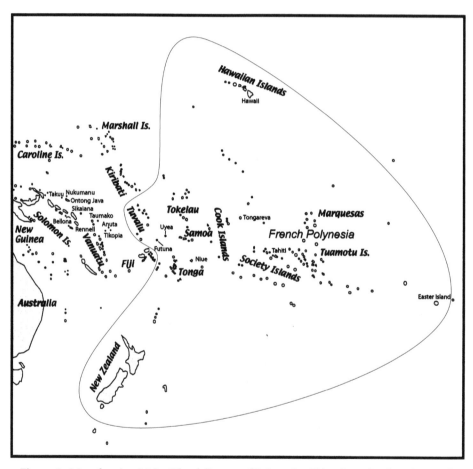

Figure 1. Map showing Major Island Groups of Polynesian Triangle and Polynesian Outliers in Solomon Islands and Papua New Guinea.

The "Eastern Pacific"

by Richard Feinberg and Cluny Macpherson

The stereotypic American image of the Pacific Islands is a Polynesian paradise. Encouraged by Hollywood films and tourist brochures, popular imagination conjures up a romantic landscape of lush tropical jungles, gracefully swaying coconut palms, hula dancers in grass skirts, and exotic alcoholic beverages. We are taught to picture dots of land framed by clear blue seas, coral reefs, outrigger canoes, and unlimited fresh fish. The prototypical Polynesian islands, according to this vision, are probably Tahiti or Borabora in French Polynesia and Maui or O'ahu in Hawai'i.

As is the case with most stereotypes, the popular image contains a kernel of truth. Most Polynesian islands *are* located in the tropics, and coconut is among the usual staples. Hula dancing is a traditional Hawaiian art form, and many Polynesians once upon a time wore leaf garments that might well be taken for grass skirts. Early European explorers, and a few anthropologists, reported Polynesian islands to be havens of uninhibited sexual freedom. Nor is the Hawaiian tourist bureau completely off the mark in claiming that a central Polynesian value involves displays of friendship, hospitality, and mutual support. On the other hand, the common apprehension of Polynesia is a gross oversimplification and—in many ways—a serious misrepresentation.

Polynesia, which literally means "Many Islands," is appropriately named. It refers to a region encompassing thousands of islands occupying a vast triangle in the eastern and central Pacific Ocean. In one corner of the triangle is Easter Island, also known by its indigenous Polynesian name, Rapanui, off the western coast of South America. At the region's northern apex is the Hawaiian archipelago, well above the equator and just below the Tropic of Cancer. The third corner is occupied by New Zealand or Aotearoa, far to the southwest, whose climate ranges from subtropical to temperate and, in the southern portion of South Island, even subantarctic. Within the Polynesian Triangle are such well-known archipelagoes and islands as Hawai'i, Tahiti, Tonga, and Samoa. The Marquesas were made famous by the writings of Herman Melville and the paintings of Paul Gauguin; and the Tuamotus endured decades of French nuclear testing. Fiji, which is sometimes classed as Polynesian, was the site of modern Oceania's first military coups in the late 1980s, followed by a third armed overthrow of a civilian government in May 2000. The major Polynesian islands are shown on the map in figure 1.

Stewart and Strathern point out in the introduction to this volume that Pacific culture areas are somewhat arbitrary designations. In many respects, some so-called Melanesian communities differ more from one another than they do from communities commonly regarded as Polynesian or Micronesian. Nonetheless, Polynesia exhibits a remarkable degree of uniformity for so vast a geographic region. Physically, Polynesians tend to have brown complexions and dark, wavy hair, and they are typically large people of muscular build. It is no accident that many Polynesians from Samoa play for the U.S.

National Football League, or that a Samoan raised in Hawai'i recently held the Japanese sumo wrestling championship.

More significant than physical appearance, language displays remarkable continuity throughout the far-flung isles of Polynesia. For example, Mauna Kea, the name for the tallest mountain on the island of Hawai'i, literally means "White Mountain"—so called because its peak, at approximately 14,000 feet above sea level, is covered with snow in the winter. On Anuta—located in the Solomon Islands, thousands of miles southwest of Hawai'i—the Hawaiian /n/ becomes /ng/ and the Hawaiian /k/ becomes a /t/. Thus, "white mountain" would be rendered in Anutan as *maunga tea*.[1]

Other traits found throughout Polynesia include the existence of highly centralized and stratified polities, led by hereditary chiefs. Particularly in pre-Christian times, Polynesian chiefs typically were thought to have close ties with divinity. The first Tu'i Tonga was said to be the son of the sky god, Tangaloa, and an earthly Tongan woman; on Tikopia and Anuta, the premier deities were ghosts of deceased chiefs.[2] Polynesian chiefs often served priestly functions, and they were said to possess a kind of awesome supernaturally derived force termed *mana*. Yet, points of variation among Polynesian communities are every bit as prominent as the areas of continuity.

Even Polynesia's geographical boundaries are somewhat problematic. Although scholars often speak of the "Polynesian Triangle," there are a number of islands whose people share Polynesian traits but which are located in territory that is usually considered Melanesian or Micronesian. These islands are termed "Polynesian outliers" because they are situated well outside of the Polynesian heartland. Among the best documented of these outliers are Tikopia, Bellona, and Ontong Java in the Solomon Islands, and Kapingamarangi in the Federated States of Micronesia.[3] One of our contributors has conducted extensive anthropological field research on the Polynesian outliers of Anuta in the Solomons and Nukumanu in Papua New Guinea.[4]

Fiji's proper designation is also problematic. Located slightly to the west of Tonga and Samoa, it shares some Polynesian characteristics, some more typical of Melanesia, and some that do not easily fit into either area. Physically, Fijians are tall and muscular like Polynesians; but their darker complexions resemble those of eastern Melanesians. Political leadership was, and to a large degree continues to be, provided by hereditary chiefs. Prior to European contact, Fijian polities presented greater centralization than is common in Melanesia, but the archipelago was less politically unified than was often the case in Polynesia. Fijians speak a number of Eastern Oceanic languages which are neither Polynesian nor Melanesian, but are related to both. Rotuma, an isolated island located in the nation state of Fiji, is usually considered Polynesian because of the community's social structure and the people's physical appearance. Linguistically, however, Rotuman is anomalous in much the same way as Fijian. The historical relationships of Polynesian languages to Fijian, Rotuman, and to one another are shown in figures 2 and 3.

Although most of Polynesia is tropical, New Zealand's climate ranges from subtropical in the north, where taro and bananas are grown, through a temperate belt in the center, to the parts of New Zealand's South Island and the Chatham and Auckland Islands which are subantarctic. Furthermore, on Polynesia's large high islands, climate and ecology may differ radically from coast to inland or from one side of an island to the other. On Hawai'i, one can play in the surf and ski the slopes of Mauna Kea on the same day. The trade winds blow roughly from east to west and pick up moisture as they sweep across the wide Pacific. Therefore, east of Hawai'i's two great mountain peaks of Mauna Loa and Mauna Kea, the weather is cool and rainy, while the western side of the island is sunny, dry, and desert-like.

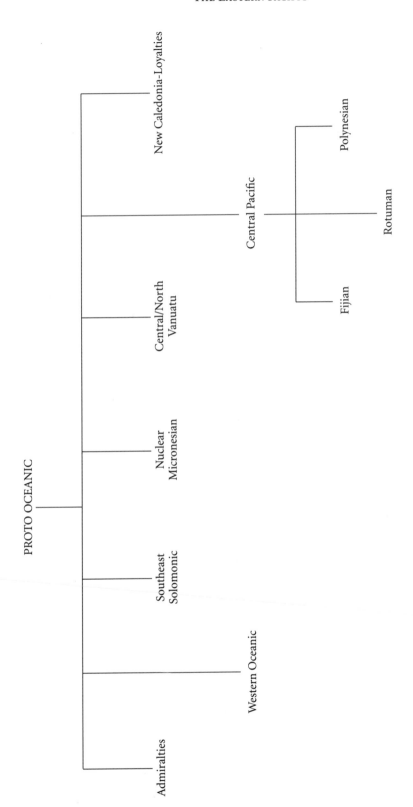

Figure 2. Subgrouping of Eastern Oceanic languages. Adapted from Kirch (2000).

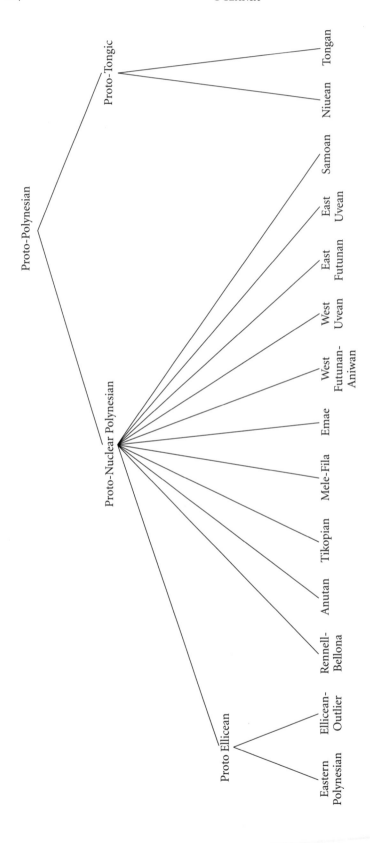

Figure 3. Subgrouping of Polynesian languages. Adapted from Marck (1996).

One of the most obvious contrasts among Polynesian environments is that between atolls and high islands. An atoll is a ring of low coral islets that protrude just above the surface of the ocean. The islets are surrounded by the ocean and, themselves, surround an inner lagoon. Since lagoons are protected by the encircling land, they tend to be relatively calm. Coral heads provide places for marine organisms to congregate and hide; thus, atolls are often blessed with an abundance of fish and shellfish. On the other hand, their sandy soil is porous and does not retain rainwater. Frequently, the highest point of land on an atoll is only a few feet above the ocean in high tide. In the absence of high peaks to stop the clouds, precipitation is likely to be sparse; and storms or tidal waves may inundate the entire atoll. Crops are limited to those that tolerate dry, salty conditions; therefore, the vegetal staples on many atolls are limited to coconut, pandanus, and a kind of "swamp taro."[5]

Polynesia's high islands are typically volcanic in origin. This means that they are the tops of underwater volcanoes that protrude above the ocean's surface. They tend to be mountainous and range from a few hundred to many thousands of feet in altitude. Volcanic islands are, for the most part, better watered than atolls; there is a greater variety of distinct ecological zones; and the soil is more fertile. As a result, crops are easier to grow and are more abundant. Typically, high islands sustain larger populations than atolls, and, as Sahlins (1958) pointed out in an important work, they are more likely to develop an elaborate division of labor and system of rank. The Hawaiian archipelago, the Society Islands (including Tahiti), the Marquesas, and Samoa are generally of volcanic origin, as are such outliers as Anuta, Tikopia, and Taumako. The Tokelaus, the Tuamotus, the entire nation of Tuvalu, and such outliers as Takuu, Nukumanu, Ontong Java, Sikaiana, Nukuoro, and Kapingamarangi are all atolls. Some groups, like the Cook Islands include a mix of high islands and atolls.

Polynesian communities also differ a great deal in their histories of European contact and their current political status. Some were sighted as early as the sixteenth century, although little contact between islanders and Europeans took place until considerably later. Others, like Hawai'i and Samoa, were not "discovered" by Europeans until well into the eighteenth century. Anuta was first sighted as late as 1791 by a Mr. Cherry aboard the *HMS Pandora* during the search for the *Bounty* mutineers.

Most of Polynesia was evangelized by Christian missions and, later, colonized by one or another of the major European powers. A few island groups, like Tonga, while successfully evangelized, were never formally brought under colonial rule. Yet, even those communities came under powerful European cultural, political, and economic influence.

Today the indigenous Maori people of New Zealand are an ethnic minority, numbering just over a half million people in a modern, independent nation state of 3.8 million. Their status and rights as *tangata whenua* "people of the land" are enshrined in the 1840 Treaty of Waitangi, which binds the state to pursue policies based on an ideal of bicultural partnership. Native Hawaiians are, by contrast, a largely impoverished and dispossessed minority in one of the fifty United States.[6] American Samoa is a U.S. territory. Tonga is an independent constitutional monarchy. Samoa (formerly known as Western Samoa), Fiji, and Tuvalu have emerged from a period of colonial domination to become independent, albeit cash poor, developing states. The Cook Islands and Niue are internally self-governing but dependent on New Zealand, which provides financial support and defense and administers their foreign policy. The Tokelaus remain a non-self-governing territory of New Zealand but are embarked on a program of constitutional change and development designed to increase their level of political and fiscal autonomy.[7] The Polynesian outliers constitute small ethnic minorities in overwhelmingly non-Polynesian (Melanesian or Micronesian) states.

Metropolitan powers, in order to protect their military and geopolitical interests, have subjected French Polynesia and the unincorporated U.S. territory of American Samoa to what Victoria Lockwood (1993a, 1993b) calls "welfare state colonialism." For many years Pagopago's harbor provided an ideal mid-Pacific naval station for the U.S. Pacific fleet; later, Pagopago provided a military airbase. Tahiti is a cosmopolitan community, much of whose income depends on the tourist trade. Mururoa and Fangataufa atolls in the Tuamotus have been used as nuclear-testing sites. The more remote portions of the Society Islands, as well as most of the Marquesas and Austral Islands, are predominantly rural and depend on agriculture, both for subsistence and commodity production.

Prehistory

Polynesians are descendants of Austronesian speakers who moved into the Pacific several thousand years ago from Southeast Asia (e.g., see Bellwood 1978; White 1979; Kirch 2000). Austronesian, prior to the sixteenth century, was the world's most widely dispersed language family, ranging throughout Polynesia, Micronesia, and Melanesia to Indonesia, the Philippines, Malaysia, Taiwan, parts of mainland Southeast Asia, and on westward to the island of Madagascar, off Africa's eastern coast.

Human settlement of the western Pacific dates back at least thirty to forty thousand years, and perhaps considerably more, with the arrival of non-Austronesian speakers on the island of New Guinea (see Kirch 2000:67–68). From New Guinea, these people migrated south into Australia and Tasmania, and eastward into the Bismarck Archipelago and Solomon Islands. Today, their progeny inhabit the interior of New Guinea and most of the large islands of Melanesia, plus a few smaller enclaves in places like the Reef Islands of the eastern Solomons.

A second wave of migration began about four thousand years ago, when Austronesian speakers settled in northern New Guinea, the Bismarck Archipelago, and Solomon Islands. These people are known archaeologically from a distinctive type of decorated pottery called Lapita (see, e.g., Green 1976, 1978; Kirch 1997, 2000). This pottery resembles ceramic styles from Indonesia and the Philippines and demonstrates conclusively that Pacific islanders originated in Southeast Asia. These archaeological finds, combined with the linguistic evidence noted above, have put to rest the hypothesis most dramatically advanced by Thor Heyerdahl (1950, 1952) and supported by the widely publicized Kon Tiki expedition of 1947, that Polynesians originally entered the Pacific from the Americas. Somewhere between 3,000 and 3,500 years ago, these makers of Lapita pottery moved eastward to Fiji, then to Tonga and Samoa where they developed the cultural characteristics that we now associate with Polynesia. By the end of the first millennium AD, virtually all the islands of Polynesia had been visited, and most of them settled, by these intrepid voyagers.

A few scholars (e.g., Bellwood 1978, 1980) are convinced that Polynesians passed through Melanesia without being significantly affected by the people who preceded them there. Most contemporary Pacific specialists (e.g., Terrell 1998) reject the idea of a sharp distinction between Polynesia and Melanesia and regard the Lapita potters as ancestral to both Polynesians and Austronesian-speaking Melanesians.

The lifestyle of these Polynesian ancestors has been reconstructed from both archaeological remains and historical linguistics. We know, for example, that they cultivated root crops and had sophisticated water craft. They depended upon fishing and, to a lesser extent, bird-hunting for subsistence. Virtually all of Polynesia's useful plants and animals (as well as many of the non-useful ones) were introduced by human beings. These include taro, coconut, breadfruit, pigs, chickens, dogs, and several pests such as the omnipresent rat. Many Polynesians developed systems for burying starchy vegetables in underground pits, where they would ferment to a form that could be preserved and eaten many years later. This preparation has been called by terms like *masi* or *ma*, and was used as a hedge against famine during periods of natural disaster. Some Polynesians ventured into subtropical and temperate climates and had to adapt their agricultural crops, practices, and technologies to the conditions that they found in their new homes. In parts of Aotearoa (New Zealand), the Maori modified pits to serve as temperature- and humidity-controlled storage areas for their root vegetables throughout the colder winters. They also discovered ways of preserving seasonal birds by encasing them in clay "shells." By the time of Christ, Lapita pottery was no longer being made, and the last Polynesian ceramics died out soon thereafter, perhaps reflecting a change in cooking technology that relied on the earth oven rather than boiling in watertight vessels. Pottery continues to be made in Fiji and some parts of Melanesia.

Early Polynesians appear to have lived in scattered settlements rather than clearly defined villages. In later times, the village became the central unit of social organization on many Polynesian islands. In some cases, the population's aggregation in villages reflected the influence of missionaries, who persuaded their followers to gather around places of worship. Some peoples, like the Maori, found it necessary to maintain both agricultural villages (*kāinga*) near their plantations and fishing grounds, which they inhabited in times of peace, and fortified hilltop villages (*pā*), to which they retreated in times of war with their neighbors.[8]

Proto-Polynesian terms for leadership positions have been reconstructed and suggest that a hierarchical social order in Polynesia dates to the period of initial settlement.[9] Such a conclusion must be hedged with a degree of caution, however, since we cannot be certain that terms had the same meaning 3,000 years ago as in historic times. It should also be remembered that hierarchy is a complex and problematic notion, and that it can take many forms. In fact, Petersen (1999) has argued that for Micronesian chiefdoms hierarchy and egalitarianism are two sides to the same coin, a point that Feinberg (1978, 1996a, 2001) has argued for Polynesia as well.

The earliest known Polynesian settlements were in Tonga and Samoa around 1000 BC (see, e.g., Bellwood 1978; Davidson 1979; Kirch 2000). Tonga, Samoa, and Fiji have been in more or less continuous contact for about 3,000 years, but they have also been developing their separate cultural and linguistic identities for a long time. Linguistic evidence suggests that Samoa was the launching point for settlement of most of West Polynesia and all of Eastern Polynesia. The Marquesas and Society Islands may have been settled as early as 200 BC, and certainly by AD 600; and it is there that the distinctive features of Eastern Polynesian culture seem to have developed. The rest of Eastern Polynesia, including Hawai'i, Easter Island, the southern Cooks, the Australs, and New Zealand were settled from one or both of these centers during the first millennium AD.

The Polynesian outliers were a point of contention for many decades. Churchill (1911) and others proposed that they were relict populations, left behind in the great eastward migration of ancestral Polynesians out of Melanesian territory. Archaeological and linguistic evidence, as well as oral traditions, however, now demonstrate conclusively that they were populated relatively recently as a result of back-migrations from the Polynesian Triangle. Most outlier languages have been placed in a "Samoic-Outlier" subgroup of Nuclear Polynesian, their closest connections probably being to the languages of Tuvalu on the Polynesian heartland's far western border (see, e.g., Bayard 1966; Pawley 1967). Oral traditions, however, indicate complex histories, with contacts and possible settlement from most of the archipelagoes of western Polynesia and, in some cases, from southeastern Micronesia as well. Anutans, for example, say that their island was colonized by voyagers from Uvea (Wallis Island), Tonga, Samoa, Rotuma, and Tikopia some ten to fifteen generations ago, with later contacts from Tuvalu and the Santa Cruz Islands of the Solomons. And in 1933, Harry Shapiro of the American Museum of Natural History even questioned whether the Ontong Javanese are physically and historically Polynesian.

One enigma in the mystery of Polynesian settlement is an apparent contradiction between legends of Tongan imperialism and the fact that only one Tongic language—Niuean—has been identified outside of Tonga proper. Some skeptics have suggested that *tonga* simply means "south" (as it does, for example, in Samoan and Maori), and that tales of invasions from "Tonga" only mean that the interlopers arrived from southern climes. However, while *tonga* is a directional indicator, it does not mean "south" in all Polynesian languages. In Anutan it is "east" or "southeast," and in Hawai'i—where *tonga* is pronounced *kona*—the *kona* coast is to the west or southwest. In other words, *tonga* seems to indicate the direction in which the Tongan archipelago actually lies.[10]

Perhaps as we obtain more detailed oral histories, linguistic and archeological data, and DNA evidence, some of the apparent contradictions will be resolved. For example, early reports about Anuta (e.g., Firth 1954) attribute to Anutans the claim that their island was originally settled from Tonga. Their language, however, is classed by historical linguists as Nuclear Polynesian, a fact which has been taken to demonstrate that Anutan oral traditions are erroneous. In reality, the Anutan language contains a good deal of Tongan, and Anutan oral traditions cite Tonga as but one of several sources of original settlement. The most important source was 'Uvea or Wallis Island, an island that was for many generations dominated by Tonga and which had extensive borrowings from the Tongan language. As Feinberg (1977) pointed out and Biggs (1980) confirmed, when these facts are put together, the Anutans' rendition of their history is consistent with the linguistic evidence (see also Feinberg 1976, 1981a, 1998).

A similar point can be made for Samoa, whose history records a period of Tongan domination which ended when the Tongans were expelled by military force. Thereafter, the relationship between the two archipelagoes was based on trade in ceremonial commodities and exchange of spouses for the aristocratic lines of both societies. Likewise, Fijian history recalls an era of Tongan domination in such regions as the Lau group in the eastern part of the archipelago. Over time, that contact came to be reflected in extensive intermarriage between the Tongan and Fijian chiefly lines. Domination via trade, marriage, and political alliances might not produce the kind of linguistic change that could result from wholesale military conquest—something that would have been difficult to maintain given the logistical difficulties of shifting large numbers of warriors around the Pacific—but it would have been no less effective.

Polynesian Seafaring

Regardless of the details of Polynesian settlement and prehistory, the overall picture is clear. The Polynesians' ancestors migrated from Island Southeast Asia to the Bismarck

Archipelago in what is now northeastern Papua New Guinea by 2000 BC. Around 1200 BC they moved out into Fiji, and then to Tonga and Samoa. During the next two millennia they spread throughout the area now known as Polynesia. Later, a series of back-migrations populated the western Polynesian "outliers." All of this was accomplished via ocean travel, a feat that required remarkable skill, courage, knowledge, and equipment. Indeed, Polynesian dispersal through the insular Pacific is one of the great maritime accomplishments of human history. In wooden boats held together with sennit cord woven from fiber found in coconut husks, and following the stars, sun, waves, and wind, they populated virtually every habitable island in the tropical central and eastern Pacific.

Some of these voyages were most likely purposeful exploratory forays. Others were undoubtedly forced migrations resulting from population pressure or political and military conflict. Some were accidental drift voyages by sailors who had lost their way, or by fishermen swept out to sea by powerful currents or inclement weather. At each stage, return voyages probably were made for purposes of trade, marriage, and exchange of information (see particularly Irwin 1992).

Thinking about Polynesian seafaring abilities has shifted several times since early European contact. The French explorer Bougainville was so impressed by the canoes he witnessed in Samoa in 1768 that he called the archipelago "The Navigators' Islands." Britain's Captain James Cook noted that Polynesian canoes were often as fast and maneuverable as his ships, and he carefully recorded Raiatean chief Tupaia's impressive geographical knowledge (Lewis 1972:293–299). Even as late as the middle twentieth century, Sir Peter Buck (Te Rangi Hiroa), director of Hawai'i's Bishop Museum, took Polynesian traditions of voyaging, exploration, migration, and settlement quite literally (Buck 1967[1938]).

The tone of the discussion altered radically with the publication in 1957 of Andrew Sharp's *Ancient Voyagers in the Pacific*. Sharp argued that, in the absence of instruments such as the sextant and magnetic compass, human beings lack the ability to navigate successfully for more than a few hundred miles when out of sight of land. In particular, he argued, one cannot detect, accurately estimate, and correct for current or leeway drift. Over distances of the many hundreds—and sometimes thousands—of miles claimed by Polynesian oral traditions, he argued, errors would have been compounded, making the prospect of intentional landfall at a planned destination virtually nil. Therefore, exploration and settlement were almost certainly the result of accidental drift voyages by sailors blown off course or forced, against their will, to put to sea. And certainly, once voyagers made safe landfall, they would have been neither interested nor able to make the return voyages necessary for systematic colonization.

This view again shifted with the pioneering ethnographic work of Thomas Gladwin (1970) on the Micronesian atoll of Puluwat and David Lewis' more wide-ranging survey of Pacific Islands seafaring practices (Lewis 1972). They and others (e.g., Alkire 1965; Thomas 1987; Feinberg 1988, 1991) have documented voyages of hundreds of miles with accuracy similar to that which can be achieved with modern instruments, as well as the techniques through which such voyages are accomplished. Most traditional-style voyaging in recent times has been conducted by Micronesians, but their techniques are similar to those employed by Polynesians in the past. This is confirmed by comments from Polynesians recorded by early European explorers, and those few Polynesian communities where traditional wayfinding techniques have been retained into the present era (e.g., see Lewis 1972:passim, 1995; Feinberg 1988, 1991, 1995a; George 2001).

A second line of argument against Sharp's drift voyage hypothesis is provided by the direction of settlement. As pointed out in the previous section, migration was predominantly from west to east, against the prevailing winds. Recorded drift voyages, by contrast, are almost always in the opposite direction. Such voyages have certainly occurred, and more than a few sailors have been lost at sea (see Feinberg 1988:154–162 for documentation of the ratio of successful to unsuccessful voyages in one Polynesian community). This however, cannot account for the overall exploration and settlement of the Pacific.

A third strand of evidence comes from computer simulations. Importantly, Levison, Ward, and Webb (1973) demonstrated—taking into account prevailing winds and currents, and comparing them with the geographical relationships of various islands and archipelagoes—that Oceanic exploration and settlement could not have come about through accidental drift, but must have resulted primarily from purposeful voyaging by skilled seafarers and navigators.

The final, and perhaps most persuasive, line of evidence affirming the proficiency of Polynesian—and other Oceanic—navigators comes from experimental voyages with replicas of traditional voyaging canoes, using traditional navigational techniques. In 1980, a group of islanders from Taumako (Duff Islands), a Polynesian outlier in the eastern Solomon Islands, built a traditional voyaging canoe (*puke*), which they successfully sailed to the western Solomons, over 500 miles away. And in 1998, as part of the locally-inspired Vaka Taumako Project, Duff Islanders sailed a newly constructed *puke* to the Reef Islands, where they visited their traditional trading partners.

Still more impressive are the exploits of *Hōkūle'a*, a replica Hawaiian double-hulled voyaging canoe, built with modern materials but to traditional design. *Hōkūle'a* has now been sailed successfully through most of Polynesia. Its first major voyage was to Tahiti, following traditionally prescribed star paths, under the guidance of Mau Piailug, a master navigator from Satawal Island in Micronesia (see Finney 1979). Later, Nainoa Thompson, a Hawaiian trained largely by Piailug, navigated *Hōkūle'a* without instruments through the major Polynesian archipelagoes, traveling as far as New Zealand (see Finney, et al. 1989; Finney, et al. 1994; Kyselka 1987). *Hōkūle'a* was succeeded by a voyaging canoe called *Hawai'i Loa*, built of traditional materials. Like *Hōkūle'a*, *Hawai'i Loa* has been successfully sailed without instruments through much of the Polynesian Triangle.

Voyages like those of the early Polynesian explorers and settlers who traversed the vast Pacific Ocean without sextant, compass, or chronometer required exceptionally seaworthy vessels. They had to be sturdy, maneuverable, resistant to being blown sideways (known technically as leeway), and, to some degree, able to sail into the wind. They had to resist deterioration from exposure to sun, wind, salt, heat, and a variety of marine organisms. And, for lengthy journeys, they had to be large enough to carry a good quantity of food, drink, and sometimes crops and livestock. This was accomplished differently in different parts of Polynesia.

Any boat needs some mechanism to keep it going straight and to prevent it from turning over. These characteristics are known as tracking and stability; and most Polynesian canoes use outriggers for those purposes. An outrigger is a buoyant piece of wood that is attached to the boat and set more or less parallel to the hull, several feet away. If the wind pushes the canoe too hard on one side, the outrigger acts as a counterweight; if it pushes on the other, the outrigger helps the boat to stay upright by acting as a float. Modern European sailing yachts accomplish these goals with a keel, a piece of metal that is attached to the bottom of the hull and sticks straight down into the water. Keels have the advantage that they enable the boat to sail fairly efficiently against the wind. However, in tropical waters that are often choked with shallow reefs, a keel that extends several feet below the surface risks getting caught on the bottom, with the result that the boat may be damaged or sunk. A sailing canoe equipped with twin hulls (see below) or an outrigger does not beat against the wind as effectively as a yacht with a deep keel. Lewis (1972:269) and Irwin (1992:44) have estimated that even the best outrigger canoes cannot sail at better than a close reach, or approximately 75° off the wind. Such boats, however, carry a significantly reduced risk of running aground with resultant injury to vessel, passengers, and cargo; and with a favorable wind they can cover well over 100 miles a day.

The commonest canoes through most of Polynesia were single-outrigger craft, ranging from small vessels paddled by one or two men (or occasionally women) for coastal travel and inshore fishing, to the great Fijian *camakau* which might approach 100 feet in length and rival European sailing ships for speed. Resembling the *camakau* were voyaging canoes of several Polynesian outliers: e.g., Takuu (*vaka fai laa*), Nukumanu (*vaka hai laa*); and the Polynesian islands of the Santa Cruz group in the eastern Solomons (*puke*). Outlier Polynesians on Anuta still make single-outrigger canoes which they have been known to sail hundreds of miles—to the Banks group of northern Vanuatu, to Vanikoro in the Santa Cruz Islands, and recently to Santa Ana and Malaita in the central portion of the Solomons (see particularly Feinberg 1991).

In the Polynesian outlier atolls, such as Nukumanu and Takuu, islanders have adapted the Fijian (and Micronesian) canoe design, in which bow and stern are exactly the same shape. The two ends are, thus, interchangeable, meaning that the canoe can be sailed with either end in front. When the sailors want to tack (that is, to change the boat's direction in relation to the wind), they do not swing the bow through the wind (a maneuver known as "coming about") as is done on conventional European sailboats or sailing ships. Instead, they move the sail to the opposite end of the vessel, and everybody turns around, thereby always keeping the outrigger upwind. On other Polynesian outliers, such as Tikopia and Anuta, the more common Polynesian pattern was adopted. Bow and stern are distinct; the outrigger is always kept to the same side (most often, to port); and the canoe is sometimes sailed with the outrigger to the lee side of the craft.

The most imposing of the Polynesian voyaging canoes undoubtedly were the great double-hulled vessels of the Polynesian heartland. Such canoes have been reported from Samoa, Rotuma, and Tuvalu, south to Tonga and New Zealand (Aotearoa), and north to Hawai'i (see particularly Haddon and Hornell 1975[1936–38]). These involved two full-sized hulls connected by a platform, and they sometimes were more than 100 feet in length. They employed large sails woven from plant material, most often leaves of the pandanus palm, for power and directional control. These canoes—one might fairly call them ships—were less maneuverable than the smaller outrigger vessels. However, for interisland voyages that could be thousands of miles, they provided necessary cargo space as well as room for a shelter and a fire pit for cooking.

Among the more specialized developments were the New Zealand Maori's large, elaborately carved, single-hulled, outriggerless canoes. These vessels used sophisticated jointing and bindings to combine a number of large tree trunks, thereby maximizing both length and stability. Some were designed to carry large numbers of warriors in coastal waters; in these, speed and the ability to turn quickly during hand-to-hand combat were critical. Others were used for extended visits to offshore fishing grounds, sometimes more than twenty miles from land. Later, such vessels were used to service the coastal trade that developed as Maori began to supply significant quantities of food to growing European settlements. Since the boats were not intended for lengthy interisland voyages, they were not designed primarily for stability. However, their handling was improved by stowing cargo, supplies, and occasionally ballast under false floors in the bottoms of their deep hulls.

The central question asked by innumerable researchers over many decades is how Polynesian navigators could find their way from one island to another when they were far out on the ocean, with no land or other stable markings visible in any direction. The answer is that they sailed (and often still do sail) primarily by the stars. Near the equator, stars rise from the east, travel more or less straight overhead, and set toward the west. The expert navigator knows the relationship between the bearings of various islands and the rising and setting points of various stars. Ideally, he identifies a star that rises or sets directly over the target island, and he points the canoe's bow toward that star. When the star rises too high to be a reliable guide, or when it sinks below the horizon, he turns his attention to another star following approximately the same trajectory. A sequence of such stars may well continue through the night, and it forms a "star path." In reality, it is unlikely for a sequence of stars to rise or set directly over the target island, so the navigator must set off the bow at an appropriate angle from the stars' actual positions. In addition, the navigator must be able to estimate the direction and speed of wind, current, and leeway drift in order to determine a proper heading.

Wind strength and direction are not overly difficult to estimate as long as one can see the stars, moon, or sun. Leeway depends on the contours of the canoe's hull and the vessel's heading in relation to the wind. It often can be gauged by the angle between the canoe and its wake. Probably the navigator's greatest problem is that if the boat is being carried by the current and there is no land to provide a frame of reference, it is difficult to know that there is any current at all; thus, estimating its direction and velocity may be nearly impossible. Yet even this is not hopeless.

First, a navigator knows the prevailing currents in the region that he plans to sail. These tend to be fairly constant at a particular time of year. The current's velocity is confirmed when the canoe is still near the point of embarkation, or when sailing over shallow reefs. The greatest danger is if currents change direction while one is in deep water, far from land. Such shifts are difficult to detect, but there are sometimes useful clues. Anutans, for example, say that when the current and wind are running in opposite directions, seas tend to be unusually steep and white-capped. Conversely, when wind and current coincide, the seas are exceptionally flat in relation to the strength of the wind. Thus, by feeling wind strength and seeing or feeling the condition of the sea, one may be able to discern the current's direction even in deep water.

Fixing one's position on the ocean is another major problem. Latitude—one's distance from the equator—can be gauged with some accuracy by identifying zenith stars. A zenith star is one that passes directly overhead and which one can see by looking straight up into the night sky. Since stars appear to move from east to west, they remain at the same latitude during the course of a night; and if the navigator can identify a zenith star, he can accurately estimate his latitude. In addition, the configuration of stars at a given latitude at the same time on any given night is identical regardless of longitude, i.e., the distance east or west of Greenwich, England. Therefore, one can estimate latitude by observing where specific stars rise and set, and how close they come to passing directly overhead.

Longitude, unlike latitude, cannot be gauged from observation of the sky and must be estimated by dead reckoning. This means that the navigator calculates the position of his canoe in relation to the islands in his universe by estimating the vessel's speed, direction, and how long it has been at sea. Dead reckoning is difficult, requiring the navigator to keep a running total of his vessel's progress at all times. One consequence is that he cannot sleep, other than occasional brief naps, even on a lengthy journey. Sharp argued that the element of human error inherent in dead reckoning is cumulative and, over a distance of many hundreds of miles, would be too great to permit accurate landfall. Empirically, it has been demonstrated, however, that the error is random and tends to cancel itself out. Therefore, the longer the voyage, the smaller the probable error (Kyselka 1987; Irwin 1992).

During the day, when stars are unavailable, Polynesian navigators use the sun. This is practical in early morning and late afternoon, when the sun is low on the horizon. Toward mid-day, however, it loses value as a navigational aid. The sky also loses its navigational value when it is obscured by clouds, whether in the day or night. Under such conditions, auxiliary techniques are needed. For example, navigators are aware of the prevailing wind patterns. If the sky is overcast, they assume that winds will remain constant until the stars and sun can once again be seen.

Still more stable and reliable are swells. A regular ground swell is produced by winds from far away, blowing over a vast expanse of ocean. Because of this characteristic, it stays constant despite shifts in local wind direction. An expert navigator can distinguish the regular ground swell from choppier seas produced by local winds. Indeed, some Micronesians have demonstrated the ability to distinguish several swells caused simultaneously by different far-off wind patterns (Gladwin 1970). Polynesian master navigators almost certainly could to the same. By holding a steady course in relation to the swell, then, the navigator maintains his bearings until celestial bodies become visible once more. In addition, sea marks such as deep reefs that can be detected from the color of the water may help indicate one's route. Use of such marks has been reported ethnographically for Micronesia (Gladwin 1970), and at least some Polynesian navigators undoubtedly employed similar techniques.

Sailing strategy, particularly for exploratory voyagers, was to sail counter to prevailing winds. This was accomplished by waiting for a westerly shift during the normally easterly trade-wind season. If landfall was not made in a reasonable amount of time, it was expected that the wind would shift again, making for an easy return home. This accounts for the generally west-to-east direction of Polynesian migration (Finney 1985; Finney, et al. 1989; Irwin 1992).

Likewise, in historic times, Anutans prefer to sail at the beginning and end of the trade-wind season, when breezes are relatively light and unstable, but the prevailing wind is from the southeast. During this period, they can usually find a period of a few days when wind of moderate strength is blowing in the preferred direction. Should it shift before they reach their destination, they can almost always return to their point of departure (see Feinberg 1988:90–91).

Irwin (1992) further suggests, plausibly although without definitive evidence, that long-distance voyagers employed "latitude sailing." This involves sailing to the latitude of the target island but at a point well to windward, then making landfall by running downwind. Sailors from all parts of the Pacific also minimized their risk by island-hopping, thereby breaking lengthy journeys into shorter segments (Gladwin 1970; Lewis 1972; Feinberg 1991). And they aimed, wherever possible, for groups of islands rather than isolated targets.

As the navigator approaches land, he uses a variety of techniques for homing in on his objective. These include attempting to make landfall during daylight to minimize the chance of either being swept onto an exposed reef or over-running the target. Then, before land is visible, it may be located via one of several indicators.

Among the most important of these is the flight patterns of birds that roost on land at night and fly to sea to feed during the day. Reflected waves are shaped differently from waves produced directly by the wind, and they can, at times, be felt at distances of more than twenty miles from land. Clouds tend to accumulate around the peaks of high islands, indicating their presence; and a greenish tint to clouds can sometimes indicate the presence of an atoll when it still cannot be seen from a canoe.

A few writers have made much of the distinction between Polynesia and other Oceanic culture areas in terms of seafaring acumen. Dodd (1990:68), for example, has suggested that the comparatively short distances traversed by Melanesians and even Micronesians means their vessels and wayfinding techniques could be less sophisticated than those of Polynesians, who sometimes had to sail thousands of miles, as they did on journeys from Tahiti to Hawai'i or to Aotearoa.

Clearly, the logistics of such lengthy voyages posed problems not faced by Micronesians sailing from the Carolines to Saipan—a distance of about 500 miles. On long journeys, for example, the importance of dead reckoning increases and a smaller proportion of the voyage is guided by land-finding techniques such as reflected waves or flight patterns of birds. However, modern ethnographic evidence from around the Pacific and beyond supports the view that navigational techniques were fundamentally similar throughout Oceania. The transferability of old skills to new locations, and their ability to meet new challenges, is demonstrated by the success of Micronesian Mau Piailug at piloting *Hōkūle'a* from Hawai'i to Tahiti and, later, of Hawaiian navigator, Nainoa Thompson, who guided *Hōkūle'a* on similar, and even more ambitious, journeys.

Subsistence and Expressive Arts

Polynesians at the time of European contact were settled agriculturalists. Most depended on marine fauna for the bulk of their animal protein. In addition, they domesticated a few animals, notably pigs, dogs, and chickens. Western scholars have long admired the Polynesians' complex and sophisticated subsistence practices; here we can only offer a cursory introduction to the activities on which islanders depended for their livelihood. For more detailed information, the reader might consult any number of archaeological, ethnobotanical, and ethnographic discussions (e.g., Handy 1940; Handy and Handy 1972; Yen 1974; Christiansen 1975; Lieber 1994; Kirch 2000).

Polynesian agriculture through the centuries has emphasized root and tree crops. Traditionally, the most important of these were probably taro and coconut. Taro is technically a corm—a swollen underground portion of stem—rather than a root. True taro (*Colocasia esculenta*) was, in many regions, the most esteemed root crop. However, it is sensitive to soil and weather problems and, therefore, difficult to grow. It requires a major investment of time and energy to keep one's garden clear of weeds and adequately, but not excessively, watered. Taro also contains a chemical substance that irritates one's hands when peeling or cutting the corm and is toxic if ingested before it has been neutralized by cooking. Other taro-like crops, particularly *Cyrtosperma chamissonis* and *Alocasia macrorrhiza*, are more resistant to inclement weather. However, *Cyrtosperma* has a stringy texture which many people dislike, and *Alocasia* is more caustic than true taro.

Other underground vegetables in the Polynesian diet include yams, sweet potato, and more recently, manioc. Yams require sandy, well-drained soil and tend to be grown at low elevations. The Polynesian sweet potato appears to be a pre-Columbian import from South America and is perhaps the best indication of contact between Polynesia and the Americas prior to the arrival of Europeans in the Pacific. It withstands cold temperatures relatively well and, therefore, became a staple in the temperate islands of Aotearoa. Manioc was introduced from South America by Europeans and has become a popular cultigen because it stands up well to salt, poor soil, and bad weather. This has made it a valuable hedge against storms and droughts. However, it has lower nutritional value than taro, yam, and sweet potato.

The Polynesians' most important tree crop is undoubtedly coconut. It grows well in sandy, salty, infertile soil. The young nut and new leaves may be chewed or eaten. Green, immature nuts contain a watery liquid that is critical to human survival on many atolls. Mature nuts provide a hard, white meat that may be eaten raw or ground and squeezed to express the rich, white coconut cream that is widely used in cooking. The meat of the dry coconut is known as copra and since the nineteenth century has been a major export of many tropical islands in Polynesia and elsewhere. Islanders make cups, bowls, and water bottles from the shell. They use fiber from the husk to fabricate a kind of rope. Dry husks burn slowly and can be used to transport fire over considerable distances. Coconut leaves are used to make baskets, floor mats, and thatch for house walls or roofs. The paperlike bast serves as a filter in preparation of sago flour and turmeric dye. And the dense, hard trunk makes house posts, digging sticks, and weapons.

In addition to coconuts, other important tree crops include a variety of fruits and nuts. Some of these predate European contact, while others are relatively recent imports. Among the more important are pandanus, banana, papaya, Malay apple, *Canarium* almond, and Tahitian chestnut. The kava plant, betel vine, and areca nut are cultivated for ritual purposes as well as their intoxicating properties. The turmeric plant is valued for its colorful and ceremonially important dye and as a flavoring in food. In addition, some Polynesians grow their own tobacco, another relatively recent American import.

Polynesian cultivators developed an impressive array of agricultural techniques including crop rotation, terracing, and irrigation. Terracing and crop rotation have been in use for generations even on such small and isolated islands as Anuta. Archaeological evidence of irrigated taro swamps has been uncovered in much of Polynesia, and some prehistoric Hawaiians developed complex networks of irrigation ditches.

The most highly valued and widely domesticated animal is the pig. Some Polynesians also raise chickens, ducks, and (previously) dogs for consumption. Many hunt birds with nets, nooses, or by hand. The Hawaiians, in a remarkable display of innovation, constructed artificial ponds where they raised mullet and milkfish. The most reliable and constant source of animal flesh for Polynesians, however, has always been the sea.

In general, Polynesian fishing techniques resemble those of Micronesians and coastal Melanesians. The most productive methods usually involve use of a hook and hand line from a canoe. These include bottom fishing over inshore reefs; deep sea fishing sometimes at depths of a half mile or more; allowing a baited hook to float freely at the end of a long line, or trolling. Casting with a pole and line (but usually no reel), either from the shore, from the reef flat into breaking surf, or from a canoe is common practice. Traditionally, hooks were made from fish bone, shell, or wood; in recent times, these have been replaced by metal fishhooks of European manufacture.

Many Polynesians still rely on fish drives, especially when rough weather makes the ocean dangerous. These are typically communal activities, involving large numbers of people of both sexes and all ages. Fish drives can take many forms, but they all work on the same principle: people make a commotion in order to frighten the fish, which seek refuge in a place that allows little freedom of movement, such as a fish trap or a hole in a rock. The fishermen then spear or net their prey—or occasionally even grasp them by hand. In addition, women, men, and even children sometimes collect shellfish on the reef flat or from rocks just above the water line, especially at low tide.

Among the most spectacular techniques is torch-fishing at night for flying fish. The fishermen paddle to the ocean with a leaf torch, flashlight, or pressure lantern. The light attracts flying fish which leap from the water. Then, while the fish are rushing toward the light, a crew member scoops them from the air with a long-handled net.

As is true of subsistence practices, we can only hint at the complexity, vitality, and diversity in Polynesian expressive arts. The most elaborate forms of artistic expression were probably music, dance, poetry, story telling, carving, and tattooing.[11] Many of these arts have survived to the present day.

Musical instruments included the human body, a variety of rattles and sounding boards, bamboo pipes, and conch shells that could be blown to produce a trumpetlike sound. With European contact, the Spanish guitar, Hawaiian slide guitar, and 'ukulele, as well as several new musical genres were added to the Polynesian repertoire.

Music was often accompanied by dances, which might be performed for a variety of ritual and social purposes. The Hawaiian *hula*, familiar to tourists in Waikiki, is only one of scores of Polynesian dance forms. Some, like *hula*, involve swaying hips and graceful, intricate arm movements, where the hips and legs keep the beat while the arms and hands tell the story. Others, like the Anutan *mataavaka*, are performed with relatively stiff legs and torso and the arms swinging back and forth in front of the dancer. Some are performed in a sitting position and primarily involve motion with the head and arms. Some employ dance paddles; others are intended to emulate battles and are performed with sticks or war clubs.

Perhaps the most elaborate of Polynesian arts are in the sphere of oral communication. Music is most often vocal, and lyrics take poetic forms. Topics range from serious love songs to sexual banter, recollections of glorious deeds or frightening encounters, commemoration of loved ones, and expressions of appreciation to gods and spirits. Some songs are intended to accompany dance; others take the form of funeral laments or chants performed to invoke spiritual assistance. Among the most impressive expressions of Polynesian poetry is a great Hawaiian epic known as *The Kumulipo*—described variously as a long chant, an origin story, and a genealogical history, all rolled into one. Samoans have fashioned political speech making into a high art, and most Polynesian communities have well-developed traditions of story telling. Anutans, for example, recognize three quite different types of story. *Araarapanga* are fairly mundane recitations of relatively recent events. *Taratupua* are tales of the more distant past and involve spiritual beings as well as great culture heroes with superhuman powers. The third category, known as *tangikakai*, are stories understood to be fanciful, usually situated in Nga Rangi "The Heavens," and told for entertainment value, particularly to help young children fall asleep.

Some Polynesian tales, especially those relating to recent history, may be specific to the local community. Others are extraordinarily widespread. A good example of the latter involves accounts of a semidivine trickster who is said to have pulled most of the Pacific islands from the ocean floor with his magical fishhook, to have forced the sun to linger in the sky for twelve hours a day, and to have performed a variety of other miraculous feats. Hawaiians know this character as Maui. The New Zealand Maori call him Maui-A-Tikitiki. On Rennell and Bellona in the Solomon Islands, he is Mautikitiki. He is called Metikitiki on Tikopia and Motikitiki on Anuta. The similarity of names and deeds associated with this character make it clear that this is a unified set of traditions (sometimes described as "the Maui cycle") that stretches thousands of miles across the Pacific, from one end of Polynesia to the other.

Visual arts are sometimes difficult to differentiate from crafts. Polynesians, like other Pacific Islanders, often put a great deal of effort and care into constructing canoes, temples, and meeting houses. In addition to obvious functional considerations, builders may devote much of their energy to the aesthetic qualities of their creations. The designs carved into Maori meeting houses are impressive by any standards. Samoa's fine mats, intricately woven from carefully prepared pandanus leaves, have become famous throughout the Pacific. A few wooden representations of Hawaiian gods have been preserved in major museums. And the enormous stone statues of Rapanui (Easter Island) have intrigued generations of observers from around the world.

For the most part, Polynesians have been less interested in painting or drawing than carving—except when it comes to using the human body as one's canvass. Polynesians developed the art of tattooing; indeed, the word itself comes from Polynesian, where it is usually some variant of *tatau*. Each community had its own distinctive style. Some, like the Maori, focused on the face; others, like the Samoans emphasized the midsection, from the buttocks, hips, and upper legs up to the waist and navel. During the twentieth century, tattooing was abandoned or at least attenuated through most of Polynesia. Toward the end of the century, however, it was reintroduced in many areas as a symbol of cultural pride and identity.

Central Themes in Polynesian Culture

Major elements of Polynesian culture have been familiar to scholars since the days of early Pacific exploration. Irving Goldman (1970) presented one of the best summaries of these elements in an important book. Themes identified by Goldman include: ritual honor; genealogical seniority; primogeniture; *mana*; sanctity (*tapu*); fighting ability (*toa*); and mastery of special skill, ranging from carpentry through tattooing to religious practice (*tohunga*). The way in which these elements were manipulated for purposes of status rivalry, Goldman suggested, led to an evolutionary progression from what he termed "traditional" to "open" to "stratified" sociopolitical systems. While Goldman's evolutionary assertions are debatable, he correctly identified most of the basic Polynesian values. Here we present the concepts cited by Goldman, with our glosses and the addition of what we will call *aloha*, the Hawaiian variant of a term encountered throughout Polynesia.

Honor

Honor is a central theme in any status system. As Goldman (1970:7) puts the matter: "By status system I mean the principles that define worth and more specifically honor, that establish the scales of personal and group value, that relate position or role to privileges and obligations, that allocate respects, and that codify respect behavior." Honor is associated with political authority and rank. It is a function both of genealogical seniority (often, but not universally, as traced through the male line) and achievement (partic-

ularly in warfare, generation of material abundance, effective stewardship of sociopolitical capital, and generosity in supporting and assisting others).

Mana

Honor in Polynesia, whether based on genealogical seniority, achievement, or some
combination of these, is associated with *mana*. Proposed definitions of this concept include "supernatural power" (Codrington 1972 [1891]), "luck" (Hogbin 1936), "efficacy"
(Firth 1967b [1940]), "potency" (Howard 1985), and "'effective' or 'godly power to act'"
(Salmond 1989:73). The term may be used as a noun, adjective, or stative verb (see particularly Keesing 1984). When used as a noun, it refers to an unusual ability to affect
one's surroundings in a favorable way. One who has (or is) *mana* can promote fertility
and growth, both of food and people (e.g., see Shore 1989). He is successful in warfare,
navigation, gardening, and other technical pursuits, but because of spiritual rather than
physical prowess—although he may also have the latter.

Polynesians attribute the ultimate source of *mana* to the spirit world (e.g., Firth
1967b [1940]; Feinberg 1978, 1981a, 1996a; Salmond 1989, Shore 1989), and spirits are
typically said to bestow it in approximate proportion to genealogical seniority. In most
of Polynesia, *mana* resides primarily in males and is obtained, above all, from one's father. Most of one's *mana*, according to the latter model, goes to one's eldest son, so there
is less available for the next and least for the youngest. The greatest *mana* is assumed to
reside in the senior male descendant of a line of eldest sons; the least rests with the junior
descendant through a line of youngest sons. In short, *mana* flows from gods, who typically are also ancestors; and ancestors have a propensity to share their power with their
closest and most senior male descendants.

Since *mana* is identified with power, efficacy, or competence, it is only recognized
when seen in action. People's competence, however, does not always vary in direct proportion to their genealogical seniority. Therefore, if things go wrong and one loses control, it is taken to be prima facie evidence that the person lacks *mana*. This can be interpreted in terms of the inscrutable will of the gods, and it opens the way for achieved
status, even in what look superficially like rigid systems of hereditary rank.

In some instances, females also are major receptacles of *mana*. Thus, Anutans describe Nau Ariki, a prominent woman who lived about nine generations back, as a person of tremendous *mana*. Similarly, many Hawaiian and Maori women had exceptional
mana undergirding their economic and political power (see, e.g., Linnekin 1990:226 and
passim; Metge 1976:24, 62–65). *Mana* also may reside in natural objects and such artifacts as weapons, head rests, or other items associated with important persons.

Mana is associated with positions of authority and honor. In Polynesian languages,
these positions usually are called by variants of *tui* or *ariki* "chief," *toa* "warrior," and *tohunga* "priest" or "craftsperson." In addition to named statuses, one might gain respect
and honor because of wisdom, expertise, oratorical and technical competence, or acquisition and distribution of wealth. All of these characteristics indicate possession of *mana*
and might be called upon for purposes of status rivalry.

Over the past several decades, most discussions of *mana* have focused on Polynesia
(e.g., Firth 1967b; Salmond 1989; Shore 1989). Yet, the concept—and even the term—is
widespread among Oceanic communities. The most widely cited early scholarly analysis
of *mana* was by Codrington in his famous account of Melanesia (Codrington 1972
[1891]:118–120, 191–208, and passim), and one of the most influential recent contributions was presented by a Melanesianist (Keesing 1984). Gegeo and Watson-Gegeo (1996)

offer a penetrating analysis of *mamana* and *mamana'anga*, cognates used by the Melanesian Kwara'ae of the Solomon Islands. And in Micronesia, the Pohnpeian concept of *manaman* is described in terms virtually identical with Polynesian *mana* (Petersen 1982:17).

Tapu

Tapu and its cognates (e.g., *tabu, tambu, ābu, kapu*) have been glossed as "holy," "sacred," "forbidden," or "demanding of respect." The concept is intimately associated with *mana* (see, e.g., Salmond 1989; Shore 1989). *Mana* can ensure fertility, nurturance, abundance, and general well-being, but it is also dangerous and, if abused, can be a powerful source of destruction. Therefore, it must be treated with care and circumspection.

Typically, the head is the most *tapu* part of the body. The body of a Polynesian chief is *tapu* and should not be touched. Objects used by someone of high rank, such as a sleeping mat or headrest, are *tapu* for others to use or touch. A high ranking person might touch a subordinate, but an inferior should not initiate physical contact with his superior. On islands with less elaborate systems of personal *tapu*, only bodily contact is forbidden; for those with the most, commoners might have to step aside, sit down, or prostrate themselves on the ground upon a chief's approach. On Tahiti, the highest-ranking chiefs had to be carried on litters, and in Samoa to this day, people lower their heads (and even their umbrellas) as they pass or sit opposite others who are their social superiors. At the opposite extreme, on Nukumanu atoll, a Polynesian outlier in Papua New Guinea, contact between members of the chiefly family and ordinary citizens is rather loose and informal, and occasional bodily contact is acceptable.[12]

As in the case of *mana*, *tapu* (and related terms and concepts) extends well beyond the boundaries of Polynesia. In the Solomons and Papua New Guinea, it is so widespread as to have been incorporated (as *tambu*) into Pijin and Tok Pisin, Melanesian pidgins that constitute the most widely spoken languages in those two countries. It is discussed at length by Keesing (1982) for the Kwaio, and Burt (1988) and Gegeo and Watson-Gegeo (1996) for the Kwara'ae (see also Codrington 1972 [1891]:215–217 and passim). It is implied by the ritual underpinnings of Godelier's "great men" and the spiritual basis underlying the Trobriand distinction between people of *guya'u* "high rank" and *tokay* "commoner" status (see particularly Weiner 1988:108–110; also Malinowski 1929:30, 457–458; Weiner 1976:43–50). Among Micronesians, it is seen in the Yapese distinction between "pure" (*tabugul*) and "impure" (*taay*) (Labby 1976:chapter 5; see also Lingenfelter 1975:96–97, 102–103, and passim). Even on the small and relatively egalitarian atoll of Ulithi, Lessa (1966:34–35) reports that the paramount chief or "king" is:

> transformed into an individual of sacred character who henceforth must live a life apart....the investiture and the observance of the taboos endow him with an aura that goes a long way towards maintaining his position of authority and responsibility.

Aloha

Aloha and its cognates (e.g., *aroha, alofa, arofa, aropa, 'ofa*) denote a pan-Polynesian concept that joins together genealogy and achievement, binding them to power, honor, mutual support, kinship, and descent. It may be glossed as "pity," "love," "affection," "sympathy," or "empathy." It denotes positive affect directed toward another being, but it must be validated by giving, sharing, or assistance in performing social, political, and economic tasks.

Typically, kin share a genealogical connection, and they should treat each other in a manner that expresses *aloha*. *Aloha* is not a secondary attribute of kin but enters into the very definition of kinship to differing degrees in different communities. In some instances, persons with no genealogical link may be classed as kin if they behave according to the proper code for conduct. For example, in Samoa people who "act as kin" (*fa'aa'aiga*) over extended periods may claim the rights of kin from nonkin. Likewise, a distinction between "near" and "distant" kin may be the product of an interface between appropriate behavior and genealogy.

In general, gods grant *mana* to the chiefs because of feelings of *aloha* for their most direct descendants. Meanwhile, chiefs return *aloha* through their worship practices. The gods show *aloha* by providing for the island's welfare, and the people show *aloha* to the gods through acts of sacrifice. Persons of high rank, particularly chiefs, have more *mana* than do ordinary people. They are expected to show sympathy (*aloha*) for people who lack the *mana* to provide for their own welfare; therefore, chiefs and others of high rank serve as protectors and providers for the rest of the community. Conversely, ordinary people feel *aloha* for persons of rank in return for their assistance and protection; and they demonstrate *aloha* through appropriate displays of obedience, respect, and loyalty, by ceding honor, and by paying tribute or first fruits.

This ideal, of course, is not always realized in practice. Sometimes chiefs become arbitrary and exploitative, and people may fail to respect their chiefs or obey chiefly edicts. An oppressive chief is likely to lose his political legitimacy. Indeed, in relatively open societies such as Samoa, families who appoint their chiefs retain the right to dismiss them if they fail to maintain or enhance the family's reputation and honor. Chiefs often have sanctions available to discipline those subjects who challenge their authority. This is particularly true if the chief has access to an economic surplus that he can use to reward the faithful and maintain a force of armed men loyal to his cause (see Malo 1951[1898]; Sahlins 1958). Otherwise, the sanctions typically depend on public recognition of, and acquiescence to, the chief's authority.

As is true of *mana* and *tapu*, discussions of *aloha* usually relate to Polynesia; but it is equally significant in the other parts of Oceania. For example, Kwara'ae leaders must be *gwaunga'i*, a term referring to respected elders. *Gwaunga'i* rank, however, is not only a matter of age; a *gwaunga'i* is expected to embody core values of Kwara'ae culture, prominent among which is *alafe'anga*. This term appears to be a cognate of *aloha* and is used to similar effect. Watson-Gegeo and Gegeo (1990:167) translate it as "love, including obligations to kin and society as well as feelings of affection." Other characteristics of *gwaugna'i* nicely complement *alafe'anga*. These include:

> (2) *aroaro'anga*, peace, peaceful behavior; (3) *babato'o'anga*, emotional and behavioral stability and maturity, dependability, settling down in one place peacefully; (4) *enoeno'anga*, humility, delicacy, adaptability, gracefulness, tranquillity, gentleness; (5) *fangale'a'anga*, giving, sharing, and receiving, as well as etiquette and manners...; (6) *kwaigwale'e'anga*, welcoming, comforting, hospitality...; (7) *kwaisare'e'anga*, feeding someone without expectation of return; and (8) *mamana'anga*, honesty, truthfulness, and power....(Watson-Gegeo and Gegeo 1990:167; see also Gegeo and Watson-Gegeo 1996)

Similar concepts are found in Micronesia, although not always designated by a cognate term. On Namoluk in Chuuk State, for example, "the word *ttong*...carries many of the connotations of the English word 'love'" (Marshall 1977:656). As with *aloha*, the same word connotes what in English is termed "love" and "pity," and "One expresses one's love through overt acts—by taking care of the object of such feelings. In Chuukese kinship, actions speak louder than words: *ttong* must be *demonstrated* by nurturant acts" (Marshall 1977:656, emphasis in original; see also 1976:39–40).

Descent

Descent is vital for transmitting *mana*, and it underpins property ownership and feelings of solidarity. Most Polynesian descent groups were initially described as "patrilineal" because of a preponderance of links through males (e.g., see Gifford 1971[1929]). Usually, however, it is possible to claim descent through links of either sex, although greater prestige accrues if one's connection to a prominent ancestor can be traced agnatically. In recent decades, groups of this sort have been called by a variety of terms including "optative descent groups" (Firth 1957), "nonunilinear descent groups" (Goodenough 1955), or "cognatic descent groups," perhaps with patrilateral skewing (e.g., Fox 1967). Arguably, they are often not descent groups at all if by "descent group" is meant a unit whose membership is determined by putative biological connections (see Feinberg 1981a, 1981b, 1990a). Rather, while descent is one criterion, one may also be recruited to a group through ties of *aloha* as expressed in economic terms: through sharing goods and work or joint relationship to plots of land.

European Contact

Europeans became aware of the Pacific early in the sixteenth century when the Spanish explorer, Vasco Núñez de Balboa, looked outward from what is now Panama and observed the erroneously-named South Sea. Magellan and his crew were the first Europeans to cross the Pacific Ocean but sailed from the southern tip of South America to the Philippines without sighting any populated island until they reached the Marianas, thus bypassing the whole of Polynesia. Most European activity in the Pacific during the 1600s was by Spain and Portugal. The former colonized the Marianas and Philippines; the latter took control of the "Spice Islands" in what is now Indonesia.

During this period, little attention was paid to the central and eastern Pacific. Alvaro de Mendaña on his first voyage, in 1567, managed to sail between the Tuamotus and Marquesas without observing either archipelago. Some twenty-five years later, he stopped in the Marquesas long enough to demonstrate the deadly force of European germs and firepower, then left to meet his own demise in the Santa Cruz Islands of Melanesia.

In the seventeenth century, the Dutch colonized Indonesia. Some of their sailors, the most noteworthy being Abel Tasman, sighted a few Polynesian islands. However, like the Spaniards, they paid scant attention to that region. Indeed, European powers made so little effort to explore the isles and seas of Polynesia that many islands were not recorded by a European until the eighteenth century voyages of Wallis, Carteret, Roggeveen, Bougainville, and Cook. The famed British captain James Cook, leading three voyages between 1768 and 1779, is credited with having been the first European to sight and document more than a dozen Polynesian islands, including Hawai'i, where he ran afoul of the local population and was killed at Kealakekua Bay.

During the eighteenth and ninteenth centuries, Polynesian islands of Hawai'i, Samoa, and Tahiti became havens of rest and relaxation for whalers, who helped introduce sexually transmitted and other infectious diseases to the islands, thereby contributing to the decimation of many indigenous populations. By the late 1800s, whalers were joined by more permanent residents: the planters and traders who came to dominate the economic and political scene in many areas. Among the most important trading firms were the Australian Burns-Philp Company and the German enterprise, Godeffroy and Sohn. The former is still prominent on many islands. The latter quickly spread out from its headquarters in Apia, Samoa, to dominate trade in such distant climes as the Micronesian Marshall Islands and the Bismarck Archipelago off northeastern New Guinea. Polynesian men signed on as deck hands aboard whaling and trading ships. Some of them returned home and introduced their communities to the many novelties they had experienced. Some also brought back diseases and firearms, thereby adding to the devastation wrought by European contact. Many never returned.

"Blackbirding," a system of labor recruitment that bordered on slave trade, was primarily aimed at Melanesia. However, Polynesians and Micronesians were recruited as "colonists" by entrepreneurs working out of Peru and Chile. In practice, the "colonists" were sold into slavery and found themselves working as domestic or agricultural laborers on Peruvian *haciendas*. A few were sent to work in Peruvian guano mines. Under pressure from English and French diplomats and the Peruvian newspaper *El Comercio*, the recruiting of "colonists" eventually stopped, and an attempt was made to repatriate some of those who had survived. Unfortunately, smallpox from an American whaler was transferred to the ship on which they were to be repatriated, and many of those aboard died. The few survivors introduced the disease into home populations with disastrous results.

Easter Island is a classic case of the disastrous social and demographic consequences of this pernicious trade. Of a total population of approximately 4,500 Easter Islanders, 2,300 were "recruited" between 1862 and 1863 to work in Peru. They then were sold for between $200 and $300 to the owners of agricultural estates. Of the one hundred who survived and were to be repatriated, 85 died of smallpox on the return voyage, and the fifteen who were repatriated spread smallpox through the home population, quickly killing another thousand (Maude 1981).

Around the same time, sugar came to dominate the lives of many islanders. Polynesians from Tikopia and Anuta, along with many Melanesians, were recruited to work on sugar plantations in Fiji and Australia. And by the late nineteenth century, sugar planters gained control of Hawai'i's economic and political systems. They acquired private lands as a result of the "Great Māhele" of 1848; limited the power of archipelago's hereditary monarchy via the so-called Bayonet Constitution of 1887; plotted the monarchy's overthrow with the assistance of U.S. marines in 1893; and orchestrated the territory's eventual annexation by the U.S. five years later.

Missionaries also had a profound effect on Polynesian societies, often unwittingly paving the way for commercial settlement and incorporation into the global economy (Gunson 1978). The first pastors from the London Missionary Society reached Tahiti in 1797. Missionaries from New England first landed in Hawai'i in March of 1820. The first permanent mission in Tonga was established by the Wesleyans in 1826. Peter Turner, a Wesleyan missionary from Tonga, visited Samoa several times before a permanent Samoan mission was established by the London Missionary Society in 1830. Tahitian and Cook Island mission teachers played a decisive role in the introduction of Christianity into Samoa; and Samoan missionaries were, from 1846 on, important contributors to the conversion of other peoples around the western Pacific. They played a critical role in places as far apart as the New Guinea highlands, the Polynesian island of Niue, and the atolls of Tuvalu and the Tokelaus.

Roman Catholics followed the Protestants into Polynesia and became a dominant religious force in such regions as French Polynesia. In some areas, a bitter Catholic-Protestant rivalry continued for decades or more. The Church of Jesus Christ of Latter-Day Saints, popularly known as Mormons, began its missionary activities in Hawai'i in the 1870s and Samoa in the 1880s. Tikopia in the Solomons was effectively missionized by the Anglicans only at the beginning of the twentieth century, after an abortive attempt by Roman Catholics in 1851–52 (Laracy 1969); and Tikopian mission teachers were responsible for the conversion of Anuta in 1916 (Feinberg 1998).

Through a combination of treaties, legal subterfuge, coercion, treachery, and outright military conquest, the major metropolitan powers of the nineteenth century managed, with varying degrees of success, to appropriate land throughout Polynesia and take political control of the islands, either as protectorates or outright colonies. In the 1840 Treaty of Waitangi, Maori chiefs ceded sovereignty over New Zealand to the British crown in return for a guarantee of "full, exclusive and undisturbed possession of their Lands and Estates, Forests and Fisheries and other properties... as long as it is their wish and desire to retain the same" (Treaty of Waitangi, 1840 [English version, article 2]) and the "benefits" of British citizenship (see Orange 1987, 1989). In 1842, France declared a protectorate over Tahiti and annexed the Marquesas. 'Uvea (Wallis Island) became a French protectorate in 1888. England took formal control of Fiji in 1874.

Britain, Germany, and the United States had interests in Samoa and almost came to blows. War was averted when a hurricane in 1889 destroyed a half dozen German and American warships in Apia harbor, caused the deaths of 150 sailors, and inspired the three Western powers to settle their differences at the bargaining table. The Treaty of Berlin, which followed in 1899, resulted in the partitioning of the Samoas: it assigned Germany control of the seven western islands, while the United States assumed possession of the six islands east of the 171st meridian. These are now, respectively, the independent nation of Samoa (formerly Western Samoa) and the territory of American Samoa. In return for relinquishing claims to Samoa, the British won recognition of their right to include Tonga within their "sphere of influence."

Hawai'i was annexed by the U.S. in 1898. The Gilbert and Ellice Islands became a British protectorate in 1892, and the islands of Tokelau became a protectorate in 1925. New Zealand gained control of the Cook Islands in 1901 and Niue in 1907, assumed a League of Nations mandate for Western Samoa after World War I, and took formal responsibility for the Tokelaus from Britain in 1948. Tonga was never formally colonized, but culturally and economically it has been under British influence since the middle of the nineteenth century. The Polynesian outlier atolls, Ontong Java, Nukumanu, Takuu, and Nukuria, were dominated for several decades in the late nineteenth and early twentieth centuries by private European-owned copra plantations. Such isolated Polynesian outposts as Tikopia and Anuta had no commercially exploitable resources, and they were left more or less untouched until the late twentieth century; but even they came under the political authority, first, of the British Solomon Islands Protectorate around 1900, and — after 1978 — of the independent nation of the Solomon Islands.

The policies that governed both annexation and the style of colonial administration varied greatly over time as metropolitan attitudes toward indigenous peoples changed. Thus, in the late eighteenth century the British were able to declare Australia uninhabited and engage in systematic removal, exclusion, and, in some cases, extermination of the aboriginal population. By the early nineteenth century, British policy had changed to one of recognition of legal rights of aboriginal peoples, and the British annexed New Zealand under a treaty that gave equal legal and social status to British and Maori partners. By the late nineteenth century, the policy had changed still further, favoring of the recognition and active protection of aboriginal rights. In Fiji, this resulted in colonial policies designed ensure Fijians an active role by in governance and to protect them from becoming landless laborers in their own islands.

At the dawn of the twenty-first century, all of Polynesia has adopted one or another form of Christianity. Yet it is a distinctively Polynesian form of Christianity. In most cases, people remain convinced that the old gods existed and accomplished most of the exploits attributed to them by traditional narratives. In many cases, traditional spirits are still thought to be actively involved in the affairs of mortal human beings and must be considered in the course of social life. Much of the old political and spatial symbolism has persisted into the present. The Christian God has taken the place of older spiritual beings as the source of *mana*, and pastors or priests have taken over some of the roles formerly ascribed to chiefs. Decktor Korn's (1978:395) reference to Tonga's "thorough indigenization of Christianity, the infusion of everyday life with religious elements, and…absorption with matters relating to church membership," can be applied with equal force today to most of Polynesia.

In most Polynesian communities, the conversion experience followed a regular pattern. Initial European contact led to depopulation and social and cultural disruption. This was accomplished through a combination of bullets and introduced disease, often compounded by internal conflict and natural disasters. With the islanders' worldview shaken, missionaries entered the scene and proclaimed that the old gods were evil or powerless, in contrast with the new religion that they offered.[13] Typically, they made alliances with one of the leading chiefs, and with European support that chief was able to become politically dominant in his island or archipelago. In return, for political and military support, Christianity gained official sanction as a state religion, and missionaries gained influence as political advisors. In some cases, the churches attempted to protect islanders from the most serious forms of abuse by traders, blackbirders, and other unscrupulous business operators. In others, like Hawai'i and Tonga, missionaries came to prominence in the worldly pursuits of money making and political intrigue.

* * *

In precontact times, Hawai'i had a classical Polynesian social, political, and religious system. Each of the major islands was divided into pie-shaped districts (*ahupua'a*), each of which included the full spectrum of ecological zones, running from the reef and the beach through the coastal flat, and on up the mountain sides. Each district was hierarchically organized. At the top were the *ali'i* "chiefs," whose awesome *mana* made them all but unapproachable by ordinary people. Beneath the *ali'i* were "administrators" (*konohiki*), who ensured that socioeconomic and ritual enterprises ran smoothly. The bulk of the population consisted of "commoners" (*maka'āinana*), who worked the land. A possible fourth group consisted of *kauwā*, who have been described as "outcastes," "slaves," or "prisoners of war" (see, e.g., Handy and Pukui 1972:204–205 and passim). Ritual specialists called *kahuna* were an additional influential group.

At the time of Captain Cook's first visit to Hawai'i, the archipelago was ravaged by civil wars, as leading chiefs contended for sovereignty. Shortly after European contact, a dynamic young leader from the Ka'ū district of the big island of Hawai'i was able to consolidate his power over the most of the archipelago, and he established himself as King Kamehameha I. At the same time, Hawai'i was subjected to depredations of whalers and of traders who had come in quest of the aromatic and commercially profitable sandalwood. The islands' population prior to European contact has been estimated at anywhere from two or three hundred thousand (Oliver 1961:256) to as many as one million (Stannard 1989:32–58; Dudley and Agard 1990:xii). Within a century it had fallen to approximately 40,000—by Stannard's calculations, more than a 95% decline.

This led to a period of doubt about the social and religious order's viability and culminated in a cataclysmic decision by the king's widow, Ka'ahumanu, and his son/successor, Liholiho (also known as Kamehameha II) to abolish the traditional religion. In 1819, a group of royal men and women feasted together on a meal of pork, violating longstanding dietary rules. The ancient gods were declared to be ineffectual and were no longer to be worshipped. And, in the blink of an eye the old religious order, known as the *kapu* "taboo" system, was abolished. The following year, the first American missionaries arrived in the islands and promptly declared that the abandonment of the old gods and worship practices was an act of divine providence, intended to prepare Hawaiians for the blessings of Christianity.[14]

During the nineteenth century, as foreign traders depleted Hawai'i's sandalwood forests, sugar emerged as the centerpiece of the islands' economy. As sugar increased in importance, the planters found themselves immersed in a struggle to obtain ever more land for their plantations, and they exerted pressure on the king to make communally owned lands available for private ownership. Meanwhile, many of the missionaries found their operations underfunded by the home church and, to try to cover the shortfall, became involved in business themselves. They used the positions they had gained as advisors to the king to convince him to redistribute land in the "Great *Māhele*," as a result of which the sugar planters were able to exercise direct ownership of Hawaiian lands that they had previously had to lease.

Toward the latter part of the century, the sugar magnates clamored for annexation to the United States so that their product could be marketed in North America without having to pay import duties. This, combined with their desire to alienate still more of the indigenous lands, and the American military's wish to control the strategically located islands along with the excellent deep-water port at Pearl Harbor, led to a series of actions intended to force the monarch to relinquish power. In the 1880s, American businessmen formed an armed militia in Honolulu and forced King Kalākaua to accept a new constitution in which the monarchy's power was significantly attenuated. In 1893, the same militia, with the support of the U.S. Marines, deposed the monarchy, imprisoned Queen Lili'uokalani in her royal palace, and paved the way for eventual annexation of Hawai'i by the United States.

Annexation was postponed for several years when President Grover Cleveland appointed a commission to investigate the circumstances of the monarchy's overthrow. The commission found that it had been a cynical act of dubious legality by greedy businessmen and politicians. It called for the United States to recognize Hawaiian independence and to restore the legitimate rulers to their rightful position.[15] But four years later William McKinley was elected president. He reversed the position of the previous administration and, with his support, Congress formally declared Hawai'i a U.S. possession.

Capitalist production, associated particularly with the sugar industry, prompted business leaders to seek new sources of cheap labor. The result was massive immigration into the Hawaiian islands, especially from Asia. This immigration, combined with decimation of the indigenous population, led to fundamental changes in the islands' ethnic makeup. Figures in the 1940 census, cited by Oliver (1961:259), show Hawai'i's population on eve of WWII to include 156,000 Japanese, 115,000 Caucasians, 100,000 Filipinos, 50,000 part-Hawaiians, 28,000 Chinese, 6,000 Koreans, and 14,999 "pure Hawaiians." The final decades of the century saw increasing numbers of immigrants from Southeast Asia in the aftermath of the Vietnam War and related conflicts in other parts of Indochina. But the overall picture, showing a large majority of Hawai'i's population to be of Asian or European descent and Hawaiians to have been reduced to a small minority in their own homeland, has remained fundamentally unchanged.

In addition to sugar, major industries in Hawai'i have included pineapple and coffee, the latter localized on the Big Island, particularly the Kona district. The U.S. military has become a major presence, controlling over 140,000 acres of Hawaiian lands (Menton and Tamura 1989:317; Dudley and Agard 1990:65, 150 n.33). And tourism, with the explosion of hotels, condominiums, and golf courses, has forever altered the physical landscape.

Over the past few decades, Native Hawaiians have organized politically in a variety of groups, and in support of a variety of causes. The dominant theme of these movements has been to achieve some form of sovereignty. Although sovereignty means different things to different people, a common thread is the attempt to gain control at least over "crown lands" set aside for Native Hawaiians in the "Bayonet Constitution" of 1887. Associated with this is a struggle to attain at least the level of autonomy and legal protection now afforded "Native Americans."[16]

* * *

The history of such places as Tonga and Tahiti differs in detail from Hawai'i, but in each case churches played a comparable political role. The first missionaries in Tahiti were from the London Missionary Society. For more than a decade they met with limited success. Conditions, however, were ripe for a religious conversion as European contact and introduced disease reduced Tahiti's population from more than 35,000 at the time of contact to about 10,000 by 1800 (Lockwood 1993a:23; Newbury 1980:32). The ancient gods, ancestral spirits, chiefs, and their *mana* had failed to forestall disaster, and confidence in the old system began to waver. Then, early in the nineteenth century, a prominent chief known as Pomare II attempted to solidify his power over all Tahiti. When his campaign stalled, the missionaries convinced him to abandon his traditional deities and turn to the Christian God. In 1812, he proclaimed his acceptance of the new faith. After a decisive military victory in 1815, he established himself as Tahiti's paramount chief or "king." Christianity was made the official religion, and the missionaries, having gained Pomare's trust, were able to establish their political position as advisors to the Tahitian royalty.

The picture was complicated by a rivalry between France and Britain for control of Tahiti and the surrounding islands, and a parallel rivalry between the Protestant and Roman Catholic missions in the Society Islands. With the establishment of a French protectorate in 1842 and annexation to France as a colony in 1881, the traditional system of chieftainship was abolished. Yet elements of the old social and religious systems can be seen even today, superimposed on the Christian veneer.[17]

* * *

Tonga, along with Samoa, constitutes the original Polynesian homeland—the place where Polynesian culture developed as a distinctive entity. Like Tahiti and Hawai'i, Tonga had a stratified political, social, and religious system. The basic social unit seems to have been the extended family. Tongans also were organized into descent groups called *ha'a*; but by the time of European contact, knowledge of *ha'a* affiliation was lost to all but the highest ranking families.

Oral traditions identify the archipelago's paramount chief during the early centuries as the Tu'i Tonga "Lord of Tonga." According to Tongan tradition, the Tu'i Tonga was descended from a line that began approximately a thousand years ago, when the first Tu'i Tonga was conceived as the child of a mortal Tongan woman and the sky god, Tangaloa. For centuries, the Tu'i Tonga held both political and spiritual sway over the archipelago. During the fifteenth century, after a series of assassinations, Kauulufonua, the 24th Tu'i Tonga, divided spiritual from temporal rule, giving "the more arduous duties of kingship" (Gifford 1971[1929]:48) to a cadet line known as the Ha'a Takalaua. The senior leader of that line, the Tu'i Ha'a Takalaua, eventually came to eclipse the Tu'i Tonga in temporal importance. Then, during the seventeenth century, the Tu'i Ha'a Takalaua Moungatonga repeated the events of two centuries before by conferring upon one of his sons a new title, that of Tu'i Kanokupolu. In time, the Tu'i Kanokupolu line came to eclipse both the Tu'i Ha'a Takalaua and the Tu'i Tonga, a trend that culminated in the ascension of Tu'i Kanokupolu Tāufa'āhau to the position of George I Tupou, the first "king" of Tonga.

Tongan social organization was, as it still is, pervaded by a rule of brother-sister avoidance and respect in which the brother was expected to defer to his sister, who was his ritual superior. The father had to be respected, and the father's sister was given even greater deference than the father. Conversely, the relationship between a boy and his mother's brother was a warm, close, friendly one, in which the nephew was permitted to take extreme liberties with his uncle, even to the extent of appropriating his property under certain circumstances. This was known as the *fahu* relationship, and it became a prime example of a common pattern discussed by Radcliffe-Brown in his famous article on "The Mother's Brother in South Africa" (Radcliffe-Brown 1952[1924]).

The Tongan pattern of relations between brother and sister, with the consequent relationships between mother's brother and sister's child, and between father's sister and brother's child, is shared by Samoa and a number of the Polynesian outliers. The Tongans, however, connected this system of respect and ritual honor with a distinctive pattern of cross-cousin marriage among the three great chiefly lines. Since a woman outranked her brother, she was expected to marry into a line superior to his. Ideally, the sister of the Tu'i Kanokupolu married the Tu'i Ha'a Takalaua, and the sister of the Tu'i Ha'a Takalaua married the Tu'i Tonga. The sister of the Tu'i Tonga, known as the Tu'i Tonga Fefine "Female Tu'i Tonga," was so sacred that there was no Tongan of sufficiently high rank for her to marry. However, a line known as the Fale Fisi "House of Fiji" was understood to be a royal lineage from the island of Lakeba in Fiji. The highest ranking man of that line was known as the Tu'i Lakepa, Tongan for "Lord of Lakeba," and he—as a non-Tongan of royal birth—was considered a suitable husband for the Tu'i Tonga Fefine. Should this couple have a daughter, she was known as the Tamahā "Sacred Child," and Tongans regarded her as the most sacred person in the entire archipelago. Gifford (1971[1929]:80–81) lists six Tamahā, four of whom were daughters of the Tu'i Tonga Fefine and the Tu'i Lakepa.

Although a number of early explorers sighted islands of the Tongan archipelago, contact was minimal until well into the eighteenth century. Among the earliest Europeans to stop there was Captain Cook, whom the Tongans entertained in such lavish style that he named the archipelago the "Friendly Islands." Three decades later, an English castaway named William Mariner was marooned in the Ha'apai group in central Tonga for several years, and he was adopted by a Ha'apai chief named Fīnau (Mariner 1817). During his time in Tonga, Mariner learned the language and became a trusted member of the community. In one of history's ironic twists, he was informed by his hosts that the Ha'apai chiefs intended to slay Cook and his crew and plunder the ship; the elaborate entertainment was intended to lull the sailors into a false sense of security. Only an inauspicious omen at the last moment kept the plan from being executed and secured the Tongans' reputation as a haven of friendship for Europeans.

As was true of Hawai'i and Tahiti, the early nineteenth century was a time of civil war and social unrest in Tonga, and this provided a convenient point of entry for the church. Tāufa'āhau, an important chief from Ha'apai, converted to Christianity, and with Western support he ultimately was able to subdue the archipelago. He established himself as George Tupou Taha "Tupou I," the first "king" of Tonga. Tupou combined the three paramount titles in his office and his person, and ensured Tonga's position as a strongly theocratic Christian state. His adoption of Wesleyan Protestantism, however, inspired his enemies to embrace Roman Catholicism, with the consequence that there developed in the islands a large Catholic minority, which continues to thrive.

As in the other major Polynesian archipelagoes, the missionaries insinuated themselves into the political system through strategic alliances with the paramount chief, and they came to be among the king's most trusted political advisors. The most notorious of these clergy-turned-businessmen-turned-politicians in the nascent Tongan kingdom was one Mr. Shirley Baker, who held a series of high government positions until he was deposed and then deported by the British High Commissioner.

In the meantime, the missionaries around Tupou convinced him to create a constitution, making Tonga into a constitutional monarchy modeled in some ways after the British system. Traditional chiefs (*eiki*) were reconstituted as "nobles," and they continue to form a politically and ritually dominant caste. Traditional indices of ritual honor, such as stepping aside at a superior's approach, have been retained in the new setting. During a visit to the archipelago in 1973, one of the present authors was driving on the main island of Tongatapu and saw a line of cars driving in the opposite direction. His companions instructed him that this was the king's motorcade, and that he must pull onto the shoulder until they had passed. The traditional and modern have also been merged in the political arena, as may be seen in the fact that the king's brother—and more recently, his son—has served for years as the nation's prime minister. At the same time, Western ideals of equality and democracy have not entirely bypassed the islands, with the result that there has been increasing social unrest and opposition to the dominance of what is sometimes characterized as an exploitative hereditary clique.

In the religious sphere, church offerings have come to replace the first-fruits offerings which traditionally had been presented to the chiefs; and the church became all-pervasive in Tongan life. Nonreligious activities have been banned on Sundays. Business may not be conducted on the Sabbath, when it is illegal even to handle money. Sunday picnics are forbidden, as is the singing of anything other than church hymns. This situation led to one of history's more creative attempts to reconcile church and state.

The Seventh Day Adventists (S.D.A.s) observe Sabbath on Saturdays and, while there was no legal prohibition against resting on Saturday, that would have meant two days a week rather than one when their members were forbidden to conduct business. According to a widely-told story, the solution was contained in the International Date Line. From a purely geographical point of view the Date Line should bisect Tonga, as it is supposed to be precisely opposite the Prime Meridian, which runs through Greenwich, England. Just west of the line it is exactly 24 hours later than it is to the east. If the line were to run through Tonga different parts of the country would have had to operate on different days, so the line was "adjusted" to go around the archipelago. Thus, by the S.D.A.s' calculation, what Tongan law regarded as Sunday was really Saturday. Therefore, they could observe their Sabbath at the same time as everyone else, abstain from business just one day a week, and satisfy the letter of both civil and religious ordinance.

* * *

In many ways, precontact Fiji resembled the archipelagoes of Polynesia proper, combining powerful chiefdoms with a system of status rivalry and with civil war. After Tupou's ascension to power in Tonga, he convinced a chief named Cakobau (pronounced Thakombau), from the small island of Bau, just off the coast of Fiji's "main" island, to adopt Christianity. With the support of Tupou, the Christian missionary establishment, and other European interests, Cakobau established his sovereignty over Viti Levu and became the most important chief in all of Fiji. This also provided an economic and political foothold for European powers in the southwestern Pacific, and in 1872 Fiji was annexed as a British colony.

* * *

In some respects Tikopia and Anuta are as different from Tonga, the Society Islands, and Hawai'i as one could imagine Polynesian communities to be. Rather than groups of large islands populated by tens—perhaps hundreds—of thousands of people, they are tiny specks of land on the fringe of Melanesia, surrounded by hundreds of miles of open sea. Yet, in crucial ways the conversion of experience was similar. In the middle of the nineteenth century, two Roman Catholic missionaries spent about a year on Tikopia, apparently without making converts. Sporadic contacts with the Melanesian Mission of the Anglican Church began in 1858, and in 1901 two mission teachers were posted on Tikopia. Their presence was tolerated; but after a few years of minimal progress, they gave up the effort. Finally, in 1907, the Anglicans sent Ellison Tergatok, a Melanesian priest from the Banks Islands of Vanuatu, to try his hand at conversion. Father Ellison discovered Tikopia to be a congenial community; he married there, and lived out the remainder of his life in his adopted homeland. He made a few converts, but the going was slow until the Ariki Tafua, one of Tikopia's four chiefs, recognized the tactical advantages of association with the church. When the Ariki Tafua converted in the early 1920s, most residents of his district—meaning close to half the island's population— followed him into the fold. Still, the island was divided, half Christian and half pagan, and plagued by uncertainty about the proper course of action. Then, in the early 1950s, Tikopia was struck by a devastating hurricane, followed by a drought and famine, which the Christians declared to be divine retribution for the pagans' refusal to give God His due. Hardly had the island recovered from this natural disaster when it was struck by another—a major epidemic. It appeared that the pagans suffered more than the Christians from the epidemic, and they lost their most important leaders. By 1955, virtually the entire island had converted.

Anuta was evangelized by missionaries from Tikopia in 1916. A loose translation of the story as related to Feinberg by Pu Nukumarere in 1972 is as follows:

> ....On May 16, a ship came. It was the *Southern Cross*, with Bishop John Wood aboard. He asked Pu Raropuko [who was serving as regent in the temporary absence of a chief] and Pu Teukumarae [heir apparent to the chieftainship], "May we establish the Christian system of prayer on this island?"
>
> Pu Teukumarae and Pu Raropuko told him it was fine. The bishop left three missionaries on this island: John Selwyn Kavarou, Robert Pakiraki, and Shadrack Ikarima. The ship returned to Tikopia. The church was established on this island.
>
> · The ship returned on June 1. By then, Pu Raropuko had died. Bishop Wood asked of the three catechists if they attempted to treat Pu Raropuko when he got sick. They said that they went to him, and when they finished praying for Pu Raropuko he recovered. Then, behind their backs, the spirit mediums returned

to treat Pu Raropuko. While they were treating him, his sickness returned and he died.

The bishop told John Selwyn that they had behaved irresponsibly out of fear. The church had been handed over to Pu Raropuko's supervision because this island followed his guidance.

When Pu Raropuko was close to death, he told Pu Teukumarae to watch his children. He should assume leadership and not permit *them* to do so. Pu Teukumarae should follow Pu Raropuko's commitments to the church. He followed these instructions.

The bishop was very angry at John Selwyn and Robert because they had allowed Pu Raropuko to die. The bishop said that they feared being attacked and had neglected to follow the way of the church. He told them to do "the work" [i.e., to promote the church's teachings] responsibly that it might flourish. He then said he would depart and leave them on this island to observe what things the pagan community was doing. If the pagans went to perform kava, they also should make sure to be present.[18] They should fix up the community properly. The island henceforth shall implicitly obey the church.

During that same year, oral traditions indicate that Anuta was faced with a hurricane, drought, and famine which resulted in starvation and reduced the islanders to eating dirt to fill their bellies. Clearly the traditional religion, which was supposed to ensure the island's prosperity, had not protected people from disaster, and they were ready to try an alternative.

Contemporary Issues

Different Polynesian communities, because of their divergent geographical and geological situations and different colonial histories, have followed disparate trajectories. Some, like the Anutans of the Solomon Islands, still live in small, isolated communities, and they continue to struggle for a cash income and access to European-manufactured commodities. Others, like the New Zealand Maori and Native Hawaiians, are fighting for official recognition, some form of sovereignty, and return of at least a portion of their ancestral lands. Samoans and Tongans are more concerned with: making ends meet in their island homes, which are becoming overpopulated; holding families together; and maintaining their cultural integrity despite extensive travel to such cosmopolitan centers as the United States and New Zealand, where many have gone in search of education and comparatively well-paying jobs. In French Polynesia, people are relatively prosperous as a result of "welfare state colonialism," but they must deal with the psychological burden of cultural stress and the knowledge that they have been condemned to a life of dependency on the metropolitan power. We will conclude this section of the book by exploring in some detail three variants of the Polynesian experience. The first is that of the New Zealand Maori, who have largely become a "Fourth World" community as a dispossessed minority in a "modern" Western nation. The second involves the Samoans, who have integrated many features of Western culture with their own indigenous patterns of political, economic, and social life to form an independent and distinctively Polynesian nation state. The third case is that of Anuta, a remote and still predominantly self-sufficient Polynesian enclave in a precariously integrated developing nation.

The Maori of Aotearoa

Around A.D. 1200, a group of Maori seafarers left the high island of Rarotonga, in what is now the Southern Cook Islands. The voyage took them south to a new home that they would call "the land of the long white cloud," Aotearoa. They claim knowledge of its existence from an earlier journey by one of their ancestors, Kupe, who had returned to Rarotonga with tales of a bounteous land in the south (Jones 1995). The voyagers would explore and settle these islands at the southwestern corner of the Polynesian Triangle, where they would be largely undisturbed by outside forces until the late eighteenth century. Why they left their former homeland when they did, however, remains a matter of speculation (Buck 1966).

Maori oral history recalls that seven double-hulled canoes (*waka*) left Rarotonga together but arrived in different parts of Aotearoa. The principal challenge for the new arrivals was to adjust their social and agricultural practices to the conditions that they found, and to explore and harness the potential of the new resources. With large areas of fertile land, mature forests, and bountiful marine resources, the new arrivals were able to increase their population quickly without exerting significant pressure on their ecosystem.[19] With room for expansion, there was. at first, little pressure on resources and little economic reason for tribes to come into conflict (Firth 1959a).

The crews of the seven canoes founded tribes that settled particular localities around the coastline. The descendants of a crew became a loosely affiliated group known as a *waka*. These *waka* grew and segmented over time into a number of *iwi* "tribes." An *iwi* might comprise descendants of the captain, navigator, or chiefs who led the expedition to the new land. The tribes from the different *waka* dispersed and settled in locales around the point of arrival. They became closely linked with particular localities, each identifying itself by reference to a river, a mountain, and a chief. *Iwi* however, grew in size and became difficult to coordinate on a day-to-day basis. They split, in turn, into *hapū* "subtribes," which became the basic economic and social units. Members of a *hapū* cooperated economically and socially to undertake tasks that were beyond the capacity of the smallest units of Maori society, the *whānau* "extended family" (Firth 1959a).

Social relationships between tribes, subtribes, and individuals were contained in, and shaped by, comprehensive genealogies (*whakapapa*) and histories that were committed to memory by chiefs and their advisors, called *tohunga* (Jones 1995). Tribes were led by higher chiefs (*ariki*) and lesser chiefs (*rangatira*). *Ariki* were connected by genealogy with gods, and they served both as chiefs and priests. Succession to chiefly office was determined by primogeniture and genealogical seniority, so that chiefs were normally the senior members of the senior male lines of tribes and sub-tribes. While the term *ariki* might apply either to a firstborn male (*ariki tamāroa*) or firstborn female (*ariki tapairu*), formal leadership typically rested with males. However, firstborn women exercised considerable leadership by virtue of genealogy. The history of the Tainui tribe shows how this division of power worked out in one major *iwi* (Jones 1995).

Over time, as populations expanded and the potential of certain areas and resources was recognized, tension increased between tribes. Under growing competitive and demographic pressure, Maori society developed a new lifestyle. *Hapū* lived in villages near their plantations and fisheries. Each village appears to have been built around a central common, known as a *marae*, where residents held meetings and performed collective activities. Some Maori also constructed fortified villages (*pā*) on nearby hilltops, to which they could retreat and from which they could defend themselves against aggressive neighbors. They kept supplies of weapons, food, water, and firewood in these *pā*. The division of activity between cultivation and defense grew so pronounced that specialization became necessary. Male children were dedicated at birth either to the skills of the god of war and were trained as warriors, or to those of the god of plantations and agriculture, and were trained as cultivators.

The wars were not immensely destructive. They typically involved relatively small forces in combat at close range, using a variety of wooden and stone weapons such as hand clubs (*mere* and *patu*) and longer spears and staffs (*taiaha*) (Vayda 1960). They did, however, lead to the taking of slaves (*taurekareka*) and property. The nature of social honor (*mana*), however, meant that acts which humiliated a tribe and its chiefs had to be avenged. This led to retaliatory military actions. While no single action was necessarily destructive, the ongoing retaliatory actions could be disruptive (see, e.g., Jones 1995). The political and economic risks of allowing unchecked retaliation were recognized, and Maori developed ways of managing these conflicts, often through strategic marital alliances between senior members of the tribes or sub-tribes involved (Biggs 1960).

Meanwhile, Maori society developed more efficient means of assuring its survival. With new means of creating and preserving food surpluses it was able to support the development of specializations such as wood and jade carving, tattooing, weaving, canoe building and decoration, and the preparation of military forces and defenses (Firth 1959a). These forms of knowledge were formally transmitted by specialists (*tohunga*) in schools known as *wananga*. Protected by remoteness from introduced diseases, the population expanded steadily by exploring and settling more remote areas without putting significant pressure on its ecosystem. But this was to end.

European Contact

After the Dutch explorer Abel Tasman "discovered" Aotearoa in 1642, James Cook visited and mapped the land during three voyages, beginning in1769. After the Cook expedition's record was published, the islands' existence and economic potential became more widely known. In the late eighteenth century, the first European whalers and sealers began to settle in relatively remote locations around the South Island. Their reports stimulated further interest in the territory and, by the early nineteenth century, informal European settlement commenced in the north. Maori leaders became concerned about the destabilizing effects of these often-dissolute elements, who introduced disease, liquor, and weapons. With access to muskets beginning in 1820, northern chiefs began a decade-long series of destructive wars against their traditional enemies.

Chiefs, and some missionaries, grew increasingly aware of the colonial powers' interests in annexing Aotearoa, and of settlers' interests in acquiring land by whatever means. A group of 35 northern chiefs declared the country's independence in the name of the United Tribes of New Zealand in 1835, in an attempt to establish their sovereignty and their right to regulate settlement and government. When this failed to have the desired effect, the British government resolved to bring New Zealand under its colonial rule (McHugh 1989). The British representatives arrived to negotiate a treaty in the same year that agents of the private New Zealand Company initiated attempts to purchase land for formal settlements.

British representatives and Maori chiefs negotiated a formal treaty in which Maori ceded sovereignty to the crown in return for undisturbed possession of all of their lands, fisheries, and other valued "assets" (Orange 1987). The Treaty of Waitangi, signed in February 1840, was supposed to create an orderly land market by ensuring that Maori sold only such land as they chose—and at an agreed price—to the crown, which would survey and resell it. This, it was thought, would improve relations between the treaty "partners," which had deteriorated over earlier unregulated land sales. While the Treaty of Waitangi was an attempt to provide an honorable solution to a problem, it could not subvert the greed of settlers who now sought land for raising crops to supply the growing market in Australia.

Maori sold some land but were reluctant to alienate parcels on which they were making significant profits by supplying food for European settlements, and which were fundamental elements of their social identity. European settlers, jealous of Maori success and hungry for agricultural land, put increasing pressure on the government to secure more land, and the scene was set for a collision of wills. The resulting wars undermined Maori society.

In 1844, wars began in the north; in 1860 in Taranaki; and in 1863 in Waikato. The Land Wars were generally considered a series of European victories. Recent research, however, has shown that Maori military and political resistance, both active and passive, continued until 1881 (Belich 1998).

After the wars, land losses continued as "legal" means were found of expropriating Maori land (Kelsey 1984). By the end of the nineteenth century, Maori had lost 20 million hectares, comprising almost the entire South Island and two thirds of the North Island, to the British crown and private European owners. Maori lost land not solely through military defeat, but by a combination of sale, fraud, legal subterfuge, governmental confiscations of land from tribes which resisted, population decline resulting from introduced diseases, and the sheer weight of growing settler numbers (Asher and Naulls 1987). The situation was made worse by systematic attempts to suppress and devalue Maori language and culture through a system of "Native Schools." A population estimated at between 150,000 and 200,000 in 1769 had declined to 100,000 by 1840 as a consequence of tuberculosis, typhoid, sexually transmitted disease, measles, and wars. By 1848, the population had declined to 60,000; and by the 1860s, Maori had become a minority in their own land as the European influx continued. The Maori decline continued until 1896, when it reached its nadir at 42,000 and led to discussions about the possible "extinction of the race."

Throughout the latter part of the nineteenth century Maori leaders attempted to recover control of their situation. Various Maori movements continued to resist European encroachment by such active means as the formation of the Kingitanga "King Movement" in the Waikato region, by passive resistance such as that by followers of the prophet Te Whiti at the Parihaka community in Taranaki, and by forming religious movements which combined Maori and Christian symbols and practices such as the Ringatu and Ratana faiths. Without a history of pantribal cooperation, and with difficult communication, united movements were always difficult to establish and manage. Limited success was attained in 1892, when Maori for the first time established their own national parliament, the Kotahitanga, to take control of their political and social situation.

It was clear to some leaders that Maori would have to press their claims through the parliamentary process. However, although Maori representation had been guaranteed since 1867, it was confined to four out of a total of 80 seats in the national parliament. As long as Maori could enroll only in certain stipulated electorates, the impact of their representation was bound to be limited. Despite Maori leaders' vision, the combination of declining population and continuing land loss saw Maori separated from their traditional leadership and economic resources. They were unable to shape their destiny and became a demoralized people. For many Maori the ideal of partnership, to which they had signed on in the Treaty of Waitangi, had been betrayed by the European partners to the Treaty (Orange 1989).

The Twentieth Century

Through the first half of the twentieth century, many Maori remained in the rural areas where their ancestors had always lived. Yet, even in the early twentieth century, land alienation continued. Maori farmers lost a further five million of their remaining eight million hectares, and Parliament continued to pass laws to get access to the rest (Asher and Naulls 1987). The Maori situation had been made worse by a combination of this "legal imperialism" and, particularly, the application of European principles of land tenure and inheritance to Maori estates by successive parliaments. Appropriation by settlers depended on the individualization of title to land so that it could be surveyed and sold. The notion of land as a commodity was new to the Maori, as were the consequences of inheritance law. Few realized that if they died without leaving a written will, their estates would be divided equally among their heirs. This process resulted over time in the fragmentation of land into many relatively small and separated holdings that were uneconomical to farm.

Some Maori leaders, such as the scholar and lawyer Sir Apirana Ngata, saw the need to use remaining Maori land more effectively in order to participate more actively in the growing economy. As a Member of Parliament, beginning in 1905, he consolidated land-holdings in his own tribal area and developed large commercial farming and forestry operations which generated new wealth and unity in his tribe. Later, as Minister of Maori Affairs he advocated consolidating other tribes' fragmented landholdings, and after 1930, with government funding, bringing land into commercial production on the same basis as their European (*Pakeha*) neighbors. Later, as a member of the opposition, he continued to work with a growing body of Maori politicians on land reform and political and economic measures designed to improve the social status of Maori. The Maori population began to grow again and, with improvements in public health and primary health care, reached its precontact levels in 1945. At the same time, 75% of the population remained in rural areas; but without access to some of their best lands many were reduced to a combination of small-farming and laboring for *Pakeha* farmers and timber millers.

World War II was a watershed in Maori social history (Sutherland 1949). Maori women became involved in war-related industries in urban centers and, after widespread opposition to serving in WWI, Maori men chose to participate in large numbers in WWII as members of a Maori battalion. The companies that made up the Maori Battalion were recruited from various *waka* areas and led by their own officers. Their gallantry and heroic deeds generated a new respect for Maori within New Zealand. Among Maori, the proud record of the 28th Maori Battalion had a profound effect in rebuilding people's self-esteem.

At the end of the war the Maori had a body of men who had served and proven themselves as leaders in the battalion and were ready and determined to play an active role among their people. There was now a group of women who had worked in the city and had enjoyed the higher wages and greater range of options that urban life proffered. These men and women were not prepared to return to life as farm labor in depressed rural areas; instead, they settled in the cities after the war. So, in the postwar period, one of the greatest transformations of Maori society began (Metge 1964).

Urbanization was possible because new jobs were being created as the country's formerly agricultural economy was becoming increasingly industrial. By the 1950s, the government had in place a comprehensive scheme for Maori who wished to move to urban centers. Maori, drawn by higher wages, new career opportunities, and better housing available on generous terms, moved to the cities in steadily growing numbers and over a relatively short time. In 1936, only about 15% of the Maori population lived in urban centers; by 1945 this had risen to 26%; by 1956 the number was 37%; and by the mid 1960s, the figure topped 61%. The urban figure continued to rise and then flattened out in the mid-1990s at around 86%.

The movement transformed Maori social organization in several ways. The rural communities lost significant parts of their populations. The loss of youth to the cities caused a profound change in the rural societies, where their energy had been a vital ingredient of economic and social life. They were the hunters, cooks, entertainers, farm workers, and grave diggers. Many activities around which rural social life revolved were more difficult to perform with smaller numbers of youth. Some of those young people who remained became ambivalent about rural life, as they compared their lifestyles with those of their urban cousins and awaited opportunities to follow them. The steady loss of mature men and women, who had proven themselves at war and in urban industries during the war, and their young families, was another serious loss to the social fabric of rural Maori society. Their leadership potential, and the future contributions of their children, were often lost to the communities as the demands of work and family reduced the frequency of their visits to home *marae*. Other families were split as parents sent their young to the city and remained behind to look after their own aging parents. Some of those who stayed in rural areas did not remain where they had grown up because the opportunities for work were limited. Many became seasonal laborers, dividing their time between home communities and work on shearing and forestry gangs, or as fruit and tobacco pickers, moving around the country to wherever there was employment.

If the impact on rural Maori tribal communities was serious, however, the impact on emerging urban Maori communities was even more so. Many Maori migrants had limited formal education, few job qualifications, and were victims of employer racism. These three factors confined the migrants to a narrow range of semi-skilled and unskilled work. By 1976, 39% of all Maori were engaged in manufacturing, and a further 29% of men were found in transport and communication. Initially, the consequences of this pattern of occupational concentration were limited. Full employment in the booming postwar economy guaranteed relatively high incomes that were protected by labor unions. The government housing programs ensured that urban Maori were relatively well housed on quite reasonable terms, with increasing numbers taking advantage of concessionary home ownership schemes to acquire urban property. Children found a wider range of opportunities in urban schools and greater access to higher education than had been available in the rural areas. Some commentators argue that Maori acceptance of this situation reflected a satisfaction with the newfound improvement of their situation. But this was not to last.

A rapidly growing, better educated, and increasingly organized Maori population, from 1975 on, was able to enroll in "general electorates." As it did so, it was able to exert increasing influence in politics. Leadership was provided both by individuals and such urban political organizations as the New Zealand Maori Council, Maori Women's Welfare League, the Maori Graduates' Organization, the Maori Organization on Human Rights, Nga Tamatoa "The Young Warriors," and the Maori branches of political parties and organized labor. These forces began to develop and to articulate their social, political, and economic claims and objectives more forcefully through the 1960s and 1970s (Te Poata-Smith 1996). A sign of growing Maori anger with the government's failure to acknowledge and redress their concerns was a "march" (*hikoi*) of some 45,000 people through the length of the North Island to Parliament. The march was led by an octogenarian who had been prominent in the Maori Women's Welfare Movement, and it was united around the demand that "not one acre more" of Maori land be alienated (Walker 1990).

A group of Maori graduates was also beginning to identify and publicize evidence of illegal and fraudulent conduct by Pakeha. In doing so, these scholars were beginning to deconstruct the ideology that had guaranteed Pakeha social and political dominance. Of these deconstructions, the most powerful was one entitled *Maori Sovereignty,* written by Donna Awatere (1984), a psychologist and former opera singer who was also a daughter of a former commander of the Maori Battalion. In that work, she took the government's own data and showed that ever since contact — and despite the Treaty of Waitangi — the Maori's social, economic, political, and epidemiological condition had deteriorated. She argued that Pakeha rather than Maori conduct was the source of the current Maori situation, and that nothing short of social, political, and economic sovereignty could lead to the restoration of their rightful position. Other Maori scholars joined in challenging the dominant ideology and called for sovereignty (Greenland 1991; Te Poata-Smith 1996).

In articulating these claims, the new Maori leaders were continuing a long tradition of seeking formal recognition and systematic enforcement of the Treaty. In 1972 the Labor government, which had forged a longstanding political alliance with the Ratana Church and was relatively sympathetic to Maori interests, promised statutory recognition of the Treaty of Waitangi in its election manifesto. In 1975, The Treaty of Waitangi Act was signed into law. It allowed for the establishment of a tribunal that could investigate claims from that date on and advise the government on appropriate forms of action and redress. But Maori pointed out that since the most significant violations of the Treaty involved land and occurred during the wars and land alienations in the 1800s, the Tribunal could do little to resolve the most longstanding and serious disputes between Maori and the crown. In 1985, the government enlarged the Tribunal and allowed it to investigate and recommend redress for all breaches that had occurred since the signing of the Treaty of Waitangi in 1840.

Historical research for Maori claims to the Waitangi Tribunal exposed the nature and extent of Pakeha fraudulence and bad faith. The proceedings of these cases were published in reports to the government, and the issue became more widely understood than had previously been the case. The reports were augmented by an increasing volume of socio-legal scholarship around the Treaty of Waitangi, and this undoubtedly led to a more widespread acceptance by Pakeha of the validity of Maori claims, as well as a more general acceptance of the need to investigate and redress them. It also strengthened Maori resolve to press for settlement, and the number of claims before the Tribunal rapidly grew to some 700. The validity of the Maori claims was confirmed in a 1987 case, *The Maori Council vs. The Attorney General*, in the Court of Appeal. The court found that a special relationship of ongoing partnership exists between Maori and the crown, requiring the partners to act reasonably and in utmost good faith to one another (Statistics New Zealand 2000a, 2000b). This bound the crown in significant ways and prevented it from disposing of crown assets that were the subject of Maori claims or could be used in settlement of claims.

A number of major claims have been heard and settled since 1984. These have resulted in settlements with the specific tribes, such as that with the Tainui Tribes of the Waikato for US$85 million, and with the Ngaitahu Tribes of the South Island for US$90 million. In each case, the settlement included both cash and assets. Some 640 other claims are pending. Because of the complexity of claims, the research for and the hearing of claims by the Waitangi Tribunal takes a great deal of time. In an attempt to hasten justice, which many Maori have sought for over 150 years, the crown has established an Office of Treaty Settlements with which Maori can, in certain cases, negotiate settlements relatively quickly. These settlements have typically resulted in the transfer of crown assets and cash to tribes in an attempt to replace the economic base that the crown undermined when it seized tribal assets earlier.

In addition to its dealings with individuals, the government has reached settlements with the Maori as a people, resulting in the transfer of rights to 10% of the total commercial fishing catch and ownership of half of the country's largest fishing company to the Maori Fisheries Commission. The commission will administer these assets on behalf of Maori until such time as assets can be divided and returned to the tribes.

The government, faced with Pakeha concern about the cost of these settlements, announced a cap of NZ$1 billion; but Maori claim that this is unrealistic and estimate the real value of losses at between US$40 billion and US$60 billion (Statistics New Zealand 2000c). It appears that the government will be forced to revise the cap figure since US$300 million has already been spent on settlements, US$100 million is committed to pending settlements, and a large number of claims remain to be settled.

Many have argued that these settlements are about the return of assets, and this is partly true; but Maori have also sought non-monetary redress, which is at least as important to them. Maori have, for instance, sought acknowledgement of the crown's bad faith and of its failure to act according to the principles of the Treaty of Waitangi. For instance, the Tainui Tribes of the Waikato successfully included a claim for an apology from the British crown for its treatment of Tainui. In another case, a tribe sought the return of a sacred mountain and its *mana* "authority" over the mountain. The tribe then returned legal possession of the mountain to the crown but retained its *mana* over it.

In an attempt to resolve the growing number of claims, the crown has instituted a government ministry, along with the Office for Treaty Settlements, to encourage direct negotiations and speed the process. This was made necessary by the inordinately long wait involved in hearings before the Tribunal (www.ots.govt.nz). In the view of many Maori, the revalidation of the Treaty's status has confirmed what they always knew, and it has given new impetus to the Maori's political and economic activism.

It seems likely that significantly more funds will be required to settle these outstanding claims in ways which are considered just and reasonable, and that the process of settlement will take longer than was originally anticipated. At the same time, growing recognition that justice delayed is justice denied, combined with growing evidence of abrogation of the Treaty, make it likely that future governments will be compelled to meet their Treaty obligations.

Since 1984, the Maori population has steadily increased. Between 1991 and 1996 it grew from 434,847 to 523,371 or 16% of New Zealand's population (www.stats.govt.nz). It is forecast to continue to grow and to reach 21% by 2051. Part of this expansion is undoubtedly the result of a new pride in identifying oneself—and willingness to be counted—as Maori. Tribal membership has increased as Maori have become energized by successes in the Tribunal, the possibilities presented by ownership and management of new assets, and the opportunities for tribes to access government funds to provide alternative social services for their members. Maori culture has also undergone a renaissance. Successive governments have pursued policies of "biculturalism" which have attempted to identify and embody Maori aspirations in government policy. The government, for its part, established in 1992 a Ministry for Maori Development (Te Puni Kokiri), which is responsible for advising the crown on means of obtaining parity between Maori and non-Maori (see www.tpk.govt.nz). Te Puni Kokiri has separate branches that are responsible for advising the government on economic development, treaty compliance, social policy, regional development, implications of law reform, and monitoring and evaluation of government agencies and programs.

Maori have demanded, and have won, opportunities to define their own objectives and to become involved in the design and administration of the processes by which these are delivered. They have also won the right to administer some government resources in order to provide services to Maori populations through "flax roots" organizations such as tribal committees (*runanga*). This policy is based on the assumption that such organizations can provide more appropriate services more effectively than outsiders, thereby improving Maori outcomes in such areas as health, education, and welfare (Te Puni Kokiri 1998). In this respect, Maori have won a much greater degree of autonomy than they enjoyed at any other time since contact. The adoption of a new electoral process has significantly increased the level of Maori representation in the nation's parliament, and the growth of Maori political lobbies has undoubtedly hastened this reform process. While progress is undeniable, however, it is not occurring as quickly as many in either government or the Maori community would like.

The possibility has also emerged that further progress may be hindered by tension among Maori, themselves. Settlement of claims has resulted in the return of assets and cash to properly constituted tribal authorities, representing descendants of the signatories to the Treaty. Many urban Maori have lost contact with their tribal roots and have become members of new urban "pantribal" organizations, which represent their interests in negotiations with government. These urban Maori organizations are seeking the right to share in the distribution of resources on behalf of their urban constituents who are, they argue, also descendants of the signatories and, therefore, entitled to share the benefits of settlements. Part of the argument advanced in support of this claim is that these new urban groups are the Maori "tribes" of the present. They live in and identify with particular locales, have a common history, have *marae* "tribal meeting places" and *whare nui* "meeting houses," which both establish their connection with the place and embody their *mana*. They provide social and economic support and leadership for their members in the ways which tribes did in earlier days.

Summary

The last two hundred years have seen major changes for the Maori population. At one point it seemed that they might lose their identity as population decline, intermarriage, and assimilationist governmental policies eroded their social structures and economic base to the point that governments were faced, at the beginning of the twentieth century, with accusations of genocide. Since then, however, Maori have made a steady recovery. They now constitute 16% of the total population and are one of the fastest growing and most politically assertive segments of the population of Aotearoa. A combination of effective Maori political activity, growing electoral power, and increasing *Pakeha* awareness of the need to redress the consequences of past actions has led to a transformation of the Maori situation at the beginning of the twenty-first century.

The gaps between Maori and non-Maori populations are closing (Te Puni Kokiri 1998), and the Maori's future as a people is assured. The Maori language has been reaffirmed as an official national language, and a network of 690 Maori language pre-schools (*kohanga reo*), along with bilingual programs in schools, universities, and Maori tertiary institutions (*wānanga*), is reviving the language. Tribal and subtribal entities are reestablishing and strengthening their leadership structures through investment in their members' human capital. They are looking to reclaim and redeploy tribal land and other assets for the benefit of their members, and to obtain funds from the government to provide alternative and more culturally appropriate services for their members. A national organization, the Maori Congress, was formed in 1990 to find ways of advancing the interests of all Maori. The Congress includes representatives of 45 tribes and provides a national forum for representatives to address economic, social, cultural, and political issues within a Maori cultural framework. The Congress also promotes constitutional and legislative arrangements designed to enable Maori to control their development and reclaim their sovereignty (*tino rangatiratanga*) within New Zealand. New Zealanders no longer debate whether Maori tribal structures will survive; the question has become the most appropriate form for these in the beginning of the twenty-first century. Most significantly, these debates are being controlled by Maori themselves.

Samoa

Samoa is one of the most famous and contentious sites of anthropological research anywhere in the world. Margaret Mead first brought these islands to wide public attention through her influential book, *Coming of Age in Samoa*. In that work, Mead confronted the commonly held view that adolescence is inevitably a time of emotional stress because of the biological changes which take place in the human body during that period. She asserted that Samoans experience their teen years as an enjoyable period of sexual experimentation, free from the pressures of social disapproval, commitment, and jealousy. The difficulties associated with adolescence in the West, she concluded, are attributable to the social pressures that we place on young people rather than any biologically determined natural process.

Mead's characterization of Samoan social life and the lessons she derived from it were widely accepted among educated readers throughout the Western world until 1983, when Derek Freeman, an Australian anthropologist, published a scathing critique of her Samoan research. In *Margaret Mead and Samoa: The Making and Unmaking of an Anthropological Myth*, Freeman accused Mead of insufficient training, biased observations, and a naiveté that enabled her informants to perpetrate an elaborate hoax. Rather than a peaceful and relaxed community in which sexual experimentation was permitted and violence virtually unknown, Freeman portrayed Samoans as stress-ridden, violence-prone, and sexually repressed to the point that "the cult of female virginity is probably carried to a greater extreme than in any other culture known to anthropology" (Freeman 1983:250).

Freeman's book set in motion a debate in the anthropological community that continues in full force almost two decades later.[20] After scores of articles, books, and documentary films, the only point upon which almost every anthropologist agrees is that both Mead's and Freeman's visions of Samoa contain significant defects. Readers interested in this controversy are referred to the extensive literature currently in print. In the following pages, we will focus on the sociopolitical history of these islands and their vibrant, energetic people.

Prehistory

The Samoan archipelago was settled from the west at least 3000 years ago by bearers of a proto-Polynesian language and culture and Lapita pottery. In that group of 13 islands, over 3000 years of continuous residence, a distinctive culture, language, and society evolved. Some 1200 years after the Samoan Islands were first settled, descendants of those settlers departed to explore and populate Eastern Polynesia. In time, their descendants moved north and south to colonize the islands of Hawai'i, Aotearoa (New Zealand), and Rapanui (Easter Island). For that reason, Samoa is commonly regarded as Polynesia's birthplace, and place names from this ancestral homeland are found throughout the Eastern reaches of the Polynesian Triangle.

After the first waves of emigrants departed for Eastern Polynesia, those who remained in Samoa settled into an apparently comfortable existence on tropical high islands with extensive fringing reefs, some flat coastal land, some streams and rivers, and relatively fertile volcanic soils for cultivating a variety of staple crops. Among the most important were *talo* "taro" (*Colocasia esculenta*), *ta'amū* (*Alocasia macrorrhiza*), *ufi* "yam" (*Dioscorea* sp.), *niu* "coconut," and various *fa'i* "plantains" (*Musa* sp.). These could be grown easily throughout the year and were supplemented by such seasonal tree crops as breadfruit. These, combined with plentiful supplies of fish, shellfish, bush rat (*'iole*), flying fox (*pe'a*), and chickens and other fowl provided ample food. Cyclones and crop failures occasionally caused famines in parts of Samoa, and Samoans identified certain wild famine foods which they could eat until their plantations recovered. Like many Pacific Islanders, they developed means of storing carbohydrate-rich fruits and root crops in fermented form in underground pits. Droughts occasionally affected parts of Samoa, but often even these places had access to coastal springs, created where rainwater was carried through lava tubes to sea level.

Initially, Samoans settled inland, near their gardens; later, more settlement occurred in villages on the coastal fringe (Davidson, et al. 1969). They apparently retained their seagoing capacity, periodically visiting the islands of 'Uvea and Futuna to the west and Tonga and Fiji to the south, in search of specific commodities and skills. Fiji, for instance, was supposed to be the source of Samoan knowledge about tattooing as well as some Samoan medical knowledge. Tonga was a source of spouses for Samoa's elite families, and of the red parrot feathers that were used to decorate the borders of the fine mats for which Samoa has become famous. Some nearby islands are thought to have been settled later by groups of Samoans that were lost at sea. One such island is Pukapuka, in what is now the Northern Cook Islands. Pukapuka is believed by both Samoans and Pukapukans to have been settled by people from the village Pu'apu'a on Savai'i, the largest island of the Samoan archipelago. In addition to these visits, Samoans regularly sailed to other islands within the archipelago in a program of organized visits, known as *malaga*. Such excursions provided an opportunity to create and maintain sociopolitical alliances among the archipelago's most influential descent lines.

The largest unit of precontact Samoan society was apparently the district (*itūmālō*). There were twenty of these, which still form the basis of political representation. Each district contained a number of villages (*nu'u*). Villages were sited around the coast, but each controlled a strip of resources that stretched from the reef opposite the village to the tops of inland mountain ranges, a practice later reproduced in Hawai'i's *ahupua'a*, described earlier. Although not all of the land available to a village was in use at any given time, villages cleared and cultivated new land for plantations as their populations expanded. Village size depended on several factors, including available land resources and the quality of leadership. Villages with significant amounts of fertile land could support relatively large populations, and those with effective leadership attracted new members from other villages. Those with large amounts of fertile land, a large fishery, and effective leadership became Samoa's most important political centers (Gilson 1970).

Each village was an autonomous polity, governed by the heads of the families living there. The leaders, known as *matai*, met regularly in a council or *fono*. This council was charged with maintaining and enhancing the village's social prestige. United villages were powerful villages, and the key to unity was effective and united leadership. The *fono* itself was a model of order: all the titles represented in a council were ranked, and their relative prestige was marked during an opening kava ceremony in a public recitation of the ceremonial "order of precedence," called a *fa'alupega*. The council, in turn, defined the village's interest. It promulgated and enforced local laws and punished those who broke them. It intervened in interpersonal and interfamily disputes. Failure to resolve disputes indicated a lack of leadership and authority. The larger villages were made up of several sub-villages (*pitonu'u*), which means literally, "end of the village." Over time, a *pitonu'u* could grow and become a village in its own right. A new village marked this event by establishing of its own *fono* and, more importantly, creating its own *fa'alupega*.

The *fono* was also empowered to plan public works, exchanges, visits, and occasionally, wars with other villages. The *fono* had at its disposal the services of several groups. Prominent among these were the *'aumāga* "association of untitled men" and the *aualuma* "association of unmarried women who belong to the village." In addition, the *fono* was assisted by the *faletua ma tausi*, an "association of the wives of chiefs and orators," and, much later, by a women's committee (*komiti o tūmamā*), established by the colonial administration to promote public health. On such occasions, the *fono* could require members of the various village groups to put labor and other commodities, such as decorated barkcloth (*siapo*) and the all-important fine mats (*'ie tōga*) at its disposal. These commodities were used in activities in which *tulāfale* "orators," acting on behalf of *ali'i* "chiefs," attempted to increase the sociopolitical capital and prestige of the village and of their families in highly public displays of wealth, generosity, and power (Gilson 1970).

Each village included several major extended families (*'āiga*), each of which was headed by a *matai*, who held its title. The most important *matai* were known as *ali'i* "chiefs," who embodied their families' dignity (*mamalu*) and authority (*mana*). In precontact society, the *ali'i*'s power and authority were substantial.

Each *ali'i* was aided in the execution of secular and political affairs by an "orator" (*tulāfale*), who acted on his behalf. An effective *tulāfale* could use his political and genealogical knowledge and oratorical skills to increase the prestige of the *ali'i* and, indirectly, that of the *'āiga* that he served. An *'āiga* was said to include all those who were bound to its land and title.

Within the *'āiga*, a distinction was made between the descendents of the male siblings of the founding ancestor, who comprised the *tamatāne*, and the descendants of the female siblings, who comprised the *tamafafine*. While much of the power appears to have resided in the *tamatāne*, the relationship was, in reality, complex. The sister and brother, and by extension the *tamafafine* and *tamatāne*, were bound to one another in a covenant (*feagaiga*), which imposed an obligation on males to honor, respect, and protect their sisters. Within an *'āiga*, the *tamafafine* enjoyed a right of veto over any decision made by the *tamatāne*, and they would exercise that veto if they believed they had not been adequately consulted.

The *tamatāne* and *tamafafine* units were frequently too large to cooperate on a daily basis. Their relevance was, therefore, confined to events that involved the entire *'āiga potopoto*, which Milner (1993:11) defined as a "Collective term for all the members of a lineage who have the right to be present at, and to take part in, the election of a new *matai*." *'Āiga potopoto* typically met to discuss matters relating to the family estate and leadership. At such meetings, these units determined the division of labor and responsibility. In daily life, they were relevant only for establishing kinship linkages and associated obligations.

Kinship was crucial in determining one's life chances. Through kinship links one could trace connections to many separate 'āiga in which it was theoretically possible to claim land rights. Individuals typically, however, claimed primary allegiance to one of these. One lived in the village of one's 'āiga and served the 'āiga's titleholder. This set of connections, through which one derived rights to agricultural land, a house site, access to a fishery, and the right to the protection of the chief and family, was said to be the individual's "strong side" (itū mālosi). In return for these rights, individuals bound themselves to serve (tautua) the chief and family. Such service included the obligation to place a certain amount of labor and agricultural production at the disposal of the matai. This included a basic expectation that some part of a person's daily production would be assigned for the chief's use as a form of rent. On special occasions, chiefs could demand additional labor or resources to permit the family or village to engage in major exchanges, such as intervillage visits (malaga) and weddings and funerals of prominent members of family and village.

These resources were designed to extend the family's influence and prestige through exchanges with other families or villages. They indirectly benefited individual members who might become associated with a respected family. Men and women had different obligations, but all had critical roles in maintaining of the family's autonomy and social honor. Women, in particular, created fine mats, which were the measure of the wealth of families and villages (Schoeffel 1999). Men produced and prepared much of the food used in exchanges. These respective contributions, the women's tōga and the men's 'oloa, were necessary and complementary elements of all such exchanges.[21]

In precontact Samoa, the families that controlled the most significant chiefly titles often came into conflict, and war was a fact of life. Families sought to minimize the threat of war by establishing political alliances through intermarriage. The existence of alliances discouraged others from precipitate action against them (Gilson 1970).

European Contact

In 1722, Jacob Roggeveen sailed by and charted Samoa. A little later, an unfortunate misunderstanding between members of La Pérouse's expedition and some Samoans in a village on Tutuila island resulted in the deaths of a dozen sailors who had gone ashore and become marooned on a falling tide. This event won the Samoans a reputation for violence and led many mariners to avoid the archipelago where possible from that time until the 1820s. Wesleyan and London Missionary Society (L.M.S.) missionaries were, however, moving slowly west across the Pacific and reached Samoa in 1830. The Reverend John Williams arrived with a group of Tahitian teachers on Savai'i and, with the assistance of a powerful chief, Mālietoa Vaiinupō of Sāpapāli'i, rapidly established a foothold in Samoa (Moyle 1984).

The rapid progress of the mission reflects two factors. First, the authority (mana) of the chiefs was such that when they were persuaded of the benefits of conversion, they could and did direct members of their 'āiga to adopt the religion. Secondly, Faueā, the Samoan who led the L.M.S. missionaries to Samoa, had warned them against wholesale condemnation of Samoan custom and practice. He alerted them to the fact that, out of deference to their chiefs, Samoans would not automatically and immediately accept the missions' authority. Since the churches would depend heavily on Samoan chiefs for support and protection, the missionaries took Faueā's advice. Although they considered the early Samoans "godless," they did not feel compelled to destroy the culture, idols, or sacred sites as they had in Eastern Polynesia. At first, they sought only to restrict warfare and certain dances, including the infamous pōula "dance-nights," which they considered indecent, and to harness their converts' energy for biblical instruction, agricultural production, and as future missionaries and teachers (Moyle 1984). Later, however, they waged war on Samoan religious practices and led Samoans to renounce their tutelary spirits, violate these spirits' taboos, and destroy the objects wherein the spirits were believed to dwell.

The missionaries returned periodically to England and spread word of their progress in order to raise funds. Among their claims was the assertion that they had paved the way for commerce by establishing respect for property and a demand for goods and services. Before long, commercial interests began to arrive in Samoa seeking cheap land and cheap labor in order to produce such tropical commodities as cotton and copra. The commercial interests' arrival profoundly altered Samoan social life by creating markets for land and labor and presenting alternatives to the traditional forms of social organization (Macpherson 2000).

Attempts by foreign business enterprises to purchase land raised fundamental questions. Could land, which had traditionally been seen as an asset in which rights were temporarily assigned to individuals on the basis of kinship, be alienated permanently to nonkin? Could land, which defined family as well as individual identity, be commodified and converted into the private property of individuals for all time? Could the production from land be then retained for the exclusive use of the "owner" without consideration for the needs of the family to which it had previously belonged? Were chiefs entitled to alienate land and retain the proceeds of land sales for themselves? As land changed hands, the previously unthinkable became reality.

The creation of a market for labor similarly challenged fundamental elements of Samoan social organization. The willingness of Europeans to purchase time from Samoans for their exclusive use was a new phenomenon. The exchange of labor had previously been defined and regulated by kinship. The product of Samoan labor had been retained and used by the *ali'i* and *tulāfale*, but always for the benefit of all members of the *'āiga*. European (*Papālagi*) settlers proposed to buy labor from nonkin, to expropriate the product of that labor, and to retain profits for their exclusive use, without consideration for the circumstances of those who had provided the labor. The notion that labor could be something other than subsistence or service to the *'āiga* was a new one.

Creation of the labor market also raised questions about the nature of authority. In precontact society, the right to demand labor derived from the authority of leadership, which derived in turn from kinship. After contact, the right to demand labor derived from the ownership of resources in cash or kind, which could be used to pay laborers for their work. As a result, individuals were frequently faced with conflicting, yet simultaneous demands for their labor as members of a kin group and as sellers of labor for cash.

The creation of commercial plantations also raised fundamental questions about the nature of community. In precontact times, people lived in villages made up of kin. Their rights and obligations were, likewise, defined by kin relationships. After contact, people had to share living quarters and work with unrelated people on commercial plantations. Rights and obligations were determined and enforced by unrelated people who could terminate relationships at will.[22]

Beginning in the mid-nineteenth century, Samoan social organization faced major challenges from Christianity and from alternative ways of viewing such basic elements as land, labor, and social relationships. Colonial powers exacerbated the disruption by attempting to exercise political control throughout the late nineteenth century. Nonetheless, Samoan social organization withstood the pressures. Initially, resistance was possible because British, German, and U.S. consuls and commercial interests were unable to cooperate, and Samoans were able to play one power off against the others. European powers exercised control in the port town of Apia, but their influence outside was confined to trade and religion.

This situation changed in 1900, when the British renounced their interest in Samoa and the islands were partitioned between Germany and the United States. The Germans assumed control in the western islands, and the U.S. assumed control in the east. From that time on, the pattern of social organization of the two Samoas diverged in important ways. We will focus here on the history of what became known as Western Samoa and, more recently, simply the nation of Samoa.

The Germans were primarily interested in ensuring political stability so that they could pursue their economic interests and guarantee the safety of German citizens. They determined that they could achieve their objectives by exercising political control, and that they did not need to subdue the populace by force (Meleisea 1992). Thus, as long as Samoan commodities were available for trade and taxes were paid, the Germans did not seek to transform Samoan social organization. As a consequence, villages and their polities remained largely autonomous. Village *fono* continued to control the life of villages, and *matai* continued to control the life of the *'āiga* that they headed. Samoans retained control of 87% of Samoan land, producing sufficient food for their needs and a surplus, which was sold to meet family needs and church commitments.

When World War I broke out in 1914, the New Zealand government assumed control of Western Samoa from the Germans on behalf of the British crown. The League of Nations later assigned New Zealand a mandate over Western Samoa. Successive administrations attempted to pursue German plans to reduce the power of many nationally significant Samoan titles and substitute their own authority. However, the New Zealand administrations proved inept. One allowed a ship bearing influenza during the infamous pandemic to land in 1918, and in the months that followed, 22% of the population died.

The New Zealand administrators' ineptitude and arrogance led to a resurgence of Samoan nationalism. In a badly mishandled protest march in Apia in December 1929, nervous New Zealand soldiers shot and killed a nationally prominent high chief, along with eleven other unarmed Samoan protesters (Meleisea 1987).[23] This incident led Samoans to intensify their resistance to colonial attempts to reform their society, and it gave added impetus to the self-government movement known as the Mau a Pule (Field 1984).

A series of New Zealand administrations also pursued the idea of land reform but failed to make significant progress. From the early 1930s until WW II, New Zealand's policy could be best described as benign neglect (Boyd 1969a, 1969b). After WW II, the old mandate was converted to a U.N. trusteeship, and New Zealand was required to prepare Western Samoa for independence (Meleisea 1987).

In the comprehensive consultations preceding independence, Samoans made it clear that they wished to retain the foundation of "traditional" Samoan social organization—their system of chiefly titles and communal land tenure—as the basis of both local and national government (Davidson 1967). While some practices had changed, kinship remained the central organizing principle of social, political, and economic life. Indigenous principles of land tenure remained largely intact, and traditional titleholders, despite some changes in the mechanisms of transmission of chiefly titles, retained control of the national and local government. Alongside these "indigenous elements" was Christianity, which had been Samoanized (see Tiffany 1978) to the point of becoming an integral element of Samoan social organization—as symbolized in the nation's motto, "Samoa is founded on God."

These key elements were ratified by constitutional conventions and embodied in the Constitution of Western Samoa (Davidson 1967). When independence was achieved in 1962, almost nine tenths of the land remained under Samoan control and traditional tenure. A significant proportion of the remainder was taken as reparations from the Germans, held in trust by the New Zealand administration, and returned to the Samoan government at independence. According to government statistics, 97% of the population at the time claimed to be living under the control and authority of a *matai*. And villages were organized around and controlled by the *fono* and the thoroughly indigenized church (Fox and Cumberland 1962).

Post-Independence

After 1962, certain central elements of Samoan social organization would change for all time. In the late 1950s, Western Samoans began to emigrate to American Samoa and New Zealand, and American Samoans began to move to the Hawai'i and the West Coast of the United States, where wage employment was available for semi-skilled and unskilled workers. By the early 1960s, migration chains linked most villages and families into the global economy. One author who located and interviewed Samoans living in places as far apart as Africa, Scandinavia, and South America called his work, *The Samoans: A Global Family* (Sutter 1981). Samoans who had moved away from their home villages were no longer economically dependent on their families for agricultural land and house sites; at the same time their support for their families grew increasingly significant to the families, villages, and nation they had left. Their continued support, reflected in the continuing stream of remittances in both cash and kind (Ahlburg 1991), despite the extreme geographical dispersal, is largely due to the family's importance to Samoans as a source of personal identity.

Many emigrants dedicated significant parts of their wages to support their non-migrant kin by sending cash, goods, and even food back home. An American anthropologist, Paul Shankman, was the first to note that these remittances were often sent directly to the migrants' parents and were not controlled by *matai*. The availability of new and significant sources of cash, which did not always pass through traditional channels, transformed the status of *matai* within *'āiga* and relations among sections of families (Shankman 1976). Families that in earlier times would not have been in a position to claim leadership could now do so, using their new assets to strengthen their claims.

Subtle but important changes in Samoan organization were also occurring as a consequence of changes in land tenure. This further eroded the influence and authority of the *matai* whose power derived, at least in part, from their control over rights to family estates. If people no longer depended on their families and *matai* for agricultural land and a house site, they could opt out of many obligations. As parents, with increasing frequency, passed land directly to their children, the *matai*'s ostensible control over the assignment of land rights has come to be honored largely in the breach. Communal land tenure is, thus, giving way to social and economic pressure for de facto individualization (O'Meara 1990, 1995).

The existence of a small but significant market in freehold land allowed some people to escape traditional authority and to achieve a degree of "independence" from the family. Individualism was further encouraged by the growing number of people who earned wages and no longer depended on the family estate for their livelihood. Some, whose work required them to live away from the family and village, acquired accommodation in the rental market or boarded with relatives in return for a cash payment.

The most far-reaching changes were produced by the electoral system of independent Samoa. The constitution enshrined the *matai*'s status in national law. Only *matai* could run for parliament in 45 of the 47 electorates, and, until 1990, only *matai* had the right to vote in those elections. Families able to deliver the most votes could reasonably expect to enjoy the attention of their Members of Parliament. In order to increase their influence in the outcome of elections, families created and registered new, spurious, chiefly titles known as *matai palota* "voting titles" to increase the numbers of family members eligible to vote (Meleisea 1987).

Eventually, Parliament recognized the potentially serious effect of the proliferation of these "voting titles" and annulled all titles that had not existed on the eve of Western Samoan independence. Families then sought to increase their electoral influence by splitting existing titles so that where, before, one person had typically held the family title, it became common for several to hold it jointly, and all were entitled to vote.

Between 1962 and 1970, the numbers of registered title holders rose from 4,000 to 11,000 (Meleisea and Schoeffel 1983). This proliferation of title holders often created tension within families. Previously, families had accepted the desirability of identifying and installing a single title holder and the right of a *matai* to appoint his successor, albeit after some form of consultation with the family. Now different branches of families often find themselves in competition for control of titles. As competition intensified, tensions grew and families found themselves embroiled in disputes, some of which could no longer be resolved internally and found their way to the Lands and Titles Court for adjudication.

Other changes also posed challenges to Samoa's cultural and social tenets. Traditionally, power had resided with elders who could understand and display competence in traditional forms of knowledge. As Samoan society grew more bureaucratic, new forms of knowledge and types of skill became increasingly important, as they could produce wealth and extend a family's influence. Families, with growing frequency, bestowed titles upon younger people with bureaucratic and technocratic skills, some of whom no longer even resided in the village. While this had happened in exceptional circumstances once before—after the 1918 influenza pandemic—and did not directly devalue traditional knowledge and abilities, it did pose an added challenge to the idea that authority derived from such abilities.

The presence of an increasingly important group of overseas Samoans posed further challenges to the old social order. Some of those who served their families from overseas with remittances have sought recognition and laid claims to titles in Samoa. This placed them in competition with those kin who had remained in the village and had served the *matai* in the traditional way. This competition has raised fundamental questions about the nature of service (*tautua*). Some migrants who succeeded to titles returned to their overseas residences, thereby separating themselves physically from those units over whom they were expected to exercise authority.

Many of the Samoans who left Samoa in the 1950s, 60s, and 70s were committed to Samoan society and its way of life (Pitt and Macpherson 1974). This was reflected in the volume of remittances that they sent to support social and economic development in Samoa, and in the number of visits that they made to Samoa to participate in family and village affairs. Whether their overseas-born children will feel so strongly committed to their parents' place of birth is not yet clear. Some early evidence suggests that they are not (Macpherson 2001).

The presence of large numbers of relatively wealthy and well-educated Samoans abroad constitutes an important force for change within Samoa. They have introduced significant amounts of money, goods, technologies, and, most importantly, new ideas, and in the process have transformed Samoan culture and society in fundamental ways.

Change is not new to Samoa, but in the past *matai* were in a position to govern the pace and direction of change to a much greater degree than is now possible. As long as they controlled access to land and livelihood, they could influence the thoughts and lifestyles of those who depended on agriculture. As dependence on land declined, their power was bound to decrease. This means that the pace of change in Samoan society is likely to accelerate in ways that could not have been anticipated even 25 years ago.

Looking toward the Future

At the turn of the twenty-first century, Samoan society continues to change under these and other pressures. Samoans continue to claim that *fa'asāmoa* "the Samoan way" is constant and, in certain respects, this is correct. Key values and institutions remain intact, albeit transformed in important ways by Christian values. Yet the ways in which these values are enacted and the institutions are organized in practice has changed. In the meantime, Samoan language and culture remain intact, and indeed vibrant, changing as they always have, and finding new means of expressing and giving form to "traditional" values in ways appropriate to a society that is increasingly exposed to global influences. The role and influence of women has grown both in traditional and non-traditional spheres as they gain formal educational qualifications and titles, which open opportunities for them in national public service and politics.

Anuta

In contrast with Samoa and Aotearoa, Anuta is a single island, just a half mile in diameter and over seventy miles from its nearest populated neighbor. Archaeological investigations show that Anuta was populated as early as 1000 B.C. (Kirch and Rosendahl 1973). Oral traditions, however, trace the present population back to a group of immigrants who arrived from the Polynesian heartland about fifteen generations ago. Those immigrants are said to have arrived from Uvea (probably east 'Uvea or Wallis Island) and Tonga. Over the next several generations, additional immigrants arrived from Samoa and Rotuma to the east and Tikopia to the west. Most of the current residents, however, claim descent from the original Uvean leader, a man named Pu Taupare.

Anuta has managed to maintain a value system and the core features of a social order that go back for many generations. Its people still depend primarily on subsistence production to sustain their livelihood. The community continues to be led by two hereditary chiefs whose genealogies are traced back to the original immigrants. The senior chief, known as Te Ariki i Mua or Tui Anuta, is said to be descended through a line of senior males from a great leader and culture hero named Tearakura, who lived about nine generations ago and was responsible for the reordering of Anutan society. After Tearakura's death, he was transformed from an exceptionally powerful human being into the most awesome god in the Anutans' traditional pantheon. As a major god, Tearakura was responsible for the distribution of *mana* and made certain that the largest portion was reserved for his most senior direct male descendant. Consequently, the senior chief holds his position because of the *mana* vested in him as a result of his genealogical connection with Tearakura. The junior chief, called Te Ariki Tepuko or Tui Kainanga, is descended through a line of eldest sons from Tearakura's younger brother, Pu Tepuko, who also went on after death to became a prominent Anutan deity.

According to Anutan traditions, Tearakura and Pu Tepuko, in collaboration with their youngest brother, Tauvakatai, and their brother-in-law, Pu Pangatau, became involved in a series of disputes with the island's other leading families. In the end, they exterminated the remainder of Anuta's male population and established the island's four *kainanga*, a term that we may very loosely gloss as "clans." Anutans identify Tearakura as the founding ancestor of the highest-ranking clan, the Kainanga i Mua. Pu Tepuko began the second-ranking clan, the Kainanga i Tepuko. The third clan, the Kainanga i Pangatau, is descended from Tearakura's two sisters, Nau Ariki and Nau Pangatau, both of whom were married to Pu Pangatau. And the lowest-ranking clan was founded by Tauvakatai.

Anuta's social order, like those of Aotearoa and Samoa, must be understood in relation to the community's kinship system. But the oft-cited Polynesian principles of genealogical connection, seniority, and hierarchy do not exhaust the meaning of kinship on Anuta. As important as genealogical connection is the principle of *aropa*—Anuta's version of the pan-Polynesian notion discussed above under the Hawaiian term, *aloha*. *Aropa* refers to an emotion that we might describe as "love," "empathy," or "compassion," But it is not simply an emotional state; unless it is expressed in concrete terms by giving, sharing, or providing mutual assistance, Anutans dismiss claims of *aropa* as empty verbiage. Sharing food is the most obvious and powerful mechanism through which *aropa* is demonstrated. *Aropa*'s centrality as an Anutan value is clear from the way in which Anutans think of kinship and the way that they define their basic units of social organization.

In the most fundamental sense, people are of two types: enemies and kin. That does not mean active conflict with nonkin, but one can only count on relatives to have one's own well-being at heart. Nonkin are likely to take advantage of you if given the chance and are not to be trusted. Conversely, one has no moral obligation to assist nonkin and is at liberty to cheat, steal from, or even kill them if it is to one's advantage. Thus, it is uncomfortable for a non-relative to stay in the community, and anyone who comes for more than a brief visit must either be killed, driven off, or incorporated into the kinship system. The first two alternatives have not been realistic options for well over a century. The last is accomplished through displays of *aropa*.

Not only is *aropa* a mechanism through which outsiders are domesticated or brought into the kinship system; Anutans distinguish close from distant kin largely on the basis of the intensity with which *aropa* is expressed. And *aropa* is the basis on which households, clans, and membership in the community are distinguished.

Anuta's four *kainanga* are subdivided into a number of *patongia* "cooperating groups" or *pare* "houses," which are the elementary units of social organization. A *pare*, when the term is used in this sense, might be characterized roughly as a patrilateral extended family. Ideally, it consists of a man, his wife and children, his brothers and their wives and children, and the wives and children of the man's own and his brothers' sons. When the daughters marry, they join the "houses" of their husbands and are no longer members of the domestic units into which they were born. Although one can describe *pare* in such genealogical terms, however, Anutans think of them as economic units constructed on the principle of *aropa*.

The *pare* or *patongia* is the elementary unit of ownership, production, and consumption. Ownership of property is not by individuals but by *pare*; and since members of the same house share all their property, *aropa* is expressed most strongly through common membership in such a unit. Brothers should feel *aropa* for one another, and children should feel *aropa* for their parents. As a practical matter, however, brothers sometimes fail to get along, and *aropa* breaks down. When this occurs, the *pare* is divided, with each brother becoming the head of his own "house." Conversely, people may become members of "houses" through mechanisms other than by birth. An "adopted child" (*kauapi*) is a member of both his or her adoptive parents' and natural parents' households. And visitors from overseas are incorporated into the community and kinship system through the expression of *aropa*, by becoming members of one or another Anutan *pare*. The *kainanga* "clan" is fundamentally a group of *pare*, all of whose leaders are descended through males from one of the founding ancestors mentioned above. And it is through membership in a *pare* and *kainanga* that one is recognized as a member of the community at large—the *kanopenua*.

In addition to the units of social organization, *mana*, chieftainship, and leadership at all levels are predicated on *aropa*. A chief's power rests on his *mana*, derived from divine sources. Because of a chief's *mana*, he has the power to bring illness or disaster to anyone who crosses him. In fact, Anutans can cite many cases in which failure to obey or respect a chief in any of the traditionally prescribed ways has resulted in disaster for oneself or one's closest relatives through the operation of *tapu*, that is, as through the automatic workings of the cosmos, irrespective of the chief's willful actions. While the chief's ability to command rests on his *mana*, however, his legitimate authority depends on *aropa*.

A good chief is expected to use his *mana* to ensure the community's health, prosperity, and general well-being. By using his supernatural force in this manner, he demonstrates his *aropa* for people weaker than himself. They, in turn, show the chief their *aropa* through their obedience and respect as demonstrated in first fruits payments, occasional feasts, modes of address, and even bodily posture when in the chief's presence. The relationship between a chief and his subjects as described here also applies to any relationship between people of different rank, although in less extreme form.

Economic and Religious Conflict

Anutan culture's central focus on *aropa* precludes economic competition, exploitation, or any attempt to profit at the expense of one's neighbors and kin. The *aropa* ethic, then, is directly contrary to market-driven principles of capitalist development. Yet, Anutans are part of the wider socioeconomic universe. Over the past century, they have learned to value a variety of material goods that must be obtained through exchange from outside the community. They regard metal knives, axes, and fishhooks, nylon fishing line, kerosene, lanterns, waterproof flashlights, and batteries as necessities. Rice, tinned meats, and other imported foods are much-desired luxuries. People also place a high value on medical care, transportation to and from the island, and formal education. These are all indices of what Anutans regard as "development," and development requires monetary resources.

The quest for money, in turn, has produced a variety of interrelated conflicts on Anuta. This was particularly true at first for those domestic units that were of low rank in the traditional sociopolitical and religious order, and who viewed the market economy as providing an opportunity for social mobility. In order to take full advantage of the money economy, their children needed an education well beyond what they could obtain on Anuta; but that required funds for transportation and tuition. As one strategy for generating the necessary cash, a few families started to sell local crops—taro, bananas, and tobacco—to others whose gardens had been less productive. This, however, was a violation of the *aropa* principle, which stipulated that anything grown on the island was to be shared freely among members of the community and not sold for cash. The senior chief, who views himself as the prime guardian of the island's custom, forbade the sale of locally produced food, but the families that had commenced the practice refused to be deterred.

This turn of events divided the island into factions that might be called progressive and traditionalist. Progressives placed their priority on social mobility in Western terms, including individual initiative and entrepreneurship; and they objected to those aspects of tradition that required the subordination of individual advancement to community well-being. The traditionalists, by contrast, regarded the community's most valuable asset as its ancient custom, the centerpieces of which were the integrity of the chieftainship and the principle of *aropa*. The progressives were challenging both of these and threatening to destroy precisely those characteristics that made Anuta special.

The dispute had ramifications that rippled through the very fabric of Anutan culture. Despite the Anglican church's establishment in 1916, the chiefs have continued to take responsibility for the island's religious rectitude. Anuta has never had its own priest, and the highest-ranking member of the community's church is normally a mission teacher or catechist.[24] The catechist is responsible for organizing church activities, preparing services, teaching Sunday School, and preaching sermons, during which he points out the community's moral failings and provides direction for correcting them. Anuta's catechist in 1972, during Feinberg's first visit to the island, was Pu Tokerau, the senior chief's younger brother. Then, shortly after Feinberg's arrival, the chief ordered construction of a second church and appointed himself catechist of the new church.

In certain critical ways, the chief was simply asserting his traditional role by making himself head of the church. After all, the power and legitimacy of a Polynesian chief derive from his connection with divinity, his god-given *mana*, and his willingness to petition the deities on his community's behalf. Anutans viewed Christianity as compatible with their traditional religious system. Anutans, without exception, appear to be convinced that the old gods and spirits existed, performed most of the deeds that oral traditions attribute to them, and must be taken into account in one's daily life. Christianity simply added a new Deity who is unique in the degree of power that He wields, and who must be worshipped in a particular way—in a special place, with special symbols, using a special language and special routines. The chief is still thought to have exceptional *mana*. The major difference is that his *mana* is now said to come from the Christian God, the ultimate "source of all *mana*," rather than the island's ancient spirits.

The chief's opponents quickly realized that they could make the church into contested ground. They invented a very non-Polynesian separation of church and state and declared that it was unacceptable for the same person to hold the positions of both chief and catechist. Thus, they pressured the chief to step down from one of his posts. They strengthened their position by enlisting on their side a number of the chief's "executive officials," known in Anutan as *nga maru*. And they attempted to divide the chiefs by proclaiming that the junior chief was the island's legitimate ruler.

The senior chief, at first, stood firm. Then, as pressure mounted, he declared that if he had to select one or the other of his positions he would abdicate the chieftainship and retain his post as catechist. The Ariki Tepuko maintained chiefly solidarity, saying that he owed his position to the senior chief, and that if there were no senior chief, there could be no junior chief either.

At one point, tensions rose so high that the senior chief built himself a small house atop the island's hill, well away from the village area. And he took to carrying an adze to defend himself from the assassination attempts that he imagined were imminent. His opponents, meanwhile, were convinced that he intended to attack them with his weapon while they slept.

The stalemate continued for several months until the island was struck by a series of natural disasters, including a drought, famine, and epidemic of dysentery and influenza. The first people to suffer were leaders of the opposition and members of their families; and, as time went on, they continued to bear the brunt of the calamity. This convinced

Anutans that the chief's *mana* remained undiminished, and that they opposed him at their peril. At that point, several opposition leaders publicly apologized for their actions, and some semblance of order was restored. However, the underlying tensions remained, festered, and continued to erupt periodically over the next two decades.

Through all this, one factor that has held the community together is its religion. From 1916 through the end of the twentieth century, the Anglican Church held a virtual monopoly on Anutan spiritual loyalty. Religion continues to dominate the rhythm of Anutan life, much as it did both in pre-Christian times and during Feinberg's first visit to the island in the early 1970s. The sun rises around 5 A.M., and people get up between 5 and 5:30. The morning service starts around 5:45 or 6 A.M. The evening prayer is around 5 o'clock and lasts about a half hour—sometimes up to an hour. All productive activities have to fit in between the two services. Fishing canoes typically come back between 3 and 4 P.M., and people working in their gardens or preparing food in their earth ovens try to finish by around 4 o'clock so they can wash in time for church. It would be an exaggeration to say that everyone goes to church every morning and every evening; but almost everyone goes almost all the time. People hold the view that the traditional gods and spirits probably exist somewhere, in some form. But the church protects its adherents from having to worry about such potentially dangerous beings. And, as in other Polynesian communities, the church has taken over some of the roles of the chiefs. The *pakaari kai* or "first fruits offering" is one prominent example.

Pakaari kai literally means "showing of food." A portion of the first crop to be harvested from a garden after a new planting is taken to the church, where it remains during the evening service. The vegetables then stay there overnight and are eventually sold to raise money for the church.

Fish, like vegetables, are often given to the church. When a canoe goes out for the first time after it has been in storage, the fishermen take some of the catch to the church. Occasionally special offerings are presented to the chiefs, particularly in conjunction with major religious holidays like Christmas and Easter. In pre-Christian times, offerings of vegetables and fish to the chiefs were a regular occurrence.

Despite the central place of Christianity, by the 1990s the island's religious unity began to splinter. A small group of Anutans in Honiara, the Solomon Islands capital, joined the Seventh Day Adventist (S.D.A.) church, then returned home and began to recruit on Anuta. The senior chief, disturbed by the challenge to his island's sense of solidarity, threatened to take his family and move to Patutaka, an uninhabited, rocky outcropping thirty miles to the southeast. After months of posturing and tense negotiations, the S.D.A. converts left Anuta with the understanding that they were not to return until they agreed to rejoin the island's established church.

Rapprochement and Continuing Stress

As of Feinberg's most recent visit to Anuta in October 2000, the community finally appeared to have reestablished a satisfactory balance. The island had enjoyed some years of relative harmony and prosperity. Crops were growing well, and fish were abundant. People had plenty to eat and most of their favorite foods were readily available. They were generally getting along well, worked together smoothly, and appreciated one another's company. People recognized and accepted the chiefs' authority and, except for church fund-raisers, the sale of locally grown foods had been abandoned. Those Seventh Day Adventists still residing on Anuta, with but one exception, agreed to put their differences aside and participate in the regular Anglican services. And as long as they attended church, no one pressed them on their innermost beliefs. If one judges by overt behavior,

Anuta's population as of November 2000 consisted of 339 Anglicans and one Seventh Day Adventist, and the latter was expected to depart the island within the coming months.

This does not mean that everyone was thrilled with all that had transpired. However, complaints were generally minor, and they were expressed quietly and in private. People recognized that things were going well, and no one wanted to be responsible for the reemergence of overt friction. In contrast with the larger Polynesian archipelagoes, division of labor on Anuta remains minimal. The chiefs engage in the same productive activities as everyone else, and they have no more personal wealth than other Anutans. They live in the same kind of house, eat the same foods, and put up with all the same discomforts. Class differentiation in the modern socioeconomic sense has not yet emerged in the community.

The most pressing problem to face Anuta at the beginning of the third millennium is population growth and population control. The community has more than doubled in size over the thirty years since Feinberg was first there, and with 340 people in residence it has an amazing population density of about two thousand human beings per square mile of land. This figure is somewhat deceptive because Anuta's effective resource base extends well beyond the island's half mile of dry land to include a vast network of offshore reefs within a two- or three-mile radius. Currently, the island can support its population surprisingly well. Everyone has plenty to eat. People appear healthy, strong, and energetic, with no obvious signs of malnutrition. However, in case of a major storm, drought, or other natural disaster, the present enviable situation could change very quickly. Perhaps Anuta can survive with a population of 340; but if the number continues to climb, it soon will reach a point of non-sustainability.

Not only will population control determine the long-term viability of the subsistence economy; overcrowding is already undermining the quality of life. People are conscious of crowding. Houses are closer together than ever before, and it is increasingly difficult to find even a few moments of privacy. As of November 2000, people were getting along well and working hard to avoid conflict. They recognize, however, that as their population increases, conflict is inevitable and will grow increasingly severe. Even now, Anutans complain about a rise in antisocial behavior such as theft and sexual misconduct; and with a larger population, social control becomes ever more problematic.

All this was true even before the outbreak of ethnic tension and virtual civil war in the Solomon Islands in 1999. That conflict involves people from the two largest islands of the Solomons, Malaita and Guadalcanal; and the fighting has for the most part been restricted to Guadalcanal, home to Honiara, the national capital. Indirect effects on other islands, including Anuta, however, have been profound. Thousands of people have fled Honiara, businesses have closed down, the nation's major income-generating projects, including oil palm plantations and a gold mine on Guadalcanal, have not been operating, and international trade has almost wholly ceased. Most commodities are in short supply or are completely unavailable, and the opportunity to sell local produce in the capital has been severely restricted. Many people who had been dependent on the cash economy have had to go back to subsistence production in their rural villages, and in the estimation of one local expert (J. Roughan, personal communication) development in the Solomons has been set back twenty-five years.

In October 2000, a peace agreement finally was signed between the warring factions, and Solomon Islanders are setting about the difficult task of rebuilding their devastated country. Should the peace hold and people once again feel safe in moving to the central Solomons, that will release some of the pressure. Anutans resident in Honiara have been working to acquire land for the community in a suburb known as Independence Valley, and if they are successful, that will provide an important safety valve. However, in the absence of population control, even that will only be a temporary solution.

Conclusion

Polynesia covers a vast area, including thousands of islands distributed around the Pacific Ocean, from Rapanui to the eastern part of Papua New Guinea, and from Hawai'i to Aotearoa and the Chatham Islands. The islands also vary in size and topography, from tiny specks of coral sand to the large, high islands of Hawai'i and New Zealand. Yet despite this geographical and ecological diversity, the region shows remarkable linguistic and cultural homogeneity.

Common Polynesian cultural characteristics include a hierarchical system of social and political relations, in which most of those who hold leadership positions were historically—and often still are—hereditary chiefs. Polynesian communities tend to exhibit political centralization, although to varying degrees. Traditionally, rank was also associated with religion, and often with genealogical seniority: the high chiefs were thought to be descended from the most important gods, and others were ranked according to their genealogical nearness to or distance from the senior line. Because of their connection with divinity, chiefs and others of high rank were said to be endowed with awesome *mana*. Their bodies were *tapu*, and their orders had to be obeyed. Opposition to a chief's instructions meant to risk serious punishment, up to and including death. Such punishment might be spiritual, secular, or in some cases both.

While chiefs commanded fear and respect, their legitimacy depended on their use of supernatural connections to ensure their people's welfare and prosperity. Typically, the community was conceptualized as a group of kin—often as a set of extended families or descent groups that cooperated, shared resources, and were mutually interdependent. The principle of mutual support and empathy that held communities together is generally denoted by some variant of the Hawaiian term, *aloha*.

Most Polynesian islands only came into regular contact with the Western world relatively late in the history of European exploration and colonization. Yet, as comparatively small, insular communities, they were vulnerable to the effects of European contact, and their sociocultural fabric was quickly disrupted to varying degrees. The ones most seriously disrupted were generally those in which the value and potential of land to colonial powers were greatest. In Hawai'i and Aotearoa, for instance, imperial powers were prepared to invest greater force to gain access to large areas of agricultural land than they were on small, isolated atolls. Western commodities were introduced, and social relations were altered in response to the money economy (Macpherson 2000). Christianity was introduced early in the history of contact and, despite denominational diversity, is now the dominant religion. It has also become a significant element in social and political organization throughout Polynesia. Nonetheless, many Polynesians have retained elements of their pre-Christian religions so that Christianity in the islands has taken on a distinctively Polynesian flavor. On most islands, chiefs have lost much of their former power to command but have continued to take responsibility for their communities' spiritual and economic well-being.

Political and economic change on many islands has resulted in the introduction of distinct socioeconomic classes. Incorporation into the global political economy has resulted in the commodification of many goods, acts, and services. The *aloha* principle has become increasingly difficult to maintain as societies are divided ever more into "haves" and "have-nots." These may become increasingly important social cleavages in the near future as recent calls for democratization show. Already, Samoa has been forced to move from a form of *matai* suffrage to universal suffrage in response to public demand, and the Tongan monarchy faces similar pressures for democratization. At the same time, population pressure has become a serious problem on most islands, and this has led to emigration. As islanders move to urban centers, often in metropolitan countries, they usually attempt to stay in contact with their families back home, sending remittances in the form of money or goods. But distance and the process of adaptation to life in a non-Polynesian environment makes continued participation in the activities of the rural village difficult. Thus, islanders increasingly find themselves struggling to reconcile adaptation to the realities of the world political and economic order with notions of identity and tradition, whether *fa'asāmoa*, *Maoritanga*, or the Anutans' *tukutukunga tuei*.

While many common themes and challenges run throughout Polynesia, it is important that we not lose sight of the region's diversity. Islands vary enormously in size, climate, ecology, and degree of social stratification and political centralization. And they differ greatly in their degree of geographical and social isolation and the availability of commercially exploitable resources. This, in turn, affects the speed of cultural and social change, and the communities' ability to retain important aspects of their traditional cultures. Thus the smaller, more remote islands have found it difficult to meet the challenge of economic "development," but they frequently have managed to retain large portions of their old sociopolitical and religious systems.

Much of this is also reflected in the islands' relationships to external political entities. Even at the dawn of the twenty-first century, some peoples—like those of French Polynesia—remain in colonial territories under the control of European powers. Others, like Native Hawaiians and the New Zealand Maori, have largely been relegated to the status of marginalized "Fourth World" ethnic minorities in relatively large and economically powerful nation states. Still others, like the Tongans, Samoans, Tuvaluans, and Cook Islanders struggle to make ends meet as citizens of independent or quasi-independent developing nations. Finally, there are the isolated backwaters, the most remote and undeveloped outposts in "developing" nations, where people may be poor but have been forced by circumstances to retain their self-reliance. Each of these variations results in a unique set of responses to the common themes, concerns, and pressures running throughout Polynesia.

1. Two generations of Samoans have now been born and educated overseas since the first migrants left the islands after the Second World War. Their lives are quite different from those of their island-born cousins. (Photo: C. Macpherson)

2. The communitarian bases of island life contrast with the more individualistic values and lifestyles of societies to which islanders migrate in search of work. (Photo: C. Macpherson)

3. Island life provides many satisfactions for young people but relatively few opportunities for wage employment and the lifestyle to which an increasing number aspire. (Photo: C. Macpherson)

4. Woman from Ontong Java Atoll in northwestern Solomon Islands, with traditional tattoo. She is sitting on a coconut grating stool. Photograph was taken on Nukumanu Atoll in Papua New Guinea in 1984. (Photo: R. Feinberg)

5. Islanders from Nukumanu Atoll in Papua New Guinea, sailing an outrigger canoe in the lagoon. (Photo: R. Feinberg)

6. Tepaona, an immigrant from Ontong Java, using a specialized adze to construct a canoe hull on Nukumanu atoll in Papua New Guinea. (Photo: R. Feinberg)

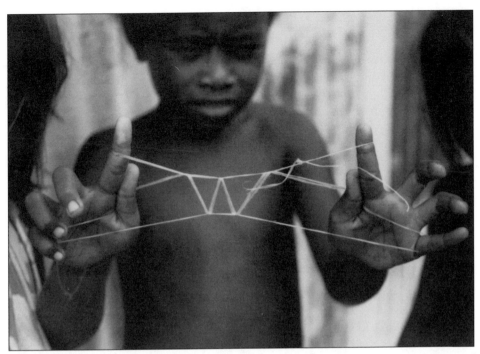

7. Nukumanu child demonstrating a "cat's cradle" string figure. This is a widespread form of entertainment among Polynesian children. (Photo: R. Feinberg)

8. Pu Teukumarae and Pu Teaokena, brothers of Anuta's senior chief, stone-boiling coconut cream in a wooden bowl. This is done by picking up red-hot stones with tongs and placing them in a bowl that has been filled with liquid. Since Polynesians had no metal or ceramic vessels at the time of European contact, they depended on stone-boiling for much of their cooking. Feinberg's (then) five-year-old son, who was about to undergo an Anutan rite of passage, stands to the right. (Photo: R. Feinberg)

9. Cyrtosperma taro arranged for distribution at a spirit releasing ceremony for a deceased chief on Takuu, a Polynesian outlier atoll in Papua New Guinea. (Photo: R. Feinberg)

10a., 10b. Men and women from Takuu Atoll dance at spirit releasing ceremony for deceased chief. This celebration marks the formal end of the mourning period. The spirit of the late chief may now pass on to the world of the dead and a new leader takes control. Takuu and Nukumanu may have been the only Polynesian communities remaining in 1984 where most islanders were not members of a Christian church, and traditional religious rites were actively practiced. (Photo: R. Feinberg)

11. Pu Parikitonga, heir apparent to the paramount chieftainship on Anuta, a Polynesian outlier in the Solomons Islands, expressing coconut cream into a wooden bowl for preparation of a banana "pudding." In foreground is Nau Paone, sister of Anuta's current senior chief. (Photo: R. Feinberg)

12. Pu Avatere (John Tope) dancing at an indoor party in Honiara, the Solomon Islands capital, in 1993. Notice the beer bottle, an essential ingredient for parties in town; alcohol is normally unavailable on the home island. Dances of this kind cannot be performed indoors on the home island because Anutans are forbidden to stand up inside a dwelling house. (Photo: R. Feinberg)

Acknowledgements

We would like to thank Andrew Strathern and Pamela J. Stewart for planning this book and organizing the team that has put it together. We are indebted to them for their constant advice and encouragement as we compiled this section. We owe a special debt of gratitude to Jacob W. Love for his careful reading of the Polynesia section and for his many helpful suggestions, both substantive and stylistic. Chris Fisher of Kent State University's anthropology department used his impressive computer skills to draw the map of Polynesia, which appears as figure 1. Finally, but most importantly, we are indebted to our many friends, informants, relatives, and "custom kin" in Samoa, New Zealand, the Solomon Islands, and Papua New Guinea, who have shared their homes, resources, kindness, and *aloha* during our years of field research in their communities.

Notes

1. Other Polynesian languages have similar sound systems and shared cognates. For example, the New Zealand Maori, like the Anutans, render a snow-capped mountain as *maunga tea*.
2. Samoan traditions, like those of Tonga, record the feats of the god Tagaloa. They identify his land of origin as Samoa and suggest that he then moved across the Pacific, creating and peopling the islands as he went.
3. For information on Tikopia, see particularly Firth (1936, 1939, 1959b, 1961, 1965[1939], 1967a, 1970, 1985, 1991), Hooper (1981), and Kirch and Yen (1982). For Rennell and Bellona, see Elbert and Monberg (1965), Monberg (1991, 1996), Kuschel (1988), and others. Ontong Java has been documented through the work of Sarfert and Damm (1929), Hogbin (1930, 1931, 1932, 1961), Shapiro (1933), and Bayliss-Smith (1974, 1975, 1978, 1987, 1988, 1990). For Kapingamarangi, see Emory (1965), Lieber (1994), and Lieber and Dikepa (1974).
4. For information on Anuta, see Firth (1954), Green (1971), Yen and Gordon (1973), and Feinberg (e.g., 1977, 1979, 1981a, 1988, and 1998). For Nukumanu, see Parkinson (1986[1897]), Sarfert and Damm (1929), and Feinberg (1986a, 1990b, 1995a).
5. The term "swamp taro" or "elephant ear taro" usually refers to *Cyrtosperma chamissonis*. However, atoll dwellers sometimes also grow true taro (*Colocasia esculenta*) in artificially created swampy depressions.
6. Whom to count as a Native Hawaiian can be a contentious issue. Legally, Native Hawaiians are persons accepted as such by the state Office of Hawaiian Affairs. For purposes of this discussion, we would include anyone who claims to be a Native Hawaiian and is accepted by others who make similar claims.
7. The populations of these states and territories are as follows: Samoa (170,000); Fiji (440,000); Tuvalu (10,800); Cook Islands (17,000); Niue (1,900), and Tokelau (1,500). These figures have been compiled from Statistics New Zealand (2000c).
8. Vowel length often carries phonemic significance in Polynesian languages. Most Polynesian orthographies indicate a lengthened vowel either by writing a double letter or a macron—a small horizontal line—above the letter that is to be drawn out in pronunciation.

9. Proto-Polynesian, commonly abbreviated as PPN, is the name for the ancestral language from which all contemporary Polynesian languages have descended. Linguists reconstruct languages such as PPN, which have not been spoken for thousands of years, from detailed comparison of vocabulary lists and grammatical features found in modern-day tongues.

10. We are indebted to Jacob Love (personal communication) for this astute observation.

11. For an exhaustive treatment of Oceanic music, see Kaeppler and Love (1998). For discussions of Polynesian poetry and oral traditions, see Andersen (1928); Dixon (1964[1916]); Beckwith (1970[1940]); Luomala (1949, 1986); Firth (1961, 1991); Elbert and Monberg (1965); Finnegan and Orbell (1995); Love (1991); and many others. A wide-ranging discussion of Polynesian tattooing may be found in Gell (1993).

12. We must, however, qualify this observation. Tepuri, the heir apparent to the position of paramount chief, insisted to Feinberg during a visit in 2000 that Nukumanu regulations regarding bodily contact with chiefs or other persons of high rank were once much stricter than they are today.

13. Variations, of course, exist on this pattern. For example, the Samoan worldview was essentially intact when the missionary, John Williams, arrived in 1830. Williams acknowledged that he would be dependent on chiefs for even a hearing of the gospel, not to mention their protection of his mission. And he expressed gratitude to God for the counsel of a Samoan who had warned him against broad and sweeping condemnations of Samoan culture and practice. However, the indigenous worldview was rapidly and dramatically transformed by Christianity.

14. There is an extensive literature on the abolition of the Hawaiian *kapu* system. Among the more influential treatments are Kalākaua (1888:431–446), Ellis (1917:91–97), Kuykendall (1938:61–70), Kroeber (1948:403–405), Redfield (1953:128–130), and Sahlins (1981:33–66).

15. President Cleveland's report to Congress on the overthrow of the Hawaiian monarchy and attempts to have it annexed by the United States is reprinted in full in Dudley and Agard (1990:25–46).

16. Dudley and Agard (1990) offer a particularly thoughtful and compelling the case in favor of Hawaiian sovereignty.

17. This is evident, for example, in much of Robert Levy's (1970, 1973) commentary on the Tahitian psyche.

18. *Pai kava* "to perform kava" is the Anutans' expression for their traditional worship practice. Kava is a plant in the pepper family (*Piper methysticum*). When mixed with water it has mildly narcotic properties, and many Polynesians drink it both for social and ceremonial occasions. In some places, such as Tikopia, the traditional worship ceremony involved pouring kava libations as an offering to the gods. Anutans report that the kava plant does not grow on their island; instead, they used plain water for their pagan worship rites.

19. After this initial period, the Maori did exert increasing pressure on their natural environment, the most notable illustration being their hunting of the *moa* bird to extinction.

20. The most recent contribution to this debate is an article in the March 2001 issue of the leading journal of Polynesian studies, the *Journal of the Polynesian Society* (Tcherkézoff 2001).

21. See Shore (1982:203–208) for an excellent discussion of these exchanges.

22. See Macpherson (2000) for discussion of European contact and the impact of commercial enterprises on Samoan life.
23. According to Rowe (1930:277), this was after a mutually violent confrontation in which a group of Samoans had stoned a soldier to death.
24. We say "normally" because, on two or three occasions, priests from other parts of the Solomons have stayed on Anuta for brief periods. These, however, have been clearly temporary arrangements.

References

Ahlburg, Denis
1991 Remittances and their impact: a study of Tonga and Western Samoa. Pacific Policy Paper Number 7, National Centre for Development Studies. Canberra: Australian National University

Alkire, William
1965 *Lamotrek Atoll and Inter-Island Socioeconomic Ties*. Urbana: University of Illinois Press.

Andersen, Johannes
1928 *Myths and Legends of the Polynesians*. New York: Farrar and Rinehart.

Asher, G. and D. Naulls
1987 *Maori Land*. Wellington, New Zealand: New Zealand Planning Council.

Awatere, Donna
1984 *Maori Sovereignty*. Auckland: Broadsheet.

Bayliss-Smith Tim
1974 Constraints on population growth: the case of the Polynesian outlier atolls in the pre-contact period. *Human Ecology* 2: 259–295.

1975 Ontong Java: depopulation and repopulation. In *Pacific Atoll Populations*, edited by Vern Carroll. ASAO Monograph Number 3. Honolulu: University of Hawai'i Press. Pp. 417–484.

1978 Changing patterns of inter-island mobility in Ontong Java atoll. *Archaeology and Physical Anthropology in Oceania* 3:41–73.

1987 Tattooing on Ontong Java, Solomon Islands. *Journal of the Polynesian Society* 96:107–110.

1988 Role of hurricanes in the development of reef islands, Ontong Java, Solomon Islands. *Geographical Journal* 54:377–391.

1990 Atoll production systems: fish and fishing on Ontong Java atoll, Solomon Islands. In *Pacific Production Systems*, edited by D. E. Yen and J. Mummery. Canberra: Department of Prehistory, Australian National University. Pp. 57–69.

Bayard, Donn
1966 The cultural relationships of the Polynesian outliers. Honolulu: Department of Anthropology, University of Hawai'i. (M.A. Thesis)

Beckwith, Martha W.
1970 *Hawaiian Mythology*. Honolulu: University of Hawai'i Press. (Original: 1940)

Belich, James
1998   *New Zealand Wars and the Victorian Interpretation of Racial Conflict.* Auckland, New Zealand: Penguin Press.

Bellwood, Peter S.
1978   *The Polynesians: Prehistory of an Island People.* London: Thames and Hudson.
1980   The peopling of the Pacific. *Scientific American* 243(5):174–185.

Biggs, Bruce
1960   *Maori Marriage: An Essay in Reconstruction.* Wellington, New Zealand: Polynesian Society.
1980   The position of East 'Uvean and Anutan in the Polynesian language family. *Te Reo* 23:115–134.

Boyd, Mary
1969a   The Record in Western Samoa to 1945. In *New Zealand's Record in the Pacific Islands in the Twentieth Century,* edited by A. Ross. Auckland, New Zealand: Longman Paul Lt. Pp. 115–188.
1969b   The Record in Western Samoa since 1945. In *New Zealand's Record in the Pacific Islands in the Twentieth Century,* edited by A. Ross. Auckland, New Zealand: Longman Paul Ltd. Pp.189–270.

Buck, Peter H. (Te Rangi Hiroa)
1966   *The Coming of the Maori.* Wellington, New Zealand: Maori Purposes Funds Board and Whitcombe and Tombs Ltd.
1967   *Vikings of the Pacific.* Chicago: University of Chicago Press. (Original: 1938)

Burt, Ben
1988   'Abu'a 'i Kwara'ae: the Meaning of tabu in a Solomon Islands society. *Mankind* 18(2):74–89.

Christiansen, Sofus
1975   *Subsistence on Bellona Island (Mungiki): A Study of the Cultural Ecology of a Polynesian Outlier in the British Solomon Islands Protectorate.* Language and Culture of Rennell and Bellona Islands, Volume 5. Copenhagen: National Museum of Denmark in Cooperation with the Royal Danish Geographical Society.

Codrington, R. H.
1972   *The Melanesians: Studies in their Anthropology and Folklore.* New York: Dover Publications. (Original: 1891)

Churchill, W.
1911   *The Polynesian Wanderings.* Washington, DC: Carnegie Institute Washington Publication 134.

Davidson, Janet M.
1979   Samoa and Tonga. In *The Prehistory of Polynesia,* edited by Jesse D. Jennings. Cambridge, MA: Harvard University Press. Pp. 82–109.

Davidson, Janet M., et al.
1969   Settlement patterns in Samoa before 1840. *Journal of the Polynesian Society* 78(1):44–82.

Davidson, J. W.
1967   *Samoa mo Samoa.* London: Oxford University Press.

Decktor Korn, Shulamit R.

1978 After the missionaries came: denominational diversity in the Tonga Islands. In *Church, Mission, and Sect in Oceania*, edited by James A. Boutilier, Daniel T. Hughes, and Sharon W. Tiffany. ASAO Monograph Number 6. Ann Arbor: University of Michigan Press. Pp. 395–422.

Dixon, Roland B.

1964 *The Mythology of All Races*, Volume 9. Oceanic. New York: Cooper Square. (Original: 1916)

Dodd, Edward

1990 *The Island World of Polynesia*. Putney, VT: Windmill Hill Press.

Dudley, Michael Kioni

1990 *Man, Gods, and Nature: A Hawaiian Nation*, Volume I. Honolulu: Na Kane o Ka Malo Press.

Dudley, Michael Kioni and Keoni Kealoha Agard

1990 *A Call for Hawaiian Sovereignty: A Hawaiian Nation*, Volume II. Honolulu: Na Kane o Ka Malo Press.

Elbert, Samuel and Torben Monberg

1965 *From the Two Canoes: Oral Traditions of Rennell and Bellona Islands*. Copenhagen: National Museum of Denmark.

Ellis, William

1917 *A Narrative of Four Years' Journey through Hawaii or Owhyhee; with remarks on the history, traditions, manners, customs, and language of the inhabitants of the Sandwich Isles*, with an introduction by Lorrin A. Thurston. Honolulu: Hawaiian Gazette Company.

Emory, Kenneth P.

1965 *Kapingamarangi: Social and Religious Life of a Polynesian Atoll*. Bernice P. Bishop Museum Bulletin 228. Honolulu: Bishop Museum Press.

Feinberg, Richard

1976 Archaeology, oral history, and sequence of occupation on Anuta Island. *Journal of the Polynesian Society* 85(1):99–101.

1977 *The Anutan Language Reconsidered: Lexicon and Grammar of a Polynesian Outlier*. Two Volumes. HRAFlex Books. New Haven: Human Relations Area Files Press.

1978 Rank and authority on Anuta. In *Adaptation and Symbolism: Essays in Honor of Sir Raymond Firth*, edited by Karen Ann Watson-Gegeo and S. Lee Seaton. Honolulu: University of Hawai'i Press. Pp. 1–32.

1979 *Anutan Concepts of Disease: A Polynesian Study*. IPS Monograph Number 3. Lā'ie: Institute for Polynesian Studies.

1981a *Anuta: Social Structure of a Polynesian Island*. Lā'ie and Copenhagen: Institute for Polynesian Studies in cooperation with the National Museum of Denmark.

1981b The meaning of 'sibling' in Anutan culture. In *Siblingship in Oceania: Studies in the Meaning of Kin Relations*, edited by Mac Marshall. ASAO Monograph Number 8. Ann Arbor: University of Michigan Press. Pp. 105–148.

1986a Market economy and changing sex-roles on a Polynesian atoll. *Ethnology* 25(4):271–282.

1986b The "Anuta problem": local sovereignty and national integration in the Solomon Islands. *Man* 21(3):438–452.

1988   *Polynesian Seafaring and Navigation: Ocean Travel in Anutan Culture and Society.*
        Kent, OH: Kent State University Press.

1990a   New Guinea models on a Polynesian outlier? *Ethnology* 29(1): 83–86.

1990b   Natural and spiritual etiologies on a Polynesian atoll in Papua New Guinea. *Social Science and Medicine* 30(3):311–323.

1990c   The Solomon Islands tenth anniversary of independence: problems of national symbolism and national integration. *Pacific Studies* 13(2):19–40.

1991   A long-distance voyage in contemporary Polynesia. *Journal of the Polynesian Society* 100(1):25–44.

1995a   Continuity and change in Nukumanu maritime technology and practice. In *Seafaring in the Contemporary Pacific Islands: Studies in Continuity and Change*, edited by Richard Feinberg. DeKalb, IL: Northern Illinois University Press. Pp. 159–195.

1995b   Christian Polynesians and pagan spirits on Anuta Island. *Journal of the Polynesian Society* 104(3):267–301.

1996a   Sanctity and power on Anuta: Polynesian chieftainship revisited. In *Leadership and Change in the Western Pacific: Essays in Honor of Sir Raymond Firth*, edited by Richard Feinberg and Karen Ann Watson-Gegeo. London School of Economics Monographs on Social Anthropology, Number 66. London: Athlone. Pp. 56–92.

1996b   Spirit encounters on Anuta, Solomon Islands. In *Spirits in Culture, History, and Mind*, edited by Jeanette Marie Mageo and Alan Howard. New York and London: Routledge. Pp. 99–120.

1996c   Outer islanders and urban resettlement in the Solomon Islands: the case of Anutans on Guadalcanal. *Journal de la Société des Océanistes* 103(2):207–217.

1998   *Oral Traditions of Anuta: A Polynesian Outlier in the Solomon Islands.* Oxford Studies in Anthropological Linguistics, Volume 15. New York and Oxford: Oxford University Press.

2001   Elements of leadership in Oceania. *Anthropological Forum.* In press.

Field, Michael J.
1984   *Mau: Samoa's Struggle Against New Zealand Oppression.* Wellington, New Zealand: A. H. and A. W. Reed.

Finnegan, Ruth and Margaret Orbell, eds.
1995   *South Pacific Oral Traditions.* Bloomington and Indianapolis: Indiana University Press.

Finney, Ben
1979   *Hōkūle'a, the Way to Tahiti.* New York: Dodd, Mead.

1985   Anomalous westerlies, El Niño, and the colonization of Polynesia. *American Anthropologist* 87:9–26.

Finney, Ben, Paul Frost, Richard Rhodes, and Nainoa Thompson
1989   Wait for the west wind. *Journal of the Polynesian Society* 95:41–90.

Finney, Ben R., et al.
1994   *Voyage of Rediscovery: A Cultural Odyssey through Polynesia.* Berkeley and Los Angeles: University of California Press.

Firth, Raymond
1936   *We, the Tikopia: A Sociological Study of Kinship in Primitive Polynesia.* London: George, Allen, and Unwin.

1939   *The Work of the Gods in Tikopia*. London School of Economics Monographs on Social Anthropology, Numbers 1 and 2. London: Athlone.

1954   Anuta and Tikopia: symbiotic elements in social organization. *Journal of the Polynesian Society* 63:87–131.

1957   A note on descent groups in Polynesia. *Man* 57:4–8.

1959a   *Economics of the New Zealand Maori*. Wellington, New Zealand: R. E Owen, The Government Printer.

1959b   *Social Change in Tikopia*. London: George, Allen, and Unwin.

1961   *History and Traditions of Tikopia*. Polynesian Society Memoir Number 33. Wellington, New Zealand: The Polynesian Society.

1965   *Primitive Polynesian Economy*. Routledge and Kegan Paul. (Original: 1939)

1967a   *Tikopia Ritual and Belief*. Boston: Beacon Press.

1967b   The analysis of mana: an empirical approach. In *Tikopia Ritual and Belief* by Raymond Firth. Boston: Beacon Press. (Original: 1940)

1970   *Rank and Religion in Tikopia: A Study of Polynesian Paganism and Conversion to Christianity*. Boston: Beacon Press.

1985   *Taranga Fakatikopia ma Taranga Fakaainglisi: Tikopia-English Dictionary* (with special assistance from Ishmael Tuki, Pa Rangiaco). Auckland, New Zealand: Oxford University Press in cooperation with the University of Auckland.

1991   *Tikopia Songs: Poetic and Musical Art of a Polynesian People* (with Mervyn McLean). Cambridge: Cambridge University Press.

Fox, J. W. and K. B. Cumberland
1962   *Western Samoa: Land, Life and Agriculture in Tropical Polynesia*. Christchurch: Whitcombe and Tombs.

Fox, Robin
1967   *Kinship and Marriage*. Baltimore: Penguin Books.

Freeman, Derek
1983   *Margaret Mead and Samoa: The Making and Unmaking of an Anthropological Myth*. Cambridge, MA: Harvard University Press.

Gegeo, David W. and Karen Watson-Gegeo
1996   Priest and prince: integrating kastom, Christianity, and modernization in Kwara'ae leadership. In *Leadership and Change in the Western Pacific: Essays Presented to Sir Raymond Firth on the Occasion of his Ninetieth Birthday*, edited by Richard Feinberg and Karen Ann Watson-Gegeo. London School of Economics Monographs on Social Anthropology, Number 66. London: Athlone. Pp. 298–342.

Gell, Alfred
1993   *Wrapping in Images: Tattooing in Polynesia*. Oxford: Clarendon Press.

George, Marianne
2001   The heirs of Lata: documenting authentic Polynesian voyaging in the *Vaka Taumako Project*. Unpublished manuscript.

Gifford, E. W.
1971   *Tongan Society*. Bishop Museum Bulletin Number 61. Honolulu: Bernice P. Bishop Museum Press. (Original: 1929)

Gilson, Richard P.
1970   *Samoa 1830–1900: The Politics of a Multi-cultural Community.* Melbourne: Oxford University Press.

Gladwin, Thomas
1970   *East is a Big Bird: Navigation and Logic on Puluwat Atoll.* Cambridge, MA: Harvard University Press.

Goldman, Irving
1970   *Ancient Polynesian Society.* Chicago: University of Chicago Press.

Goodenough, Ward H.
1955   A problem in Malayo-Polynesian social organization. *American Anthropologist* 57(1):71–83.

Green, Roger C.
1971   Anuta's position in the subgrouping of Polynesian languages. *Journal of the Polynesian Society* 80:355–370.

1976   Lapita sites in the Santa Cruz group. In *Southeast Solomons Culture History*, edited by R. C. Green and M. M. Cresswell. Pp. 245–275. Wellington, New Zealand: Royal Society of New Zealand, Bulletin Number 11.

1978   New sites with Lapita pottery and their implications for an understanding of the settlement of the western Pacific. Auckland, New Zealand: Auckland University Working Papers in Anthropology, Number 51.

Greenland, Hauraki
1991   Maori ethnicity as ideology. In *Nga Take: Ethnic Relations and Racism in Aotearoa/New Zealand*, edited by P. Spoonley, D. Pearson, and C. Macpherson. Palmerston North: Dunmore Press. Pp. 90–107.

Gunson, R. Neil
1978   *Messengers of Grace: Evangelical Missionaries in the South Seas, 1797–1860.* Melbourne: Oxford University Press

Haddon, A. C. and James Hornell
1975   *Canoes of Oceania.* Three Volumes. Honolulu: Bishop Museum Press. (Original: 1936–1938)

Handy, E. S. Craighill
1940   *The Hawaiian Planter.* Bernice P. Bishop Museum Bulletin Number 161. Honolulu: Bishop Museum Press.

Handy, E. S. Craighill and Elizabeth Green Handy
1972   *Native Planters in Old Hawaii: Their Life, Lore, and Environment.* Bernice P. Bishop Museum Bulletin Number 233. Honolulu: Bishop Museum Press.

Handy, E. S. Craighill and Mary Pukui
1972   *The Polynesian Family System in Ka-'u, Hawai'i.* Tokyo: Charles E. Tuttle Company.

Heyerdahl, Thor
1950   *The Kon-Tiki Expedition.* London: Allen and Unwin.

1952   *American Indians in the Pacific.* London: Allen and Unwin.

Hogbin, H. Ian
1930   The problem of depopulation in Melanesia with special reference to Ontong Java. *Journal of the Polynesian Society* 39:43–66.

1931   Social organization of Ontong Java. *Oceania* 1:399–425.

1932   Sorcery in Ontong Java. *American Anthropologist* 34:441–448.

1936   Mana. *Oceania* 6:241–274.

1961   *Law and Order in Polynesia*. Hamden, CT: Shoe String Press. (Original: 1934)

Hooper, Antony
1981   *Why Tikopia has Four Clans*. London: Royal Anthropological Institute of Great Britain and Ireland, Occasional Paper Number 38.

Howard, Alan
1985   History, myth and Polynesian chieftainship: the case of Rotuman kings. In *Transformations of Polynesian Culture*, edited by Antony Hooper and Judith Huntsman. Auckland, New Zealand: Polynesian Society Memoir Number 45. Pp. 39–77.

Irwin, Geoffrey
1992   *The Prehistoric Exploration and Colonisation of the Pacific*. Cambridge: Cambridge University Press.

Jones, Pei
1995   *Nga Iwi o Tainui: The Traditional History of the Tainui People*. Translated by B. G. Biggs. Auckland, New Zealand: Auckland University Press.

Kaeppler, Adrienne and Jacob W. Love, eds.
1998   *The Garland Encylcopedia of World Music: Australia and the Pacific Islands*. New York: Garland.

Kalākaua, David
1888   *The Legends and Myths of Hawaii, the Fables and Folklore of a Strange People*, edited and with an introduction by R. M. Doggett. New York: Webster.

Keesing, Roger M.
1982   *Kwaio Religion: The Living and the Dead in a Solomon Island Society*. New York: Columbia University Press.

1984   Rethinking mana. *Journal of Anthropological Research* 40(1):137–156.

Kelsey, J.
1984   Legal imperialism and the colonisation of Aotearoa. In *Tauiwi: Racism and Ethnicity in New Zealand*, edited by P. Spoonley, Cluny Macpherson, D. Pearson, and C. Sedgwick. Palmerston North, New Zealand: Dunmore Press. Pp. 15–43.

Kirch, Patrick V.
1982   A revision of the Anuta sequence. *Journal of the Polynesian Society* 91:245–254.

1984   The Polynesian outliers: continuity, change, and replacement. *The Journal of Pacific History* 4:224–238.

1985   On the genetic and cultural relationships of certain outlier populations. *American Journal of Physical Anthropology* 66:381–382.

1997   *The Lapita Peoples: Ancestors of the Oceanic World*. Oxford: Blackwell.

2000   *On the Road of the Winds: An Archaeological History of the Pacific Islands before European Contact*. Berkeley, Los Angeles, and London: University of California Press.

Kirch, Patrick V. and Paul H. Rosendahl
1973   Archaeological investigation of Anuta. In *Anuta: A Polynesian Outlier in the Solomon Islands*, edited by D. E. Yen and J. Gordon. Honolulu: Pacific Anthropological Records, Number 21. Department of Anthropology, Bernice P. Bishop Museum. Pp. 25–108.

Kirch, Patrick V. and Douglas E. Yen
1982   *Tikopia: The Prehistory and Ecology of a Polynesian Outlier.* Bernice P. Bishop Museum Bulletin Number 238. Honolulu: Bishop Museum Press.

Kroeber, Alfred L.
1948   *Anthropology.* New York: Harcourt, Brace.

Kuschel, Rolf
1988   *Vengeance Is Their Reply: Blood Feuds and Homicides on Bellona Island.* Two Volumes. Copenhagen: Dansk Psykologisk Forlag.

Kuykendall, Ralph S.
1938   *The Hawaiian Kingdom 1778–1854, Foundation and Transformation.* Honolulu: University of Hawai'i Press.

Kyselka, Will
1987   *An Ocean in Mind.* Honolulu: Bishop Museum Press.

Labby, David
1976   *The Demystification of Yap: Dialectics of Culture on a Micronesian Island.* Chicago: University of Chicago Press.

Laracy, Hugh M.
1969   The first mission to Tikopia. *Journal of Pacific History* 4:105–109.

Leach, Edmund R.
1962   Review of *History and Traditions of Tikopia* by Raymond Firth. *Journal of the Polynesian Society* 71:273–276.

Lessa, William
1966   *Ulithi: A Micronesian Design for Living.* New York: Holt, Rinehart and Winston.

Levison, Michael, R. Gerard Ward, and John W. Webb
1973   *The Settlement of Polynesia: A Computer Simulation.* Minneapolis: University of Minnesota Press.

Levy, Robert I.
1970   Tahitian adoption as a psychological message. In *Adoption in Eastern Oceania*, edited by Vern Carroll. ASAO Monograph Number 1. Honolulu: University of Hawai'i Press. Pp. 71–87.

1973   *Tahitians: Mind and Experience in the Society Islands.* Chicago: University of Chicago Press.

Lewis, David
1972   *We, the Navigators.* Honolulu: University of Hawai'i Press.

1995   The heirs of Lata. *Cruising World*: 56–62. (February 1995)

Lieber, Michael D.
1994   *More than a Living: Fishing and the Social Order on a Polynesian Atoll.* Boulder, CO: Westview Press.

Lieber, Michael D. and Kalio H. Dikepa
1974   *Kapingamarangi Lexicon.* Honolulu: University of Hawai'i Press.

Lingenfelter, Sherwood Galen
1975   *Yap: Political Leadership and Culture Change in an Island Society.* Honolulu: University of Hawai'i Press.

Linnekin, Jocelyn
1990   *Sacred Queens and Women of Consequence: Rank, Gender, and Colonialism in the Hawaiian Islands.* Ann Arbor: University of Michigan Press.

Lockwood, Victoria S.
1993a   *Tahitian Transformation: Gender and Capitalist Development in a Rural Society.* Boulder, CO: Lynne Reindeer.

1993b   Welfare state colonialism in rural French Polynesia. In *Contemporary Pacific Societies: Studies in Development and Change,* edited by Victoria S. Lockwood, Thomas G. Harding, and Ben J. Wallace. Englewood Cliffs, NJ: Prentice Hall. Pp. 81–97.

Love, Jacob Wainright
1991   *Sāmoan Variations: Essays on the Nature of Traditional Oral Arts.* New York and London: Garland Publishing.

Luomala, Katharine
1949   *Maui-of-a-thousand-tricks: His Oceanic and European Biographers.* Bernice P. Bishop Museum Bulletin Number 198. Honolulu: Bishop Museum Press.

1986   *Voices on the Wind" Polynesian Myths and Chants.* Bishop Museum Publication 75. Honolulu: Bishop Museum Press.

Macpherson, Cluny
2000   Changing contours of kinship: the impacts of social and economic development on kinship organisation in the South Pacific. *Pacific Studies* 23(2):71–95.

2001   One trunk sends out many branches. In *Tangata o te Moana Nui: The Evolving Identities of Pacific Peoples in Aotearoa New Zealand,* edited by Cluny Macpherson, P. Spoonley, and Melani Anae. Palmerston North, New Zealand: Dunmore Press. Pp.66–80.

Macpherson, Cluny, P. Spoonley, and Melani Anae, eds.
2001   *Tangata o te Moana Nui: The Evolving Identities of Pacific Peoples in Aotearoa New Zealand.* Palmerston North, New Zealand: Dunmore Press.

Malinowski, Bronislaw
1929   *The Sexual Life of Savages.* New York: Harcourt Brace and World.

Malo, David
1951   *Hawaiian Antiquities (Moolelo Hawaii)*, translated by Nathaniel Emerson. Honolulu: Bishop Museum Press. (Original: 1898)

Marck, Jeff
1996   Kin terms in the Polynesian protolanguages. *Oceanic Linguistics* 35(2):195–257.

Mariner, William
1817   *An Account of the Natives of the Tonga Islands with a Grammar and Vocabulary of their Language.* Compiled from the Communications of W. Mariner by John Martin. Two Volumes. London: J. Martin.

Marshall, Mac
1976   Solidarity or sterility? Adoption and fosterage on Namoluk Atoll. In *Transactions in Kinship: Adoption and Fosterage in Oceania,* edited by Ivan Brady. ASAO Monograph Number 4. Honolulu: University of Hawai'i Press. Pp. 28–50.

1977   The nature of nurture. *American Ethnologist* 4:643–662.

Maude, Henry E.
1981   *Slavers in paradise: the Peruvian slave trade in Polynesia, 1862–1864.* Stanford, CA: Stanford University Press.

McHugh, P. G.

1989   Constitutional theory and Maori claims. In *Waitangi: Maori and Pakeha Perspectives of the Treaty of Waitangi*, edited by Ian Hugh Kawharu. Auckland, New Zealand: Oxford University Press. Pp. 25–63.

Mead, Margaret

1928   *Coming of Age in Samoa*. New York: William Morrow and Company.

Meleisea, Malama

1987   *Lagaga: A Short History of Western Samoa*. Suva: Institute of Pacific Studies, University of the South Pacific.

1992   *Change and Adaptations in Western Samoa*. Christchurch: Macmillan Brown Center for Pacific Studies.

Meleisea, Malama, and Penelope Schoeffel

1983   Western Samoa: like a slippery fish. In *Politics in Polynesia*, edited by A. Ali and Ron G. Crocombe. Suva: University of the South Pacific.

Menton, Linda and Eileen Tamura

1989   *A History of Hawai'i*. Honolulu: Curriculum Research and Development Group, University of Hawai'i.

Metge, Joan

1964   *A New Maori Migration: Rural and Urban Relations in Northern New Zealand*. London School of Economics Monographs on Social Anthropology, Number 27. London and Melbourne: Athlone Press and Melbourne University Press.

1976   *The Maoris of New Zealand, Rautahi*. London: Routledge and Kegan Paul. (Original: 1967)

Milner, G. B.

1993   *Samoan Dictionary*. Auckland, New Zealand: Polynesian Press. (Original: 1966)

Monberg, Torben

1991   *Bellona Island Beliefs and Rituals*. Pacific Islands Monographs Series, Number 9. Honolulu: University of Hawai'i Press.

1996   The Bellonese: high, low—and equal: leadership and change on a Polynesian outlier in the Solomon Islands. In *Leadership and Change in the Western Pacific: Essays in Honor of Sir Raymond Firth* on the Occasion of his Ninetieth Birthday, edited by Richard Feinberg and Karen Ann Watson-Gegeo. London School of Economics Monographs on Social Anthropology, Number 66. London: Athlone Press. Pp. 187–204.

Moyle, Richard

1984   *The Samoan Journals of John Williams 1830 and 1832*. Canberra: Australian National University Press.

Newbury, Colin W.

1980   *Tahiti Nui: Change and Survival in French Polynesia, 1767–1945*. Honolulu: University Press of Hawai'i.

Oliver, Douglas L.

1961   *The Pacific Islands*. Garden City, NY: Doubleday Anchor Books and the American Museum of Natural History. (Original: 1951)

O'Meara, Tim

1990   *Samoan Planters: Tradition and Economic Development in Polynesia*. Fort Worth: Holt, Rinehart and Winston.

1995   From corporate to individual land tenure in Western Samoa. In *Land, Custom and Practice in the South Pacific*, edited by R. G. Ward and E. Kingdon. Cambridge, UK: Cambridge University Press.

Orange, C.
1987   *The Treaty of Waitangi*. Wellington, New Zealand: Allen and Unwin.

1989   *The Story of the Treaty*. Wellington, New Zealand: Allen and Unwin.

Parkinson, Richard H. R.
1986   Ethnography of Ontong Java and Tasman Islands with remarks re: the Marqueen and Abgarris Islands. Translated by Rose Hartmann. Introduced and edited by Richard Feinberg. *Pacific Studies* 9:1–31. (Original: 1897)

Pawley, Andrew K.
1967   The relationships of Polynesian outlier languages. *Journal of the Polynesian Society* 75:259–296.

Petersen, Glenn
1982   *One Man Cannot Rule a Thousand: Fission in a Ponapean Chiefdom*. Ann Arbor: University of Michigan Press.

1999   Sociopolitical rank and conical clanship in the Caroline Islands. *Journal of the Polynesian Society* 108:367–410.

Pitt, David, and Cluny Macpherson
1974   *Emerging Pluralism: The Samoan Community in New Zealand*. Auckland, New Zealand: Longman Paul.

Radcliffe-Brown, A. R.
1952   The mother's brother in South Africa. In *Structure and Function in Primitive Society* by A. R. Radcliffe-Brown. New York: Free Press. (Original: 1924)

Redfield, Robert
1953   *The Primitive World and its Transformations*. Ithaca: Cornell University Press.

Rowe, N. A.
1930   *Samoa under the Sailing Gods*. New York and London: Putnam.

Sahlins, Marshall D.
1958   *Social Stratification in Polynesia*. American Ethnological Society Monograph Number 29. Seattle: University of Washington Press.

1981   *Historical Metaphors and Mythical Realities: Structure in the Early History of the Sandwich Island Kingdom*. Association for Social Anthropology in Oceania Special Publication Number 1. Ann Arbor: University of Michigan Press.

Salmond, Anne
1989   Tribal words, tribal worlds: the translatability of tapu and mana. In *Culture, Kin, and Cognition in Oceania: Essays in Honor of Ward H. Goodenough*, edited by Mac Marshall and John L. Caughey. American Anthropological Association Special Publication Number 25. Washington, DC: American Anthropological Association. Pp. 55–78.

Sarfert, Ernst and Hans Damm
1929   *Luangiua und Nukumanu*. Two volumes. Hamburg: Friedrichsen, De Gruyter.

Schoeffel, Penelope
1999   Samoan exchange and 'fine mats': an historical reconsideration. *Journal of the Polynesian Society* 108(2):117–148.

Shankman, Paul
1976   *Migration and Underdevelopment: The Case of Western Samoa*. Boulder, CO: Westview Press.

Shapiro, Harry L.
1933   Are the Ontong Javanese Polynesian? *Oceania* 3:367–376.

Sharp, Andrew
1957   *Ancient Voyagers in the Pacific*. Harmondsworth, Middlesex: Penguin Books.

Shore, Bradd
1982   *Sala'ilua: A Samoan Mystery*. New York: Columbia University Press.

1989   Mana and tapu. In *Developments in Polynesian Ethnology*, edited by Alan Howard and Robert Borofsky. Honolulu: University of Hawai'i Press. Pp. 137–173.

Stannard, David E.
1989   *Before the Horror*. Honolulu: Social Science Research Institute, University of Hawai'i.

Statistics New Zealand
1996   *New Zealand Census of Population and Dwellings*. Wellington: Statistics New Zealand.

2000a   Maori. In *New Zealand Official Yearbook, 2000*. Wellington, New Zealand: Statistics New Zealand and David Bateman Ltd. Pp. 136–140.

2000b   Maori society. In *New Zealand Official Yearbook 2000*. Wellington, New Zealand: Statistics New Zealand and David Bateman Ltd. Pp. 141–150.

2000c   *New Zealand Official Yearbook 2000*. Wellington, New Zealand: Statistics New Zealand and David Bateman Ltd.

Sutherland, I. L. G.
1949   The Maori revival. In *Yearbook of Education*. London: Evans Brothers. Pp. 213–221.

Sutter, Frederic Koehler
1981   *The Samoans: A Global Family*. Honolulu: University of Hawai'i Press.

Tcherkézoff, Serge
2001   Is anthropology about individual agency or culture? Or why "Old Derek" is doubly wrong. *Journal of the Polynesian Society* 110(1):59–78.

Te Poata-Smith, Evan S.
1996   He pokeke uenuku i tu ai: the evolution of contemporary Maori protest. In *Nga Patai: Racism and Ethnic Relations in Aotearoa New Zealand*, edited by P. Spoonley, Cluny Macpherson, and D. Pearson. Palmerston North, New Zealand: Dunmore Press. Pp. 97–116.

Te Puni Kokiri (Ministry for Maori Development)
1998   *Progress Towards Closing Social and Economic Gaps Between Maori and non-Maori*. Wellington, New Zealand: Te Puni Kokiri.

Terrell, John Edward
1998   The prehistoric Pacific. *Archaeology* 51(6):56–63.

Thomas, Stephen D.
1987   *The Last Navigator*. New York: Henry Holt and Company.

Tiffany, Sharon
1978　The politics of denominational organization in Samoa. In *Church, Mission, and Sect in Oceania*, edited by James A. Boutilier, Daniel T. Hughes, and Sharon W. Tiffany. ASAO Monograph Number 6. Ann Arbor: University of Michigan Press. Pp. 423–456.

Vayda, Andrew P.
1960　*Maori Warfare*. Wellington, New Zealand: The Polynesian Society.

Walker, Rangiui
1990　*Ka Whawhai Tonu Matou: Struggle Without End*. Auckland, New Zealand: Penguin.

Watson-Gegeo, Karen Ann and David W. Gegeo
1990　Shaping the mind and straightening out conflicts: the discourse of Kwara'ae family counseling. In *Disentangling: Conflict Discourse in Pacific Societies*, edited by Karen Watson-Gegeo and Geoffrey M. White. Stanford, California: Stanford University Press. Pp. 161–213.

Weiner, Annette
1976　*Women of Value, Men of Renown: New Perspectives in Trobriand Exchange*. Austin: University of Texas Press.

1988　*The Trobrianders of Papua New Guinea*. New York: Holt, Rinehart and Winston.

White, J. Peter
1979　Melanesia. In *The Prehistory of Polynesia*, edited by Jesse D. Jennings. Cambridge, MA: Harvard University Press. Pp. 352–377.

Yen, Douglas
1974　*The Sweet Potato and Oceania: An Essay in Ethnobotany*. Bernice P. Bishop Museum Bulletin Number 236. Honolulu: Bishop Museum Press.

Yen, Douglas E. and Janet Gordon
1973　*Anuta: A Polynesian Outlier in the Solomon Islands*. Pacific Anthropological Records, Number 21. Honolulu: Department of Anthropology, Bernice P. Bishop Museum.

Part III

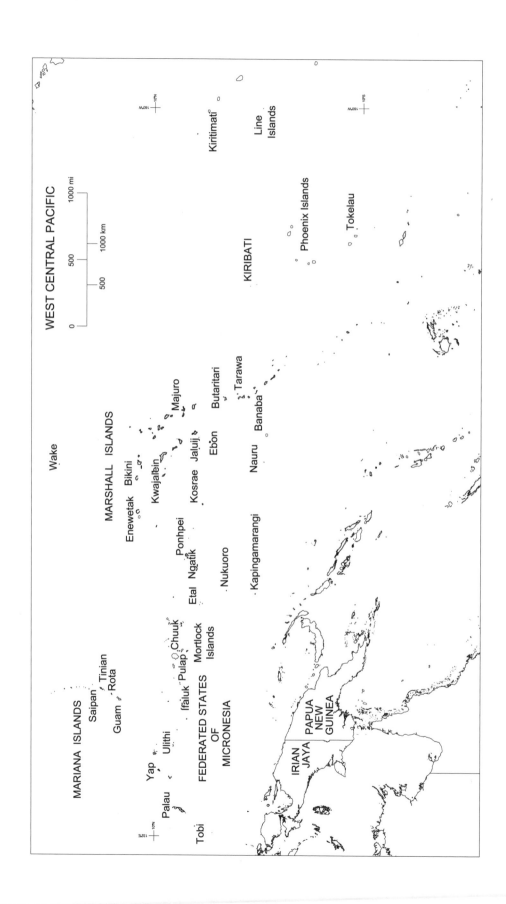

WEST CENTRAL PACIFIC

The West Central Pacific

by Laurence M. Carucci and Lin Poyer

Ecology and Society

The region that Europeans came to call Micronesia consists of a huge ocean-scape, stretching from Christmas Island and the other atolls that Europeans called the Line Islands (now part of Kiribati at 160° West Longitude), across the International Date Line to Tobi at the western fringe of the Pacific (part of Belau at 145° East Longitude). The region extends from the southernmost sectors of Kiribati at approximately 7° South Latitude to the Northernmost Mariana Islands at about 17° North Latitude. This huge expanse of ocean is larger than the United States, but with a total combined landmass no larger than a square of land approximately 30 miles on each side. With this vast expanse of ocean serving to interconnect residents held momentarily at a distance by the small spits of land on which they reside, it is little wonder that Micronesian people are some of the finest seafarers in the world.

The sea that links people together (Carroll [1972]; Hau'ofa [1993]) is an intricately charted web of predictably mobile swells, currents, and waves that inform the experienced mariner of the location of land unseen. It is overflown by birds with patterned paths of flight, some navigators themselves, others linked to shorelines to which they must return nightly. And the expanse of sea is illuminated by stars and culture-specific constellations, often the residues of deity-chiefs of ancient times, who delineate, in the stories of their travels, the mariner's paths which are well known to the experienced sojourners of the west central Pacific.

The land, too, is varied, with high islands, complex atolls, and strings of sandspits strewn around the hidden rims of subsurface volcanoes. On account of their limited size, in part, these snippets of land are critically valued by local peoples of Micronesia who embed fragments of their own histories and identities in features of the land, the reef, and the lagoon. The soil quality of the continental islands and high volcanic islands ensures a relatively rich array of resources in comparison with coraline atoll lands, while a complex atoll like Chuuk, with both high islands and reef islet, offers the most diverse environmental circumstance. Even though the recent colonial and post-colonial eras, the advent of world capitalism, and the deep-pockets of the military, have culturally re-contoured environments like Kwajalein and Guam, local ecological circumstances continue to have substantial impacts on how humans conduct their lives in Micronesia.

Anthropologists have long recognized the relationship between the simplicity or elaboration of social organization and the ecology of particular areas. In the islands of the west central Pacific, differences in environmental circumstance are important considerations that allow for more complex sorts of social organization. In a classical sense, high island societies, with a much more diverse array of resources and a greater ability to support large, concentrated populations, allow for more elaborated and hierarchical forms of social organization. Atolls with limited land and small lagoons or coral pinnacles with difficult access to the sea are far less likely to be the centers of developed chiefdoms with numerous specialized social roles and substantial hierarchy. Equally critical, however, high island inhabitants do not *necessarily* develop more hierarchical forms of social organization than do atoll-based societies. If the initial impressions of European explorers are correct, social hierarchy in Chuuk—a large complex atoll, with high central islands and smaller, fringing islets, as well as distinct surrounding atolls—was no greater than in Kiribati or the Marshall Islands, comprised entirely of atolls. Nevertheless, the societies displaying the greatest social complexity at the time of European contact are thought to be Pohnpei, Kosrae, and the high island societies west of the Andesite Line: Yap and Belau, and the Mariana Island groups. As noted, archaeological evidence suggests that during earlier historical eras, high island locations like Saipan may have supported societies of even greater complexity than those first encountered by early European explorers. Environment therefore fosters or enables greater population concentration and social elaboration, but does not, in and of itself, cause it to come into being. The Andesite Line, which separates the islands that are geologically part of the Asian continent from the sub-surface mountains of the Pacific basin, is critical in this region not only because it separates human groups with different settlement histories, but also because the disparate ecological circumstances of eastern and western Micronesia have dissimilar potentials for human habitation. Many of the large high islands with rich soils fall west of the Andesite Line, and most of the atolls and smaller volcanic high islands lie to the east of it.

More nuanced ecological factors are equally important. Like Nauru, just off the equator, several inhabited parts of Micronesia fall within the tropics where high rainfall and periods of doldrums make the landspaces lush and productive but, during parts of the year, sultry and steamy. Near the equator, rainfall approaches or exceeds 200 inches per year, the vegetation becomes more lush, and the array of food crops that can be raised— tapioca, taro, papayas, bananas and others—becomes more diverse. As one travels farther north of the equator, particularly in the coraline soils of the northern Marshall Islands, rainfall decreases and dry season winds can be blustery. Lacking the deep humus that allows root crops to flourish, these locations are ecologically more restrictive. The range of food crops that can be grown in these drier climes (with 50–100 inches of rainfall per year) is much narrower—pandanus, coconut, arrowroot, squash, certain types of breadfruit and, occasionally, dry-land taro—and even this restricted array of staples are grown with more difficulty than in latitudes closer to the equator (Mason 1947). Particularly on the atolls in these latitudes, people become more dependent on the sea and, not surprisingly, this increasing dependence on the sea combined with relative isolation means that some of the finest sailors find their homes in the small atolls of the west central Pacific. As Feinberg notes (1995), the inverse relationship between sailing skill and available land mass is a general pattern that seems to typify all parts of Pacific and, perhaps, maritime regions throughout the world. At the opposite pole, larger scale horticultural societies could only develop on high islands that had the landmass and lush soils that could sustain a substantial population.

Typhoons represent a further constraint on social organizational complexity that has had devastating effects on many parts of the region, but which have dealt their most severe blows on small atolls. The central sections of Micronesia, from Yap north to Guam, tend to be hardest hit by severe tropical storms, but typhoons are of considerable concern elsewhere as well.

Subsistence

Like most residents of the Pacific, people in the west central Pacific have long subsisted as gatherers, small-scale horticulturalists, and fisherfolk. Nevertheless, few domains of life in Micronesia have been transformed as radically in the past century as has subsistence. If large centers like Nan Madol and Lelu were supported by products from the hinterlands, Micronesia's current urban residents are highly dependent upon products from large Pacific countries like New Zealand and Australia, and the Philippines, and upon nations on the Pacific Rim: Japan, Taiwan, mainland China, and the United States. While residents of the typhoon-vulnerable outer atolls once suffered from risk of cyclical food shortages, urban dwellers now are at greatest risk from an epidemic of "first world" diseases like Type II Diabetes, heart disease, high blood pressure, and hypertension. These illnesses are the result of colonially-constructed dependence on outside foodstuffs, correlating directly with the trend toward urban living in the government and economic centers of the region (Pollock 1992; Carucci in press). Current day staples include polished rice, granulated sugar, and bleached flour. High fat canned meats often complement these staples, and high fat cooking techniques are often the easiest option for urban dwellers without access to firewood. Outer island residents, who blend imported foods with nutrient-rich local products, and who prepare foods in traditional ways, are typically less affected by diet-related health problems. Not only are health problems of this sort predominantly urban, they also are far more frequent in the former American-administered Trust Territory of the Pacific Islands than in Kiribati, where British colonialism produced far less dependence.

High ranked imported foods (culturally valued because of their rarity) have long been a part of Pacific patterns of consumption. Only as concomitant lifestyle changes have accompanied urbanization, however, have the negative health consequences of this pattern become evident. During the Japanese era many residents recall the varied and aromatic array of foods that were available from Koror, Belau to Jaluij, Marshall Islands. And even nineteenth century exchanges between explorers, entrepreneurs, missionaries, and local people commonly included foodstuffs. During these pre-colonial and early colonial times, however, Micronesians were more often the providers of goods for European and Japanese markets. In contrast, in the American era, Micronesians were brought into exchange networks primarily as consumers. Food and other sorts of "development aid" are among the principal exchangeables. The local "product" of greatest interest to the U.S. has been Micronesia's strategic position, both as a pathway to the Japanese homeland during the war and as a buffer against perceived communist threats from the Soviet Union during the cold war and largely from China in the current day.

The movement of food across the Pacific began with the settlement history of Polynesia and Micronesia, and food exchanges have long linked residents of different islands and atolls together. Many of these exchanges are closely tied to the subsistence potential of different environments, with atoll dwellers being highly dependent on the products of the sea, and the residents of high islands being far more committed to plant foods. Each subsistence strategy carries some risk, and all are at some risk from typhoons. High island residents rely on tapioca, taro, breadfruit and—in the case of Saipan—rice, foods that are far more dependable and far more productive than is the atoll dwellers' higher level of dependence on the products of the sea. Nevertheless, atoll dwellers are extraordinarily adept at exploiting marine resources. In fishing, numerous strategies are utilized to harvest fish, including several varieties of traps and weirs, nets, spears, hook and line techniques specialized for a variety of reef fishing, bottom fishing, and trolling situations, hand-capturing fish, and attracting fish, dolphins and whales using light or sound before dispatching them with efficient weapons (Lieber 1994 describes many of these for Kapingamarangi). Group fishing methods are often used, and the surround technique is a highly productive method that allows hundreds or thousands of fish to be concentrated in an increasingly small section of shallow water prior to being killed. Fishing for flying fish is a particularly exciting endeavor. The fish are attracted to a source of light at night and trapped by fishermen with small Lacrosse-like nets while perched on the edge of a sailing canoe or small motor craft as sharks, attracted to the commotion, attempt to secure their share from below. Not uncommonly men are associated with the sea and are the only ones allowed to fish outside of the reef. Women are more likely to be associated with the land and the products of the land. This division of labor is also common in many parts of Polynesia. Nevertheless, in some Micronesian locations women do much of the fishing, serving to remind us that there is no natural or necessary determination of gender roles.

Land foods are commonly grown on family-owned land parcels which, at one time, were divided so as to give each group access to resources from the various ecological niches. On high islands, this typically meant families had access to a wide array of sea products, to firewood, building materials, medicinal plants, and other resources in the highlands, and to the planting and residence zones in between. On atolls, land parcels typically run from lagoon to ocean, with habitations concentrated along the lagoon shore and crop lands toward the ocean. In many cases, atoll dwellers have access to lands on main and outer islets, or on different sections of main islets that possess resources not available on the residence parcel. As populations have increased beyond the productive capacity of an island, the need to maintain resource balance among subsistence units is no longer of concern. Many people have become dependent on outside resources, and some family members become specialists, holding government jobs, working in businesses, or providing specialized products for market. With these changes, extended families commonly divide their lands with an eye to new goals. Access to a road or to local stores may now be more critical than the foods one grows on one's family's land. Since subsistence practices vary, land tenure in the current day may well deviate from the time-tested schemata that once ensured a balance between family land parcel contours and the productive capacities of the land.

Residents of Micronesia are renowned for their in-depth knowledge of the sea (Johannes 1981), and this knowledge is particularly sophisticated among atoll dwellers who are highly dependent on marine resources for their sustenance. Islanders who depend on land resources, however, are equally adept at developing sophisticated cultural procedures for the use of those products. In many parts of the region, coconut is a core product, brought into prominence at the end of the whaling era as a new source of oil for European markets. By the1860s, coconut oil production was widespread, soon to be replaced by the export of dried coconut (copra) for processing elsewhere. With the prominence of copra, many people came to think of coconut as the most important resource in their environment. Coconuts could be used at every part of the developmental cycle as a food source. Green drinking coconuts, typically harvested by highly skilled tree climbers, provide liquid sustenance even in areas where no potable water is available.

The soft meat is also consumed at this stage, using "spoons" fashioned from the husk. Brown copra-stage coconuts, fallen to the ground, provide food during times of shortage. Transformed into grated coconut with coconut scrapers, coconut milk or cream can then be squeezed out of grated coconut. The refuse is commonly used as pig fodder, or made into copra cake, an excellent fertilizer. Coconut cream, used in the preparation of taro, breadfruit, pandanus and other staples, is then rendered into oil which local people use for cooking, lamp oil, as skin conditioner, hair tonic, and, in its purest state, as the base for many local medicines. Once the nut has sprouted, both sprout and the developing endosperm within are used as food, either raw or in various cooked forms. In many locations, coconut trees are also tapped for toddy (Marshall, 1975, 1976; Carucci 1987), a high-nutrient drink which is also fermented into an alcoholic beverage. Special types of coconut husk are edible, and early stage coconut liquids are frequently employed as the emulsifier for medicines. The fronds of the coconut are used for weaving rough-hewn mats, for thatching short-term shelters, or processed for weaving the finest handicrafts. The spathes of the coconut are used as fuel, and as (initially) fire-resistant wrap to transport live coals. Heart of palm is also a delicacy, which requires the sacrifice of a tree, and the wood of the coconut, once cured, will become extremely hard. This wood was once used to manufacture weapons. Coconut trees and products are often the sites where highly elaborated myths and stories are developed to articulate the interactions between sacred ancestral beings and current day humans, or to weave the histories of the human past into important features of the surrounding landscape. Other products of the land—taro, tapioca, breadfruit, pandanus—provide similar sites of cultural elaboration when they are prominent in local people's lives.

Prehistory

Introduction to the Archaeology of Micronesia

Archaeological research in Micronesia has undergone a major expansion over the past three decades. Although a few islands saw earlier work by German, Japanese and American archaeologists, only since the 1970s have we had enough information to seek to integrate the prehistory of Micronesia into the broader story of the Pacific region. In Geoffrey Irwin's *The Prehistoric Exploration and Colonization of the Pacific* 1992:117), he termed Micronesia's prehistory "largely unknown, and its role in Pacific colonization most problematical." Yet the past decade of work has brought an outline of Micronesia's human origins into focus.

The most important fact to keep in mind in understanding anything about Micronesia—from its prehistoric settlements to its modern politics—is that "Micronesia" does not exist. Of course all such units are lines on a map, but Micronesia has less reason for existence than most (Hanlon 1989). In his review of the region's archaeology, Paul Rainbird (1994:296) reminds us that "There is no cohesive 'Micronesian culture'; the area in question is marked not only by its geographic and ethnic diversity, but by its obvious connections with places external to the conceptual construct reified by a line on the map"—that is, it is colonial history that has produced the modern political geography of Micronesia.

To study prehistory, Rainbird (1994) suggests we look at this area in biogeographical, geological and linguistic terms. When we do this, we can see two groups of islands: in the west, the large continental islands of the Marianas, Palau and Yap; and the central and eastern islands (the Marshall, Kiribati, and eastern Caroline groups). None of these islands were occupied during the initial settling of Australia and New Guinea more than 40,000 years ago, and the region remained undiscovered during the initial settlement of Melanesia. Then, around 5,000 years ago, another group entered the Pacific from southeast Asia, the speakers of proto-Austronesian who were the ancestors of Polynesians and, in part, of Micronesians (Kiste 1994a:9).

At this point, the prehistory of the far western, and the central and eastern, Micronesian islands must be examined separately. Evidence to date suggests that the Marianas, Palau and Yap were settled earlier and from a different source than the rest of the Carolines, the Marshalls and Kiribati. (Nukuoro and Kapingamarangi, two Polynesian outliers, have their own distinct prehistories.) While one path into Oceania can be traced through Lapita culture, another entered the Pacific earlier, and directly from island southeast Asia (Oliver 1989:21,25).

Western Micronesia

Our current understanding is that the first settlement of the area now called Micronesia was in the westernmost islands. Radiocarbon dates from the Marianas go back 3500 years, with evidence suggesting that Yap and Palau were settled somewhat later. But dates may well be pushed back by new archaeological and paleoenvironmental research; it is not clear that there was a single settlement event, or several; nor is it clear whether these three island groups were settled from the same sources.

If people settled the Marianas at about 3500 BP (around 1930–1630 B.C.), that would mean that they were moving north at about the same time the Lapita pottery people were moving into Melanesia, and the settlement of western Micronesia was part of the same expansion out of island southeast Asia and eastern Micronesia that produced the Lapita colonization. (Archaeologists working in Micronesia are willing to speculate that evidence may eventually show human settlement of western Micronesia before the Lapita expansion [Kirch 2000:173]).

Where was this southeast Asian source of western Micronesian settlers? Archeologists have proposed several possibilities; an origin in the Philippines would fit Irwin's (1992) model of Pacific colonization; ceramic and linguistic comparisons also hint at links between the Marianas and Taiwan (Kirch 2000:172). Studies of pottery from the Marianas might eventually allow us to identify a specific homeland, but perhaps the Marianas were settled by people from various origins (Butler 1994). Palau and Yap were settled slightly later and perhaps from different origins—Palau may have been settled directly from the Indo-Malaysian archipelago, perhaps the Celebes, at about 2000 BP; Yap may have been settled directly from the Bismarck Archipelago. But these scenarios of the initial settlement of Micronesia are tentative, subject to change as more archaeology is done (Howe 1984:11–12; Kirch and Weisler 1994; Kirch 2000:170).

Evidence for the lives of the first settlers of the Marianas remains scarce, probably because of erosion and coastal alluvial deposition. A detailed study of four prehistoric villages on Rota (Butler 1988:xxix–xxxii) showed occupation from about 2000 BP to 1680–1700 AD, when Spanish forcibly relocated the indigenous Chamorro people to Guam. This study indicates how prehistoric Chamorro culture changed as the pioneer population expanded and settled into its new home. Ancient Chamorros relied on marine resources—deep-sea and reef fish and shellfish. They used Tridacna-shell adzes, and stone flakes for cutting and scraping (some of the stone imported from other is-lands). The first latte structures were built in this area about AD 1000–1200. People buried their dead beneath or near the lattes. Analysis of burials reveals a population that suffered great mortality in the childhood years, but reasonably good health for adults. Starting about 1000 AD, an earlier style of plain pottery, consisting of mostly shallow bowls and pans, gives way to tall globular vessels with a roughened finish, suitable for carrying and storing water or for boiling food. After AD 1200, inland villages appear, suggesting that population growth was forcing some people to live away from the sea, and to rely more on agriculture and new cooking techniques (indicated by the change in pottery). In the last centuries before Spanish contact, Butler and his associates found an increase in slingstones and in artifacts that indicate greater reliance on taro and bread-fruit, such as pounders, pestles and mortars. Rice may have been cultivated, but we do not know when this might have begun (Rainbird 1994:333).

Latte stones—tall carved stone columns with capstones that supported wood-frame structures—are unique to the Marianas. They first appear around 900–1000 BP, and were a prominent feature of Chamorro life at the time of Spanish contact. Large sites in-cluding groups of rectangular structures marked by six to fourteen pairs of latte columns (ranging in height from three to sixteen feet) are found in population centers on the large islands of the southern Mariana Islands. Archaeologists and others have proposed many ideas about what sorts of structures these represent and how they are linked with social status, ritual, everyday activity or mortuary practice (Rainbird 1994:329–333). For example, latte structures were thought to have been ritual or mortuary sites, but new ev-idence shows that burials are found near or beneath latte stones at coastal sites but not inland sites, and recent excavations have found domestic artifacts and debris associated with latte sites. Current thought is that latte were the foundations of the houses of im-portant families or some other social unit. Wooden structures would have been built on latte columns, and cookhouses or other working areas would have been beneath or near them on the ground. We do not yet know much about prehistoric Chamorro society be-fore the proto-historic era. It was hierarchical, though we do not know if there were two classes or three, or how they were structured. Perhaps, like modern Yap or Palau, hierar-chies of villages framed the social order; or perhaps locally organized villages or other social units were autonomous and regionally competitive. There is no evidence of a sin-gle political power controlling large areas of the Marianas, or even of any single island, in contrast to the complex chiefdoms that developed on Pohnpei and Kosrae (Rainbird 1994:333–4; Morgan 1988:115, 119–149; Kirch 2000:184–87).

Little is yet known about the early prehistory of Palau and Yap, though archaeology and linguistics agree that the two are very different. The earliest archaeological dates for Palau are around 2000 BP, but again paleoenvironmental research suggests an environ-mental change a thousand years or more earlier, which might have been caused by human settlement (Kirch 2000:172). The most dramatic evidence of Palau's prehistory are the monumental sculpted and terraced hills that extend across large areas of the landscape, especially on Babeldaob. These have been dated to 785–1230 BP (perhaps 500 AD–1400 AD). Lower terraces might have been agricultural; the shaped hilltops might have been used for defense or ritual, but debate continues about their function (Rainbird 1994:303–4; Morgan 1988:29; Kirch 2000:187–190). The massive sculpted forms surely required a large labor force, but no contemporary settlement sites have yet been found for study. These "marvelous architectonic works," as archaeologist Patrick Kirch (2000:188) calls them, "remain an enduring puzzle of Oceanic prehistory, for little is cer-tain regarding their construction or function" (Kirch 2000:188). Palau's terraces were no longer in use by the seventeenth century AD, when present-day village sites began to be occupied. These villages consist of dwellings and community houses (*bai*) on stone platforms, threaded with stone paths (Rainbird 1994:306). Yap and Palau, like the Marianas, did not possess a single large administrative center in late prehistory. At the time of European contact, and into the present, traditional rankings and alliances of villages maintained social order (Morgan 1988:29).

Palau's prehistoric remains also include megalithic sculptures, huge stone carvings of human faces; the most impressive is an arranged set of 52 megaliths at a leveled plaza at the north of Babeldaob. The chronology and significance of these megalithic faces is unknown, but they are named and possess specific symbolic and legendary associations for modern Palauans (Rainbird 1994:306–7; Morgan 1988:13–17; Kirch 2000:190). In fact, Richard Parmentier's (1987) study of modern Palauan understandings of history emphasizes the importance of spatial relationships and physical remains, such as architecture in the Palauan view of the past.

Like Palauan villages, historic and modern Yapese settlements consist of extensive stonework, including elevated house foundations with large sitting platforms, raised pathways, graves, sea walls, docks, piers and fish traps, and like Palau, Yap's polity is organized in terms of the ranks and relationships among villages (Morgan 1988:56). But archaeology suggests that Yap's modern arrangement of villages is relatively recent (dating back no more than 500, or even perhaps 250, years ago), and we do not yet have much archaeological evidence of the lives of the ancient people of Yap. The earliest archaeological dates are about 2000 BP (1 AD), but paleoenvironmental evidence showing a forest destruction and fire beginning around 3100 BP might indicate human presence (Kirch 2000:173). Ceramic studies have established a chronological sequence of three types of pottery: Calcareous Sand Tempered (CST) (used from first settlement around 2000 BP to around 600 BP), Plain Ware (most common 800–600 BP) and Laminated Ware. Like the rest of the Carolines, ancient Yapese depended on shell and bone artifacts, with little use of stone tools; in late prehistory, stone was brought to Yap from Palau's Rock Islands (Rainbird 1994:208–9).

Eastern Micronesian Prehistory

The dates for first settlement of the rest of the Carolines and Marshalls appear to be similar to those for Palau and Yap, at around 2000 BP, though the origins of the settlers of the two regions (western and eastern Micronesia) differ. In excavations with the earliest dates for the high islands of Yap, Chuuk, Pohnpei and Kosrae, we find similar CST (Calcareous Sand Tempered) pottery, with roughly contemporaneous radiocarbon dates.

It might be thought that central Micronesia was settled by the Marianas-Palau-Yap settlers moving east, and some archaeologists have proposed this in the past. But differences in the prehistoric pottery of Yap, Kosrae and Pohnpei do not support a simple west-east flow across these islands, and the linguistic data counters that scenario. Most now think that the settlers of eastern Micronesia came from the south, with ceramic and other evidence suggesting that at least some came from the Lapita region of island Melanesia, perhaps the Fiji-West Solomons area, or the southeast Solomons-Vanuatu area (Rainbird 1994:299–300; Kirch and Weisler 1994:292–93; Kirch 2000:173; Oliver 1989:25).

Until a good deal more archaeological research has been done, we will not even know which islands were settled first. While people in western Micronesia continued to make pottery until European trade goods replaced indigenous production, pottery was not made anywhere in central or eastern Micronesia in historic times. The presence of pottery in archaeological sites on Pohnpei, Kosrae and Chuuk suggests one of these high islands as the first point of settlement, but some archaeological and linguistic evidence points to the Marshall Islands and Kiribati as the most likely areas of initial occupation for the region (Peoples 1993; Kirch 2000:173).

Pottery was used longer on Pohnpei than on the other eastern Carolines—from initial settlement until around 1500 AD. The earliest sites dated on Pohnpei are 5 BC–240 AD, and this early pottery resembles late Lapita plain wares in the southeast Solomons or northern Vanuatu (Kirch 2000:174, 177). Archaeology on Pohnpei focuses on the thousands of stone structures across the landscape: platforms, tombs, and features associated with agriculture, indicating a population that expanded and intensified its use of the land. We don't know what sort of social system the first settlers of Pohnpei had, but an elaborate prestige system that persists in modified form into the present emerged after 900 A.D. By the time the labor-intensive megalithic construction began at Nan Madol (twelfth or thirteenth century AD), Pohnpei was ruled by the *Saudeleur*, a paramount chief who, with his followers, remained the elite until roughly the early seventeenth century AD, when they were conquered by the incoming hero Isokelekel (Hanlon [1988:4–25] summarizes the Pohnpeian oral history of these events). Isokelekel is said to have established the modern political system, based on a division of Pohnpei into five polities, each ruled by a paramount chief. In addition to the major site of Nan Madol (see below), research in the 1980s explored a major stone complex on the hilltop site of Sapwtakai, which included platforms, tomb, wall, and other features, as well as kava-pounding stones (Rainbird 1994:321–3; Scarr 1990:46).

The archaeology of Pohnpei and Kosrae are often discussed as similar, because Kosrae also has a large stone "capital city," called Lelu, on its eastern coast (described below). But the archaeological sites with the earliest dates on Kosrae are in the upland valleys, not near the coast. Kosrae's earliest sites date to 108BC–244 AD, with pollen evidence supporting changes in island vegetation and the introduction of cultivated plants at the same time, making this likely to be the date of initial colonization (Kirch 2000:174). Researchers have suggested that Kosrae experienced rapid population expansion about 550–450 BP, leading to the emergence of a hierarchical social order with the megalithic complex of Lelu at its pinnacle (Rainbird 1995:325).

Chuuk has seen less research than Pohnpei or Kosrae, but the data we have indicate an initial settlement of about 2000 BP at coastal locations, followed by the abandonment of pottery after about 500 years, then an archaeological "silence" of a thousand years, with (at present) no sites known from about 500 AD–1300 AD. Perhaps people lived a more mobile lifestyle harder to see archaeologically during this time. When evidence picks up again there has been a shift in settlement pattern, with middens and defended sites on the hilltops of lagoon islands, and long-term settlement on coasts and hill slopes. Archaeologists suggest that the adoption of breadfruit as a staple crop allowed the establishment of settled communities, leading to greater territorial control of resources and perhaps warfare; this would explain the defended hilltop sites and increased use of stone for walls and house platforms (Rainbird 1994:317–19).

Atolls (and a few isolated raised coral islands) make up a good portion of the Caroline Islands and all of the Marshall Islands and Kiribati, posing a special challenge to archaeology. Until Janet Davidson's pioneering work on Nukuoro Atoll in 1965, archaeologists had dismissed the likelihood of significant preservation of earlier materials on these low islands, constantly washed by waves and storms. But Davidson showed that atolls can hold significant archaeological resources, and subsequent work in the Marshalls and Gilberts has extended our knowledge of the prehistory of these small islands.

One might expect the larger high islands to have been settled before the atolls, but early dates attributed to sites in the Marshalls challenge this expectation. Yet environmental factors call early atoll dates into question. Studies of sea level changes over time indicate that atolls could not have formed until sea level stabilized at about 1 AD; "Thus the Micronesian atolls were in their initial stages of sub-aerial formation and stabilization when late Lapita populations began to explore the seaways north of the equator" (Kirch 2000:174). And atolls require human manipulation to develop soil and plant resources to the point where they can sustain permanent human occupation. Kirch (2000:175) suggests that the atolls were first exploited seasonally or temporarily by nearby high islanders, until they could sustain permanent habitation.

Most dates from the Carolinian and Marshall Islands atolls suggest use starting about 2000 BP. (There are a few earlier dates from the Marshall Islands, but these are debated.) Early human presence is known for both eastern and western atolls, with evidence of 1900 years of use on Maloelap and Majuro in the Marshalls, and Fais in the western Carolines. But other atolls were occupied later; Nukuoro, for example, not until 1237 BP. "In short, atoll colonization was probably continuous, with the full spectrum of Micronesian atolls not occupied by humans until the last millennium" (Kirch 2000:175). Atolls are not isolates; archaeology as well as ethnography and history reveal their place in exchange networks linking them with other atolls and with high islands. Fais, Lamotrek and Ulithi deposits hold ceramics from Yap, and Satawan, Lukunor and Etal were tied with the high islands of Chuuk Lagoon and the central Carolines (Rainbird 1994:311–14). The sophisticated navigational knowledge and long-distance sailing technology of atoll Caroline Islanders is world-famous.

Topics in Micronesian Archaeology

In concluding his review of the prehistory of Micronesia, Rainbird writes that more archaeological information is needed in order to establish chronologies for each island and to explore interesting patterns, such as the loss of ceramics in the eastern Carolines, reminiscent of its loss in Western Polynesia. Work on other material culture, such as adzes, is just beginning.

> At this stage, the prehistory of the small islands of the tropical northwest Pacific provides more problems than solutions…Basic requirements are large-scale excavations which allow for a greater understanding of site use rather than occupation dates only; the collection of palaeoenvironmental data; a critical approach to radiocarbon dates, which may reveal further gaps; a consideration of the range and use of rock art on the island groups; a greater emphasis on atoll archaeology; a broadening of interpretative approaches to allow for multiple voices; and an avoidance of simplistic applied models. (Rainbird 1994:340)

In arguing against "simplistic applied models," Rainbird refers to the danger of letting a few dominant ideas lead us to limit prematurely our interpretations of prehistory. Much of the archaeology of Micronesia is still in the stage of constructing culture history, that is, building a chronology and description of life during the time that each island has been occupied. Yet, despite limited information, archaeologists working the region have already begun to ask larger questions. Two topics that have received special attention are complex chiefdoms in Micronesia, and exchange and trade in the region. Interest in these topics reflects the general interest of American and other Anglophone archaeologists in the emergence of sociopolitical complexity, and in the role of trade and exchange in shaping social change.

Micronesia's Complex Chiefdoms

The study of the development of sociopolitical complexity has long been a topic of interest to anthropologists. The Pacific Islands are noted in ethnographic literature for the existence of complex chiefdoms at the time of European contact, and researchers are interested in how this political form emerged and developed over time. Archaeologists see monumental architecture as an important part of the answer, with "the potential to inform on processes of hierarchical development and political control and competition" (Kirch and Weisler 1994:301). The two major sites of Nan Madol on Pohnpei and Lelu on Kosrae have been the focus of research inquiring into the development of complexity.

> Because they have common origins in a late phase of Lapita expansion, the complex societies of Pohnpei and Kosrae may be compared with the classic high-island chiefdoms of Polynesia...structural similarities between these sets of societies may inform us about underlying processes of social change... (Kirch 2000:194)

Nan Madol is an extensive site consisting of 92 artificial islets, connected by canals, constructed on the southeast edge of Pohnpei. This impressive complex has been a focus of Pohnpeian traditional history and legend, and of European admiration. "Indeed," writes architectural scholar William Morgan, "no greater record of prehistoric achievement exists in all of Micronesia than the ninety-two islets of ancient Nan Madol." Pohnpei is the largest island in central Micronesia, and it may have had a prehistoric population of 20,000–30,000. While the site was occupied earlier, construction of the artificial islets began at around 1500 BP, and continued for many centuries. (The first dates at Nan Madol match those for the first colonization of Pohnpei, at around 1 AD.) The megalithic architecture that remains so impressive was probably accomplished about 1200–1600 AD, and is associated with the rule of the Saudeleur. It is not clear when the site was abandoned; perhaps around the late seventeenth century; or we might say that it has never been abandoned, since it is still well-visited by both tourists and Pohnpeians (Rainbird 1994:320–21; Hanlon 1988:9; Morgan 1988:85).

The study of Nan Madol over the past hundred years has produced a multitude of artifacts and a series of revelations about the complexity of the site. Like Lelu on Kosrae, Nan Madol was both a government and a religious center, as well as a residence for nobles and their courtiers and servants, with a resident population of probably less than one thousand. Parts of the site have been identified as priests' dwellings, special-purpose areas (such as for canoe making or food preparation), administrative areas and mortuary areas (one islet is said to contain the tomb of the legendary Isokelekel). Nan Madol also has canals, seawalls and breakwaters surrounding and protecting the artificial rectangular islets, which are made of retaining walls of basalt boulders and immense basalt prisms. Archaeologists have found tombs containing thousands of shell beads and other artifacts, including shell jewelry, rare basalt adzes and obsidian flakes (Morgan 1988:63–82, 85; Rainbird 1994:322)

Kosrae's megalithic site of Lelu was still in use at the time of European contact; French and Russian explorers left good descriptions of it in the early nineteenth century. Morgan (1988:89–115) uses archaeological and historical evidence to describe Lelu. In the early nineteenth century, "the island city consisted of more than one hundred walled enclosures" with basalt walls up to 21 feet high. Here lived the paramount chief, nobles and servants, though most commoners lived on the main island from which they sent canoe-loads of food to supply Lelu. Initial occupation of the site was in the first century AD, but the first phase of construction began around 1250–1400 AD. Slow expansion of foundation platforms continued until monumental construction about 1400–1600 AD; the last compounds were built 1650–1800 AD. Lelu was the major settlement on Kosrae, and it was at its height as an administrative center at the time of European contact, a city of high walls, a 3000-foot long canal through its center, paved streets connecting compounds to boat landings, hundreds of wooden dwellings and feast-houses topped by graceful high roofs. There were also tombs, sacred enclosures, and unwalled areas where commoners lived (Morgan 1988:89–115; Kirch 2000:201–04).

Lelu has obvious parallels with Nan Madol—both are administrative-ritual centers built on the east side of islands, made on artificial islands and walled with basalt—but the sites are significantly different. Kosrae is smaller than Pohnpei, and its prehistoric population is unlikely to have been higher than around 6,000. There is no clear evidence that the two islands were in contact during the times these centers were built (though some have suggested links with western Polynesia [Kirch 2000:200, 205–6]). They appear to be parallel developments, with major construction on Lelu beginning perhaps two centuries later than at Nan Madol, inviting questions about the overall development of local hierarchies in the region (Rainbird 1994: 326; Morgan 1988:85; Kirch 2000:201–02).

As in Polynesia, the existence of a region with shared ancestry but different histories poses a research opportunity for enquiring into what variables shape the sociopolitical outcomes. In Micronesia, much of this work has involved archaeologists, who use evolutionary theories to explain the development of complex chiefdoms. Rainbird (1994:336–7) summarizes this approach: "Successful adaptation [to a local environment] leads to agricultural intensification, the production of surplus, and, in turn, greater social complexity." While archaeologists, as Rainbird points out, seldom state this framework explicitly, it undergirds much of their work.

The case for examining Micronesian societies in terms of evolutionary political theory is presented explicitly by James Peoples, an ethnologist (Peoples 1993). Peoples argues that Nuclear Micronesia (Kiribati and the Marshall Islands, the Carolines excepting Yap and Palau-since Yap, Palau and the Marianas have different settlement origins) can be examined as a population sharing a common ancestry. Thus, he uses controlled comparison to study differences in their political organizations. In particular, he asks why the greatest political complexity or hierarchy is found in eastern Micronesia (notably Pohnpei and Kosrae), with social, political and economic differentiation much less developed in the central and western Carolines.

Peoples discounts the simple argument that the explanation is the difference between high islands and atolls (after all, Chuuk was not politically complex; the southern Marshalls were). Rather, he proposes an integrated theory about population growth, conflict, the fate of defeated groups, intensified production, and strategies for maintaining control. The relevant variables, he concludes, were that natural hazards were more frequent and severe in the central and western Carolines (making higher levels of complexity less likely), and the costs and risks of a defeated group fleeing its homeland rather than accepting subjugation were also high (if the costs and risks are high, as in the eastern Carolines, defeated groups are more likely to stay in place, with the result of increasing political complexity) (Peoples 1993:11–13).

Questions about origin and development of political complexity are likely to accompany future research into Micronesia's past. Rainbird (1994:337) however, offers a caution to archaeologists who rely too much on social-evolutionary adaptation models, arguing that "Little attempt has been made to explain historical trajectories of islands within different interpretive frameworks." New theories may cause us to reconsider what the archaeological record tells us about the development of social organization in Micronesia.

Exchange and Inter-Island Contacts

Perhaps recent inquiries into the role of trade and exchange relationships within and among Micronesia's prehistoric societies will produce alternative frameworks for interpreting the region's prehistory. Kirch and Weisler (1994:298) write that, "In Micronesia, exchange and interaction studies have been limited, due in part to the lack of basic geological data for many islands" which inhibits analysis of pottery and volcanic artifacts. Further development of our ability to analyze the regional connections among artifact types and raw materials might also illuminate the early settlement history of the islands.

Research on the western Carolinian atolls shows the usefulness of studying pottery and adze imports in examining the prehistory of exchange systems linking those islands with Yap, and perhaps allowing us eventually to learn the origin of the "Yap empire" or (more modestly) the "Yap interaction sphere" as known historically and ethnographically. Quarried stone discs ("stone money") came to Yap from Palau; Yap itself carried on a tribute and exchange system with 14 atolls stretching as far east as Namonuito. Since the people of the atolls speak a language not mutually intelligible with Yapese, the origins of Yap's relationship with these islands is not self-evident. Excavations on Lamotrek unearthed ceramics from Yap and Palau and volcanic rock from Chuuk; work on Ulithi, Fais and Ngulu also showed links with Yap. This regional exchange system has been explained as a way to increase the political power of groups on Yap and as maintaining a security net for atoll-dwellers who could turn to Yap for help after typhoons or other disasters. Cases from elsewhere in the Carolines show that modern inter-island links have a long history: a survey of Ant Atoll showed close ties with Pohnpei (as well as intensive occupation over at least a millennium), and Satawan, Lukunor and Etal show links with Chuuk Lagoon and the central Carolinian atolls (Rainbird 1994:209, 311, 313–14; Kirch and Weisler 1994:298; Kirch 2000:191–193).

In the Marianas, ceramic studies are expanding from the basic work of chronology to questions of regional interaction. In the Latte period, separate ceramic traditions developed on the large islands of the southern Marianas, while groups maintained some contact (Rainbird 1994:334–5). While early interpretations of Marianas prehistory based on ceramic studies explained variation by replacement, migration, or developmental change, Graves, Hunt and Moore (1990) suggest that the variation reflects changes in regional social relations. In early prehistory, the widespread dispersal of vulnerable populations across the Marianas produced high rates of inter-community interaction, but only "moderate" exchanges of pottery. In late prehistory, larger populations and more settled communities reduced inter-island contact but maintained intraisland exchange and increased internal variation. Perhaps, with the emergence of hierarchical social relations (indicated by the presence of latte structures about AD 1200), ceramic variation became a way to identify different communities, reflecting "conscious efforts to produce and maintain geographically-based social distinctions."

This sort of analysis allows us to compare Micronesian prehistory with that of the rest of Oceania. In contrast to the Lapita area, which shows widespread exchange of pottery in some cases, Graves et al. (1990) see the early period of dispersed settlement and relatively similar pottery in the Marianas as a desire to minimize the potential impact of environmental variability (high rates of interaction, but no extensive exchange of pottery). In the late prehistoric Marianas, we see relatively high population density, numerous aggregated settlements, hierarchically organized social groups—all conditions associated with competition between and within social groups, producing geographically distinct forms of pottery. As archaeological research and analysis continues in Micronesia, we can expect to see both an increase in the specific detail of culture histories of each island and island group, and a continuing effort to put Micronesian settlement and prehistory into the regional and global context.

Linguistics

Other sections of this volume have described how linguistic studies help elucidate the relationships among various peoples in the Pacific. Remember that all languages of the Pacific are classified as "Austronesian" or "Non-Austronesian," and that in Melanesia the study of these differences has been essential to understanding prehistory. All of Micronesia's languages are Austronesian. Remember also that "Linguistic diversity in the Pacific is directly related to the duration of human settlement in the different island groups" (Kiste 1994a:10–11). Melanesia, settled for the longest period of time, is linguistically the most complex; Polynesia, the last settled, the most homogenous.

At the time of European contact, the people of Micronesia were speaking between 11 and 13 different languages and many dialects (depending on how linguists classify them). A closer look at those languages will reinforce what we have already learned about the region's prehistory. The languages of the western islands, the Marianas, Palau and Yap form a subgroup, though they are quite different from each other. These are the oldest languages in the region. The other Micronesian languages are classified as "Nuclear Micronesian" (Pohnpeian, Kosraean, Trukic, Kiribati, Marshalls, and probably Nauruan; Nukuoro and Kapingamarangi are Polynesian languages).

Historical linguists try to reconstruct ancient forms of the Oceanic languages in order to learn the relationships among them, and to search for the Pan-Austronesian "homeland." In a 1993 review of Austronesian historical linguistics, Pawley and Ross (1993:443–44) review this work, for example proposals that shared semantic terms indicate that the ancestral culture had hereditary ranks and land-holding descent groups. The existence of the Oceanic subgrouping of languages "indicates a period of Oceanic unity, most likely in western Melanesia, where Oceanic has its immediate external relatives, followed by the breakup of Proto Oceanic into a number of widely dispersed subgroups…"

> The ancestors of the Proto Oceanic speech community may not have brought all their culture with them but they brought a large part of it. There is an impressive persistence of vocabulary for various cultural domains in some contemporary Oceanic languages of Melanesia, in most of the Nuclear Micronesian languages, and in all of the Polynesian languages. (Pawley and Ross 1993:446, 447).

Pawley and Ross discuss various theories about the subgroupings within Austronesian, which presumably indicate the dispersal of ancient populations across Southeast

Asia and the Pacific. The predominant current view is that "the Melanesian, Polynesian, and all but a few Micronesian languages fall into a single subgroup (today called "Oceanic") apart from all Western AN [Austronesian] languages." The exceptions are Chamorro, Palauan and possibly Yapese. If, as the linguists propose, "all AN languages of the southwest and Central Pacific derive from a single linguistic interstage exclusive of the rest of the family, the implication is that there was a single effective AN colonization of this area" (Pawley and Ross 1993:433). And the implication for Micronesia, as we have seen, is that its westernmost islands were settled in a different way, from a different source, than the rest of the island Pacific.

Linguistic evidence does support the approach of two separate settlement histories for Micronesia. Historian Deryck Scarr writes of a "linguistic divide" that "runs between the Caroline Islands and the Marianas."

> The prehistory of both areas as yet remains obscure, but it does seem clear that Micronesia was settled from opposite ends. In the west, settlement was from Island South-East Asia, and on the evidence of the greater internal divergencies in their Austronesian languages, it occurred earlier than in Islands to the east. Their inhabitants, also Austronesian speakers, are likely on linguistic grounds to have come up from the south through eastern Melanesia to occupy Kiribati, the Marshall Islands and the eastern Carolines. (Scarr 1990:17)

Irwin (1992:130) calls this the "orthodox settlement model" of Micronesia, and suggests that it may change in the future. The archaeological and linguistic evidence for the western islands, though, seems to agree: Chamorro and Palauan are not Oceanic languages, but belong to a different Austronesian subgroup, western Malayo-Polynesian, with their closest relatives in the Philippines and Indonesia (and it has been suggested that Chamorroan has links to the Formosan languages of Taiwan). (Kirch 2000:167). Yap's linguistic affiliations are still under discussion, but it may be an Oceanic language with its most direct link to the Admiralty Islands in the Indian Ocean (suggesting a third population movement into Micronesia); Yapese is difficult to categorize in part because the language has borrowed heavily from Nuclear Micronesian (Kirch 2000:169–70).

Within the Oceanic subgroup, Nuclear Micronesian is a fairly well-marked set, generally recognized as comprising the remaining Micronesian languages. The shared features of grammar and vocabulary of the Nuclear Micronesian languages "appear to reflect a common origin in eastern Melanesia" (Kiste 1994a:11). As archaeological evidence also shows, it seems that eastern Micronesia's cultural-linguistic origins can be traced to Vanuatu and beyond that to the Fiji-Western Polynesian area, linking them with the region of initial Lapita expansion (Kirch 2000:167). The "center of genetic diversity" for Nuclear Micronesian—which historical linguists take to indicate the region of oldest settlement—is in eastern Micronesia, "in the region of Kiribati, Kosrae, Pohnpei, and the Marshalls" (Pawley and Ross 1993:439).

There are current ideas about relations within Nuclear Micronesian. The first (described in Rehg 1995), commonly presented until the 1980s, is a "flat tree" model, indicating that these languages form a sub-group (Proto-Micronesian), but without indicating possible relationships among Trukic, Pohnpei, Marshallese, Kiribati and Kosraean. Viewed as historical linguistics, this model proposes that a group of original settlers sharing a Proto-Micronesian language spread across the central and eastern islands very rapidly, and that subsequent linguistic distinctions arose as a result of subsequent patterns of isolation and interaction. As more research is done on the Nuclear Micronesian languages, this scenario seems implausible.

Work in the 1980s proposed subgroupings which might provide insights into the settlement of Nuclear Micronesia. The languages of Kiribati, the Marshall Islands and Kosrae form one subgroup (these were perhaps the first to split off from a Proto-Micronesian ancestor language). The four languages of the Pohnpeic subgroup and the Chuukic dialect chain of some 60 distinctive forms might have developed from a mutual ancestor (Rehg 1995:311–319; Kirch 2000:169). "Given the considerable diversity of Micronesian languages," Rehg (1995:319) concludes, "a date of AD 0 for Proto-Micronesian is almost certainly too recent"—that is, the languages are too different not to have been separated for a longer time. Rehg's examination of the archaeological evidence from a linguistic perspective leads him to expect more dates closer to 3000 BP in central and eastern Micronesia (Rehg 1995:318–21). Yet the differences within the Nuclear Micronesian languages are considerably less significant than those within the Polynesian language group. Linguistics and archaeology both suggest that the settlement of the central and eastern Micronesian islands took place rapidly, without an opportunity for the languages to diverge significantly through isolation over a long period of time (Kirch 2000:175).

While historical linguistics provides valuable clues to prehistory, studies of modern language tell us about more recent historical and cultural processes. Trade and exchange among the islands, especially by the long-distance sailing of the atoll-dwellers of the Caroline and Marshall Islands, maintained mutual intelligibility even while dialects were forming. Links beyond the region are also reflected in language, as well as material culture and ideas. When non-Pacific Islanders entered the region, Spanish, English, German and Japanese vocabulary came with them, and the various rulers often insisted that schooling and official business use the colonial language.

As in the case of archaeology, linguistic research in Micronesia lags behind the amount of work done on Polynesian and some Melanesian language regions. In the early 1970s, the U.S. TTPI (Trust Territory of the Pacific Islands) and the University of Hawai'i sponsored a series of linguistic studies which were the most comprehensive that had been done (Morgan 1988:xi). A great deal more descriptive and historical linguistics is needed for us to understand Micronesia's languages more completely.

Today, the languages continue to be learned as first languages (Chamorro is a partial exception), and retain their vitality. English is the common language of the region, learned in school, and at home by children of inter-lingual marriages. In some political units, minority-language speakers learn the majority language as well (for example, most Nukuoro and Kapingamarangi people speak Pohnpeian; some people in the western Caroline atolls speak Yapese). Outer-islanders have ongoing links with nearby high islands, which are usually the site of government, health and education services, so dialects intersect and change with continual interaction. Political units are only partly congruent with language. While Marshall Islanders all speak a mutually intelligible language (with dialect differences), the people of the Federated States of Micronesia include speakers of Yapese, Trukic, Pohnpeian, Kosraean, Nukuoro and Kapingamarangi, as well as dialect variations within some of these; the shared language is English. In the central and western islands (less so in the Marshalls, and not at all in Kiribati), Japanese is a favored third language, as Micronesians strengthen personal and businesss ties with that country (some elderly people still speak Japanese learned in school).

Although Micronesians are fully literate and write in both English and their first languages for personal use, publication is mostly in English; the emergence of Micronesian written literature lies in the future. Artistic expression "remains largely in the more ephemeral realms of oratory, dance, or dramatic performance" in indigenous languages (Hereniko 1994:424). How the popular media handle local languages will be an important part of their future. In most islands, radio programs are in both local language(s) and English. The Marshall Islands' television station runs some programming in Marshallese (television on other islands relies on taped programs imported from the U.S). Marshallese and Palauans can also read newspapers and government informational publications in their own language; these are less available in the languages of the Federated States of Micronesia. Most internet sites dealing with Micronesia are in English, even when they are run by Islanders (to maintain intelligibility across different language communities), but the internet, in the future, may become a place where even smaller languages can flourish.

Chamorro has been the most endangered of the Micronesian languages, as its speakers suffered the devastating Spanish conquest of the Marianas, followed by 200 years of colonial rule and a half-century of intense acculturative pressure by U.S. administration. While the people of Guam maintained their language by speaking it at home throughout the Spanish era, the combination of official hostility to Chamorro and the pervasive influence of American culture meant that by around 1960 Chamorro was no longer the first language of most Guam natives. (It was in part the efforts of Catholic priests, who shifted from Spanish to Chamorro in churches in the American era, that helped preserve it [Rogers 1995:158–159]). A strong cultural identity movement emerging in the 1980s seeks to maintain Chamorro through education and public use.

Internal differences in patterns of language use, along with specialized vocabularies and speaking styles are important ways that speakers of most west central Pacific languages use to construct, maintain, and perpetuate meaningful social distinctions. So-called "high" speech forms are now subtly communicated, but in the past were widespread and highly elaborated restricted codes used by persons of rank as markers of elevation and social separation. Other specialized codes were used by navigators, sailing specialists, medicinal curers, and oral historians to communicate sacred information or to protect and perpetuate the high social value of restricted forms of knowledge. Given the importance of face-to-face interactions in relatively small scale social situations, it is not surprising that speaking style is closely linked with identity at the most local levels as well as at the atoll or island and regional level. Numerous social distinctions of importance to Micronesian residents are communicated in linguistic terms.

Micronesians emigrate to Guam, Hawai'i, and the continental U.S. in large numbers; it is not likely that most children of this emigrant generation will learn their parents' language. Yet, in the islands, there is every likelihood that the indigenous languages will continue. An essential part of their persistence, however, is the recognition by Micronesians that language is a key element in maintaining cultural identity.

Identity — Carolines and Marianas

If prehistory indicates that the people of the western and eastern parts of Micronesia have different origins, and linguistics assures us that their languages are diverse, it is only the continuation of a theme to say that their colonial history has also been varied, and their contemporary political relationships complex. In understanding the processes that have, over the past few hundred years, created the modern identities of people in the Marianas and Caroline Islands, we must take into account both the dynamics of internal continuity and change that have shaped their lives, and their links with the broader systems, both Micronesian and foreign, that they have encountered.

The Mariana Islands

It was only after 30 years of annual trading visits by Spanish ships that a permanent Spanish settlement was established in the Marianas, and that was spurred by the desire of the Jesuit priest Diego Luis de San Vitores to establish a mission on Guam. The Spanish presence was well-established in the Philippines, but since the Marianas had no permanent Spanish population, there was little pressure to extend control to those islands. San Vitores went ashore in 1668 with priests, catechists and soldiers who presaged the future of Guam in their complex identities: they were Filipinos, Spanish and Indian-Spanish mestizos from Mexico. Over the next four years, these men became embroiled in Chamorro politics, and San Vitores organized and used his small military force. In 1672, San Vitores and a catechist were killed. "While San Vitores was alive," writes historian Robert Rogers (1995:57), "the islanders could refuse conversion without retaliation by the Spaniards. After San Vitores' death, the Chamorros no longer had a choice: either they accepted Christianity, or they were killed by the Spanish military, whose presence and authority expanded as a consequence of his martyrdom." San Vitores' death precipitated the conquest of the Marianas, a hard-fought and bloody war lasting until 1698. The Chamorros were not united under a single ruler, but fought under a number of heroic rebels; they resisted to the point of suicide. But in the end, the Spanish *reduccion* gathered up the few hundred survivors to live in Spanish-controlled settlements on Guam. The rest of the archipelago was left uninhabited, except for a few refugees (Rogers 1995:41–73; McPhetres 1992).

Pre-European Chamorro culture virtually disappeared. Almost all of material culture, subsistence practices and settlement patterns was lost or remained only as fragmentary folk knowledge. Chamorros constructed a new life shaped by Spanish governance and the Roman Catholic faith. Many Chamorro women married the Tagalog, Mexican and Spanish garrison troops. Elite women married higher-status immigrants. The resulting lifestyle was not Spanish, but became a cultural melding (later called "neo-Chamorro," for example by Rogers 1995) that took place over many generations from about 1720 to 1886 (McPhetres 1992:244).

Because the Marianas offered little wealth, few Spanish settled there, so Chamorro land was not completely alienated (as in other Spanish colonies); but Spanish custom altered land tenure. As the matrilineal clan structure disintegrated, male primogeniture became the pattern of inheritance. In the town of Agana a landowning elite developed, a small group of families called "high people" (*manak'kilo*) who "adopted Spanish and Filipino manners and clothing," married Spaniards and separated themselves from the predominantly Chamorro rural families (Rogers 1992:74–5). By the end of the eithteenth century Guam had a *hacienda* system (with *manak'kilo* and the Catholic church as owners). Landless Chamorros lived in villages and worked as hired laborers or tenants on farms or cattle ranches.

Despite the upheavals, some aspects of Chamorro culture persisted, though greatly altered. The people of mixed ancestry that made up Guam's new population used traditional healers and practiced reciprocity in gifts and labor. Historian Robert Rogers (1992:102–3) argues that the Chamorro language, though adopting much Spanish vocabulary, retained its grammatical foundation; it was "maintained through maternal control of family life," a familiar habit among the formerly matrilineal Chamorro. The foreign men who married Chamorro women customarily lived in the wife's village, another way to ensure some continuity in cultural transmission. Catholic reverence for the Virgin Mary honored women's role in the home, letting them pass on Chamorro language and heritage to their children (Rogers 1992:102–3; McPhetres 1992:244).

Rogers argues that Chamorro absorption of introduced customs (such as the Spanish ideas of godparenthood and the importance of the extended family) shows them not as passive victims but as "agents of their own transformation," maintaining the core of their language and family life through women's domestic role.

> Largely by means of this language-family linkage, and because Guam was a poor and isolated island, the Chamorros were neither totally Hispanicized nor replaced by a hybrid nonindigenous population, as occurred in Cuba and Puerto Rico. Instead, the Chamorros absorbed immigrants into a neo-Chamorro society with new attributes but still permeated by a distinctive uni-vocal Chamorro consciousness at the grassroots level. (Rogers 1992:104).

Yet, in their households and communities, Chamorro social organization at the end of the Spanish era "had become in appearance closer to that of lowland Filipinos than to any traditional Oceanic society." Although, as Rogers writes, "neo-Chamorros never lost their roots," they did in many ways lose their similarity to and familiarity with other Micronesian cultures.

And, because of political and historical events, Chamorros lost contact with each other when the archipelago was split as a consequence of the Spanish-American war. Spain relinquished Cuba, Puerto Rico and Guam to the U.S., and sold the Marshalls, Carolines, Palau and the rest of the Mariana Islands to Germany (Rogers 1995:111–13). What had been a common history of Chamorros under two hundred years of Spanish rule diverged sharply. Guam became isolated from the rest of Micronesia as it underwent Americanization; the repercussions of this separation continue into the present (McPhetres 1992:245–46).

Guam

President William McKinley placed Guam under the control of the U.S. Navy. With this decision, Chamorros' relationship to the U.S. government became a unique, ambiguous, and in the long term troubling and contested one. The first naval governor sought to alter Guam immediately, implementing laws to reduce the role of the Catholic Church, eliminate debt peonage, improve health care and plan an English-language school system (Rogers 1995:119–121). American rule developed infrastructure and opened some economic opportunities, but "local customs remained an ultraconservative mix of neo-Chamorro and Spanish traditions" (Rogers 1995:142). One significant change was that, as American enlisted men married Chamorro women, a new set of families developed as an economic and political elite (Rogers 1995:141).

The U.S. had captured Guam in war, and Guam's history has continued to be shaped by military needs. Through the start of the twentieth century, as American strategists eyed the growing threat of Japan, the governing of Guam changed little. The navy pursued a policy of acculturation. Chamorros learned English, in part because of the navy's push to suppress Chamorro: forbidding it in schools and, in the 1920s, even collecting and burning Chamorro-English dictionaries. Golf, Coca-Cola, and the Guam Chamber of Commerce showed that "Agana and Sumay, but not the rural villages, were becoming more Americanized every year" (Rogers 1995:147–48).

Yet if the navy intended Chamorros to become Americans culturally, they did not mean them to become so officially. Chamorros' relations with the U.S. began to focus on politics; if religion had been the refuge of dissatisfied Chamorros under the Spanish, political protest was the avenue of choice under American rule. In the 1920s, Chamorros began formally petitioning for U.S. citizenship, first denied by Congress at the navy's request in 1927. Despite the efforts of an activist governor and of petitions to Congress in 1933, 1936 and 1939, the requests failed in the face of navy opposition. Yet the new generation of Chamorro leaders that had grown up under U.S. rule were intensely interested in their political standing; despite the impending Pacific conflict, Chamorro rights would never again be off the American agenda in Guam. Puerto Ricans and Virgin Islanders had already received citizenship, and the Philippines was moving towards independence. Guam's leaders began to sharpen their opposition to navy authoritarianism and emphasize the uniquely ambiguous position of Chamorros (Rogers 1995:148–49, 152, 154–6).

By the time of the Pacific War, Rogers writes, "Acculturation of the Chamorros into the American ethos was already deeper than their absorption into the Spanish culture in all social aspects except religion," with English more widespread than Spanish had been, and increasing acceptance of American lifestyles and values (Rogers 1995:157–9). The Japanese invasion and occupation of 1941–1944 was powerfully effective in solidifying the commitment of Guam's people to an American identity. More than fifty Chamorros were killed in the first day of Japanese invasion, and legends of patriotic actions took root, lauding Chamorro loyalty to the country that had not yet granted them citizenship. In all, several hundred Chamorros died during the occupation and in the U.S. reinvasion of Guam in July 1944, when Chamorros actively aided U.S. troops. While Chamorros welcomed the return of American rule, circumstances put Guam once more under the sole control of the U.S. Navy. As the navy prosecuted the war from Guam, it confiscated land and moved civilians without regard for ownership and civil rights, setting up land tenure snarls and war claims that would persist into the next millennium.

While the rest of Micronesia came under U.S. control after the war as a United Nations trust, Guam's status as a U.S. territory did not change. Post-war strategy called for Guam to be permanently fortified and linked with U.S. bases in the newly independent Philippines. For Chamorros, this meant that the navy had even greater control of Guam—in terms of demography, landownership, and legal authority—than it had had before the war (Rogers 1995:207–8). While Chamorros' daily style of life became increasingly similar to that of the U.S. mainland, the navy controlled and restricted the island's economy and political development.

The influence of the old *manak'kilo* elite was waning, and new leaders emerged. The years between the war and the passage of the Organic Act in 1950, which finally granted citizenship to Guamanians, were exciting ones for Chamorro activists and formative ones for Guam's political scene, as the Guam Congress mounted resistance to navy policies on landownership, wages, immigrant labor and civil rights (Rogers 1995:210–223). While Chamorros were not united on every issue, these years generated public awareness of the contradictions of American rule and the peculiar nature of the Chamorro-American relationship. The Organic Act created a civil government for Guam, removing the island from U.S. Navy rule, but not from its influence. By the late 1960s, Rogers writes, "the Americanization of Guam was becoming irreversible in cultural as well as in political matters." While Chamorro customs and the extended family remained important, people relied on salaried employment and lived full-time in villages or in the city. Chamorros were now free to travel, and thousands moved to the U.S. With the legislature at last wielding real power, "Politics became one of the most popular activities on the island, with Guamanians tending to vote in family blocks through the Chamorro *pare* [extended family] system for favorite personalities who functioned as *patrones* rather than on issues" (Rogers 1995:234). By 1966, Guam had a Democratic and a Republican party. Guam's polity looked like California, but the principles on which it ran remained distinctively Chamorro.

Guam's public life over the last thirty years has been shaped by external events (the war in Vietnam, the escalation and collapse of the Cold War, U.S.-China relations) and by internal processes, including infrastructure development, financial difficulties, lively and personal political theater, and recurrent typhoon destruction. "GovGuam" has continually expanded, making public service employment the dominant wage sector; federal aid created dependence on U.S. subsidies and welfare programs (Rogers 1995:250–264). Though the Organic Act provided welcome changes, as Chamorros became more familiar with American politics they realized the Act's limitations in ensuring civil rights and self-government; "many now consider themselves "second-class" Americans"(Rogers 1995:226).

In 1972, the Northern Marianas began negotiating with U.S. officials to become a commonwealth. The people of Guam were taken aback as they watched the neighboring Chamorros quickly negotiate for more money and more local autonomy than Guam had ever had, and as they were readily granted U.S. citizenship, a goal that had taken Chamorros on Guam fifty years to achieve. It seemed unfair, especially in light of the patriotism and wartime suffering of Guam's people. The formation of the Commonwealth of the Northern Marianas spurred Guam's search for a status change, but internal politics and the lack of a shared vision hampered progress (Rogers 1995:250–54). After a series of task forces and commissions, Guam's most recent quest for commonwealth collapsed in 1997. Guam continues to explore the options of statehood, independence, and free association with the U.S., while consulting with U.N. committees on decolonization (Shuster 2001).

Meanwhile, tourism and Japanese investment have transformed Guam's landscape, bringing haphazard urbanization and pollution along with low unemployment and high wages (Rogers 1995:245–89). Today, Guam looks even more like a California or Hawai'i suburb, and the new interest in Chamorro self-determination seems to parallel the trend to complete Guam's Americanization. "Indeed," writes anthropologist Larry Mayo (1992:240), "Guam has become integrated into the fabric of American society. All institutions are based on an American model. The population is ethnically diverse."

The diversity of Guam's population is a matter of concern to most Chamorros. The demands of military labor and recurrent typhoon devastation have required a constant flow of imported workers, since Chamorros have consistently refused to become a workforce of manual laborers. Immigration from the Philippines began in the seventeenth century, and continued, until "Americans of Filipino origin became the largest ethnic minority on Guam, with about one-quarter of the island's population" (Rogers 1995:236). Guam's most recent economic expansion coincided with the 1986 end of the Trust Territory of the Pacific Islands. Thousands of Micronesians, mostly from Chuuk, have come to Guam, joining Korean, Japanese, Chinese, and Filipino immigrant workers.

Today, the Chamorros of Guam face the problem of how to maintain political control of their island while adhering to American ideas of ethnic pluralism. They struggle with the desire to achieve the material standard of living common to other Americans, while maintaining a distinctive culture. The economic and social transformation of Guam over the past fifty years has made it in many ways "where America's day begins" (as Guam's *Pacific Daily News* declared each morning). Yet Catholicism still dominates the public conscience, and saints'-day festivals draw crowds. Chamorros still seek prestige through generosity, as did their ancestors (Rogers 1995:38–9). In the centrality of kinship and religion, the primacy of personal relations in business and politics, and in its core values, neo-Chamorro culture remains distinct. The Chamorros of Guam have not yet found a united vision for their political future, but they remain assured in their desire to affirm the survival of their identity.

Northern Marianas Islands

While Spain governed Guam's developing neo-Chamorro community, the rest of the Marianas were largely unpopulated, apart from a small group of Chamorros on Rota. In the early 1800s, islanders from central Caroline atolls, fleeing typhoon and tidal wave destruction, received permission from Spanish authorities to settle on Saipan. After 1886, Chamorros from Guam were permitted to resettle the north, moving primarily to Tinian and Saipan. Thus, by the 1898 negotiations ending Spain's interests in Micronesia, there were two very different populations in the northern islands. "By this time," historian Sam McPhetres (1992:245–46) writes, "Chamorros were practically indistinguishable from Filipino peasants in their dress, customs, and lifestyles," while Carolinians "had maintained their tradition and custom almost undiluted."

While Guam experienced forty years of American influence, the rest of the Marianas experienced 15 years of German and 30 years of Japanese colonial rule. The German administration here, as throughout Micronesia, was one of "benign commercialism," encouraging land surveys, private ownership, and quota production for the market (McPhetres 1992:246). Because the Chamorros were more acculturated than other Micronesians, Germans deployed them as traders and small businessmen in Yap and Palau, where they formed small expatriate communities until the U.S. Navy returned them to the Marianas after World War II.

The greatest transformation occurred under Japanese rule, when the islands became a sugar-cane production region worked by immigrants from Okinawa and Japan. By 1937, of a total of 46,708 residents in the northern Marianas, only 4,145 were Chamorro and Carolinian (Poyer, Falgout and Carucci 2001:21–22). Like Chamorros on Guam, those in the northern Marianas were not attracted to agricultural or manual labor. They found their economic niche in leasing their land to immigrant sugar-cane farmers, and themselves living at the edges of Japanese towns. Like most Micronesians in Japanese territory, the Chamorros of the northern Marianas began the war with a sense of loyalty and confidence in the victory of Japan. Though most were not actively involved in the conflict, some volunteered or were conscripted into the Japanese armed forces, and some were sent into Guam as scouts and interpreters during the invasion on December 8, 1941, and served there during the war. Their actions created resentment that extended long into the post-war period.

When American troops conquered Saipan and Tinian in mid-1944, Chamorros of Guam and the northern islands were once again united under the same government, but the distinctions shaped by history and politics precluded any simple reunification. Chamorros who had lived for 30 years under Japanese rule were a very different people from the Americanized Chamorros of Guam. Now the U.S. Navy had two sorts of Chamorros under its charge, and the term "Guamanian" came into general use to distinguish them from "Saipanese" (Rogers 1995:200).

After the war, Marianas Chamorros faced an empty land, as Japanese and Okinawan troops and settlers were repatriated, even those who had married Chamorros. The U.S. Navy resettled Chamorros from Yap and Palau to Tinian, where they struggled with the navy's desire to see them become farmers and their own desire to work in a wage economy. In a way, northern Chamorros had to construct a new identity. For decades, their identity had been submerged under massive Japanese acculturative pressure that was—because of the overwhelming presence of immigrants—even more compelling than that experienced by Chamorros on Guam.

Like Guam, the future of the rest of the Marianas was shaped by U.S. military decisions. While the rest of the TTPI was turned over to the U.S. Department of the Interior, the northern Marianas (except Rota) returned to navy control in the early 1950s. The CIA used Saipan as a secret guerilla training camp, mostly for Chinese Nationalists. The operation was closed in 1962, and the TTPI headquarters were moved into the former CIA buildings on Saipan. The military presence gave Saipan the best infrastructure in the TTPI, including schools, roads, water and sewage systems, housing, and jobs—which gave people a chance to interact more often with Americans, thus solidifying their identity as more acculturated (or "less primitive") than other Micronesians.

In the 1960s, as Guam was becoming strategically central to geopolitical developments in east and southeast Asia, the TTPI began to move towards dissolution. The better education and employment opportunities that they had enjoyed under separate U.S. Navy administration and as capital of the TTPI, encouraged the people of the Marianas to opt out of joining with Palau, the Carolines and the Marshall Islands in the negotiations. Since the beginning of the Trust Territory, the people of the Marianas District had sought closer affiliation with the U.S. They felt that their economy was more developed, and they themselves more sophisticated, than the other Micronesian islands, and that those islands were taking advantage of the strong Marianas economy (Hezel 1995:336; McPhetres 1992:252).

While the rest of the TTPI sought independence or free association with the U.S., the Northern Marianas favored unification with Guam. But the people of Guam voted against that, because of memories of Saipanese and Rotanese actions on Guam during the war, and fear that the islands would be a drag on Guam's economy (Rogers 1995:249–50). The Northern Marianas then requested commonwealth status, and the U.S., wanting to retain the islands for security reasons, agreed. Established in 1975, the Commonwealth of the Northern Marianas (CNMI) gained financial assistance from the U.S., considerable local autonomy and American citizenship (finalized in 1986, when the UN Trusteeship ended). "By being united but flexible in negotiations with the United States, the Northern Marianas moved ahead of Guam in political development" (Rogers 1995:253)

The CNMI now faces its own challenges, some of them similar to Guam's. As a U.S. commonwealth, there is no preference for Chamorros in jobs or contracts, and Chamorros have come to resent "outsiders" (U.S. citizens, but not local Chamorros) taking active roles in government and business. Islanders question whether all U.S. laws should apply to the CNMI, and do not appreciate the oversight role of mainland federal agencies. Taking advantage of customs regulations, Asian-owned garment factories have brought in a large labor force, often young women from the Philippines or China, and problems of enforcing U.S. labor laws have made headlines. Legally, only people of Northern Marianas descent (Chamorros or Carolinians) can own land, but long-term leases have allowed foreign investors to take over, especially on Saipan, leaving local families not only landless but often (after they have spent the payment) destitute. Japanese investment has built large beachfront hotels, but local people are seldom directly involved with these economic initiatives. "Class distinctions are beginning to form, based not on traditional family stratification or on caste, but on whether or not the family has land to lease" (McPhetres 1992:259). McPhetres also identifies the possibility of a military base on Tinian, the ever-growing impact of alien labor, and the challenge of applying U.S. federal laws (for example, in a series of corruption trials) as future challenges for the CNMI (McPhetres 1992:252–60).

Central Micronesia

The peoples of the Marshall Islands, the Caroline Islands, Palau and the Northern Marianas were held together by the administrative order of the Trust Territory of the Pacific Islands, itself an artifact of earlier colonial history. As the years of negotiation and discussion passed in the 1970s and 1980s, Micronesia's leaders came to see that there could be no single "Micronesia" as a political entity. As early as 1961, the people of the Northern Marianas had expressed interest in integration with Guam or outright annexation by the U.S., and the district had repeatedly asked the U.N. to allow it to pursue a separate destiny from the rest of Micronesia. Despite their repeated statements of their wishes, many Micronesians and some American negotiators still hoped for a united Micronesia. In 1971, the tension reached a crisis: the Marianas District Legislature actually threatened to secede from the TTPI by force if necessary, and the destruction by arson of the Congress of Micronesia chambers the next day made the point (Hezel 1995:337). Separate negotiations then culminated in the establishment of the CNMI.

But it was not only the Chamorros who felt that they had interests separate from their neighbor Islanders. The early 1970s were a time of enormous political ferment in Micronesia, as a post-war generation affected by American political rhetoric explored the options of independence and free association. Each group of islands had its own concerns, and the United States had different strategic interests in each island group. Like the Northern Marianas, Palau and the Marshalls were most vocal in expressing their divergence from the attempts to create a unified Micronesian nation; after 1978, they too began separate talks with the U.S. What was left—Chuuk, Pohnpei, Kosrae, Yap, and the atolls around them—formed the Federated States of Micronesia (Hezel 1995:345–367).

Palau began writing its own constitution in 1978. Though traditionally a hierarchical society, Palau never united under a single ruler; its political life has always been a matter of competition and alliances among ranked villages and titles. In modern politics, that translated into factions that disagreed on foreign economic investments, relations with the U.S., and whether to allow the U.S. military to store or test nuclear and chemical weapons in Palau. A series of referenda were held over the next dozen years in order to approve a constitution; Palau's "tradition of balanced opposition," which worked well to maintain competition without allowing concentration of power, dramatically slowed its ability to create a nation-state (Hezel 1995:357).

Palau's long fight over its constitution produced intense conflict, including the assassination of one president and the suicide of another, threats of violence, corruption, and intimidation of citizens. While global anti-nuclear activists became involved with Palau because of that issue, many Palauans were more concerned with the possibility that the U.S. military would take Palauan land, as it had done on other islands. In the end, political maneuvering and Palau's need for foreign aid meant that "independence was achieved on United States terms" (Firth and van Strokirch 1997:336). Palau was the last unit of the old TTPI to disappear when it became independent in 1994.

The dissolution of the TTPI emphasized the distinctive identities felt in each island and region of Micronesia. The political units formed out of the TTPI are no more "natural" than was the TTPI itself, and within those units smaller communities continue to press for greater political independence to match their sense of uniqueness. Micronesia's modern cultures are the result not only of ancient communities of shared language and custom, but are also the outcome of the colonial eras. Chamorro people feel themselves distinct not primarily because of the unique heritage of Chamorro culture, the culture of latte and matrilineal clans that disappeared soon after 1668; rather, it is their experience of acculturation under Spanish, American, German and Japanese rule that has created their unique identity, and that sets them apart from other Micronesians. The same can be said for other peoples. Cultural identity does not refer to an unchanging body of tradition inherited by each island population. Rather, each Micronesian community has a sense of itself that is composed of its ancient heritage, its colonial experience and its modern circumstances.

If we look at the history of the Caroline Islands in segments, snapshots that take in perhaps fifty years at a time, the sum of changes over the past two centuries would seem to have been enough to have totally transformed these cultures. The era of beachcomber trading and whalers in the first half of the nineteenth century brought disease, violence, a revolution in material culture and irreversible commitment to commerce. Traditional leaders used the new resources to pursue their own agendas; local politics underwent upheavals as epidemics and access to guns upset existing power bases. The second half of the nineteenth century brought Christian missionaries to the Carolines, offering solutions to disease and violence, introducing literacy, and bringing new problems of balancing missionary ideas against the traditional order. These decades also brought a new commercial era, as traders, backed by international firms, developed markets for copra, beche-de-mer, lumber and other goods. Commerce and missionization did cause "striking changes in the externals of life in the islands" but "in most important respects life was lived very much as it had been in past centuries." Access to Western goods had the potential to revolutionize the relationship of chiefs and commoners, but that potential would not be realized for another generation (Hezel 1992:207–08).

In the first half of the twentieth century the Germans and Japanese pressed acculturative agendas. The Germans promoted economic development and fought Pohnpeian resistance; they limited chiefly power and tried to absorb chiefs into a colonial administrative order, made patrilineal inheritance the law and drew the Carolines into a global colonial network. Japan turned Pohnpei, Kosrae, Yap and Chuuk into profitable units of empire, where plantations, industry, and a large population of immigrants pushed Micronesians to the edges of their own islands. Then Japan prepared for war and the Carolines were transformed into military bases. Both military and civilian areas were destroyed in the war, and left unreconstructed by a U.S. government that wanted to keep the islands secure, but not to pay to rehabilitate them. In the last half-century, Caroline Islanders have struggled both for and against modernization, facing overwhelming changes as their economy shifted from post-war poverty to post-Kennedy affluence, and their social organization and political lives see-sawed between forced acculturation and isolation, between chiefly rule and democracy.

While the indigenous society and culture of the Marianas were largely destroyed, to be recreated in a new form, the social organization of the Carolines retains greater continuity. Kosrae's chiefly system was abandoned under the impacts of depopulation and conversion to Christianity, but elsewhere traditional chiefs remain influential, though their powers are limited (Kiste 1994a:16). One ongoing discussion in creating new forms of self-government for the Caroline Islands has been whether to give traditional leaders an official role in the new political structures. Is tradition enough to maintain chiefly power? Or do they need support from law?

At any point over these past two centuries outside observers might have said, and many did say, that "traditional culture" of this area is "disappearing," that the Caroline Islanders are "losing their old ways." Yet as we look at the Carolines today we see communities whose sense of heritage and tradition is very much intact, though altered in manifestation. Languages remain vital; social organization remains resilient and responsive to local needs; a sense of identity at the level of the community, the island, and the island group, is freely expressed.

In fact, within the islands that make up the Federated States of Micronesia (FSM, consisting of Chuuk State, Yap State, Kosrae State, and Pohnpei State), cultural diversity and political tension is so great that some think disintegration is likely. Far from becoming homogenous and deculturated, the different islands insist on maintaining their distinctiveness. Political anthropologist Glenn Petersen described the "structural and ethnic tensions among the states and between the states and the national government" apparent at the FSM's second constitutional convention in 1990.

> Although the peoples of Micronesia's many islands and island groups have always traded and intermarried with one another, their societies have been developing there for at least two thousand years, and they tend to view themselves in terms of what scholars call distinct ethnic identities. As one delegate had stated at the beginning of the convention, "We are different peoples, speaking different languages, with different cultures." (Petersen 1994:359)

The most populous of FSM's states is Chuuk; at more than 55,000, it overshadows the other three states and one of their political concerns is curbing the power of Chuuk's majority. Yet Chuuk State itself contains a great deal of diversity. The Mortlock Islands speak different dialects from those in Chuuk Lagoon; within the Mortlocks each atoll has its own identity. To the west, Puluwat, Pulap, and Pulusuk also speak a distinct dialect, and they differ among themselves. Within Chuuk Lagoon each island has a distinct identity, and the western part of the Lagoon has repeatedly sought to break off into a separate state within the FSM.

In contrast to Hawaiians, Maori or Chamorros, Caroline Islanders seldom publish critiques or manifestos on their cultural identity. Yet we might see public politics itself as a commentary on cultural identity, as Caroline Islanders continue to ask whether they should and how they might form a single nation from diverse but linked cultures.

Marshall Islands Identity

As in many parts of Micronesia, Marshall Islands residents are committed members of extended families and clans that are linked closely to the lands on which they reside. The primacy of household and family commitments is notable, and substantial communal sanctions keep in check any idea that personal needs and desires might supersede those of the group. Age and gender are primary materials out of which identities are shaped within any family or clan. As Marshall Islanders move to other parts of the globe, this sense of communal identity is being challenged yet, even in those distant locales, new Marshallese communities are often fashioned with similar ideologies. Indeed, close interpersonal relationships are incredibly important, so much so that they are deeply embedded in the linguistic categories of Marshallese. An elaborated set of possessives and pronouns, along with complex contextual rules of etiquette, humor, and sanctions for social improprieties, indicate how cautiously individual desires and aspirations must be situated among a wide set of interpersonal identities. These identities are fashioned out of multiple social materials, from association with a particular clan and a particular atoll down to a certain household and extended family.

At least since the emergence of copra production in the late nineteenth century, a focal point of each Marshall Islander's identity has been vested in a clan. Clans determine the essential, core features of one's person (what Europeans and Americans might call the core personality), and each person gets his/her clan identity through one's mother. In contrast, the external features of person are shaped by, and transmitted through men. In many parts of the Marshall Islands, lands are held by matri-clans. Yet while residents commonly rationalize their rights to reside on land through women, the labor of the male members of each clan creates a continuity of identity between clan members and the soil that has been transformed by clan labor. By working land, eating the products of the land, and dying and being buried on that same land, an intimate link is created between Marshall Islands soils and souls. Land and people are one. On Enewetak and Ujelang, Marshall Islands outliers, these identity relations that inextricably link people with the lands on which they reside are equally valid, though both males and females have rights on the lands they work, and these rights can be transmitted to male and female offspring for as long as they continue to vest their labor in the land (Carucci, in press). Even though districts and large segments of land are held in common by members of a single clan, each person resides and works on lands as members of particular households and particular extended families. Experiments with individual ownership and long-term land leases are of recent vintage. Not uncommonly, disputes arise as a result of the conflict between European-American ideas about fee-simple ownership, and local ideas that unify notions of land and persons.

Marshall Islands chiefs have different relationships to land, relationships that have changed significantly with the arrival of Europeans. As living deities (*irooj*), descendants of primordial god/chiefs who shaped many features of the earth, chiefs were too sacred to own land. Chiefs, however, were given the rights to oversee all of the lands of their domain, and to adjudicate all disputes over those lands, by the commoners who supported (nutritionally, politically, and militarily), their god/chiefs. Chiefs had no need to control land since they were fully supported by commoners (Carucci 1999). In the nineteenth century, German explorers and entrepreneurs came to see Marshallese chiefs in European feudal terms (Erdland 1914; Kramer and Nevermann 1938). They depicted chiefs as the owners of the lands they oversaw and, with the emergence of the copra trade, chiefs and their local land heads (*alab*) were given new power as intermediaries in the production of coconut oil. In the German feudal interpretations, chiefs owned the land and the commoners were but surfs who lived under them (Mason 1947). Rank relations were considerably altered during the German copra era. With warfare outlawed, late nineteenth century chiefly lines became ossified. The introduction of European vessels, weapons, and supplies, led to the expansion of chiefly domains, and chief-commoner relations became increasingly institutionalized along feudal lines (Tobin 1956).

Identity constructs continued to change with new waves of colonial influence. Japan seized control of the German colonies in the west central Pacific soon after Germany became involved in World War I. If German interests had been largely entrepreneurial and economic, Japan saw the region as an expansion of its own limited territories. Micronesians became citizens of the Japanese empire (even if of low class), and Japanese flooded into the territory, soon numbering more than a thousand in the Marshall Islands and outnumbering indigenous residents in Belau and the Mariana Islands. For the first time, virtually every young Marshall Islander attended primary school (for three years), and the best students were given opportunities to continue with higher levels of education, often attending a trade school in Koror, Belau. Students learned some Japanese, bowed daily toward the deified Japanese emperor, and began to develop a sense of themselves as part of the Japanese empire. If these trends resituated most people's view of themselves as small contributors to an unfathomably large Japanese state, the institutional authority of Marshallese chiefs that had been expanded during German times became far more ambivalent under the Japanese. The divine emperor had to be positioned in relation to Marshall Islands *irooj*, and thus the relative authority of Marshallese chiefs came to be questioned. On a day-to-day basis, Marshallese chiefs continued in positions of privilege, and, when they proved useful, they continued their intermediary functions under Japanese rule. At the same time, however, new domains of civil authority, including local magistrates, police, and civil clerks were established. These alternate routes of governance ultimately led to a significant realignment of relationships between chiefs and commoners. Land tenure also shifted substantially during Japanese times, with as much as one third of all land coming under governmental control.

If local warfare was outlawed by colonizers of the region, the foreigners' wars became a central force shaping the physical and social contours of the western Pacific. The islands and atolls of Micronesia were critical to Japan's expansionist dreams and, by 1940, what had begun as public works projects in the Marshall Islands were turned to military ends (Poyer, Falgout & Carucci 2001). By the end of 1941, with the bombing of Pearl Harbor (with support from bases in Micronesia), Japan was at war with the United States. Marshall Islanders' lives were often re-contoured during the preparatory phases for war, with young men and women recruited from local villages to work as laborers and support personnel on those atolls where military facilities were being built. The largest of these bases were on Jaluij, Mili, Maloelap, Wotje, Kwajalein, and Enewetak. Retaliatory strikes for Pearl Harbor included bombings of Jaluij and Kwajalein in 1942, but it took the United States more than a year to prepare to fight simultaneous wars in Europe and the Pacific. The Allies, headed by U. S. military forces, did not return to Micronesia until the end of 1943. This time they arrived with an apocalyptic force that devastated those communities in Kiribati and the Marshall Islands that were settled near Japanese bases at the same time that they destroyed Japanese forces.

The northern road to Japan that ultimately led Allied forces to Japan in 1945 began in Kiribati in 1943. The Allied assault on Tarawa was a disaster, pointing out how little the Allied military knew about atoll environments. With inadequate consideration given to tide levels, many soldiers lost their lives as assault craft could not get them anywhere near the shore. Nevertheless, Kiribati residents, who had remained under British governance until overrun by the Japanese, were happy to be freed from harsh Japanese military treatment.

After their experiences in Kiribati, U. S. forces developed an island-hopping strategy that allowed them to take critical military bases in the rest of Micronesia and bypass others, isolating and bombing bypassed Japanese bases. This strategy resulted in three very different experiences of the war in Micronesia, with concomitant differences in islanders' views of Americans, Japanese and, ultimately, of themselves. As on Butaritari and Tarawa in Kiribati, Kwajalein and Enewetak residents in the Marshall Islands experienced the effects of a direct invasion. Residents of the bypassed atolls which housed Japanese military contingents experienced daily bombing runs, lengthy periods of hardship and hunger, and threats of abuse and death at the hands of starving Japanese troops. On atolls that had only a few Japanese weather watchers and scouts, life often went on without major disruptions. The abuses of Japanese troops typically moved local people to welcome the Americans as saviors on bypassed atolls. Kwajalein and Enewetak residents are more divided. Families whose members were eradicated during the invasion often harbor negative or ambivalent feelings about Americans, while others commonly share the salvational images of Americans held by those on bypassed atolls. And on the atolls without Japanese contingents, there is little historical experience to ground impressions of outsiders.

With the arrival of the Americans, the word "freedom" began to alter Marshall Islanders' views of themselves. Americans told people they were now "free," and local interpretations of freedom became linked to a variety of changes in relation to people's lives under the Japanese. Vivid images of freedom included the fact that black soldiers could eat next to white, women could wear men's clothing and occupy statuses typically associated with men, and chiefs were demeaned by Americans: somehow they were seen as contrary to American freedoms. But, if Japanese had enforced regulations with a strict and authoritative hand, American freedom was taken to mean that people could do as they wished, an anarchic state soon viewed as far more dangerous to Marshallese notions of communal identity than was life under the disciplined Japanese. And if chiefly hierarchy was bad, why would the rule of magistrates, church officials, and persons who hoarded their wealth be better? Today, Marshallese identity resides in this ambivalent condition, seeking a space between the socially sensitized ideas deeply embedded in Marshall Islands history, the feudal and formalized hierarchies reformulated during German and Japanese times, and highly libertarian interpretations of freedom fashioned after the war.

The church, too, has become a site where Marshall Islanders root an important component of their respective identities. Not unlike Hawaiians, who were first confronted with missionaries from the American Board of Commissions for Foreign Missions ("the ABCFM": a conservative New England-based mission group who were precursors of today's far more liberal United Church of Christ [Hezel 1983]), Marshallese were reticent to accept ABCFM Christianity until the accession of their chiefs. Nevertheless, between 1857 (on Ebon) and 1926 (on Enewetak) nearly all Marshall Islanders began to think of themselves as good Christians, freely weaving local ideas about deities and proper religious comportment with the teachings of the ABCFM (see below). Only on Likiep, an atoll in the central Ratak chain "purchased" by early European entrepreneurs, was a competing Roman Catholic identity developed. In many ways, a shared Christian identity (as opposed to the "non-Christian" Catholics!) bound Marshall Islanders from different atolls together through the middle years of the twentieth century. Beginning in the 1960s, however, new religious sects arrived in Majuro and Ebeye, and have begun to proliferate throughout the Marshall Islands, fueling often contentious disagreements in formerly unified local communities. In time, these religious wars will undoubtedly die down but, in the current day, they provide a critical point of rupture as Marshall Islanders experiment with more differentiated personal and interpersonal identities (Carucci 2000).

Case Study:

Ritual Practice and the Projection of Local Identity

In *Nuclear Nativity* (1997), Laurence M. Carucci explores the way in which Ujelang and Enewetak residents in the Marshall Islands have contoured their celebration of

Kūrijmōj "Christmas" into a festive event that seeks the renewal of life on earth at the same time it projects the community's identity to surrounding people of importance in their current day world. At one level, this four month ritual weaves elements of indigenous religious practice with Christian themes first suggested by Micronesian representatives of the ABCFM mission. The primordial tale of Jebero, younger sibling chief whose rule of the Marshall Islands was secured through acts of kindness and consideration, is juxtaposed with the story of Christ, the biblical second son, whose stories of love and kindness were first told by resident missionaries.

The celebration also incorporates elaborated ritual forms that project an empowered sense of atoll identity to other communities in the Marshall Islands. For example, Enewetak's celebration is not only the longest in the Marshall Islands, it is also the most elaborate. It shares with other Marshallese festivities public presentations of song and dance practiced by members of competing song fest groups. On Enewetak and Ujelang, however, these song fest groups compete among each other for months prior to December 25th, presenting food and other gifts to one another along with their most recently composed songs. These encounters are called *kamolu*. The group with the best songs, the most elaborated speeches, and the most highly perfected songs win these small encounters and encourage the counterpart song fest group to respond with an even more highly elaborated presentation in the days to come. Increasing the difficulty and the fun (for one core value of the celebration is to promote happiness), the ritual games of *karate* and *kalabūūj* make it ever more difficult for a song fest group to ensure success as they plan a presentation for another group. In *karate*, the women from one group use typically male strategies to steal the foods from returning fishermen from another group, thereby making the other group's plan to *kamolu* much more difficult. *Kalabūūj* adds even more complexity. In *kalabūūj*, the men from one song fest group steal women from another group who are returning from collecting materials to make gifts to be given by their group during their community-wide presentation on December 25th. The humor is increased as men use typically female strategies to place their victims "in jail", treating them like the most highly ranked chiefs who they have taken in as marriage mates. Only after a week or two of feasting are the marriage mates returned, cross-dressed in garb of the opposite gender so as not to dissolve the union. Not only do these games increase the difficulty of the competitions and greatly increase the fun, they also represent eras of community history, *kalabūūj* referencing the earliest era of Spanish colonial influence, and *karate* conjuring up the Japanese era, through this locally renowned mode of self-defense.

The highlight of Christmas, Ujelang and Enewetak style, comes on December 25th, when each group presents all of its songs and dances and each family prepares a huge basket of food to exchange with members of another song fest group. In addition, each group presents its *wōjke* "tree", a huge piñata-like construction on a biblical theme that must be magically exploded from a distance by a youthful team of military personnel. The *wōjke* is a money tree, filled with dollars, soap, matches, and other valuables to be given to the minister, the earthly representative of God. It, too, has great historical symbolism, condensing images of local people's encounter with Christianity with the community's thirty year exile on Ujelang, during the years that the United States military exploded nuclear devices on their home atoll, Enewetak. Having witnessed these nuclear explosions, events that for local people represent the most potent, apocalyptic, and potentially most destructive force on earth, members of the community capture and use this force as a way to secure the renewal of life during the celebration of *Kūrijmōj*. The Ujelang-Enewetak "Christmas" does not end until well after New Year, after visiting deities and ancestor spirits have been chased from the village during a Halloween-like New Year's ceremony, and after the ritual softball and volleyball games have provided additional entertainment and a further source of ranking among the song fest groups. The final event, "the front of the year", provides a time when people begin the New Year with a display of their best demeanor as another way to ensure good fortune in the year to come (Carucci 1993; 1997).

Kiribati Identity

The Marshallese tale of Lijbake tells of the descent links that tie Marshallese to the residents of Kiribati, and recent stories, such as those that trace escapees from Japanese oppression in Kiribati to the southern Ratak chain during World War II, continue to reassert the long-established connections between the Marshall Islands and Kiribati. Issues of Kiribati identity have not been explored in as much depth as have Marshallese studies; nevertheless, some critical similarities and differences are worthy of note.

The intimate connection between land and identity, explored in some detail above, is an idea first elaborated by Martin Silverman in relation to Banaba (1971). Known to anthropologists as the "mud and blood" hypothesis, it is a concept that, in some form or another, was thought to unite all of the societies from the central Caroline Islands studied by Schneider (Silverman's mentor who worked in Yap) and Goodenough (who worked Chuuk), to the far reaches of Eastern Micronesia (Banaba). Whereas land is transmitted through males in most parts of Kiribati, on Banaba the bilateral pattern prevailed (Grimble 1989: 60). This parallels the contrast between the isolated atolls of Enewetak and Ujelang, where land rights are held bilaterally, and other parts of the Marshall Islands where extended rights to land are held primarily through females. It is clear that different historical experiences, with greater or lesser institutionalization of enterprizes such as copra production, have had substantial effects on current-day land holding practices. Nevertheless, the high valuation of land, due in part to its shortage and its centrality to the way in which Micronesian people make a living in the pre-colonial, colonial, and post-colonial eras, has provided a context in which issues of personal and communal identity are deeply rooted in the soils and landscape of this region. On Banaba, this connection between land and identity was fractured during the British administrative era. A case study of Banaba, including issues concerning identity, can be found in the section on globalization.

Classic Themes in Micronesian Identity

Anthropologists have long known that critical features of identity are shaped by household and family groups as well as clans. In a classical study (1955), Ward Goodenough demonstrated that the internal dynamics of small population groups could shift very rapidly. Clans, for example, could move from being quite prolific to extinction in just a few generations. As a result, social groupings in small Micronesian communities like those Goodenough encountered in Chuuk, utilized an array of flexibility features to seek a sustainable balance between resources and group size. Since land was often held by reason of a person's membership in a certain family within a certain clan, for example, the exchange of children among different clan or family groups allowed communities to maintain a reasonable balance between resources and the currently living members of the society. The high rate of adoption is a recognized feature of Pacific societies (Carroll 1970), though adoption often involves shifting residence from one group of parents to another or adding a new group of relatives to already established kin (rather than being raised exclusively with parents other than one's biological mother and father). In Goodenough's view, this was one of the critical flexibility features of societies in this part of the world.

In the view of David M. Schneider, the members of each cultural group have their own unique ways of identity fashioning based on principles that are far from universally shared. In *A Critique of the Study of Kinship* (1984), Schneider uses the work of David Labby (1976) and others of his students, to show that his own earlier analysis of kinship relations on Yap were highly biased by long-established anthropological ideas about the universality of the concepts of consanguinity (blood relationship) and affinity (marriage). Schneider contends that Yapese have different ideas that balance local understandings of the *tabinau* and the *genung*, along with a series of interlinking relationship terms that can only be understood in relation to these two counterbalanced concepts. *Tabinau*, for example, refers to many concepts simultaneously including: a house/dwelling, a group related by shared identity through land/house/dwelling, a foundation or dwelling platform, the possessors of *tabinau* names (living or dead), a marriage (those who share residence in such a dwelling). While Schneider had once called the *tabinau* a patrilineage and a patrilocal extended family, these concepts are clearly inadequate to local understandings, since people who are not linked by any sort of blood relationship can be *tabinau* members. European and American theories of consanguinity and affinity simply cannot be used to explain Yapese identity constructs. While Schneider certainly recognizes that members of other societies in the west central Pacific have historically related ideas, he argues that each society must be understood in terms of its own categories of relationship, categories that are not easily translated in a poetic manner into the concepts of an unrelated society. Likewise, Schneider argues that the set of Yapese categories of interpersonal relationship that are built up of and around *tabinau* and *genung* cannot be called "kinship" terms since kinship, by definition, has to do with consanguinity and affinity. On the basis of this work, anthropologists have been forced to look beyond kinship to discover other views of identity, not only those shared by all members of a culture at one moment in time, but the views of persons from different parts of the social order acting in different social settings, during particular historical moments in time.

The Winds of Change: "Freedo-Pendence" and the Global Marketplace

As human societies spread themselves across the globe, the islands of the west central Pacific were among the final settlement frontiers. In addition to geological instability, their small physical size, relative isolation, and restricted land resources postponed human settlement. These same factors, as well as the small scale of the human societies that established themselves in this part of the world, made them among the final locations to enter the post-colonial era. If India's post-war independence from Britain set the course for decolonization in the era following World War II, it was not until the 1970s and 1980s that most of the emergent nation-states of the west central Pacific became political realities (Kiste 1993). Many argue that even in the current day, these nation-states are only politically decolonized and remain dependent economically on larger nations on the Pacific Rim. Nevertheless, the pace of social change has been extremely rapid in this part of the Pacific, and social, cultural, and ecological integrity have often suffered.

The forces of social change brought about by colonialism are particularly notable in Kiribati and the Marshall Islands. While the mineral and timber wealth of New Guinea and parts of the Solomon Islands have become the most recent sites of plunder, the extraction of phosphate and the fate of location itself—highly isolated yet precisely centered in the cold war conflict between the United States and the former Soviet Union—made Kiribati and the Marshall Islands irresistible to colonizers. While many policies of colonial control continue to haunt the newly-established island nations of the west-central Pacific, new scenarios have also become apparent. As is so often true, common people have often been disenfranchised by all-too-greedy chiefs and government officials, and intermediaries. Equally, however, unregulated fishing and experiments with tourism have begun to place the fragile ecosystems of this region at risk.

Case Study:

Banaba

In *Disconcerting Issue*, Martin Silverman describes the plight of the people of Banaba, who were forced to leave their primordial homeland as the result of the near total destruction of their land by the British Phosphate Company (BPC). The extraction of phosphate began in 1900, and in December 1945 they were forced into exile on Rambi, an island some 1600 miles from Banaba (located off of the eastern tip of Vanua Levu, Fiji). While the abuses of colonialism and of state sanctioned capitalism are somewhat obscured by Silverman's reliance on systems theory applied largely internally, he nevertheless describes the radical changes in Banaban's ways of fashioning their identities and world view as a result of their imposed exile and colonial legacy. As is often the case, he demonstrates how Christianity serves as the first step in the colonization of Banaban's views of their world. Silverman suggests that missionization introduced the residents of Banaba to a universalizing moral framework and to an individualizing world view that considered the rights, responsibilities, and choices of persons in ways very different from the essentialized traditional Banaban view he sketches. The BPC followed close on the heels of missionaries and, with the extraction of phosphate, core notions about the relationship between identity and land had to be retooled. A view of Banaban identity rooted in residence as well as blood is transformed first, into a more alienated view of the relationship between land and identity, and second, into a formalized separation of collective (subsurface) and individual (surface) land rights. What is more, during the era of phosphate mining, Banaba people became a minority on their own homeland. As in so many Pacific locations, most notably Hawai'i and Aotearoa, but equally Koror, Belau and Saipan during Japanese times, or Enewetak, Bikini, Kwajalein, and Guam in the American colonial era, the idea of being a minority in one's own land has radical implications in terms of the formulation of identity. Minority status speaks of substantial inequalities of power, and ultimately leads to cries of outrage on behalf of those who have been the victims of colonial abuse.

The possibility of moving to a new island in Fiji forced Banaba people to rationalize critical features of their identity. In a manner precisely analogous to that of Enewetak, Bikini, and Ebeye residents in the Marshall Islands, they focused on the ambivalent fea-

tures of identity that had resulted from the colonial legacy. They wished to retain ownership and visitation rights to Banaba. While worried about preserving Banaban practices
in the future, they wished to remain distinctly Banaban. At the same time, they wished to
continue to have the benefits of European life. With their move to Rambi in 1945, however, Banaba people experienced other levels of disenchantment, for they were confronted by the loss of additional sources of residual empowerment that they had formerly been able to maintain. On Banaba they were treated as land owners, rather than
just workers. This placed them well below the foreign officials who managed the phosphate enterprise, yet in a category of privilege vis-à-vis the Chinese and other expatriot
laborers. In exchange for the persistent destruction of their land they, like their phosphate rich cousins on Nauru (160 miles west of Banaba), had access to a relatively cosmopolitan life, a meager side benefit of phosphate mining. On Rambi, Banaban identity
again had to be significantly rethought. While the land space here was large, it was on the
margins of the much larger emerging nation state of Fiji. And being a landowner on
Rambi entitled one only to cut copra. It carried few of the entitlements that being a
landowner had conveyed on Banaba. Situating one's identity as a Banaban-in-exile required new negotiations vis-à-vis Fijians and Gilbertese who were in-married (but without Banaba land rights) or who followed the community as friends. It involved a stage of
noted lawlessness in a community that had been renowned in pre-World War II days for
being particularly law-abiding. It included disputes with the appointed government ad-
visor. Most importantly, it involved re-formulations of a personal and communal identity that had been incorporated in land, land one resided on and worked on a daily basis.
Primordial sentiments of attachment to one's homeland had to be brought into align-
ment with another home land. Images of these two spaces and of the different identities
they evoked were frequently overlaid in people's minds, yet impossible to co-join either
geophysically, or in other important ways. Having separated a people from their culturally inscribed place, having extracted the very soul from the Banaban landscape, the Banaban community is left with the dilemma of how to resettle a new space, to imbue it
with Banaban sensibilities and align it with this other, now distant, mythical place that is,
in some residual ways, also truly their own.

This tale of colonial abuse is hardly unique in the west central Pacific. Not only is a
fair segment of Banaban history replicated on Nauru; Ebon, in the Marshall Islands, also
had its own brief encounter with phosphate (as well as a particularly intimate encounter
with Christianity). Equally disquieting, however, has been the history of nuclear testing
in the northern Marshall Islands and the correlative effects on the residents of Kwajalein
Atoll in the central Rālik chain.

Case Study:

Bikini (and other S/Pacific Locations: Enewetak, Rongelap, Utedik, and Kwajalein)

When the United States dropped atom bombs on Hiroshima and Nagasaki, Japan in
1945, the Pacific War was brought to a sudden end. In spite of the fact that knowledge
about radioactivity was at an infantile stage, and the human risks of such testing were
only beginning to become evident, a decision was made to move further atomic tests

from the deserts of the American Southwest to the distant isles of the Marshall Islands, islands controlled by the United States Navy after the battles with Japan. The United States was granted the authority to administer these islands under a special strategic trust, an agreement under which the U. S. could continue its military experiments at the same time it promised to protect local islanders and further their best interests. These were clearly antithetical courses of action. With established U.S. military bases on Kwajalein and Enewetak, nearby Bikini was chosen initially as the atomic test site. Beginning in 1946, with the Able test, nearly seventy announced tests took place in the Marshall Islands. The largest of these nuclear blasts was nearly 200 times more powerful than the bombs that had been dropped on Japan. Bikini people were forced into exile, first on nearby Rongedik; then, ravaged by famine and fearful of the foreign spirits who had primordial rights to Rongedik lands, they were taken to Kwajalein until they could be resettled on Kili (Mason 1947). At the time of their removal from Bikini, residents were told that the tests were to promote the well-being of humankind. Clearly, the well-being of Bikini people was considered far less critical.

In less than two years, the residents of Enewetak followed Bikini people into forced exile, also, they were told, to promote the betterment of humankind. The pace of nuclear testing had to be increased and, in the Americans' eyes, Enewetak's isolated location was ideal for additional tests. Bikini people were placed on Kili, a coral pinnacle in the southern Marshall Islands. Kili had rich soils, as advertised, but the lack of a lagoon and of any good anchorage during the dry, windy months of winter left the fishing-oriented community of Bikini people dejected and without outside support (Kiste 1974). Enewetak people, placed in exile on Ujelang, fared no better. Nearly 650 miles from the governmental center, it was rarely visited by a supply boat and, while Ujelang did have a lagoon, the usable fishing area was only about 1/14th the size of that of Enewetak, the land area was also much smaller, and Ujelang's soil was strewn with coral rubble from an 1860s typhoon. As a result, within two or three years, Enewetak people faced repeated cycles of famine on Ujelang, where they remained for thirty-three years.

Finally, in 1980, they returned to their home atoll after years of struggle on Ujelang. In a way quite comparable to Banaba, however, the soils of the Enewetak homeland had been radically transformed by the nuclear tests. Soils dredged from the lagoon were used to create a flattened land surface that could support a lengthy runway. In the process, all of the sacred historical sites on the main islet that bore the imprint of Enewetak history and consciousness had been destroyed. A second major islet had been transformed into a military city for 10,000 personnel during the height of nuclear testing. The island's contours, boundaries, and culturally significant features were obliterated. The atoll's soils were radioactive, meaning that foods grown in it were unsafe; only four of the atoll's 48 islets had been thoroughly cleaned of radioactive soils and replanted, leaving residents with an even smaller usable area than they had had on Ujelang. Food crops proved difficult to reestablish on nutritionally depleted and contaminated soils. People have been forced to depend on imported foods, resulting in epidemic levels of formerly unknown illnesses such as adult-onset diabetes and heart disease. In 2000, the Nuclear Claims Tribunal established to settle all nuclear testing related grievances in the Marshall Islands, judged that a fair settlement to rehabilitate Enewetak and compensate people for their suffering would cost the United States 341 million dollars. To date, the United States Congress has not provided these funds (Carucci 1999; in press).

Bikini has fared no better. The Nuclear Claims Court recommends an even larger compensation settlement for Bikini, since its soils are more widely contaminated than those on Enewetak. A brief attempt at repatriation in the 1970s proved unsuccessful, since the clean-up of radioactive materials was entirely inadequate. As a result of ingesting local foodstuffs, Bikini people were soon showing evidence of thyroid cancers and had to be removed from their home atoll. Some returned to Kili, while others moved to the islet of Ejij in the government center, Majuro, since their life on Kili was too unbearable. Yet others have taken up residence in Hawai'i or in the continental United States in hopes of fulfilling some of the dreams of freedom that were to have been an integral part of the American approach to justice.

The legacy of nuclear testing extends also to the people of Rongelap and Utedik who were exposed to high-level doses of radioactivity during the 1954 Bravo Test. While conspiracy theorists contend that the test was perpetrated *in order to* see what the radioactive effects on humans might be, United States government authorities insist it was accidental. Recently declassified documents make it clear that, if accidental, the decision to conduct the test was based on a series of bad judgements. As a result of radioactive exposure, members of the Rongelap and Utedik communities suffered medical injury and, in some cases, death. Community members were relocated to Kwajalein for up to three years after Bravo, and the Rongelap community moved from their home atoll in 1985 as a result of their fears of residual radioactivity in Rongelap soils and food plants. While rehabilitation efforts have begun on Rongelap, much of the community continues to reside on Mejatto islet on Kwajalein. Marshallese tell stories of the "jelly-fish babies" aborted by expectant mothers after the Bravo test, and young mothers today continue to express fears about birthing aberrant young. Other stories describe a wide array of malformed subsistence plants and creatures of the sea. The members of these communities live with fears that have resulted from the nuclear tests. They must live with constant medical check-ups, with surgically altered bodies, and with Synthroid, a medicinal substitute for the thyroids they have sacrificed to remain cancer free. Community members who are too young to have been alive in 1954 question the safety of their soils, the lagoon waters, and the products of the land and sea. Others express their fear of local foods and subsist on the only imports they can afford, often subjecting themselves to the same dietary illnesses that have become epidemic on Enewetak.

The military testing era has also inscribed its motifs on Kwajalein, the support base from which nuclear tests were conducted and, more recently, a tracking station for intercontinental ballistic missiles and test site for "Star Wars" interceptor missiles. William Alexander (1978) and David Hanlon (1998) describe aspects of life on Epjā (known as Ebeye since World War II), the Marshallese enclave that provides labor support for the military base on Kwajalein Atoll. Laurence M. Carucci (1997) overviews the contradictions between locations of value to Kwajalein people and American military spatial designs on the atoll. To outsiders, Ebeye is the largest urban slum in the west central Pacific, a site plagued with extreme overpopulation and extraordinary problems meeting the basic needs of human life. Often without water, without operational sewers, with only the most overburdened and marginal medical facilities, the islet presents a despicable image. Contributing to the image of degradation is the monstrous contrast with life on Kwajalein islet, U. S. Army headquarters just a short boat-ride across the lagoon. Hanlon typifies Kwajalein as patterned on a typical Southern California suburb, with a golf course, snack bar, and Macy's West. Indeed, as a military-governed entity, Kwajalein's strict rules contribute to an atmosphere that, while oppressive in some respects, is hyper-idealized in others. Each emasculated coconut has been pruned in mock-Waikiki style, and every lawn is trimmed in a timely manner. Each residence is regularly refurbished, and food, either prepared or grocer's fresh, is bargain priced. Little wonder that jobs on Kwajalein are at a premium, and Marshallese who are allowed to live on Kwajalein often find the opportunity irresistible, in spite of isolation from kin and from Marshall Islands' life (even the rare drinking coconut on Kwajalein could not be harvested since climbing trees is tabu).

In spite of such changes, Kwajalein people talk of life on their atoll as following a primordial path. In ancient times the atoll was known as *Aelōñ in Tarlōñ* after a famous coral head in the middle of Kwajalein lagoon. On one side, the coral head is filled with fish, on the other it lacks any sea life. This, people say, is like life on the atoll today. In many senses, the ambivalences of life on Kwajalein provide an ideal condensation symbol for Marshallese life at the beginning of the twenty-first century. Under the tutelage of the Americans, Marshall Islanders were convinced of the value of following a path that would lead to freedom and democracy. Yet, having acceded to being led down that path, in fact they have found themselves on a trail that spells greater dependency. At the moment a Kwajalein resident spends hard-earned compensation money from the rental of Kwajalein lands to fly on a U. S. airline to Hawai'i, the choice feels something like freedom. But, in the next moment, as one recalls the inability to visit one's own land parcel on Kwajalein islet, or the extreme restrictions on fishing or visiting family lands in the largest segment of Kwajalein, the Mid-Atoll Corridor, also leased to the U. S. Army, the feeling is one of being dependent and dominated. As an Ebeye resident, one lives on dreams of Marshall Islands foods, while consuming an over-priced can of fatty corned beef. Who would have predicted how convoluted the contours of this particular path to "freedo-pendence" might become? Yet the path has been well-trodden in the Marshall Islands and, to some extent, throughout the west central Pacific, where strategic location is the most highly desirable export, and where the currency of military or capitalist (ab)use disrupts the way in which local people see the features of the landscape and the sea, which have been shaped by their lives from ancient times until the current day.

Case Study:

Econ 101, Pohnpeian Style

If Micronesian residents have been confronted head-on with the forces of global capitalism, they have certainly not been consumed by principles of economic gain. Rather, they have reshaped exchange principles to align with local valuations and local understandings. In the exchanges of Enewetak *Kūrijmōj*, described above, the aim is similar to that of Ongka and other center persons or big men in Highland New Guinea. The way to gain rank is through giving, and the only way to "win" the encounters among song fest groups is to give far more than one receives from other groups. It is the accumulation of rank and renown rather than the accumulation of goods that is of local value. In a similar way, Glenn Petersen (1993) describes the repeated life cycle of small businesses in Pohnpei. Petersen notes that most businesses are started with a small capital outlay, expand, and then, within a few years, realize their demise. This cycle, Petersen argues, is not evidence that Pohnpei entrepreneurs lack business acumen. Rather, the expansion cycle of small businesses typically includes the extension of credit to purchasers, typically relatives and close friends of the entrepreneur. As goods are distributed, the rank of the entrepreneur increases and, of course, goods are distributed among a broad network of community members in a manner that is of benefit to everyone. The entrepreneur gains rank by giving away what he owns. What looks to economists like another Pohnpeian business "failure", in other words, is actually a Micronesian success involving the perpetuation and expansion of long-standing Pohnpeian exchange networks and the operation of a local theory of social value.

Religious Change through History and Revitalization

Religious Background

Pre-Christian Micronesian religions shared the common Oceanic concern with spirits, with the influence of ancestors and other supernatural beings present in the world. It is generally said that Micronesian religions were less complex than those of Polynesia, but this may just reflect the lack of recent scholarship on the topic. It is true that formal religious ideologies, ranked pantheons of deities and powerful priesthoods, were less obvious in Micronesia and were most elaborated only on the islands with a highly stratified social order. But throughout the islands, the world of the spirit was linked with the human world through prayer and ritual, and Oceanic ideas of *mana* and *tapu* were part of everyday life. Spirits were (and are) associated with landscapes, natural objects and certain activities: building houses and canoes, navigation, healing and divination. Islanders still treat sacred places with respect and caution; these may be places where spirits are known to dwell, or where important mythical events took place. Chants, offerings, and taboos on food and sexual activity were ways people could interact with spirits. Micronesians practiced shamanism, spirit-mediumship, divination and sorcery, and fear of magical retribution controlled some sorts of social interactions (Kiste 1994a:16; Alkire 1977:16–17, 51–52). Today, almost all Micronesians consider themselves Christians, and their personal and community lives are linked with Christian institutions. Yet Islander ideas about the spiritual dimension remain distinctive. Later in this section, we will return to the role of non-Christian religious ideas in modern Micronesian life.

The Introduction of Christianity

It is curious that, just as Micronesia was first settled by different groups arriving separately from southwest and southeast, so Christianity first arrived from different directions and different sources: Spanish Catholicism was the first and strongest influence in the western islands; American Protestantism in the east.

The history of the Roman Catholic Church and the Chamorro people is a complex one. The church was undoubtedly part of the oppression of the people of Guam — it was a major landowner in the *hacienda* system; responsible for education, it failed to educate any but the elite; it supported a government infamously harsh and repressive. Yet "religion, not political reform, was the refuge of the poor on the island, and all Chamorros remained devout."

> At first a scourge, then a refuge against natural calamities and the follies of alien humans, the fierce embrace of suffering and fate that is Roman Catholicism became an abiding spiritual heritage of the people of the Marianas. Of all the legacies of Spain — which included the *patron* system with its privileges and elitism, the *pare* [extended family] system with its bedrock reliance on family ties, and

macho enthusiasm for military service—the Christian religion would be the most enduring for the Chamorros. (Rogers 1995:105–6)

When the U.S. took control of Guam after the Spanish-American war, the mostly Protestant U.S. Navy officers distrusted Spanish Catholicism and sought to separate church and state. The first Protestant missionaries came to Guam in 1901, but Protestantism remained a minority religion in western Micronesia.

Protestantism was and remains strongest in the eastern islands, where it arrived in the mid-nineteenth century. While British Protestants had missionized most of Polynesia, American missionaries converted the Hawaiian Islanders. The young Hawaiian Christian churches joined forces with the children of the pioneering missionaries on Hawai'i and with the American Board of Commissioners for Foreign Missions (ABCFM) to evangelize Micronesia. In 1851, three American missionary couples and two native Hawaiian pastors and their wives sailed for Kosrae and Pohnpei, where they struggled not only with what they saw as native heathenism, but also with the evil influences of traders and whalers, alcoholism and disease and depopulation. (The Hawaiian missionaries also had to struggle with being seen as servants rather than partners of the Americans.) On Pohnpei, a 1855 smallpox epidemic proved a crisis in which the missionaries were able to help, and over the next decade teaching, preaching, translation, astute alliances with high-ranking Pohnpeians and medical service brought the ABCFM missionaries to the point that one could write, "the great mass of the people have abandoned heathenism" (Hezel 1983:142–70; Garrett 1992:136–60).

On Kosrae, early support from the paramount chief furthered Christian teaching. By 1869, the Christian church had asserted its ascendancy over both spiritual and secular matters; the paramount chief's son had been ordained as the first Kosraean deacon. In 1874, the traditional chiefly system was abandoned, and Kosrae's new ruler was chosen by democratic election. The American Protestant missionaries had created a blend of church and state that would persist for a century, and still shapes Kosrae's society.

Micronesian converts themselves carried Christianity throughout the Carolines. Pohnpei's mission school produced a generation of pastors, and in 1874 sent Pohnpeian missionaries to the Mortlock Islands and, later, to Chuuk Lagoon. The first American missionary to Chuuk arrived in 1884 to find four churches already established and chiefs eager to host more teachers. A Nukuoro woman named Siakwe, converted on Pohnpei, returned home to convert others. Her son Lekka was educated at the mission school on Kosrae and returned to Nukuoro as both an ordained minister and chief; he later sent missionaries to Kapingamarangi. Catholicism reached the Mortlocks in 1911, when Mortlockese on Pohnpei invited a priest to found a mission there; a year later, Catholic work began on Chuuk (Garrett 1992; Hezel 1983:62–70, 142, 258–261).

The Protestant pattern of training Micronesians to carry on the missionary work was also successful in the Marshall Islands, where work began at Ebon in 1857, again as a partnership between American and native Hawaiian missionaries. Hezekiah Aea, who volunteered to serve in Micronesia in 1860, was the "outstanding missionary builder of the Marshallese church", and was followed by six other Hawaiian couples. Aea "used pre-Christian forms of social organization and festivity, giving local customs a fresh Christian meaning"(Garrett 1982:147) and setting the Marshall Islands churches on a trajectory of independent development. Mission-educated Marshallese soon evangelized the rest of the archipelago. As the Hawaiians died or left, Marshallese took over the churches, which soon became self-governing and self-supporting (Hezel 1983:200–210; Garrett 1982:146–48).

The successful mission school at Ebon was moved to Kosrae in 1879, and Kosrae became a center of Christian activity in the Carolines and Marshalls (and, for a time, Kiribati as well). Pastors, their future wives and other future Micronesian leaders were trained and sent throughout the region. The mission school was a place where Islanders formed inter-ethnic friendships and marriages and constructed a new Christian Micronesian identity that reached far beyond their home island to the Carolines, the Marshalls, Kiribati, Hawai'i and the United States—and, later, to Germany and Japan as well.

Kiribati also received its first missionary visits from the Hawaiian churches in cooperation with the ABCFM, though later church development took place under the direction of Samoan pastors from the London Missionary Society, moving north into Kiribati from Tuvalu. But, Garrett writes, "Through the Hawaiian presence and example Gilbertese Christianity would early aspire to an identity of its own" (Garrett 1982:153, 149–54). This identity became more complex when an I-Kiribati ruler encouraged Belgian and French Catholic missionaries who arrived in 1891, opening a contest of Christian faiths in Kiribati. The Northern Gilberts, centered at Abaiang and maintaining French links, became and remained more Catholic; the south, centered at Rongorongo, more Protestant.

Christianity under Colonial Rule

In 1885, the Carolines came under newly active Spanish rule, and the Marshalls under German control. Now the churches had to deal with colonial authorities as well as indigenous leaders, and for the first time Protestants and Catholics came directly into competition. The new Spanish governor of Yap went ashore accompanied by priests and a garrison of Filipino troops, in an eerie reminder of the Mariana Islands two centuries before. Yapese responded politely but without great enthusiasm to the government-supported missionary efforts. In Palau, Catholics began to work in 1891, setting up churches and schools, but neither the church nor the Spanish government was a strong presence (Hezel 1983:313–15; 1995:9–24, 70–84; Garrett 1992:313).

On Pohnpei, where Protestantism was well rooted, the arrival of Spanish officials and missionary priests in 1887 was more problematic. More than half of Pohnpeians belonged to Protestant churches, and there were several mission schools. Spanish Catholic missionaries were energetic proselytizers, but religious tension was only part of the volatile situation on Pohnpei. When Pohnpeians resisted government demands with a violent uprising in mid-1887, the American Protestant missionaries ended up helping the Spanish officials, while the Catholic priests fell out of favor with the government. The Catholics became allied with the paramount chief of Kiti, whose chief rival was Henry Nanpei, a young man who was to become a Protestant pastor and the most influential man on Pohnpei. Thus the Catholic-Protestant rivalry of Europe became enmeshed in the traditional politics of Pohnpei.

The northern part of Pohnpei (where the beleaguered Spanish took refuge in their Kolonia fort) became largely Catholic. Henry Nanpei responded by using his business and political leadership skills to strengthen Protestantism. The lines of political-religious conflict became sharper, erupting into violence first in a Catholic Pohnpeian uprising against Spanish forced labor, then in a 1898 Protestant attack on a Catholic mission station, for which the American missionaries were blamed and expelled. The Spanish were unable to control Pohnpei, and their introduction of Catholicism had added fuel to internal rivalries (Hezel 1995:25–44, 81–93; Garrett 1992:300).

German emphasis on economic development threatened Pohnpei's traditional land tenure and tribute system, limiting chiefly power and introducing taxation and corvee labor as a way for people to pay the imposed taxes. The changes, plus competition between Pohnpeian leaders, produced a tense situation which in 1910 erupted into the "Sokehs rebellion." The leaders and many involved with the rebellion were Catholics; some were executed and others exiled. (Hezel 1995:94–105, 132–144; Garrett 1992:283–86, 302).

When Germany annexed the Marshall Islands in 1885, it continued a process already underway, developing its links with the global copra market. In fact, under an agreement with the German government, the Jaluit Company actually governed the Marshalls, running the area "like the company store" (Hezel 1995:48). Marshallese became deeply involved with copra production; traditional chiefs became wealthy from it; churches benefitted from German trade policies while opposing imports of alcohol and tobacco. In the first decades of the twentieth century, "Marshall Island Protestantism, at the atoll level, was already rooted in the daily life of the people through relations with chiefly leaders and, more significantly, through strong church committees composed of deacons, which governed the internal affairs of the church and were linked together in many ways through shipping and trade" (Garrett 1992:438; Hezel 1995:45–55, 124–5; Garrett 1997:129–30).

The Japanese Era and the Pacific War

Japanese officials at first welcomed Christianity's role in acculturating Islanders to western ways, and subsidized Catholic and Protestant churches. Spanish Jesuits in Tokyo supervised the Northern Marianas, the Japanese Congregationalist South Seas Mission, *Nan'yo Dendo Dan*, eventually took over the Protestant mission work in Micronesia, and Seventh Day Adventists from Japan responded to an invitation to work in Palau.

On Kosrae, neither the Spanish nor the German governments had a strong presence. The Protestant church continued to shape Kosrae's social fabric and politics. In these years, Hezel writes, "the island population was being remarkably transformed" into a "startling blend of prosperity and piety" (Hezel 1995:55–62). The harshness of the local Japanese colonial official encouraged the already established tendency to handle secular matters through the Protestant church rather than the government, further solidifying the Kosraean melding of church and state—especially since most Japanese were non-Christian. Kosrae's mission school brought in two Japanese Congregationalist women to run it, and continued to graduate pastors and their wives.

On Yap and Palau, Catholic missionaries at first worked largely with the church's core of immigrant Chamorros. The German and then the Japanese push to modernize was countered in Palau by political and spiritual opposition, beginning a thread of revivalism that was to characterize Palau for another century through the political/religious movement called Modekngei (see below). Yapese practiced passive resistance to Japanese assimilation efforts, and "began converting to Catholicism, which served as a buffer between them and the foreign government much as Protestantism was on Kosrae" (Hezel 1995:179). The Japanese government was supportive, using Catholicism to undermine the traditional clan system, until growing nationalism turned the official attitude to one of suspicion and harassment (Garrett 1992:453–55; 1997:141–42).

During the 1930s, the Japanese government embarked on a plan of immigration and economic intensification for Micronesia, bringing tens of thousands of Japanese and Okinawan settlers to the high islands and transforming the face of the region. Then, as war approached, the Japanese colonial policy of assimilation became more threateningly nationalistic. Christianity was seen as a foreign influence; yet, as battles neared, for Islanders, their faith was also to become a mode of resistance. The Japanese did not actively try to convert islanders to State Shinto, but they encouraged (and sometimes forced) participation in its nationalistic rituals. Christian activity was restricted, and increases in the number of Japanese missionaries was insufficient to stop the pressure on the missions' work (Hezel 1995:209–217).

The danger and stress of World War II caused people to turn to Christian churches and, in some places, to non-Christian spirituality, while the Japanese military saw the churches as a security threat, forbidding services and confiscating church property. With foreign missionaries expelled, imprisoned or executed, Micronesians gained experience in church leadership under the harshest conditions. In the Marshalls, as Japanese policy became more warlike in the late 1930s, "Marshall Islanders drew inward, away from the tensions generated by the two introduced cultures." Marshallese culture and Christianity "became a refuge" from war (Garrett 1997:127). But in Chuuk, "The disillusionment of the laity, Catholic and Protestant, extended to both the contending military powers which had rendered their daily life almost insupportable. Many people defected from the churches and invoked old local spirits" (Garrett 1997:137; Hezel n.d.).

Garrett (1992:46) writes that World War II brought the "period of greatest change" to Pacific churches, as it did to all of Micronesian society (Poyer, Falgout and Carucci 2001). In the war, "The idea of sin took on new dimensions," and caused Islanders to view foreigners with new eyes. As Micronesians emerged from the war years, they were seeking more control over their spiritual lives, as well as over their temporal fortunes.

Micronesian Independence and Indigenous Churches

As Americans moved into areas formerly under Japanese control, the initial U.S. Navy military government restored the opportunity to worship openly. Both Catholic and Protestant missionaries returned after the war, but soon Micronesian churches, like those in the rest of the Pacific, began to move more assuredly to local control. Decolonization in the political realm was paralleled by "de-missionization" in the religious realm, as island churches declared their independence from foreign organizations. The Second Vatican Council and the ecumenical movement reduced Protestant-Catholic hostility. In 1966, the Pacific Council of Churches was formed (the Roman Catholic church joined in 1975), bringing church leaders and policy-makers together from around the region (Garrett 1997:311–312).

As Hezel (1978) points out, "indigenization," the creation of "native churches", has always been, in some sense, a goal of foreign missionaries. American Protestants put a high priority on training native ministers, along with wives, and on making local churches self-governing and self-supporting. Catholic missions were less aggressive in establishing a native ministry; the long training to become a priest is one reason that the first Micronesian priest, Paulino Cantero from Pohnpei, was not ordained until 1940. Yet, despite their desire to encourage local leadership, neither Catholic nor Protestant missionaries encouraged a genuine synthesis of indigenous culture and Christian philosophy. Not until the postwar global changes described above was it possible for native churches to link their Christian faith with their cultural identity. "Today," Hezel (himself a Jesuit priest in the Carolines) writes, "Catholic missionaries profess salvation for both the islanders and their cultures" (Hezel 1978:273).

In 1971, the first Guamanian bishop of Guam was appointed, Monsignor Felixberto Camacho Flores (the first diocesan priest of Chamorro ancestry, Jose Bernardo Palomo y Torres, had been ordained in 1859). While the Catholic Church became more local, its

predominance was challenged in the late 1960s and 1970s as new denominations and religions came to Guam (Episcopalians, Seventh Day Adventists, Lutherans, Mormons, Baha'is), and from there influenced the rest of Micronesia (Rogers 1995:100, 291, 244–45).
Both Protestant and Catholic churches have expanded their work in the Carolines. The
arrival of an energetic set of post-Vatican II Jesuit missionaries in the 1960s produced
new initiatives, including the establishment of the elite Xavier High School in Chuuk
and the Pohnpei Agricultural Training School on Pohnpei. Pohnpeian priest Paulino
Cantero, trained in Spain, returned to Pohnpei, and the first Chuukese priest, Amando
Samo, was ordained in 1977; many Chuukese women have joined Catholic orders.
Catholic efforts in Chuuk and Pohnpei have also been helped by the ordaining of permanent deacons, who are allowed to marry (Garrett 1997:291–94, 440).

The first Palauan priests were ordained in the early 1960s. Palau experienced a period
of political disturbance from 1960–1990; perhaps reflecting this, Modekngei also flourished, even establishing a high school, but the movement collapsed again in the early
1980s. The career of Palauan priest Felix Yaoch opened "a new vista for the church in
Palau, with the insights of the Second Vatican Council and aspects of Modekngei, becoming in the process a Palauan Catholic Church, loyal to the spirits of the ancestors"
(Garrett 1997:302). The first Yapese priest, Nicholas Rahoy, was ordained in 1977, with
two others in the 1980s. Palau's Protestant church, which trained a generation of civil
servants in Bible-study schools, continued the tradition of indigenous proselytization
when it sent two Palauan men and a German couple as the first Protestant missionaries
to Yap in 1952. And, in the post-war years, the last outer island communities in the central and western Carolines became Christian (Garrett 1997:299–305).

Religion continues to shape the modern politics of Kiribati, as both Protestant and
Catholic church leaders hold positions in the *maneaba* (village meeting house), and the
geographic-religious split sowed the seeds of two post-war political parties. The political
and theological changes since the 1960s have reduced hostility between Catholic and
Protestant (as has a mutual interest in economic development and competition from the
Church of the Latter Day Saints), but the political ramifications of the distinction have
been slow to disappear. There are many I-Kiribati ministers, and I-Kiribati priest Paul
Mea was ordained bishop in 1979, just before independence (Garrett 1992, 1997).

The Marshallese church followed U.S. Congregationalists into the United Church of
Christ in 1957, and became independent in 1972; most missionaries left. The Marshallese Protestant church today retains its important status and resources, despite a decline in membership. In 1992, the United Church of Christ comprised only about 52% of
the Marshallese population, due to the growth of the Assemblies of God, a Pentecostal
group that arrived in the 1960s and drew many adherents in urban area Majuro, a center
of rapid social change. Marshallese have also joined several other newly introduced
Protestant denominations, or become Baha'is. (Catholics, who began work in the Marshalls in 1899, remain a minority, with only modest growth.) Garrett speculates that the
"disaffection" from the established church may be due both to the firmly centralized
governance and to the progressive Americanization of the Marshalls (Garrett
1997:431–3).

Contrast this with Kosrae, where the close identification of Kosraean identity and
polity with the Congregationalist church created strong resistance to the introduction of
other religions, despite American promotion of religious liberty. In the 1990s, 98% of
Kosraeans belonged to the four main Congregationalist churches (Garrett 1997:436).
Other islands have also sought to limit proselytizing for new faiths, which Micronesian
anthropologist Joakim Peter (1996) sees as an example of how indigenous people exert

control over what began as an imported religion. Small atoll communities, especially, see their social harmony as linked with unity of religious affiliation.

Both the Church of the Latter Day Saints (LDS [Mormons]) and the Seventh Day Adventists (SDA), as well as smaller Christian denominations and Baha'is, began teaching actively throughout the Pacific in the 1970s. Some of these (especially LDS and SDA) built schools and emphasized educational opportunities; all suffered opposition from established churches. The LDS arrived in Micronesia first in Kiribati (established from Tonga); in the early 1980s, "small, well-funded groups" were established in Guam, the Northern Marianas, the Marshalls and the FSM (Garrett 1997:428). Another innovation, Pacific Missionary Aviation, was founded in 1974 and now has a significant presence throughout the region; "a blend of classic evangelical mission with modern technology" (Garrett 1997:435, 437).

Although global changes in Christianity affected Micronesian churches, "After 1960 the overall U.S. modernizing of Marshallese life dwarfed the relatively minor visibility of the church" (Garrett 1997:430). This was true throughout Micronesia—the massive increase in money and programs poured into Micronesia has made "government," rather than church, the primary source of social change throughout the region.

Religion as Resistance

As in other parts of the Pacific, one way people responded to the stresses of social change was to phrase their emerging understandings and resistance in religious terms, taking the form that social scientists call revitalization movements. Such movements occurred in Micronesia during the Spanish, German and Japanese eras. In 1889, only a year after the first Christian missionaries began work on Yap, earthquakes were interpreted as ancestral anger and produced spirit-possession movements (Garrett 1992:312). In 1903, a revivalistic movement spread through the Mortlocks and revived intermittently until 1908. Missionaries called it "a wave of heathenism," and it involved the practice of old dances, traditional dress, the use of turmeric, contacting the spirits through mediums, and celebrating non-Christian marriages. The German government suppressed the movement, not out of religious concerns, but to prevent the neglect of crops and the depletion of resources in feasting (Hezel 1995:98–99). German officials on Pohnpei were constantly monitoring for opposition, and disbanded several secret societies of young men that "observed such rituals as scarification, eating raw lizards, and sexual promiscuity, and went by names like the Typhoon Society and the United States Company" (Hezel 1995:141). In 1930, a local prophetic movement on Beru, Kiribati, led by a Protestant minister, ended in fighting against Catholics, with two deaths (Garrett 1992:432–33).

The most influential indigenous religious movement in Micronesia is Modekngei on Palau. At the end of the nineteenth century, Palau was perhaps the least modernized area of Micronesia. In 1905, an enthusiastic German governor, aided by a high-titled Palauan man named Louch, changed that in a burst of reform aimed at traditional customs. Palauan religious leaders, spirit mediums, mounted increasingly open protest as the government pressed its reforms, and in 1906 they urged chiefs to support an uprising. The chiefs informed the Germans, who exiled six ringleaders, banned the spirit mediums completely, and destroyed their shrines (Hezel 1995:111–120).

The Japanese were even more zealous in their desire to modernize Palau. Religious opposition resurfaced through a man named Temedad, who, between 1912 and 1916, had first experienced visions and claimed supernatural powers. Temedad, and a man named Ongesi, together created Modekngei (from "Ngaramodekne," meaning "it is bound together"). Modekngei preached the existence of a single God—one of the local Palauan deities equated with Jesus; its symbol was the cross and its meetings were similar to Christian services. Temedad exorcised spirits and abolished totemic food taboos, but his most important ceremonies were for healing. (The philosophy and history of Modekngei has been described by both Japanese and American researchers; see Aoyagi 1978; Barnett 1949, 1979; Shuster 1982a,b; Useem 1946; Vidich 1980[1952]:228–44).

The German administration had opposed Modekngei, and the Japanese administration also sought to suppress it, partly at the urging of Palauans who supported the "civilizing" efforts of the colonial rulers (some traditional chiefs and healers also opposed Modekngei). Adherents were jailed several times during the 1920s; Temedad died in prison soon after his last arrest. His successor, Ongesi, rebuilt Modekngei after his release from prison in 1925.

Under Ongesi, Modekngei became explicitly nativistic and opposed to acculturation, banning foreign goods and opposing Japanese schools, health care, labor conscription, and changes in Palauan customs. The approach touched a chord; in late 1937, according to Vidich (1980:233), Modekngei "was in complete control of all native political power in Palau." It then faced another period of suppression by Japanese officials helped by Palauans who favored modernization and held positions with the colonial administration. By late 1940, "Modekngei had been thoroughly repressed and Japanese authority was firmly entrenched"; Ongesi was jailed again (Shuster 1982a:77; Hezel 1995:161–66).

During the last year of war, the main islands of Palau were isolated and suffered continual American bombardment. With large numbers of troops and civilians trying to live off the land, and communication disrupted, Japanese authorities become ineffective in governing Palauans (Nero 1989). Palauans turned to Modekngei, which offered reassuring prophecies of future well-being, cures for the wounded and protective charms. As Allied success weakened Japanese effectiveness, Modekngei grew in power, even making efforts to control Palau's traditional chiefs and interfering with Japanese war work. By September 1945, Rnguul, who replaced the imprisoned Ongesi, "was acting as the undisputed political leader and policy maker for Palau" (Vidich 1980:246).

After the war, over 700 Palauans told American census takers that they were members (Useem 1946:76). But conditions were soon to prove less favorable to Modekngei. While pre-war Palau had been the capital of Japanese Micronesia, Palau under American rule became a backwater. American policy restored the power of traditional chiefs (who had lost power under Japanese policies); this "broke the chiefs' link to the Modekngei and was the first step in the post-war decline of the movement" (Shuster 1982a:129).

Despite its post-war loss of power, Modekngei remains active in Palau. In 1963 a district publication claimed that a revived Modekngei embraced about a third of the population. Modekngei members affected elections to the Congress of Micronesia throughout the 1960s by regularly voting in a bloc. Modekngei established businesses and a school, and played a role in the 1974 Constitutional Convention and the 1980 Palauan presidential elections. By the 1980s factionalism and a decrease in membership had limited its influence.

In a current website, Modekngei is called by a Palauan student-researcher "just another religion among the many in the world," and "a combination of all the religion[s] that were introduced to Palau in the early 1900's." But the text also presents Modekngei's claim to cultural authenticity, stating that "the Modekngei religion was continually practiced until foreigners introduced their religions to Palauans, diverting most of the society from its traditional religion" (www.geocities.com/SouthBeach/palms/6757/modekngei.html, research by C. Adelbai).

Christianity and Cultural Identity

We have seen that indigenous religions were a focus of resistance to acculturative pressures in pre-war colonial Micronesia, and that Modekngei became an established church that maintains Palauan traditional culture as part of its creed. Micronesians have also used Christianity as resistance.

> As a political strategy, religious conversion to Christianity allowed Micronesian peoples to contain the demands of foreign authority by permitting communication and negotiation with colonial representatives through a higher, mutually shared body of religious beliefs. In this way, the more oppressive aspects of the colonial presence could be blunted. (Hanlon 1994:101).

In reviewing the impact of Protestant Christianity on the Caroline and Marshall Islands in the nineteenth century, Hezel (1983:315–317) describes achievements in health care, literacy and eliminating warfare in some regions, while acknowledging that their efforts to change cultures were not successful. "Kinship, land tenure, and political authority—the bedrock of the cultures—were almost entirely unshaken by missionary conversions." That European and American missionaries saw their task as "civilizing the heathen"—changing cultures as well as hearts—is certainly true. The effect of delivering Christian teachings from ethnocentric and even racist perspectives was undeniably destructive to indigenous cultures and psyches. As James Nason (1978) explains for Etal, foreign Protestant missionaries to the Mortlocks set the goal of changing a wide range of Micronesian beliefs and institutions. Yet "the actual extent to which they were able to change the basic social organization of the island of Etal appears to have been slight." Changes in material culture and social organization would have happened, he concludes, whether the missionaries were there or not. What Christianity did provide was a "new religious framework" allowing Etal people to undertake social change.

Despite common ideas about missionary conversion "destroying" indigenous societies, that does not seem to be the case. Peter Black (1978) studied why Tobi Islanders became Roman Catholic quickly and profoundly during a single visit by a Jesuit priest from Palau, and concludes that, in this case, conversion was chosen as a way to maintain indigenous ways of thinking about the world. Michael Lieber (1994) similarly shows how the adoption of Christian belief, and even church organization, did not alter essential elements of Kapingamarangi worldview.

Joakim Peter, himself an Etal Islander, recounts the story of the founding of Catholicism on Etal in terms of family politics. He writes, "I contend that Ettal Islanders are much in control of their situation and that the Catholic Church grew out of Ettal Islanders' propensity for change, for redressing some perceived political imbalance" (Peter 1996:285). As John Barker (1990:1) points out, images of primitive cultures and rigid white missionaries are anachronistic. "Christianity is today the most widespread and pervasive religion in the region, and the original peoples of the South Pacific are steadily making it their own" with national churches, creative syntheses of indigenous and Christian symbols and philosophies, and political uses of Christian values. Micronesians even use Christianity to critique their own cultures. Women took active roles in the churches from the start, using these new institutions to exert effective power in cultures that limited their public roles. Micronesian women today attend international conferences and use links with global organizations to address local issues. In Chuuk, women's organizations took on problems of alcohol use and domestic violence, pushing their nearly all-male local governments to implement controls (Marshall and Marshall 1990).

Juliana Flinn (1990:221–235) describes how the people of Pulap Atoll west of Chuuk use Catholicism to maintain traditional values. Pulapese converted to Catholicism only in the late 1950s. Today, they use Catholicism to promote their adherence to core values of sharing, nurturing, and cooperation. Late conversion allowed Pulapese to benefit from a twentieth-century Christianity that did not require them to abandon their previous identity. They distinguish between elements of their culture that are "pagan" (to be discarded) and elements that are "custom." In fact, Pulap people see themselves as the most traditional in Chuuk State. As part of their self-conscious claim to a cultural identity that includes traditionalism, Pulapese say they exhibit the ideal of *tong* "love, pity, mercy, compassion", and they claim that Catholicism promotes this. Catholicism also has practical advantages in education and other resources through the church. Catholicism, Flinn writes, "plays a role in allowing Pulapese to be both traditional and modern."

While Micronesians have taken Christianity as part of their own identity, they think about the spiritual world in ways that are different from orthodox Western Christianity. Micronesian ideas of "soul" and understandings of the intangible aspects of human beings have been described under the rubric of psychological anthropology (Black 1999), but it is difficult to summarize these briefly. Micronesian belief includes a concept of the personal soul which moves into a spiritual life after death, but its potential for interaction with the living is a continual source of concern for Micronesians. Describing modern ideas about spirits on Ifaluk Atoll, Catherine Lutz writes:

> Although particular spirits may be either benevolent or malevolent, named or unnamed, ancestors or not, in general they are much more likely to intend harm or cause fright than are humans. They do, however, share many of the motivations and traits of people. They can be envious, righteously indignant, or compassionate, and, in the case of ancestor spirits, retain the personal characteristics that they were identified as having when alive. (Lutz 1988:87)

Spirits communicate with humans through dreams, apparitions, and spirit-possessions, as well as less directly through their impact on health and fortune or misfortune. Ifaluk people, Lutz (1988:191) writes, perceive spirits "as one of the central dangers in their lives." The same could be said in most of Micronesia. Anthropologists have understood the Micronesian concern with spirits as, in part, a way to encourage harmony in tight-knit small island communities.

Hezel and Dobbin (1996) describe how, in modern Chuuk, spirits remain important in people's lives; personal spirits and Christian faith in God "do different kinds of work." Spirits adjudicate family conflicts; "God plays a more important role in the community at large, and may be called upon to control spirit activities, or evoked to drive out possessing spirits." In pre-Christian Chuuk, a variety of spirits interacted with humans. Early accounts of spirit mediums describe the medium seated with family in a lineage meeting house, being possessed by a dead relative and—trembling and speaking in a spirit-language translated by an expert. Modern spirit possession, though fairly common, is quite different. It is usually women who are possessed; the spirit speaks directly through them (rather than through an expert) at a family gathering, about a family issue. While Chuukese call on Christian clergy to bless the women, they recognize that it is usually a family problem that precipitates an episode; most commonly "squabbles over land or fractiousness over family responsibilities" but also the sudden death or suicide of a family member or pregnancy of an unmarried woman.

Why is it women who act as messengers from dead relatives to deal with these family issues? In Chuuk, gender roles are strongly differentiated. Women are expected to be quiet and strong, the peacemakers at the center of family life. Hezel and Dobbin suggest that "spirit possession has become a cultural vehicle that women utilize under stress to express grievances and resolve family tensions" brought on by modernization. Possession brings attention to women, allowing them to voice grievances in a culturally acceptable way (Chuukese men use drunken behavior, mental illness, or suicide to manage stress; e.g., Marshall 1979). Unlike male strategies, which may help individuals cope but create problems for others, women's spirit possession actually is "a means of resolving family conflicts" as family members are encouraged to respond to the concerns voiced by the spirits.

Although in some communities Christian teaching has largely effaced non-Christian understandings of the spiritual world, most Micronesians' ideas about the "big issues" of life, death and fate are constantly evolving philosophies including both Christian and indigenous elements. In the prolonged Christmas-linked ritual on Enewetak in the Marshall Islands discussed above, Laurence M. Carucci (1997) explores the combination of indigenous ideas of time, space, deities, exchange, gender, good and bad fortune, beauty and happiness, with Christian theology and recent historical events on Enewetak. The elaborate and joyful Enewetak celebration of *Kūrijmōj* demonstrates how untrue it would be to say that Micronesians have "lost their culture" by adding Christianity to it. The people of Enewetak, Chuuk, Pulap, Etal and the rest of Micronesia continue to maintain and deepen their understanding of traditional myths, cosmology and sacred landscapes. At the same time, they value and commit themselves to Christian devotion and church community.

Reification of Culture and the Politics of Tradition

For much of Micronesia, the emergence of political self-determination has generated increasing self-consciousness about cultural identity.

In Guam, the first local gubernatorial election and the naming of the first Guamanian bishop marked a turning point in self-rule at the start of the 1970s. At the same time, "much of what remained of traditional neo-Chamorro culture—the language, family ties, and retention of land—was being threatened by Americanization, development, and by tourism. A cultural watershed was passed sometime in the late 1960s when English began to replace Chamorro as the main language in a majority of island homes" (Rogers 1995:245). In 1984, more than 50% of Guam's land was held by the state, military, or federal government; despite intermittent efforts to return land to private owners, the situation has not changed much from 1946 (Rogers 1995:266).

In addition to acculturation and loss of land, Chamorros worry about the large numbers of immigrant Filipinos and Micronesians, and growing Japanese tourism and investment. Chamorros made up only 40% of the 1990 population of 133,000. (Chamorros were emigrating as well; by 1990 more than 25,000 lived permanently in California.) Immigrants filled labor needs, but they also added to welfare rolls and pressured educational, health, criminal justice and housing capacities (Rogers 1995:251, 273).

Indigenous rights groups on Guam became more visible in the 1970s, encouraging or forcing public discussion about rapid economic and cultural transformation. Guam's Chamorros worry that they are on the brink of losing political and cultural control of the island as immigrants, mainland Americans and military personnel continue to arrive, and Chamorros continue to leave (Rogers 1995:273–74). Indigenous rights was an issue in the 1979 referendum on Guam's draft constitution; rhetoric heated up through the 1980s as Chamorro and Washington politicians negotiated changes in Guam's status. Resulting factionalism and U.S. resistance to a vehement indigenous-rights movement meant that, after 10 years of work, "Guam's quest for commonwealth was in serious doubt of ever being realized" (Rogers 1995:271–275). A tragic symbol of the dilemma was the suicide of former Governor Ricky Bordallo. In a drama phrased as cultural identity, he set out hand-lettered placards calling for "justice and a halt to the deculturation of the Chamorro people" and draped a Guam flag about his shoulders before shooting himself (Rogers 1995:289).

Chamorros of the Northern Marianas share some of these concerns. Today, about as many Chamorros live in the U.S. as in the CNMI, and most educated Chamorros speak English to their children, both factors hastening assimilation. Like Guam, the Northern Marianas is experiencing an economic boom which has brought Filipino construction workers, Japanese associated with tourism, and garment-factory workers from east and southeast Asia. "Understandably, tensions exist between local residents and the hordes of outsiders, and the Chamorro people are fearful, and very much in danger, of losing control over their own affairs," with only 18,000 Chamorros in a population of 50,000 (Kiste 1994b:238). Dependence on federal funding, the overwhelming pace and scale of foreign investment and the transformation of Saipan's landscape are forcing awareness of cultural identity. "Chamorros hold effective political power but are losing economic and social power rapidly to overwhelming forces of international capital and U.S. law" (McPhetres 1992:263) By entering into long-term leases, Chamorros lose control over their land. Before the boom, Chamorros and Carolinians were at odds, with Chamorros unwilling to welcome Carolinian differences and Carolinians resenting Chamorro assumptions of superiority. Now the two Marianas populations find themselves allied against the flood of more recent immigrants.

> It is safe to say that this is a period of confusion in the community. The opportunity to strike it rich pervades the whole society, from the poker machine addicts to the land speculators. Preservation of the culture is not a very high priority in capitalist culture. Perhaps preservation is not even possible among the vicissitudes of changing fashions in commodity production in a monetized economy. (McPhetres 1992:263)

While the people of Pohnpei also worry about immigration and loss of political control (as the capital of the FSM, Pohnpei hosts government employees and politicians, as well as immigrants from nearby atolls), in other respects the situation in the Caroline Islands is quite different. The CNMI resolved its economic difficulties through subsidies from the U.S. and inviting foreign investment. The FSM and Palau also receive financial support, but the question remains of how to create an adequate economic future. As elsewhere in the small-island Pacific, Micronesians faced an economic dilemma: "The population had acquired an expensive taste for modernity, but it was unclear just how nation-states that lacked a substantial resource base would support these tastes under their own government" (Hezel 1992:218).

The flow of dollars after the 1960s transformed economies and lives. Today, two-thirds of all Micronesians live in urban centers. The Marshall Islands, Guam and Saipan have dense populations in their capital cities, while rural areas are emptying. Relocation for schooling, employment, health care or pleasure scatters communities. It separates the young and middle-aged from elders and children, interrupting the transmission of language, skills and cultural knowledge. Growing up in a city or a suburb, "many younger islanders could no longer sustain their existence in a subsistence economy" (Kiste 1994b:236).

Those who live far from town continue to rely on farming and fishing for subsistence, though they need cash to purchase imported goods. But in the urban and peri-urban areas most Micronesians today rely on a paycheck, usually from the government. "Indeed," writes Hezel (1992:217), by the time of independence "the shape of their families was being altered to accommodate the reality of a regular cash income, just as their chieftainships had been changed in an earlier age to allow for modern political apparatus." As the Chamorros have learned, changes in social organization need not mean the destruction of a culture, but the transition is a challenging one.

Carolinian atoll populations participate in the ongoing creation of new identities in the post-colonial context. Atoll communities in Pohnpei, Chuuk, and Yap States of the FSM—in contrast to high islanders—favor a strong national government. Otherwise, their interests are overwhelmed by the larger and more influential population of the high islands which are urban centers and seats of government. Lieber (1994) describes how the lack of control over outside resources experienced by Kapingamarangi people, a minority in Pohnpei State, did not change once the FSM became independent; "as colonial powers are succeeded by emerging nations, monocultural communities [like Kapinga] face a series of political crises attendant precisely on their places in these emerging nations" (Lieber 1994:205). Kapinga, and other small ethnic communities, must produce capable political leaders who can negotiate with the new power-brokers of their nation.

While high islanders seek to maintain control of their land, Micronesians from atolls seek access to the essential resources that are only available in the urban areas. Kolonia on Pohnpei, Kolonia in Yap, and Koror in Palau—are these places that "belong" to everyone in the state or the nation? Or do they remain under the control of those whose ancestors lived nearby?

The same questions affect other resources, such as reefs or historical sites. Nan Madol, Pohnpei's spectacular ancient city, is of interest to international tourism and archaeology, as well as Pohnpeians. "Current disputes over control of the site," writes Petersen (1995:105), "verify the existence of precisely the threats Nan Madol warns against: the dangers of big government." The paramount chief of Madolenihmw has been fighting claims to control Nan Madol from state, national, and international interests. This, says Petersen, is a metaphor for Pohnpei resistance to large-scale hierarchical government. "Modern-day Pohnpei read their island's natural and cultural landscapes as commentaries not only on the past and its many vicissitudes but also as a guide to contemporary political life: on the island, within their new republic, and in the world at large."

The world at large has not had very much interest in the Caroline Islands. The people of the Marshalls have developed their modern life in no small part due to the international interest in the fate of the nuclear atolls and the future of weapons testing. Palau has also received attention from international anti-nuclear activists, and Greenpeace has worked in both places. But the Caroline Islands rarely receive global attention. An exception is the traditional navigators of the central Caroline atolls, who have become world-famous for their skills through participation in long-distance Pacific Islands voyages. Robillard (1992:8–9) cites reports of how the publicity given to the famous navigator Piailug of Satawal angered the traditional chiefs (Piailug is not a chief), creating a self-consciousness about how publication worked "to propel and fix the construction of the identity of the chiefs and Piailug into a social circuit, a symbolic code, far beyond the interactional grasp of the Satawalese." Islanders are unable to control the way they are represented by foreign politicians, tourists and anthropologists. A look at tourism-oriented websites of the Micronesian nations, though, shows some of the ways in which they are attempting to take control of public representations of their identity.

Navigation is a good example of an element of traditional culture that has come to have meaning in the realm of public representations of identity, as well as in its own local significance. Despite many predictions of its loss, central Carolinian navigation appears healthy, with the number of active navigators in 1992 only one less than in 1972. Asking why some islands continue to train navigators, while on others the tradition has lapsed, Ridgell, Ikea and Uruo (1994:181) conclude that navigation "was and remains more important culturally on those islands where its practical value is greatest," on atolls where people sail to isolated islands and fishing banks. But cultural identity also plays a role:

> For the people of Polowat [Puluwat], a keen sense persists that indigenous navigation is something that is truly theirs and that although new methods and new vessels may be employed, all the traditional skills of the navigation system continue to be important. To give up navigation would be tantamount to giving up being a Polowat Islander. (Ridgell, Ikea and Uruo 1994:206).

As traditional navigation vividly proves, Micronesians have never seen their islands as "isolated," though foreigners often use the word. The ancestors of today's Micronesians were linked into long-distance networks of trade, marriage and political ties along familiar seaways. Today travel is by air and new destinations have been added, but Micronesians still participate in far-flung networks. With the status changes following the dissolution of the TTPI, Micronesians (except I-Kiribati) are free to travel to Guam, Hawai'i, and the U.S. mainland. Large communities of Chamorros and Marshallese have settled in Hawai'i and California, and Chuukese in Guam. Individuals and families with Micronesian origins now live throughout the U.S. mainland.

The MIRAB (Migration, Remittances, Aid, and Bureaucracy) economy of Micronesia does not look quite like that in the more southern parts of the Pacific. Some Marshall Islanders *send* money to their relatives in the mainland. Few communities have enough relatives living abroad to provide a dependable flow of income from remittances. But these expanding connections have made young Micronesians more aware of their place in the global system, and fostered a more American-style idea of "ethnic" identity. When Chamorros started to move in large numbers to the U.S. in the 1970s, they formed culture clubs and learned about political organizing from other Pacific immigrants.

> New layers of inauthenticity then became apparent-home island Guamanians' private doubts about the authenticity of Chamorro festivals in California, and the degree to which other Islanders recognized Chamorros at home or in the United States as having a unique Pacific culture (Nero 1997:450).

But Chamorros are used to challenges to their cultural vitality. While outsiders have predicted for years that Chamorro culture is on the brink of demise, Vicente Diaz argues that they have created a discourse of survival. Chamorro culture, he says, had maintained itself precisely by engaging in language, activities and ideas that are non-Chamorro. It uses the fact of resistance to assimilation itself as a part of what it means to be Chamorro. In the post-war world, that ability to maintain cultural identity within foreign frameworks is being stretched to its limit.

An unprecedented political and cultural predicament faces the Chamorros today: there are many non-Chamorros in the land while many Chamorros no longer have access to land. There are also more Chamorros in other lands than there are Chamorros in Guam. And there are many Chamorros, in Guam and elsewhere, who are not fluent in the Chamorro language. Chamorro survival appears especially urgent, and the stakes appear even greater today than ever before in Guam's long colonial history. (Diaz 1994:53)

Diaz sees Chamorros responding with "a revival, a concerted effort to design Chamorro cultural projects that dare compete with MTV and video games for the next generation's attention." Within the wider Pacific, Chamorros who once sought an American identity now cultivate a Pacific one, despite the fact that their "traditional culture" is very different from that of most Polynesians, Melanesians and other Micronesians. At the 1980 Pacific Festival of the Arts in Port Moresby, Karen Nero reports, "Islander participants had difficulty crediting the modern dance performances offered by the Guamanian troupe as authentically 'Pacific.'"

By the 1988 festival, however, other nations started moving beyond the strict constraints of traditional pasts. In large part it was due to Chamorro activist and educator Laura Torres Souder's capable explanations that Pacific audiences began to appreciate Guam's syncretic offering of dances as speaking to the shared histories of many Pacific peoples. Participants began to recognize that the ability to incorporate and benefit from newcomers is a strength of Pacific cultures. (Nero 1997:450)

The homecoming of Chamorros to a self-consciously Pacific Islander identity may be the strongest sign that the tide of acculturation has turned.

Images of the Future

We write these final paragraphs in the days immediately following the September 11th, 2001 airplane bombing of the World Trade Center and the Pentagon, moments when all of us are filled with serious questioning about a humanitarian future. This moment, however, perhaps brings most of us closer to the feelings shared by many residents of the west central Pacific during this period when the Compacts of Free Association that linked the United States with the Federated States of Micronesia and the Republic of the Marshall Islands are being renegotiated. Indeed, while in all likelihood the Compacts of Free Association with the United States will be renewed, current negotiations have brought to the forefront important concerns about national sovereignty and self-determination. The United States contends that, under the original compact, programs were mismanaged and funds often siphoned off for the benefit of a few empowered elites. They demand better accounting of expended funds and are pressing for greater accountability over a much more narrowly focused set of programs such as education, health care, and specific genres of economic development. In contrast, Micronesian residents note that it will take many years to rehabilitate island economies too long overlooked during the years of Trust Territory governance. They argue for patience and for continued support of programs that have had the most direct and positive effects on particular families and communities. For some, this means the continuation of programs that have allowed family members to attend college in Guam, Hawai'i, or the United States. Others benefit from the relatively open immigration and residence policies established by the original Compacts of Free Association. Yet others are particularly concerned with U. S. promises to settle nuclear claims or to renegotiate conditions of military use. Many outer islanders agree with United States demands for greater accountability, hoping that funds for future programs may extend beyond the grasp of urban elites. Others, however, see those same demands for accountability as a continuation of U. S. paternalism: the desire to impose conditions on a formerly dependent territory, and a failure to grant those now mature states the right to govern their own affairs.

If these are uncertain times, however, the residents of the west central Pacific face the future with confidence and determination, having existed for centuries with uncertainty. Many have survived the destruction of typhoons and the ravages of occasional famines. Most have lived through the abuses or neglect of one or more of the multiple colonizing nations to have inscribed fragments of their own desire on the lands and seas of the region. More than a few have come face-to-face with death and suffering during World War II, while others have had their lives and identities fully contorted and re-contoured as a result of nuclear and military testing. The outcomes of the compact renegotiations are, in many ways, beyond local control. They rest on the uncertain value of strategic position in imagined confrontations between powerful nations in distant locales. They rely on the needs of the United States to be viewed as a humanitarian power by other nations in the world community. The risks to local styles of life from the rising tides of a much-discussed era of global warming are equally in the hands of the United States and other large nations who continue to feed on their fetish for fossil fuels. Yet, listening to the voices of Micronesian residents, there is no aversion to potential risks. Like many Pacific peoples, these are groups with vital futures. Facile and adaptive, some construct identities out of practices designed to align with tested symbols of an imagined past deeply rooted in the soil and swells of places long traversed. Others, following the course of sailors of old, travel the globe quite freely, fashioning their own imagined futures as Chamorros or Marshallese, from cultural materials of disparate source, yet constantly re-tooled with outlines of authenticity anchored in an equally-valued past.

> Living in this last-settled region of the globe
> My head resting on a spit of sand
> washed hither by the sea.
> The crashing waves resonate
> with sounds of other shores.
> A traveler
> moves within the global sea
> of humanity.

> —L. M. Carucci

1. Roman Catholic church and school, Weno, Chuuk, Federated States of Micronesia. (Photo: L. Poyer)

2. Traditional-style house in Yap, Federated States of Micronesia. (Photo: L. Poyer)

3. Toloas (Dublon), Chuuk, Japanese-developed area after U.S. attack, April 1944. (Photo: U.S. Navy, National Archives photo #80-G-227331)

4. Fishing forms a central part of daily life for many residents of Micronesia. (Photo by L. M. Carucci)

5. Copra production transformed the course of daily life in many parts of the West Central Pacific. (Photo by L. M. Carucci)

6. Men's activities in many parts of Micronesia often revolve around canoe craft, sailing, and the sea, as is the case for these men in the Marshall Islands. (Photo by L. M. Carucci)

7. *Kūrijmōj* on Ujelang, Marshall Islands. The Children's Group performs their songs. (Photo by L. M. Carucci)

8. The contrast between the wealthy and the poor has become a critical issue for many Micronesian residents. (Photos by L. M. Carucci)

a. Dilapidated dwellings and overcrowding on Ebeye, Marshall Islands.

b. Distinctive dwellings are used to display newly fashioned differences of wealth or class on Majuro, Marshall Islands.

References

Alexander, William J.
1978   Wage Labor, Urbanization and Culture Change in the Marshall Islands: The
            Ebeye Case. Ph.D. Dissertation. Political and Social Science. The New School
            for Social Research.

Alkire, W.H.
1977   *An Introduction to the Peoples and Cultures of Micronesia*, 2nd ed. Menlo
            Park, CA: Cummings.

Aoyagi, Machiko
1987   Gods of the Modekngei religion in Belau. In *Cultural Uniformity and Diver-
            sity in Micronesia*, ed. by I. Ushijima and K. Sudo, *Senri Ethnological Studies,
            No. 21*, Osaka Japan: National Museum of Ethnology, pp. 339–361.

Barker, John
1990   Introduction: ethnographic perspectives on Christianity in Oceanic soci-
            eties. pp. 1–24 in J. Barker, ed., *Christianity in Oceania: Ethnographic Perspec-
            tives*, ASAO Monograph #12, Lanham MD: University Press of America.

Barnett, Homer G.
1949   *Palauan Society: A Study of Contemporary Native Life in the Palau Islands*. Eu-
            gene, OR: University of Oregon Publications.

1979   *Being a Palauan: Fieldwork Edition*. New York: Holt, Rinehart & Winston.

Black, Peter W.
1978   The teachings of Father Marino: Christianity on Tobi Atoll. Pp. 307–354 in J.
            Boutilier, D. Hughes & S. Tiffany, eds. *Mission, Church, and Sect in Oceania*.
            ASAO Monograph #6, Ann Arbor: University of Michigan Press.

1999   Psychological Anthropology and its discontents: science and rhetoric in
            Postwar Micronesia." Pp. 225–53 in R.C. Kiste and M. Marshall, eds., *Ameri-
            can Anthropology in Micronesia*. Honolulu: University of Hawai'i Press.

Butler, Brian
1994   Early prehistoric settlement in the Marianas Islands: new evidence from
            Saipan. *Man and Culture in Oceania* 10:15–38.

Butler, Brian M., ed.
1988   *Archaeological Investigations on the North Coast of Rota, Mariana Islands*. Mi-
            cronesian Archaeological Survey Report No. 23. Southern Illinois University
            at Carbondale, Center for Archeological Investigations Occasional Paper No.
            8.

Carroll, Vern
1970   *Adoption in Eastern Oceania*. Honolulu: University of Hawai'i Press.

1972   Comments from a discussion at the Pacific Atoll Population Conference,
            27–30 December, 1972.

Carucci, Laurence M.
1987   *Jekero*: symbolizing the transition to manhood in the Marshall Islands, *Mi-
            cronesica* (20): 1–17.

1993   Christmas on Ujelang: the politics of continuity in the context of change, in *Contemporary Pacific Societies*, Victoria S. Lockwood, Thomas G. Harding, and Ben J. Wallace, eds. Englewood Cliffs, N.J.: Prentice Hall.

1996   *In Anxious Anticipation of Kuwajleen's Uneven Fruits: a cultural history of the significant locations and important resources of Kuwajleen Atoll.* Huntsville, Alabama: USASSDC.

1997   *Nuclear Nativity: Rituals of Renewal and Empowerment in the Marshall Islands.* DeKalb IL: Northern Illinois University Press.

1997b   Measures of chiefly ideology and practice in the Marshall Islands. In *Chiefs Today: Traditional Pacific Leadership and the Postcolonial State*, M. Lindstrom and G. White, eds. Stanford, California: Stanford University Press.

1999   *Ien Eñtaan im Jerata*: times of suffering and ill fortune: an overview of daily life on Ujelang and Enewetak since 1946. A Presentation to the Nuclear Claims Tribunal. Majuro: Marshall Islands.

2000   *Mōn jaar eo*: The church as an embodiment and expression of community on Wōjlañ and Āne-wetak, Marshall Islands, presented for a Working Session entitled The Cultural Construction of Space. The Association for Social Anthropology in Ocean. Vancouver, British Columbia.

in press   The transformation of person and place on Enewetak and Ujelang Atolls in *Pacific Island Societies in a Global World*, Victoria Lockwood, ed. Englewood Cliffs, N.J. Prentice Hall.

Diaz, Vicente M.
1994   Simply Chamorro: telling tales of demise and survival in Guam. Pp. 29–58, *The Contemporary Pacific*, 6(1): Spring 1994.

Erdland, P.A.
1914   *Die Marshall-Insulaner.* Munster, Germany: Aschendorffsche Verlagsbuchhandlung.

Feinberg, Richard
1995   *Modern Pacific Seafaring.* Dekalb, Illinois: Northern Illinois University Press.

Firth, Stewart and Karin von Strokirch
1997   A nuclear pacific. Pp. 324–358 in D. Denoon, ed., *The Cambridge History of the Pacific Islanders.* Cambridge: Cambridge University Press.

Flinn, Juliana
1990   Catholicism and Pulapese identity, pp. 221–235 in J. Barker, ed. *Christianity in Oceania: Ethnographic Perspectives*, ASAO Monograph #12, Lanham MD: University Press of America.

Garrett, John
1982   *To Live Among the Stars: Christian Origins in Oceania.* Suva: Institute of Pacific Studies, University of the South Pacific.

1992   *Footsteps in the Sea: Christianity in Oceania to World War II.* Suva: Institute of Pacific Studies, University of the South Pacific.

1997   *Where Nets were Cast: Christianity in Oceania since World War II.* Suva: Institute of Pacific Studies, University of the South Pacific.

Goodenough, Ward
1955   A problem of Malayo-Polynesian social organization. *American Anthropologist* 57: 71–83.

Graves, Michael W., Terry L. Hunt, and Darlene Moore
1990   Ceramic production in the Mariana Islands: explaining change and diversity in prehistoric interaction and exchange. *Asian Perspectives* 29(2):211–233.

Grimble, Arthur Francis
1989   *Tungaru Traditions: Writings on the Atoll Culture of the Gilbert Islands*. Edited by H. E. Maude. Carlton, Victoria, Australia: Melbourne University Press.

Hanlon, David
1989   Micronesia: writing and rewriting the histories of a nonentity. *Pacific Studies* 12(2):1–21.

1994   Patterns of colonial rule in Micronesia. Pp. 93–118 in K.R. Howe, R.B. Kiste and B.V. Lal, eds., *Tides of History: The Pacific Islands in the Twentieth Century*. Honolulu: University of Hawai'i Press.

1998   *Remaking Micronesia: Discourses over Development in a Pacific Territory*. Honolulu: University of Hawai'i Press.

Hau'ofa, Epeli
1993   Our sea of islands, in E. Waddell, V. Naidu, and E. Hau'ofa, eds. *A New Oceania:Rediscovering Our Sea of Islands*. Suva, Fiji: University of South Pacific, pp. 2–16.

Hereniko, Vilsoni
1994   Representations of cultural identities, pp. 406–434 in K.R. Howe, R.B. Kiste and B.V. Lal, eds., *Tides of History: The Pacific Islands in the Twentieth Century*. Honolulu: University of Hawai'i Press.

Hezel, Francis X., S.J.
n.d.   The Catholic Church on Truk. Ms. seen at Micronesian Seminar, Chuuk (now in Kolonia, Pohnpei).

1983   *The First Taint of Civilization: A History of the Caroline and Marshall Islands in Pre-Colonial Days, 1521–1885*. Honolulu: University of Hawai'i Press.

1987   Indigenization as a missionary goal in the Caroline and Marshall Islands. Pp. 251–273 in J. Boutilier, D. Hughes & S. Tiffany, eds. *Mission, Church, and Sect in Oceania*. ASAO Monograph #6, Ann Arbor: University of Michigan Press.

1992   The expensive taste for modernity: Caroline and Marshall Islands. Pp. 203–219 in A. B. Robillard,ed., *Social Change in the Pacific Islands*, London; Kegan Paul International.

1995   *Strangers in Their Own Land: A Century of Colonial Rule in the Caroline and Marshall Islands*. Honolulu: University of Hawai'i Press.

Hezel, Francis X. and Jay D. Dobbin
1996   Spirit possession in Chuuk, pp. 195–212, in J.M. Mageo and A. Howard, eds., *Spirits in Culture, History, and Mind*. New York: Routledge

Howe, K. R.
1984   *Where the Waves Fall: A New South Seas Islands History from First Settlement to Colonial Rule*. Honolulu: University of Hawai'i Press.

Irwin, G.
1992   *The Prehistoric Exploration and Colonization of the Pacific*. Cambridge: Cambridge University Press.

Johannes, R. E.
1981   *Words of the Lagoon: Fishing and Marine Lore in the Palau District of Microne-sia*. Berkeley: University of California Press.

Kirch, Patrick V.
2000   *On the Road of the Winds: An Archaeological History of the Pacific Islands be-fore European Contact*. Berkeley: University of California Press.

Kirch, P.V. and M.I. Weisler
1994   Archaeology of the Pacific Islands: an appraisal of recent research. *Journal of Archaeological Research* 2(4):285–328

Kiste, Robert C.
1974   *The Bikinians: A Study in Forced Migration*. Menlo Park, California: Cum-mings Publishing Company.

1993   New political statuses in American Micronesia, in *Contemporary Pacific Soci-eties*, Victoria S. Lockwood, Thomas G. Harding, and Ben J. Wallace, eds. En-glewood Cliffs, N.J.: Prentice Hall.

1994a   Pre-colonial times. Pp. 3–28 in K.R. Howe, R.B. Kiste and B.V. Lal, eds., *Tides of History: The Pacific Islands in the Twentieth Century*. Honolulu: University of Hawai'i Press.

1994b   United States. Pp. 227–257 in K.R. Howe, R.B. Kiste and B.V. Lal, eds., *Tides of History: The Pacific Islands in the Twentieth Century*. Honolulu: University of Hawai'i Press.

Kramer, August and Hans Nevermann
1938   *Ralik-Ratak*. Elizabeth A. Murphy translation available at the Hamilton Li-brary Pacific Collection, University of Hawai'i.

Labby, David
1976   *The Demystification of Yap: Dialectics of Culture on a Micronesian Island*. Chicago: The University of Chicago Press.

Lawrence, Roger
1992   Kiribati: change and context in an atoll world. Pp. 264–299 in A. B. Robillard, ed., *Social Change in the Pacific Islands*, London; Kegan Paul International.

Lieber, Michael
1990   Lamarckian definitions of identity on Kapingamarangi and Pohnpei. Pp. 71–101 in J. Linnekin and L. Poyer, eds., *Cultural Identity and Ethnicity in the Pacific*. Honolulu: University of Hawai'i Press.

1994   *More than a Living: Fishing and the Social Order on a Polynesian Atoll*. Boul-der: Westview Press.

Lutz, Catherine A.
1988   *Unnatural Emotions: Everyday Sentiments on a Micronesian Atoll and Their Challenge to a Western Theory*. Chicago: University of Chicago Press.

Marshall, Mac
1979   *Weekend Warriors: Alcohol in a Micronesian Culture*. Palo Alto CA: Mayfield Publishing Company.

Marshall, Mac and Leslie B. Marshall
1975   Opening Pandora's bottle: reconstructing Micronesians' early contacts with alcoholic beverages. *Journal of the Polynesian Society* 84(4): 441–465.

1976   Holy and unholy spirits. *Journal of Pacific History* 11(3–4), 135–166.

1990   *Silent Voices Speak: Women and Prohibition in Truk.* Belmont CA: Wadsworth Publishing Company.

Mason, Leonard

1947   *Economic Organization of the Marshall Islands.* Honolulu: U.S. Commercial Company

1948   Rongerik report. Honolulu: University of Hawai'i. Archived in the Pacific Collection, Hamilton Library, University of Hawai'i.

Mayo, Larry W.

1992   The militarization of Guamanian Society. Pp. 220–240 in A.B. Robillard, ed., *Social Change in the Pacific Islands.* London: Kegan Paul International.

McPhetres, Samuel F.

1992   Elements of social change in the contemporary Northern Mariana Islands. Pp. 241–263 in A.B. Robillard, ed., *Social Change in the Pacific Islands.* London: Kegan Paul International.

Morgan, William N.

1988   *Prehistoric Architecture in Micronesia.* Austin, University of Texas Press.

Nason, James D.

1978   Civilizing the Heathen: missionaries and social change in the Mortlock Islands. Pp. 109–137 in J. Boutilier, D. Hughes & S. Tiffany, eds. *Mission, Church, and Sect in Oceania.* ASAO Monograph #6, Ann Arbor: University of Michigan Press.

Nero, Karen L.

1989   Time of famine, time of transformation: Hell in the Pacific, Palau." In *The Pacific Theater: Island Representations of World War II*, ed. By G.M. White and L. Lindstrom, Honolulu: University of Hawai'i Press, pp. 117–147.

1997   The end of insularity. Pp. 439–467 in D. Denoon, ed., *The Cambridge History of the Pacific Islanders.* Cambridge: Cambridge University Press.

Oliver, Douglas

1989   *Native Cultures of the Pacific Islands.* Honolulu: University of Hawai'i Press.

Parmentier, Richard J.

1987   *The Sacred Remains: Myth, History and Polity in Belau.* Chicago: University of Chicago Press.

Pawley, Andrew and Malcolm Ross.

1993   Austronesian historical linguistics and culture history. *Annual Review of Anthropology* 22:425–59.

Peoples, James G.

1993   Political evolution in Micronesia. *Ethnology* 32(1):1–17.

Peter, Joakim Manniwel

1996   Eram's Church(Bell): local Appropriations of Catholicism on Etal. *Isla: A Journal of Micronesian Studies*, 4(2): dry season 1996:267–287.

Petersen, Glenn

1993   Some Pohnpei strategies for economic survival, in *Contemporary Pacific Societies*, Victoria S. Lokwood, Thomas G. Harding, and Ben J. Wallace, eds. Englewood Cliffs, N.J.: Prentice Hall.

1994   The Federated States of Micronesia's 1990 Constitutional Convention: calm before the storm? *The Contemporary Pacific* 6(2):337–369.

1995   Nan Madol's contested landscape: topography and tradition in the Eastern Caroline Islands. *Isla: A Journal of Micronesian Studies* 3(1), rainy season 1995: 105–128.

Pollock, Nancy

1992   *These Roots Remain: Food Habits in Islands of the Central and Eastern Pacific Since Western Contact.* Laie, Hawai'i: The Institute for Polynesian Studies.

1996   The impact of mining on Nauruan women, *Natural Resources Forum* 20(2): 123–134.

Poyer, Lin, Suzanne Falgout and Laurence M. Carucci

2001   *The Typhoon of War: Micronesian Experiences of the Pacific War.* Honolulu: University of Hawai'i Press.

Rainbird, Paul

1994   Prehistory in the tropical Northwest Pacific: the Caroline, Mariana and Marshall Islands. *Journal of World Prehistory* 8: 293–349.

Rehg, Kenneth L.

1995   The significance of linguistic interaction Spheres in reconstructing Micronesian prehistory. *Oceanic Linguistics* 34(2):305–325.

Ridgell, Reilly, Manny Ikea and Isaohsy Uruo

1994   The persistence of central Carolinian navigation. *Isla: A Journal of Micronesian Studies* 2(2), dry season 1994: 181–206.

Robillard, Albert B.

1992   Introduction: social change as the projection of discourse. Pp. 1–32 in A.B. Robillard, ed., *Social Change in the Pacific Islands.* London: Kegan Paul International.

Rogers, Robert F.

1995   *Destiny's Landfall: A History of Guam.* Honolulu: University of Hawai'i Press.

Scarr, Deryck

1990   *The History of the Pacific Islands: Kingdoms of the Reefs.* Melbourne, The MacMillan Company of Australia Pty Ltd

Shuster, Donald R.

1982a   Islands of Change in Palau; Church, School, and Elected Government, 1891–1981. Ed.D. dissertation, University of Hawai'i.

1982b   State Shinto in Micronesia during Japanese rule, 1914–1945 *Pacific Studies* 5(2):20–43.

2001   Guam: Micronesia in review: issues and events, 1 July 1999–30 June 2000, pp. 203–211. *The Contemporary Pacific* 13(1), Spring 2001.

Silverman, Martin

1971   *Disconcerting Issue.* Chicago: University of Chicago Press.

Teaiwa, Teresia K.

1994   bikinis and other s/pacific n/oceans. *The Contemporary Pacific* 6(1), pp. 87–109.

Tobin, Jack A.
1958   Land tenure in the Marshall Islands, in *Land Tenure Patterns: Trust Territory of the Pacific Islands* (Volume I). Guam, Mariana Islands: Office of the High Commissioner.

Useem, John
1945   The changing structure of a Micronesian society. *American Anthropologist* 47(4):567–588.

1946   *Report on Yap and Palau*. U.S. Commercial Company Economic Survey of Micronesia, Report No. 6. Honolulu: U.S. Commercial Company. Mimeo.

Van Trease, Howard
1993   From colony to Independence, pp. 3–22, in H. Van Trease, ed. 1993 *Atoll Politics: The Republic of Kiribati*. Canterbury, NZ: Macmillan Brown Centre for Pacific Studies.

Vidich, Arthur J.
1980   *The Political Impact of Colonial Administration*. New York: Arno Press. (Reprint of The Political Impact of Colonial Administration, Ph.D. dissertation, Harvard University, 1952.)

About the Authors

Andrew Strathern and **Pamela J. Stewart** are a husband and wife team, and are both in the Department of Anthropology at the University of Pittsburgh. They have published many articles and books on their fieldwork in Papua New Guinea and Scotland. Their most recent co-authored books include: *Curing and Healing: Medical Anthropology in Global Perspective*. (1999, Durham, N.C.: Carolina Academic Press); *Collaborations and Conflicts: A Leader Through Time*. (1999, Fort Worth: Harcourt Brace College Publishers); *Arrow Talk: Transaction, Transition, and Contradiction in New Guinea Highlands History*. (2000, Kent, Ohio and London: Kent State University Press); *The Python's Back: Pathways of Comparison between Indonesia and Melanesia*. (2000, Westport, Conn. and London: Bergin and Garvey, Greenwood Publishing Group); *Stories, Strength and Self-Narration: Western Highlands, Papua New Guinea*. (2000, Adelaide, Australia: Crawford House Publishing); *Humors and Substances: Ideas of the Body in New Guinea*. (2001, Westport, Conn. and London: Bergin and Garvey, Greenwood Publishing Group); *Minorities and Memories: Survivals and Extinctions in Scotland and Western Europe* (2001, Durham, N.C.: Carolina Academic Press); and *Remaking the World* (forthcoming [Spring 2002] Washington, D.C. and London: Smithsonian Institution Press).

Stewart and Strathern have also recently co-edited three further volumes: *Millennnial Countdown in New Guinea* (Special Issue of *Ethnohistory* Vol. 47. No. 1, 2000, Duke University Press); *Identity Work: Constructing Pacific Lives* (2000, ASAO (Association for Social Anthropology in Oceania) Monograph Series No. 18. Pittsburgh: University of Pittsburgh Press);and *Anthropology and Consultancy* (Special Issue of *Social Analysis* Vol. 45. No. 2, 2001, Adelaide University). They have served as Editor (AJS) and Associate Editor (PJS) for the Monograph Series of the Association for Social Anthropology in Oceania.

Laurence M. Carucci is professor of anthropology at Montana State University, where he has been a member of the faculty since 1985. He was raised in Colorado, earned his BA in anthropology at Colorado State University (1968), and his M.A.(1972) and Ph.D. (1980) at The University of Chicago. Carucci has conducted research with ethnic groups in Chicago, has worked on historical materials in Hawai'i, and has lived and worked repeatedly with members of the Enewetak community and with other Marshall Islanders since 1976. He has published numerous articles on the Marshall Islands. The following books are also based on the several years of field research experience that Carucci has had in the Marshall Islands: *Nuclear Nativity: Rituals of Renewal and Empowerment in the Marshall Islands* (Northern Illinois University Press, 1997), *In Anxious Anticipation of the Uneven Fruits of Kwajalein Atoll* (USASMDC, 1997), and *The Typhoon of War: Micronesian Experiences of the Pacific War* (with Lin Poyer and Suzanne Falgout; University of Hawai'i Press, 2001). He has worked closely with members of the Enewetak community as they seek compensation for damages to their atoll during the years of military testing on Enewetak and works with several Northern Marshall Islands communities in their attempt to deal with medical problems that have resulted from their shared nuclear legacy. In addition, Carucci has been an officer and serves on the board of the Association for Social Anthropology in Oceania.

Lin Poyer is Associate Professor of Anthropology at the University of Wyoming. She is the co-author of *The Typhoon of War: Micronesian Experiences of the Pacific War* (with Larry Carucci and Suzanne Falgout; University of Hawai'i Press, 2001) and co-editor of *Cultural Identity and Ethnicity in the Pacific* (with Jocelyn Linnekin; University of Hawai'i Press, 1997). In addition to the numerous articles that she has written on her research she has authored *The Ngatik Massacre: History and Identity on a Micronesian Atoll* (Smithsonian Series in Ethnographic Inquiry, Smithsonian Institution Press, 1993) and *Micronesian Resources Study, Marshall Islands Ethnography*, Republic of the Marshall Islands: Micronesian Endowment for Historic Preservation, U.S. National Park Service, 1997. She has served as a board member and as Chair of the Association for Social Anthropology in Oceania.

Richard Feinberg is professor of anthropology at Kent State University, where he has served on the faculty since 1974. Born in Virginia, he grew up in New York City, earned his AB (1969) in anthropology at the University of California, Berkeley, and his MA (1971) and Ph.D. (1974) at the University of Chicago. Feinberg has conducted field research among the Navajo Indians and with Polynesians of Anuta (Solomon Islands) and Nukumanu (Papua New Guinea). Among his publications are *Anuta: Social Structure of a Polynesian Island* (Brigham Young University-Hawai'i and the National Museum of Denmark, 1981), *Polynesian Seafaring and Navigation* (Kent State University Press, 1988), *Seafaring in the Contemporary Pacific Islands* (Northern Illinois University Press, 1995), *Leadership and Change in the Western Pacific* (co-edited with Karen Watson-Gegeo, London School of Economics Monographs on Social Anthropology, 1996), *Oral Traditions of Anuta* (Oxford University Press, 1998), and *The Cultural Analysis of Kinship* (co-edited with Martin Ottenheimer, University of Illinois Press, 2001). He has served as an officer of the Association for Social Anthropology in Oceania and the Central States Anthropological Society. In addition, he has been involved in university governance at Kent State University, serving several years on the faculty senate executive committee and one year as the senate's chair.

Cluny Macpherson is a professor of sociology at the University of Auckland in New Zealand. Born and educated in New Zealand, he took a BA in Social Anthropology and Maori, an MA in Social Anthropology, and a Dphil.in Sociology. His current research and teaching and consultancy interests are in the political economy of the Pacific and social and economic relations between island and metropolitan states. He usually works and writes with his wife La'avasa. He has served on national Social Science Research, and Health Research funding agencies and the Board of the Association for Social Anthropology in Oceania. He was Rockefeller Fellow at the Center For Pacific Island Studies, at the University of Hawai'i and has co-authored *Emerging Pluralism: Samoan Community in New Zealand* (with D. C. Pitt), *Samoan Medical Belief and Practice* (with La'avasa Macpherson) and has most recently co-edited a series of four books on ethnicity and ethnic identity in Aotearoa/New Zealand.

Index